JON, WHY ARE YOU CRYING?

A Work of Non-Fiction

BY

DAVID KEY PARRISH

First Edition

Green Feather Publishing
Columbia

Published by Green Feather Publishing
P.O. Box 370
Columbia, Maryland 21045

First Edition

Printed in the United States of America

ISBN   0-9647772-3-1

Library of Congress Catalog Card Number 95-78631

10 9 8 7 6 5 4 3 2 1

There is no miracle - nothing on this plane is supernatural. What we see now and what we have read of in ages past are but the operation of law which has not yet been studied and defined. Already we realize something of its possibilities and of its limitations, which are exact in their way as those of any purely physical power. We must hold the balance between those who would believe nothing and those who believe too much. Gradually the mist will clear and we will chart the shadowy coast.

Sir Arthur Conan Doyle
The Edge of The Unknown

Miracles fall like drops of healing rain from Heaven on a dry and dusty world, where starved and thirsty creatures come to die. Now they have water. Now the world is green. And everywhere the signs of life spring up, to show that what is born can never die, for what has life has immortality.

From *A Course in Miracles* VOL II, Pg 473
©Copyright 1975
Reprinted by Permission of the
Foundation for Inner Peace, Inc.,
PO Box 1104, Glen Ellen, CA 95442

Preface

Every word in this book is honest. What is true is a question for God.

I have changed many names. I have changed the names of people who might be embarrassed or whose privacy would be invaded, people who could be physically harmed, and people who might sue me. I've spent enough time in courts in the past few years. I don't like those places, even though I've never been at the center of what was being done there.

I also have changed a few insignificant details for all the same reasons. I try to make it clear each time I have felt the need to change a name or a detail. These slight revisions do not detract from the story except, perhaps, for those who would like to point fingers, to lay blame. I have tried, recently at least, not to contribute to such things. I can only hope I have succeeded more often than I have failed.

I dedicate this book to myself. If I had known what I was getting into, I never would have done it; and if I hadn't, there would have been no self to whom I could dedicate this book, and no book.

And to Jon.

1 At 11:39 p.m. on Friday, January 5, 1990, a young woman who was the night clerk at the Red Roof Inn on Route 1 just outside of Columbia, Maryland, placed the call to the Howard County Police Department. A man answered.

"Howard County Police. May I help you?"

"Yes. This is the desk clerk at the Red Roof Inn."

"Yes?"

"I'd like to know how often you send policemen here to do rounds?"

"Do you mean to stop in and check?"

"Yes. Do they patrol the area?"

"Yes, that's something they do whenever they're free. They check out spots, drive by, whatever's called for. I don't think they have a specific number of times. They're just supposed to do it."

"Well, see, I just came on duty, and the girl that was here didn't tell me that anything was going on, but a guest just called and said there was a party or something going on in one of the rooms."

"Well, I mean..."

"I'm the only person on duty right now, and I didn't want to go out there."

"Well, I mean, are there narcotics involved? I mean, what..."

"I have no idea."

"Is it a bad party? A good party?"

"He just said there was a bunch of noise."

"You have a noise complaint? Do you have the address?"

She gave it. "I mean, I get a lot of calls," she said.

"You're the only person working there tonight?"

"From eleven to seven there's only one person."

"Good grief. What's your last name?"

She gave it.

"First name?"

She gave that, too.

"And your phone number there?"

She gave him the number.

"Let's see. I guess that's a loud party. Right?"

"From what he's saying. I don't know. I didn't want..."

"You know, it's good to be able to describe to me what's going on, because I don't like to send police into situations..."

"Noise complaint."

"Yeah."

"He said it sounded like a party was going on."

"Was it loud music, or..."

"He didn't tell me. I can call him back and ask for more specific information."

"Are you the night manager?"

"No, I'm not the manager. I'm the desk clerk."

"Okay. You'll be at the front desk?"

"Okay."

"Okay, I'll send somebody over."

"All right. Thank you."

"Thank you. 'Bye."

I was a kid myself a few decades ago, and I know a kid who is partying thinks the whole world is partying. Kids don't think. That's just the way it is.

It wasn't even a party at first. A few guys got together at the home of a kid named Chris and hung around in the basement shooting pool and talking junk. For a few weeks they had tossed around the idea that it would be fun to rent a motel room. They could drink beer and not worry about driving home or getting hassled.

Carl Jonathan "Jon" Bowie and his identical twin brother, Mickey, and some of the other guys went out for beer and got a case. A case wasn't much for the number of people who eventually showed up, but kids don't think.

When they returned to Chris's they left the case in the car. Chris's parents were out for the evening, and Chris didn't want his parents to come home and find a bunch of guys drinking beer in the basement. A few of the guys, including Chris, each snuck a beer into the house, but most of them didn't think to do it. They called some more guys, and some girls. There had to be girls.

At between 10:15 and 10:30 p.m. they met in the parking lot of the Red Roof Inn in Jessup, a mile or so east of Columbia on Route 1. One of the girls went in the office and tried to rent a room, but she came back out into the parking lot exhaling white air and saying that you had to be twenty-one. A kid I'll call Eddie Vickers lived next door to Jon and Mick. Eddie was the only one who was twenty-one. He went inside and came back out waving a room key.

The room was on the first floor. The front door faced a sidewalk, the front parking lot, and a grassy hill that sloped down toward Route 1. The room was the unit next to the end unit. It was about as far away from the office as you could get.

As the kids entered the room, they were looking down the end wall on the right and endways over a low dresser with a tv on it. Inside the door, to the left, there was a round table with two chairs. The head of the double bed was pressed against the center of the far-left wall, and the bed all but filled the room. Those who hadn't brought beer begged favors. A couple of the girls had pitched in for a twelve-pack, but there wasn't much beer to go around. Not everyone drank, which was seen as something of a benefit for those who did.

One kid, the kids wouldn't say which one, brought a pipe that belonged to someone that kid knew. It was a tobacco pipe, but it was the kind of pipe that could be used to smoke marijuana. There was no marijuana smoked that night, and the only drug in the motel room was alcohol, but the kid brought the pipe and showed it around in a bragging sort of way.

Someone switched on the television. Most of the kids sat on the bed and talked as they waited for Arsenio to come on. In 1990, the Arsenio show was new to the area, and it came on at eleven.

There were fifteen people in the room - eight girls and seven guys. The girls were all of average height, or smaller. At six-two, Chris was the largest of the guys. Jon and Mick were the next largest at about five-ten. The rest of the guys were between five-six and five-eight. One girl was seventeen. Eddie was twenty-one. The rest were mostly eighteen and nineteen. One of the guys, Puffy, was black. Another, Chong Ko, was Korean. The rest were white.

They had been there a half hour or so when the phone rang, and Eddie answered it. He hung up saying it was the front desk and they had to keep it down. They tried, and did for a while.

Either a girl named Becky or her sister, Jennifer, had brought a camera. At one point in the evening Jon held the camera at arm's length in front of his face and took his own picture. Jon sometimes did things like that.

Eddie made a pass at one of the girls. His girlfriend, a slender blonde we'll call Pamela, got angry and ran crying into the bathroom. Eddie left in a huff and then there were fourteen. Eight girls, six guys.

A couple of the girls went into the bathroom to tend to Pamela. Mickey didn't know Pamela that well, but he followed the girls in to see if he could help, leaving the door open behind him. Mickey couldn't see that he was helping much. He was coming out of the bathroom when someone shouted, "Cops."

The police have their own official version of what happened. Four months later, almost to the day, when Jon was dead, and for months after that, the official version would appear in dozens of articles in the Howard County, Washington and Baltimore newspapers. It would appear in numerous television stories on the Baltimore and Washington stations. Few people I talked with actually believed it, but it kept appearing. That version was that the police were just doing their jobs, and that nobody understood.

The kids' version got less coverage. When I had pieced together their official statements and had added details from quite a few conversations I had with different ones, I got closer to what I believe actually took place. I'm not saying it's exactly what God saw, but all I could do was get as close as my own limitations permitted. I wasn't there.

A kid named Danny was leaving with a kid name Kristin to take her home. They had pulled on their coats and were stepping back from the door as Mickey looked up. Two police officers were in the room near the door. One was a muscular white guy in his upper twenties. He was big and really tall. Six-seven. The other was a black guy who was pushing thirty and about halfway between five and six feet. There was immediate confusion. Kids shouted, "Cops," and the officers shouted, "Out of the bathroom. Everybody, out," and "Sit. Everybody on the bed." Mickey came around the end of the bed and sat down, and the girls followed him out of the bathroom. Someone had moved one of the chairs closer to the door. Chris was sitting there, and he got up and went to the bed and sat beside Pamela, who was still sniffling. Puffy was standing near the door and he sat in the chair Chris had vacated. Chong was sitting near the door in the other chair.

The black officer, I'll call him Lenny Hamilton, stayed near the door, which remained propped open. The tall, white officer, I'll call him Roland Meyers, went around the bed and checked the bathroom. He came back and began asking for identification, and no one produced any. He ordered the person who had rented the room to stand up. The kids said he had left. This seemed to make the officers angry, as if they didn't believe it.

Hamilton read a statement about the legal consequences of underage drinking. Then he said there was no commissioner on duty that night to sign the necessary paperwork, so anyone who didn't have identification would have to spend the week-end in jail. Some of the girls started crying. Guys looked at the floor.

Jon was sitting on the heating unit behind Hamilton. When Hamilton said they might spend the week-end in jail, Jon said, "Yeah, right. You can't do that just because we don't have identification."

Hamilton turned sharply to face Jon.

"Shut the fuck up."

Jon looked at his chest and looked up again.

"You can't do that."

"'You got a problem?" Hamilton snapped.

Chris was a tall, blonde kid with the slow, easy athleticism common to good first basemen. Chris said later he had known Jon a long time, which he had, and he could tell that Jon knew he had gotten himself into something he wished he hadn't gotten into. Chris said Jon raised both hands and slumped back against the wall, which Chris knew wasn't at all like Jon unless Jon was a little nervous and wanted to get out of something.

A girl named Nula didn't remember later exactly what was said, but she thought Jon was being smart with Hamilton, sort of showing off, and

Hamilton got angry.

"Hey, no problem. No problem," Jon said.

"Let me talk to you outside," Hamilton said.

Chong Ko snickered. Chong was a stocky, black-haired kid who stood about five-seven. His Korean name was Chong and his American name was Steve. His friends called him Chong. He was sitting in the chair to the left of the door and, when he snickered, Meyers shot him a look.

"So you're a smart ass," Meyers said. "Stand up."

Chong stood up. Jon had also started to stand up and Hamilton gave him a shove and Jon sat back hard on the heating unit. Hamilton frisked Chong. Hamilton stopped his hand at Chong's jacket pocket and said, "What's this?" Chong took out an unopened pint of grain alcohol and set it on the table among the opened beer cans. Then he sat back down.

Hamilton turned to Jon again and motioned for Jon to get up. Jon got up and turned to start walking toward the door. Hamilton grabbed Jon's sleeve and jerked him hard in the direction of the door, and Jon stumbled.

I want to inject here that, so far as Mickey was concerned, you didn't touch Jon. Jon could take care of himself, but it was a thing about Mickey that was a part of who he was. It didn't matter who *you* were, and Hamilton had touched Jon *twice*.

Mickey was off the bed and behind Hamilton in a step. Mickey put a hand on Hamilton's arm from behind, to get Hamilton's attention, and Hamilton stopped and turned around. Hamilton glared at Mickey and Mickey ignored him. Mickey looked at Jon and said, "No. Don't go outside with him."

Hamilton looked down at the hand on his arm and said, "Get the fuck off my arm. Don't you know you can't touch a police officer?" Hamilton jabbed his night stick at Mickey's hand.

Mickey looked at Hamilton and took his hand away. "Where are you taking him? Outside, where you can hit him and nobody can see?"

This seemed to surprise Hamilton. "'Ain't nobody goin' to get hit," he said. "We're goin' outside to calm him down."

A flash of black passed in front of Mickey's face. The night stick pressed hard against his adam's apple, shutting off his air. Meyers, who was almost a foot taller than Mickey, lifted Mickey up and back with the stick. Mickey's air supply was shut off and he grabbed at the stick with both hands and caught hold of it at each end. Mickey pressed forward hard with his hands and body, trying to get the stick away from his throat. Then he and Meyers were stumbling about, and Hamilton jumped forward excitedly and struck Mickey hard in the eye with his night stick. Pain came from everywhere and centered in Mickey's face, but Mickey couldn't relax. He had to get air.

Jon was standing half outside the room in the doorway. He stepped backward out of the room as Mickey and Meyers came stumbling toward him. Mickey and Meyers took a few short steps and fell. Meyers released his grip on the night stick as they fell, and Mickey fell through the door sideways onto the sidewalk. He landed on his side and rolled from his side onto his back.

Meyers fell through the door and landed on the sidewalk beside Mickey. Meyers immediately sprang to his feet and jumped onto Mickey's stomach, straddling him. As Meyers landed on Mickey, he struck Mickey in the eye with his fist.

"Shit," Mickey said. "What are you doing?" Meyers drew back his fist and Mickey pressed up hard with his chest in an effort to flip Meyers off him before Meyers could strike him again. Meyers was too large and too heavy and he hardly budged.

"You're under arrest," Meyers shouted.

Mickey immediately went limp. Meyers rolled Mickey over and handcuffed Mickey's hands behind his back and Mickey lay still, face down on the sidewalk.

Other officers already were on the way as Hamilton and Meyers had arrived. Official records say that at some point after Meyers and Mickey fell outside, Hamilton called for backup. It's not clear from the records exactly when there would have been time to do that. There was a state police barracks hardly a mile up the road from the motel, and state troopers soon were arriving as well. The first of the officers other than Meyers and Hamilton began arriving at about the time Meyers was handcuffing Mickey.

To Mickey, the next blow felt like a forearm. It struck the back of his head and drove his chin into the sidewalk, tearing open the flesh.

"Damn," Mickey said. "Are you nuts?"

More blows followed. More officers arrived. Mickey turned his face sideways and braced himself. "You're real tough," he said, "beating on a kid with handcuffs on." Meyers hit him again and Mickey said, "Come on. Is that the best you can do? Give it your best shot." Meyers hit him again and Mickey laughed. "Tough guy," he said. "Real tough guy. Try again."

Chong watched in astonishment from his seat inside the door. He said later that Mickey was trying to act tough because he was getting hit and because, maybe, he didn't want to cry in front of the girls.

Jon was standing beside the door with his back to the brick wall. Hamilton shouted, "Back up. Back up." Later, when I read the transcripts, I wondered if Hamilton ever actually called for backup, or if this order to Jon somehow got turned into that.

"Where?" Jon said. "I'm as far back as I can get." They stared at each other and Jon said, "How about if I just lie down?"

"Right," Hamilton said. "Lie down."

Jon lay down next to where Meyers straddled Mickey's back.

"Not there," Hamilton shouted.

Jon got up and stepped farther down the sidewalk, out of sight to the kids in the room.

"How about here?"

"Yeah, there."

Jon lay spread-eagle on the sidewalk with his feet toward Mickey and

Meyers and his head facing south down Route 1, toward the nation's capital.

Meyers got off Mickey and ran to the door of the motel room. He shouted to the kids inside, "Put your hands on your heads." Some of the kids responded more slowly than others and Meyers shouted again, "Put your hands on your fucking heads."

Several officers gathered at the motel door with their backs to it. Chong and Puffy still could see a little of what was going on because they were sitting in the two chairs near the door. The others in the room were sitting on the bed and they could not see anything.

Mickey looked up and saw Meyers standing near the door. "What did I do?" Mickey asked. Meyers came over and gave Mickey a light kick, nothing particularly sharp, and said, "Shut up." Mickey was angry, and he started shouting, "Get their badge numbers. Get their badge numbers."

Jon raised himself up on one arm and shouted at Hamilton, "Y'all aren't smart enough to catch rapists and murderers, so you just break up parties and beat people up. Y'all can't do this just because you have badges."

An officer Jon didn't recognize reached down and struck Jon's arm with a night stick, sweeping Jon's arm out from under him, and Jon fell back to the sidewalk.

"Shut up," the officer said.

Jon raised his head and said, "But y'all can't do this. I'm telling you that you can't do this."

Hamilton leaned down and struck Jon in the mouth with his night stick, and blood began seeping from Jon's gums and through his lips. Jon winced and shut his eyes. Hamilton said, "If you say one more word you'll be arrested, too."

Jon opened his eyes and looked up at Hamilton. He raised his head and pulled his hands together behind his back.

"Arrest me then."

Neither Puffy nor Chong saw Hamilton hit Jon in the mouth. Puffy was not referring to that, but to the entire scene playing out before him, when he looked across the doorway at Chong and asked, "Did you see that?"

"Yeah, I saw it," Chong said. "and it's real. This is no movie." Mickey still was shouting, "Get their badge numbers," and Chong called out through the uniformed backs of the officers blocking the doorway, "Mickey, shut up. You're just making it worse."

One of the officers with his back to the door, call him Parker Howe, turned abruptly and stepped into the room. He shot the tip of his night stick at Chong's face. As Chong later told it with much animation, Chong opened his mouth in surprise as Howe came toward him and Howe crammed the night stick deep into Chong's mouth. Howe told investigators later that the timing was unfortunate, that Chong leaned forward just as Howe pointed the night stick. The way Howe told it, maybe a little of the tip touched Chong's mouth. Maybe a little went inside. Whichever, Howe shouted, "Shut the hell up." He jerked the night stick away and turned and left the room.

An officer we'll call Sam Long was standing near the outside wall. Jon recognized him as an officer who worked nights as a security guard at the Oakland Mills Village Center. "Hey, I recognize you," Jon said. Jon would tell investigators later that he didn't actually know Long; he was just glad to see a familiar face. Long walked toward him.

"Shut up," Long said.

Long stepped around Jon and the night stick pressed down hard against Jon's neck. In an effort to breathe, Jon twisted his neck until his face was pressed straight into the sidewalk.

Hamilton was watching and Mickey called to Hamilton, "If you didn't have that badge and gun, I'd fuck you up."

Meyers came over to Mickey and, with his boot, he pressed the side of Mickey's head down against the sidewalk. Meyers twisted the boot as if he was putting out a cigarette. Mickey braced himself against the boot as the sharp surface of the sidewalk cut into his cheek and head.

"Tough guys," Mickey muttered. "Real tough guys."

A high, wide passageway on the ground floor of the motel led through the center of the building to the rear parking area, where several police cars were parked. As Meyers escorted Mickey through the passageway, Mickey asked again, "What did I do?"

Mickey's hands still were handcuffed behind his back, and Meyers was holding Mickey by an arm and a wrist. Meyers said, "Shut up," and he slammed Mickey face-forward into the brick wall. Mickey raised his head to protect his nose from the bricks. His mouth struck the wall and the bricks cut him above his upper lip.

A K-9 unit and several other officers were waiting behind the motel with the patrol cars. As Meyers walked Mickey toward a police car, two officers came over to assist. One officer opened the door of the police car and Mickey bent down to get in. As if on cue, the other officer pushed Mickey hard in the back. The top of Mickey's head struck the molding above the door, and Meyers and the other two officers laughed. Mickey stood up and looked at the officer who had pushed him.

"You motherfucker. Why did you do that?"

The officers laughed again. Mickey bent down again to get in, and the officer pushed him again. The top of Mickey's head struck the door a second time.

Mickey stood and slowly straightened his back. He looked at the officers as if he was going to say something more. As they waited, still chuckling, Mickey quickly dropped backward onto the seat. He jerked his feet into the car and turned to face the front before the officers could assist him further.

Meyers leaned across Mickey to fetch the loose end of a seat belt. As he pulled the belt across Mickey's lap, Meyers elbowed Mickey in the mouth, splitting Mickey's lip.

"Damn," Mickey said. "Why did you do that?"

"Sorry," Meyers said. "It was an accident." He laughed.

An officer we'll call Tim Burns escorted Jon to a patrol car behind the motel. Burns was a fiercely muscular man with reddish blonde hair. I'd put him at the time in his late twenties or early thirties. As Burns led Jon through the passageway to the rear of the building, Meyers met them. Meyers brushed against Jon and looked down at him.

"You want some, too?"

Jon ignored him and Burns nudged Jon forward.

"Go ahead," Burns said. "Keep moving."

An officer came in the room and told the kids they could lower their hands. Officers searched under the bed and in the dresser drawers and began the gathering of names. Some referred to Chong with mocking names such as "Ching-Ching" and, "Boing-Boing," and "Ping-Pong." A girl asked if any citation against her could be sent to her college address rather than to her home. An officer laughed at her and said he would make a point of sending a letter to her home.

Meyers came back in the room and joined in the searching and name taking. He extracted the pipe from between the mattress and box spring and asked whose it was. No one responded, and he put the pipe in a sack. He took out a small pad and pencil and, as he asked for names, his hands shook noticeably.

No one except Chris produced any sort of identification. Meyers asked Chris for identification and Chris pulled out his driver's license. Meyers said, "I think I recognize you. I attended a party at your house. Right?"

"Yeah," Chris said. Chris remembered Meyers, but he didn't want to get into a conversation with him. Chris said later that Meyers looked, "Pos-i-tive-ly crazed."

"Your license says you were born in 'seventy," Meyers said. "We can change that to 'sixty-eight and charge you as an adult."

Chris forgot his determination not to speak to Meyers and said, "You can't do that."

Meyers laughed and handed the license back to Chris.

"Shut the fuck up," Meyers said.

No one was charged with underage drinking. The officers finally told those in the room they could leave. Chris was feeling a little drunk and he didn't want to drive, but he wanted even less to mention it.

Chong and Puffy and one of the girls stood around talking for a few minutes in the parking lot, waiting to see what would happen to Jon and Mick. An officer called out from the room, "Hey, you." Chong pointed to himself and the officer said, "Yeah, you," and motioned Chong back into the room.

Later, Chong would say that the officers singled him out because he wasn't afraid of them, and they didn't like that. Chong went back inside and sat in the chair by the door. Pamela, Eddie's girlfriend, was sitting in the other chair, and several officers stood around her. Pamela pointed at Chong and said, "Yeah. It was him. He brought the pipe in."

He didn't, and neither did Jon or Mick, and that's all I have to say about that.

"What are you talking about?" Chong said.

"Stop denying it," Pamela said. "You know you did it," and she started crying.

"She's crazy," Chong said. "Did you guys make her say that?"

Meyers strip-searched Chong in the bathroom and then told him he was under arrest.

"For what?"

"You'll find out at the station."

Pamela stayed behind to clean up the room, and Officer Tim Burns offered to drive her home. Hamilton drove Jon to the police station and Meyers drove Mickey.

Mickey had waited in the police car for about forty-five minutes. The handcuffs were tight, and his wrists hurt. Meyers had pulled out of the parking lot and was heading toward the police station in Ellicott City when Mickey asked Meyers if the handcuffs could be loosened or moved. Meyers said they would be at the station soon. Mickey asked again why he had been arrested.

"If you don't shut up I'll charge you with this," Meyers said, holding up the sack with the pipe in it so Mickey could see the pipe from the back seat.

"You can't do that."

"Haven't you ever heard of possession of drug paraphernalia?" Meyers asked.

"Yeah, I've heard of it. If you charge me with it, I don't suppose there's anything I can do about it, but it's not mine."

At the station, Jon and Mickey and Chong were finger-printed. They argued and asked what was going on. Officers laughed. Chong protested about the pipe, saying it wasn't his.

"Listen," Meyers said to Chong. "You're lucky we like you, or you'd look like your two buddies."

Jon's girlfriend, Jennifer Hollywood, was one of the young people who had been in the motel room. Jon told Meyers he wanted to call Jennifer's dad and have him come for him and Mick and Chong. Meyers looked at his notes.

"I think we'll call your parents."

"Don't do that," Jon said. "My mom'll just get all upset. It's my phone call. Let me decide who I call."

Meyers laughed and picked up the phone.

2 Sandra hadn't so much given up on the notion of getting married again as she had given up thinking about it. You could give yourself an ulcer.

Sandra was a petite woman with sharply outlined features. She would say in her native West Virginia twang that she had large ears and that her nose was bent a little to one side. Women worth knowing sometimes talk about themselves like that. She had long, auburn hair that she often wore straight down her back and, as often, wore in a loosely tied bun. She was inclined toward tight blue jeans and men's shirts and dangling earrings. She had the kind of figure that made other women look to see where their husbands were looking. She had dark brown eyes and one occasionally drifted almost imperceptibly to the outside just enough to give her a mysterious look.

Seven years earlier, in February of 1983, Sandra had come down with a sore throat and a headache and had slept away two days. On the morning that she re-emerged into the world, an unpredicted snow had fallen. Front doors were completely covered by drifts. Attics with ventilation louvers situated the wrong way into the wind let in a foot or two of snow. People shoveled their roofs so the roofs wouldn't collapse. The official snowfall was close to three feet, but homeowners in Columbia measured four feet in the flattest areas of their yards. Sandra came into the living room in her housecoat and Jon and Mick said they couldn't find her car. Sandra didn't know it had snowed and she thought the boys meant the car had been stolen. She bundled up and started down the open-air stairway that separated the two halves of the building. When she saw the white mounds in the parking lot she realized the car hadn't been stolen and she went back inside for a broom.

Jim Keyser, tall and lanky and with an almost incessant country boy smile, delivered the mail on Sandra's route. Jim also was divorced. To please his first wife he had joined her church, driven the church bus, taught a Sunday School class and almost completely given up beer. Then his wife ran off with a beer truck driver and Jim gave up church and started spending his Sundays playing golf.

Jim had spent the night with a fellow mail carrier in an apartment in another building in the complex where Sandra lived. Most of Sandra's neighbors were outside digging out cars and shoveling sidewalks, and Jim and his friend had joined in. The two men saw Sandra stumbling about in the snow, stabbing her broom at cars and occasionally bursting into tears. They came over and offered to help. Sandra accepted and Jim took the broom and began sweeping off cars, asking, "Is it this one? This one?"

Finally, Jim found it and, for a while, Sandra made an effort at helping clean it. She still felt weak from her cold and she cleaned and cried, cleaned and cried. She eventually apologized and went back inside and watched from her third-story window. The two men cleaned the snow from around the car, shoveled a path behind it, and then came up the stairs, knocked on the door and asked for the key. They went back downstairs and warmed the engine and then drove the car to the main street and parked it. When they returned with the key Sandra invited them in for coffee. In his somewhat shy, do-it-anyway manner, Jim told Sandra he had noticed her. He said he admired how she and her sons seemed to enjoy themselves. He asked if she was married. When she said no, he asked if he could call her sometime.

Jim and a group of his friends from work sometimes played darts at a local bar and restaurant called The Last Chance Saloon. After darts and a few beers worth of courage one night, Jim called Sandra and asked if she would like to go out for a drink. She said she would. Jim picked her up and they rejoined Jim's friends at The Last Chance. He had another beer. She had a glass of wine.

They were married in May of 1985. What tipped the scales in Sandra's mind was how respectful and accepting Jim was of her children. Her first husband, Carl, had custody of her daughter, Carlen, and, when Carlen visited and Jim came over, Jim treated Carlen like family. Jim bought Carlen an old and rusted orange Toyota and spent hours sanding and painting it. Carlen said she'd always wanted a gold car so Jim painted the Toyota gold. Carlen named it Fred. It embarrassed Jim that Carlen and Sandra made such a big deal of the way he had fixed up the car. It was something that was needed and he could do, so he had done it.

Jim had his concerns before the wedding. Sandra was college educated and smart and pretty. Jim didn't want to go away to Never-Never Land and then wake up one morning and find that he had only dreamed it. Sandra liked him, though. She had told him, and he thought he saw it sometimes in her eyes. She had said a bit awkwardly that she loved him, too, and he had gathered himself when he thought it had to be done and said it to her, and that also was important, he supposed.

Jim sold his house and they bought a townhouse in the Oakland Mills neighborhood in east Columbia. When Sandra's relatives from West Virginia asked what a townhouse was, Jim or Sandra explained. Theirs was the third unit down in an eight-unit row of two-story, connected dwellings. Jim and his two sons, Joe and Mike, and Sandra and Jon and Mickey, moved in. When Carlen came to visit, the family was complete.

Sandra was casual about housekeeping and Jim took up the slack. She filled the garbage and he took it out. Her gifts were more toward the artistic side of things, his toward the practical. Sandra dried flowers and hung them in wicker baskets from the artificial beams in the kitchen ceiling. Jim showed her how to fasten the baskets so they wouldn't fall. Sandra bought antique oak furniture at flea markets at bargain prices. Jim hauled it. Sometimes he made breakfast and sometimes she did. They had their arguments, but their arguments never woke the neighbors, and the arguments usually had a reassuring lack of a final edge. Both Sandra and Jim had been through it before. They knew how to leave each other alone, sometimes, and other times not at all.

When the phone rang at around midnight that Friday night, Sandra was upstairs trying to sleep. She had called the parents of practically all of Jon's and Mick's friends in an effort to find out why her sons weren't home yet, and she was certain her sons would be angry at her for making the calls. She worried that she was overly protective, and she worried that she had given up calling too soon and was not protective enough. She worried that she wasn't a good enough parent. She worried that they might be hurt, and if they weren't then she would give them what for. Sandra rolled over and fumbled on the dresser for the receiver.

The caller was a woman we'll call Katy Vickers, Eddie's mother.

"Now, don't get upset," Katy said in a shrill and excited tone, "but Jon and Mick have been arrested for assault and battery of a police officer."

"What?"

Sandra jerked up onto an elbow.

"Pamela, Eddie's girlfriend, told me. A police officer brought her here."

When Katy hung up, Sandra went down to the basement to tell Jim. She was suddenly angry and confused and, needing a place for the anger and confusion to land, she was angry at her sons. If they had done something they shouldn't have done, they *should* be in jail.

Jim was half awake in a recliner in the basement, watching an instructional videotape on golf.

"Calm down," Jim said. "We don't know the whole story yet. All we know is that Pamela told Katy something and Katy told you. That's third hand at least."

Then Sandra was angry at Jim.

"I'm calling the police department right now," Sandra said.

"Wait an hour," Jim said. "If the boys haven't come home by then, or if we haven't heard anything, then call."

"Oh, you just want to finish watching your tape," Sandra said.

"No, if you want to call now then call now, and we'll go up there if we need to. I'm just saying we should wait an hour."

The phone rang at around one o'clock, and Sandra answered it.

"This is Officer Meyers of the Howard County Police Department. Your sons have just been arrested for assaulting a police officer."

"I know," Sandra said.

"How do you know?" Meyers asked.

"A neighbor told me. I've been waiting to hear from the police."

"Oh," Meyers said. "Well, Jon's here, and he wants to talk to you."

There was a pause and then Jon said, "Mom?"

"Are you all right?" Sandra asked.

"No, I'm not all right, and Mickey's really upset. You can probably hear him yelling in the background." Sandra switched her attention but she couldn't hear Mickey. "We've both been beat up really bad," Jon said. "My mouth is all ripped up inside. Somebody needs to look at it."

Sandra heard Meyers yell, "Get him back in his cell. He's out of control." Then Meyers was on the phone again. "Mrs. Keyser," he said, "I can assure you that your boys don't have a scratch on them, and they do not need medical attention. All they need is an alcohol and drug abuse program."

"I'm coming down there," Sandra said.

"Don't do that," Meyers said. "They won't be released for at least six hours, and you can't see them. All you can do is sit out front and wait. If you want to do something, go to the Red Roof Inn and pick up their car."

"I don't think that will be necessary," Sandra said, "since their cars have been sitting in front of our house all night."

"Oh."

"If it's going to be six hours, then, okay, but I want to be called immediately when they are released, and I'll come get them."

"They're big boys," Meyers said. "They can walk home," and he hung up.

Sandra paced, talked with Jim about it, and then she went to bed. She drifted in and out of sleep throughout the night, wondering what her sons had gotten themselves into. At 6:00 a.m. she was sitting on the side of her bed looking out the upstairs window onto the parking lot when Puffy's older brother, Dennis, dropped the boys off. She went downstairs and met them at the door.

"Oh, my," she said. "What kind of party did you go to?"

Mickey's eyes were swollen nearly shut. One cheek bulged away from his face. His chin had crusted blood on it and looked ground like hamburger. Jon's face was puffy and his lower lip was red and swollen. There was wet blood in the cracks of his teeth. Jon and Mick looked angry. They brushed aside her question and went upstairs to shower and fall into their beds.

Sandra fretted about the house all day Saturday. From time to time she looked in on her sons as they slept. Had they had weapons of some sort? It was a preposterous thought, but why else did they look the way they did unless the police had to take weapons away from them?

When Jon and Mickey came downstairs at around five o'clock, Sandra was making spaghetti in the kitchen. Her sons were sullen, and they seemed angry at her.

"Tell me what happened?" she asked, but they wouldn't talk. They sat at the kitchen table staring at her and then looking at each other. "Are you angry at me?" she asked.

"Of course we're angry at you," Jon said. "What kind of mother tells the police that her sons are big boys and they can walk home? They took me back in the cell and I told Mickey and Mickey was as mad as I was."

"I couldn't believe it, " Mickey said.

The gears spun freely in Sandra's mind for a moment and then engaged as she realized what had happened.

"I didn't say that," she said. "That's what that policeman, that Officer Meyers, said to me."

The air gradually cleared between them and Jon and Mickey told her what had happened.

"Did you have guns?"

"What?" Mickey asked.

"You know, weapons of some kind?"

"Are you kidding? Nothing, Mom. It was just like we said."

"You believe us, Mom?" Jon said. "You do believe us?"

Sandra didn't know what to think. Why would a police officer play such a nasty trick as to tell her sons she had said something he had said himself? Why did her sons' faces look the way they looked if they hadn't had to be stopped from doing something really awful?

Sandra went to the table to look at Jon's mouth. He winced and leaned back and she pulled his lip down as gently as she could. Pieces of flesh inside his mouth were torn away and dangling.

"This is going to need stitches," she said.

"They can't stitch inside your mouth," Jon said. "Can they?"

"You have to have it looked at," Sandra said.

"I don't want anybody looking at it except Jennifer's mom," Jon said. "She's a nurse. I trust her."

Sandra looked at Mickey's face and she couldn't decide what to do.

"You and I are going to the doctor's office on Monday," she said to Mickey.

"Mom," Mickey whined.

Sandra found her Polaroid camera and took the boys into the back yard and took pictures of their faces. Jon and Mickey had a friend who had a friend who had been given a 35mm camera for Christmas. Jon called the friend, who borrowed the camera and came over, and Sandra took more pictures. Jon called Jennifer and Jennifer's mother was working the late shift and wouldn't be home and awake until Sunday.

Jon and Mickey knew about a Saturday night party at some friend's house that night, but they didn't go. They didn't want the people at the party to see them looking the way they did. They went to see a friend who's father was a police commissioner, a man whose job it was to sign the papers that said charges the police or anyone else made against someone were credible. They told the friend's father what had happened and he said he was shocked.

"You guys have to press charges against those cops," he said. "We can't have this kind of thing going on."

On Sunday, Jon went to Jennifer's. Jennifer's mother, Claudia, looked at Jon's mouth.

"This is serious," Claudia said. "You have to go to the emergency room and get stitches."

Jennifer went with Jon to the emergency room. When the nurse called for Jon, Jennifer went into the examination room with him. Jon sat on the examination table and waited.

The nurse was an attractive and slightly plump black woman in her late twenties. We'll call her Yvonne Last. She asked Jon, "Who did this to you?"

"Lenny Hamilton," Jon said.

"Oh, I know him," Last said. "I've dated him. He's bad news. He likes to act like a bad ass, beating up on people and then wanting to brag to me about it. You know."

Jon said, "Tell me about it."

3 I knew the Bowie twins because of baseball. Except for one year of Little League, and a few decades of softball, I didn't play organized ball. I was a decent enough player and had a basic understanding of the game, but I never got deeply involved with it. I certainly would not have considered coaching young people. I didn't have the background for it. Then a coach shouted at my oldest son.

I had hurried thirty miles home from Washington as quickly as a person can hurry in two to four lanes of stop and go traffic. By the time I finally got to the grassy field next to a local elementary school, the game was underway. Michael was seven at the time. His team was in the field and he was playing shortstop. A batter hit a screaming high popup that clearly would come down near Michael. Parents and coaches on the other side of the field were screaming to the runner at second base, "Run, he's going to drop it," and,

"Don't run. Tag." Parents and coaches on our side of the field were screaming, "Catch it," and "Don't drop it." Mike and I had played enough catch in our small back yard for me to know he could catch the ball. Whether he would in the middle of all that racket was a different matter. I watched the flight of the ball and held my breath. The ball finally came down and Michael caught it. He turned beaming to the sidelines to accept the cheers.

There weren't any. Parents on the other side were shouting to the runner at second, "Run to third," and, "Tag. Go back to second." Parents on our side were shouting at Michael, "Tag him out," and "Throw the ball." The runner had passed in front of Michael on his way to third base. He turned, ran past Michael again toward second, turned again and started for third, and then started for second again. Michael chased him for a few steps and then threw the ball to the second baseman. It arrived just after the runner returned safely. I tried not to smile too openly and made a mental note to go over that particular rule with Michael. The coach for Michael's team, an athletic, blonde-haired man wearing a royal blue jogging outfit, suddenly rushed onto the field. He ran up to Michael and shook a finger in his face. His face was red with anger and he screamed, "Don't you know anything about baseball? You have to throw to the base before the runner tags."

After the game, Michael and I rode home alone. I talked to him about how adults don't always behave the way they should and how kids have to learn to enjoy the game regardless of how other people act. What I didn't say was how angry I was at myself that I had stood and watched a grown man scream at my seven year old son without doing anything about it. I felt I had let him down. I didn't start coaching until the next season, but it was that night that I decided to do it. Plenty of people knew more about baseball than I did, but I couldn't let my children be treated like that.

Mike is two-and-a-half years older than my younger son, Dan, and after Dan started playing I would coach Mike's team one year and Dan's the next. I was coaching a team of ten and eleven year olds the first year that Dan, who was ten, and the Bowies, who were eleven, were on the same team for the first time. The Bowies were the kind of kids other kids wanted to be like. They enjoyed themselves, were good at what they did, and when it was over they forgot about it and did something else. Jon was the closest to a genuine free spirit I'd ever encountered. Mickey, although he usually had less to say, was also more fiery and more physical. Although their personalities differed, I still got them confused after I'd known them for years. They were both sandy haired with dark eyebrows and had a glint of the devil in their eyes. Later, after Jon's death, Mickey told me that sometimes he and Jon switched positions for the fun of it and Mickey played catcher and Jon went to shortstop. I never caught them at it.

During the first summer I knew them, I also met their mother, Sandra. She is Sandra Keyser now, but she hadn't met or married Jim Keyser at the time. She was a single, divorced parent and went by her maiden name, which was Aylor. I kept forgetting it and, like almost everyone else, referred to her as Sandra Bowie. She was six months older than I was, so she would have been in her middle thirties when I first met her. She came to every game to watch her sons play and she cheered vigorously from the sidelines. The first conversation with her that I recall followed an afternoon practice. She informed me in sweet tones to be reckoned with that, although Mickey was a good pitcher, a coach in West Virginia had overused him and his arm had been injured. I knew immediately that having Mickey pitch would be a serious mistake, and I didn't consider doing it. Some people might have thought I was looking out for my player, but I was looking out for myself.

A second popup story happened during the first season I knew the Bowies. We were playing a team coached by a local psychologist. The game was close that day, and, about halfway through it, one of his players hit a popup that went almost straight up and obviously would come down near the pitcher's mound. A kid named Ahmed was pitching the game for us. Ahmed was a good athlete and was likely to catch the ball. The psychologist began screaming across the field to the runner at first base, "Run. He's going to drop it. He's going to drop it." I watched the ball and listened as the psychologist tried to intimidate Ahmed into dropping the ball. By the time the ball came down I was pretty aggravated. Ahmed caught the ball, and the runner, who probably knew Ahmed, had been smart enough not to listen to his coach. As Ahmed caught the ball, a flash of auburn hair and blue jeans crossed in front of him and rushed in a straight line to the other side of the field. The coach looked around and Sandra was shaking a finger up at his face. She shouted, "Don't you play those mind games with our kids. You save it for the people on your couch." In truth, *people* is not the word she used, but let's just leave it at that. Sandra turned and marched back across the field, leaving everyone who saw it more than a little stunned. A league rule prohibited parents from coming onto the field, but no one thought to bring that up.

When Mike was about fourteen, he asked me not to coach him anymore. He didn't like the feeling of being the coach's son. He said I was too hard on him in an effort to be fair, and he couldn't feel that anything he accomplished was clear-cut when his dad was deciding when he played and when he didn't. It sounded reasonable to me, and I agreed and began coaching Dan's team each year.

The Bowies were a year older than Dan. Some years the age brackets were such that they played in the same league, and some years the Bowies played in an older age group. Whenever I could I got them on my team, which happened to be every time their ages fit.

When Jon and Mick were fourteen, I ran into Jon one day at the mall. It was a year when he would be in the right age group to play on Dan's team, and I mentioned baseball. By that age the kids were selected by draft, and Jon told me he didn't plan to play that year unless I drafted him. His varsity coach also coached in the league. Jon was afraid his varsity coach would draft him as a catcher, and he wouldn't get to pitch. I told him I would do what I could.

The league draft was held in the Commissioner's kitchen, and I suggested to the other coaches that we draft pitchers and then catchers and then the other players so the league would be somewhat balanced. The others agreed, and I drew the third or fourth pick. Jon was a catcher of considerable reputation in the county, and he was likely to be the first pick in the second round, when we had agreed that catchers would be picked. When I picked Jon in the first round as a pitcher, the other coaches spit beer all over the Commissioner's kitchen curtains. Jon's varsity coach immediately picked Mickey in retaliation. I was reasonably certain that neither Jon nor Mick would play unless they were on the same team, and I had to trade the equivalent of half of a county all-star team to get Mickey. Jon's varsity coach kept insisting that Jon was not a pitcher, so, to sweeten the dealings and work on his ego some, I finally promised him that Jon would pitch when we played his team.

Jon, who didn't know any of this, practically begged at the first practice to pitch against his varsity coach's team. I promised that he could on the condition that he not have anything to say to his varsity coach during the game beyond normal courtesies. He promised. By the middle of that game we had scored quite a few runs and the other team hadn't scored any, and had hardly gotten a hit. With the game well in hand, Jon left the mound at the end of an inning and walked to the wrong sideline. I took a deep breath and watched. Jon walked in the direction of his varsity coach. When he was a few feet away from the man, Jon turned and came back to our side of the field. As he arrived I asked him, "What did you say?" "Nothing, Coach," he said, with a surprised and innocent look that had that slight hint of devilment in it. Then he grinned. "I just winked at him."

We got knocked out of the championship series in the semifinal game that year because I was saving Jon to pitch the championship game. Things got out of hand and I brought Jon in too late and we never got to the championship game. After all these years, Dan still reminds me occasionally that I should have started Jon in the semifinal game, and that it was a coach's loss. What can I say?

And there was, of course, the Great Potato Play. I had read of a similar incident in *Reader's Digest*, and I would learn later that Jon and Mick had read the same story. The kids were sixteen or so, and Jon suddenly stood during a game from his position as catcher and threw a peeled potato six feet over the third baseman' head into left field. Mickey ran from his shortstop position out toward the outfield after the potato and the left fielder ran in after it. The baserunner on third stutter-stepped toward home, looked back at Mickey and the left fielder running wildly after what the runner thought was the ball, looked toward home plate again, looked back into the outfield, and finally started jogging in to score. Just before the runner reached home plate, Jon reached behind his waistband, pulled out the ball and tagged the runner. The umpire got pretty steamed at Jon.

There were more seasons and more stories and then the kids started graduating and going off to college or getting jobs. Jon and Mickey got full scholarships to play baseball for a school in North Dakota. Mickey also planned to play football in college, and, before school started, Mickey left for North Dakota to start football practice. Two weeks later, Sandra and Jim and Jon rode up to North Dakota together. Jim and Sandra had decided to make a vacation of it and tour the area after the boys were settled. Mick and Jon put their heads together that first day and then announced to Jim and Sandra that they had decided not to go to school there after all. It was too cold, they said, too far from home, too whatever. Jim and Sandra talked about it and decided that maybe the boys were just getting cold feet. Sandra told the twins that she and Jim weren't going to abandon their plans for a vacation, and that, if the boys weren't staying, they simply would have to get themselves home. She thought that would be the end of it. She and Jim toured the area and Jon and Mickey took a Greyhound home. Sandra eventually got over it, and Jon and Mickey started school at a local community college.

I didn't know any of this story of the entrance and fast exit from college when, sometime in January, I was at the town mall and I ran into a kid I had coached. He asked if I had heard that the Bowies had given up their scholarships and come back to Columbia. I was so distracted by it that I forgot my errands and returned home. I found the Bowies' phone number on an old roster and called. Jon answered.

"Hey, Mick," I said.

Jon laughed. "Nah, Coach. This is Jon. 'You want to talk to Mick?"

Once I knew I was talking to Jon, I thought I could distinguish his slightly higher, slightly clearer voice. That's what I told myself, anyway, and I was irritated at myself and a little embarrassed that I had mixed them up again.

"Not particularly," I said. "I mean, either one. I just called to find out what's going on."

"'You mean about school?"

"Yeah. What's the story?"

I don't recall Jon ever hesitating to search for an answer, and he didn't this time, either.

"It's too cold in North Dakota."

I did hesitate.

"Were the books giving you trouble?"

"Nah, that wasn't it. Like I said, it was just cold."

"What about Mickey? Was he having trouble?"

"Nah. They told him he probably would make the football team, and I'm pretty sure I was going to make the baseball team. We just talked about it and decided to come home."

We talked for several minutes and I became begrudgingly convinced that Jon was comfortable with the decision.

"I don't suppose your mother took it too well."

He laughed. "She'll get over it."

"So everything's going all right, then?"

"Well, almost. Mick and I got beat up by some cops over the holidays."

I couldn't imagine Jon and Mick being beaten up by anyone. They weren't giants, but their agility and athletic prowess had provided the substance for a small local legend.

"How? I mean, what did you do?"

"Nothing," he said. "Seriously. I mean, we had a party at a motel, and there was some beer, but the cops just got crazy and started hitting us."

"Did you hit them back?"

"Nah. I'm not stupid. You can't hit a cop. I would have liked to, but they had badges, you know. One of them was pretty big, but I think we could have taken them in a fair fight."

This wasn't sinking in. I paced back and forth in the kitchen, searching for an appropriate thought.

"Did you get hurt?"

"Yeah, some. Mickey's face was all cut up and bruised, and he got black eyes. They hit me with a billy club a couple of times and cut my mouth and stuff."

I was at a complete loss as to where to take my end of the conversation. It was simply outside my frame of reference.

"We can't have that," I finally said. "Is there anything you can do about it?"

"We've got attorneys, and we filed complaints. The police department is investigating it."

"Well, good. We just can't have that sort of thing." Then I changed the subject. "How's Mickey doing?"

"To tell you the truth, I'm not sure. He doesn't seem to have his head together. He just lays around and hangs out."

"Well, you know Mick. He'll sort things out and he'll be all right."

"I guess. I don't see how there's anything I can do about it, regardless."

"Well, tell him I said hello."

"Okay, Coach."

"And you're sure everything's all right?"

"Sure, Coach. I'm sure."

We said goodbyes and take cares and then hung up. I didn't exactly forget about what Jon had told me about the motel incident, but I did assume it was taken care of. Later, I would think of this as the last conversation I would ever have with Jon Bowie.

4 During the week following the motel incident, Jon read a feature article in a local paper about the Reverend Doctor John Wright, the outgoing head of the county chapter of the NAACP. Wright, the article said, had a reputation for taking on local agencies, including the police, and for a willingness to help anyone, race aside. Jon figured that maybe Wright knew how to go about filing complaints against the police, and Jon wrote Wright a letter. Jon looked up the address of Wright's church in the phone book. He drove to the address on a rural road south of Columbia to deliver the letter himself. Wright wasn't there and Jon left the letter in the church door. Jon checked the next day and the letter still was in the door. He put a stamp on it and put it in the mailbox of a home across the street.

Jon's determination made Sandra doubt her own doubts. Still, she couldn't feel certain that her sons were justified in filing complaints against the police. She knew people could get excited and see what they wanted to see. She neither encouraged nor discouraged Jon and Mickey, and she kept expecting the issue to go away in some natural way that wasn't clear at the time.

Wright called Jon and told him it didn't matter that Jon and Mickey were white. The NAACP was interested in hearing their story. Jon and Mickey met with Wright and Wright recommended an attorney, Jo Glasco, who was a member of Wright's congregation. Sandra reluctantly agreed to go along with Wright's suggestions, but she said the boys would have to pay for the attorney themselves. She secretly thought this would end the matter, but the boys immediately began saving money. They met with Glasco, who recommended a second attorney for Jon. Glasco explained that there was some legal necessity, which Sandra didn't completely follow, for the boys to have separate attorneys.

With the attorneys' guidance, both boys filed formal complaints at the police department against Officers Roland Meyers, Lenny Hamilton and Sam Long. This would lead to an internal police department investigation of whether the officers had used excessive force or violated any other police department policies or procedures.

The boys also filed formal assault charges against the officers at the courthouse. These charges put the case in the normal judicial process and would lead, they thought, to a day in court, when they could tell their stories to a judge.

The police department, meanwhile, charged Jon and Mickey with various offenses such as assault on an officer, hindering an officer in the performance of his duties and resisting arrest. These charges were expected to lead to trials in which Jon and Mickey would be defendants.

Reverend Wright arranged an evening press conference in the basement of his church. Reporters came from the Baltimore Sun, the Washington Post and the Columbia Flier. Most of the kids who had been at the motel were there. Sandra was the only parent who came. Jon, Mickey, Chong Ko and Reverend Wright sat at a table in front of the room, and everyone else sat facing them in card chairs. Wright made an opening statement saying this was not a race issue. The reporters asked questions and took notes. After the meeting, the boys felt upbeat about the exposure, but none of the papers printed anything about the meeting or about the incident at the motel.

At Wright's suggestion, Jon and Mickey visited the local Human Rights Commission. The Commission met in a conference room in an office building in an industrial complex in north Columbia. Commission membership was an appointed county position, and the members volunteered their time, so no one on the Commission was present to speak with them. A woman instructed the boys to fill out a form. The woman said that someone from the Commission would get in touch with them. The form asked for the nature of the complaint and, on a separate line, asked for the reason it might have happened. Jon and Mickey couldn't think of any reason why it had happened, so they wrote *Age*.

In early February, a police officer I'll call Nelson Graham interviewed Jon and Mickey and most of the other kids who had been at the motel. Graham was the head of the Internal Affairs Division of the county police department. The Internal Affairs Division, or IAD as it's often called, was the part of the police department that investigated complaints against police officers. Jon and Mickey told Sandra that the interviews went all right, although Graham kept trying to get them to say they had drunk more beer than they had and to say they had been some sort of ring leaders in the group.

Reverend Wright also suggested that the boys contact the FBI, because that agency investigated complaints against officers. Sandra hadn't known that. Sandra took off from work one afternoon and went with the boys to the local office of the FBI. The FBI office was on the outskirts of Baltimore in a large, one-story, pebble-finish building that sat in a graveled parking lot. Sandra waited inside in the large reception area as a black agent I'll call Sutherland interviewed the boys. Sandra put Sutherland at about thirty-six. She thought he had good eyes. Sutherland interviewed Mickey first and then Jon. He talked to each of them for well over an hour. Sutherland invited Sandra to participate in the interviews, but she declined. Jon and Mick were nervous, and Sandra thought she should wait with each son as he waited to be interviewed. After the interviews, Sutherland told Sandra he wanted the photographs that were taken at the motel. He came by their home a few days later to get them.

A few weeks passed. One evening Sutherland and his boss, a tall and trim grey-haired man in his middle fifties, came to the house. Sandra immediately sensed bad vibrations and noticed that Sutherland wouldn't look her in the eyes. She led the two men into the kitchen and called the boys. She sat at the table with Sutherland's boss. Jon stood across the kitchen with his back to the counter, and Mickey sat at the table. Sutherland stood at the kitchen door, hardly coming into the room.

"Mrs. Keyser," Sutherland's boss said, "We've looked into this matter, and our investigation shows that there was no wrong-doing on the part of the police officers." Sandra stared at him without responding, and, after an uncomfortable silence, he continued. "You have to understand, Mrs. Keyser, that police officers have bad days, too."

Sandra was immediately furious, and she sat in silence as she tried to control her emotions. The thought that went through her mind was, "I work with children all day. If I had a bad day and hit one of them, I'd be out of a job. What kind of explanation is that?" She didn't say it. When she sensed that the blood in her face had begun to cool, what she said was, "What else can we do?"

"If I were you, I'd just drop it," Sutherland's boss said.

"You don't believe us?" Mickey asked.

Sutherland's boss stood as if he had been about to leave. He said to Mickey, "Young man, you should understand that you have to listen to what a cop says. You have to learn to respect authority."

Mickey went, "Pffft," with his lips and waved an arm in the agent's direction. "Forget it," he said.

Sandra saw the disappointment behind her son's nonchalance. She saw it in Jon's face, too. As calmly as she could manage, she said, "Why don't you give the boys a lie detector test? Then make up your minds what happened."

Sutherland's boss gave Sandra an icy stare and said, "It is our experience that habitual liars can pass a lie detector test."

The lid nearly blew off of Sandra's calm, but she had to save the situation if she could for the sake of her sons. She tried to keep her voice from trembling, and said, "What do you think the chances are that there were fourteen habitual liars in the same motel room?"

Sandra still wasn't one hundred percent convinced her sons were doing the right thing by pursuing their complaints against the police officers, but the meeting in her kitchen with Sutherland and his boss was something of a turning point for her. Regardless of the merits of the case, she didn't think the FBI had taken the matter seriously. They hadn't done their jobs. They had walked into her kitchen as representatives of everything she believed about America, and they had left mumbling about police officers having bad days.

When the FBI agents had left, Sandra went back into the kitchen thinking that she knew a bit about what it felt like to be a black person in America. Jon asked her if she believed them.

"Yeah," Sandra said, slowly, and with less than complete conviction.

Mickey looked at Jon.

"I still don't think she believes us," Mickey said, "but she's in."

One evening in March, Mick was getting ready to go to a party at Chong Ko's sister's apartment. Chong's sister, who was planning to move, would be out of town. She said the kids could use her apartment. Jon was getting over a bad case of strep throat, and he didn't think he would go. Before leaving for the party, Mickey reminded Jon that Loyola Marymount was playing basketball on television in the NCAA basketball tournament. Even though Loyola Marymount's star, Hank Gathers, had died suddenly, the team still was scoring around one hundred points a game, and people were starting to wonder if the team could win it all that year. Jon decided to go to the party.

There might have been as many as three dozen people at the party. They wandered in and out of the rooms watching television and talking. The doorbell rang at about ten o'clock and somebody said the police were at the door. Chong said he wasn't putting up with anymore of this and answered the door. He stepped outside closing the door behind him, and Jon and Mickey stood at the door watching through the peep hole. It was Meyers and another officer, a black guy the kids didn't recognize. Meyers wanted to know how many people were in the house, and Chong wouldn't tell him. He said he didn't know. Meyers said everyone had to leave, and Chong said, "Fine, but you're not coming inside. I've had enough of you guys."

Meyers asked, "Are the Bowie twins here?"

"They might be," Chong said, "and they might not be. You're not coming in to find out. I'll tell everyone to leave, but you're not coming in."

When Jon and Mickey heard Meyers ask for them, they ran through the apartment and out the back door. Other people also were starting to leave through the front and rear doors. Meyers called out for the officer with him to go around back and look for two brothers who were twins and hold them, because Meyers wanted to talk to them.

Jon and Mickey ran through the woods and several of the others ran with them. About ten people stopped on a hill in the woods and watched as the officers came around back and shined their flashlights onto the back of the building and into the woods. Jon's car and Mickey's car were parked at the apartment, and they weren't sure what to do. A kid named Sean, a large black kid who played football and looked it, said that, since the officers were looking for twins, Jon and Mickey should split up. That way, the officers wouldn't know if they were twins even if they saw one of them. Sean walked with Mickey the several miles back to Mickey's house. Mickey had been home about a half hour when Jon arrived and came into the kitchen.

Jon said he had gone to a friend's home in a nearby apartment complex called Copperstone, and Meyers had showed up there. Jon and his friend Chris and the friend who lived there had been outside in front of the apartment, and Meyers drove up in his police car. As Chris told it later, Meyers looked over at them and then went into another building across the parking lot. It scared Jon that Meyers had asked for him at the party and then had showed up where they'd gone after the party broke up.

The next day, Sandra called Sergeant Graham of the Internal Affairs Division. Sandra told Graham she wanted Meyers to stay away from her sons. Graham told her Meyers couldn't have been at the Copperstone complex because it was not Meyers' patrol area. Sandra said, "That's ridiculous. Police cars have wheels the same as any other car. If Jon says Meyers was there, then he was there. I'm telling you that I want him kept away from my sons."

Sutherland, the FBI agent, came by several days later to return the photographs, and Sandra told Sutherland about the party.

"It sounds like Meyers is feeling guilty about something," Sutherland said.

"I don't care what it sounds like," Sandra said. "My sons have told the police department and the FBI what happened at that motel, and nobody believes them. Now this guy Meyers shows up at a party looking for them, and then he shows where Jon went after the party. I tell the police and they don't care. I tell you about it and you just shrug it off. What does it take to get you people to pay attention?"

5   It was mid-April when Sandra, Jon, Mickey and several of the kids from the motel incident went to the courthouse. Jon and Mickey were to be tried for assaulting a police officer and such.

Sandra and the others got there early and were sitting in the lobby or mingling about when Sergeant Graham arrived. Graham came over to where Jon and Sandra were sitting. Graham shook Jon's hand and said, "You and I need to talk." Graham stepped around the sofa and Jon followed him. They stopped a few feet away, and Sandra listened to their conversation.

"I've got a problem with what you had to say about Officer Long," Graham said.

"What kind of problem?"

"Well, are you sure he was the one who stuck the night stick against your neck?"

"Yeah, I'm sure," Jon said. "I know him from the village center. It was him."

Sandra was convinced that Graham told Jon that Long couldn't have been at the motel because Long wasn't on duty that night. What Graham said was not clarified by the official records, which did make it clear that Long was present at the motel. Graham and Jon finished talking, and Jon returned to his seat next to Sandra.

"What was that all about?" Sandra asked.

"I don't know," Jon said. "I think he wants me to drop the charges against Sam Long. I'm not sure what to do."

From what Jon and Mickey had told her, Sandra didn't think Long had been the main culprit at the motel. She had heard stories that led her to believe that Long wasn't the kind of person who should be a police officer, but, if the police department wanted to protect Long for some reason, then going along might help in some way. She told Jon this.

"I don't know," Jon said. "I don't like it. I know what happened."

"Do what you do," Sandra said. "I'm just telling you what I think."

Sergeant Graham, meanwhile, was having a conversation with Jon's attorney, the woman Jo Glasco had recommended. Jon's attorney was a former assistant state's attorney, which meant she had once worked for the side she now was opposing. She knew many of the police officers in Howard County, and she knew Meyers fairly well. Graham told her that most of the police officers in the county were not happy with her for taking the case.

In time I would have reason to have a few conversations with Graham. In the early seventies he was the first black officer hired by the Howard County police department, and that set of circumstances took some courage and a lot of determination on his part. I liked the guy. I didn't think he was the sort to try intentionally to intimidate anyone. Still, intentional or not, it can come out the same.

As Sandra and the kids filed into the courtroom, another case was underway. The room looked almost like a small chapel with its white walls, high, narrow windows and light-oak pews. Sandra didn't want to disturb the proceedings, so she sat with several of the kids toward the end of the last row, away from the center aisle. Jon and Mickey sat in the row in front of her. Sandra's hair was gathered in a pony tail, and, from the rear, she would have looked like one of the young girls in the group.

A big, tall police officer came into the court room. He looked at the large representation of young people sitting in the rear of the court room and then went to the front and spoke in whispers to the county attorneys. He returned to the rear of the room and stood behind Sandra with his back to the wall. Sandra had never seen this big and extremely tall officer before, and she paid no particular attention to him. Perhaps a minute had passed when there was a thump against the seat immediately behind Sandra. She ignored the thump and kept looking forward. Then there was another thump, and another. Keys jangled behind her. She heard a low, guttural, growling sound. After several minutes the officer pushed himself away from the wall and walked up the aisle toward the front. As he passed the kids he looked over at Jon and grinned. He continued on to the front, sat in the row behind the county attorneys and leaned over and whispered to them again.

Puffy was sitting in the end seat in front of Mickey. He turned around and whispered to the kids behind him, "Did you see that?"

"Yeah, I saw it," Jon whispered back in an excited tone.

Sandra leaned forward across the seat back. Jon's face was turned slightly away, and she saw tears swelling in his eyes.

"Who is that?" she asked.

"Don't you know?" a kid named Charlie asked. "That's Meyers."

"So what," Mickey said. "He's nothing."

"Like hell," Charlie whispered. "That man's dangerous."

Sandra sat back in her seat and looked at the gigantic man sitting with the county attorneys in the front of the room. In that instant her nagging doubts disappeared. She thought, "These kids really are telling the truth."

The case in progress dragged on. Meyers got up and came to the back again and leaned against the wall behind Sandra and the kids. He thumped the back of the seat several times with his knee, jangled his keys, and made low, growling noises. Sandra and the kids stared intently forward. After a few minutes, Meyers pushed himself away from the wall and started back for the front. As he walked past Mickey, he bumped Mickey's shoulder. Puffy was sitting at the end of the row in front of Mickey with one arm propped on the end of the seat. As Meyers passed Puffy he swept out a hand and knocked Puffy's arm off the seat.

Sandra was up and moving before Puffy had recovered.

"Excuse me. Excuse me," she whispered as she made her way to the center aisle. She found Jo Glasco and the woman who was Jon's attorney just outside the courtroom in the large waiting room. She hurried up to them and told them what had been happening.

"Somebody has to do something," she said. "That idiot is terrifying those kids. Somebody has to do something or..." She took a breath. "Somebody has to."

"You go back inside," Jo said. "We'll talk to Sergeant Graham."

Sandra returned to her seat. Graham came in the courtroom and went to the front and motioned for Meyers to come with him. They were gone several minutes and then Meyers came back inside. Meyers turned inside the door, walked along the rear wall and stopped immediately behind Sandra. He leaned against the wall and jangled his keys loudly.

Sandra jumped to her feet, excused her way to the far end of the row again, and went around the row to the rear wall. She stopped beside Meyers and turned, facing the front of the room. Her intention was to stand beside him as long as he stood there. She was not going to put up with his trying to intimidate her or the kids.

As Sandra stood facing forward, she was struck with how large Meyers was. Her head hardly came up to his chest. Meyers stood with his arms folded across his chest, now looking intently forward himself. Sandra folded her arms across her chest, mimicking his position. Her legs began to shake and her heart pounded. For a long moment she was afraid she might faint. From the corner of her eye she saw Meyers slowly turn his head and look down at her. She sensed that he wanted her to look back at him, and she kept looking forward.

Jo Glasco and Jon's attorney came into the room, and Graham followed them in. Meyers looked over at Graham coming into the room and Meyers jerked away from the wall. He hurried to the front and sat down, and Sandra returned to her seat.

The court clerk called the state's case against Jon and Mickey, and attorneys made their ways to the front. That almost took longer than the case itself. An assistant state's attorney, a dark-haired man in a navy suit, said the county was not prepared to go forward. Sandra's sense of it was that the state's attorney was surprised that so many of the young people who had been at the motel had showed up to testify.

Jo Glasco objected that she wished to proceed. She said there was reason to believe that the safety of some of the young people was at risk. The judge, a thin, grey-haired man with wire-rimmed glasses, brushed that off and saw it the state's way. The case was continued.

The kids and Sandra grumbled to each other as they left the courtroom. Sandra and Jon and Mickey waited in the lobby for others to catch up. Sergeant Graham came out of the courtroom and saw them, and he waited with them until Meyers had left. As Meyers walked past them, he crouched down into a slumped posture, ducked his chin down close to his chest, and held his palm sideways to his face, like a blinder on a horse's bridle.

"What a wise ass," Graham muttered.

Sergeant Graham had already interviewed many of the kids who had been at the motel, including Jon. A few days after the case was continued, Graham had Jon return to the police station for a second interview. Graham led Jon into the interviewing room and closed the door. Graham talked with Jon for a while and then turned on the tape recorder.

"Okay," Graham said, "After we had some discussion, you said there is a chance that Long may not have been the person that put the night stick up against your neck."

"Right," Jon said.

"Okay, and can you tell me what you base that on?"

"Okay, 'cause when I was laying on the ground and I looked up, and I told Officer Long that I knew him, and that I knew where he worked, he walked over to me in a loop where his face got out of my sight. But I saw his feet walk around. And then an officer, it could have been another officer, put a night stick to my neck."

"Okay. When Sam..." Graham stopped and corrected himself. "When Officer Long walked around you, how long was it before another officer, ah, approached you and put the night stick against your neck?"

"It was right as he got right next to me and stopped."

"Could you see the officer's face?"

"No, I couldn't. I could see his hand, and the outside was pressing down with his night stick."

"He was actually pushing your neck with the barrel of the night stick?"

"Yeah."

"You said you were laying on the ground outside the motel room, facing toward Washington. Right?"

"Yeah."

"Where was Officer Long when you saw him?"

"He was standing next to the door. I told him I recognized him from the village center."

"And what did he say?"

"'Told me to shut up."

"Were you saying anything else?"

"Nah. After I said that, he just told me to shut up and started walking around towards me, and I didn't say *nothing*."

"And then you saw him walk toward..."

"Walk around, like towards me, and stop."

"Did you watch him to see where he went?"

"Yeah, I saw his feet, and then, after that, I just looked at the wall again and then somebody came up and put a billy club on..."

"Okay, so your eyes went away from his body, from his feet, for a period of time."

"Yeah, they did."

"And then someone, some officer, came up, placed a night stick..."

"Yeah."

"And you assumed it was Long in the beginning because he had been the one standing between you..."

"Yeah, 'cause he stopped right next to me, and I assumed it was him."

"Okay. So you're really not sure if Long was the one who put the night stick up against your neck?"

"Yeah. Since I looked away, I guess not."

"The only thing that you said when you were lying on the ground was, looking up at Officer Long, saying, 'I know you from Oakland Mills'?"

"Yeah."

"You did that because you didn't want him to do anything to you, and you wanted him to know that you knew who he was?"

"Yeah. It was like, 'Good, at least I know somebody here.'"

Following this interview, charges against Officer Long were dropped.

6 One day out of the blue, Jon said to a friend, "I don't think I'm going to live much longer."

This surprised the friend, who asked, "Why would you say that?"

"I don't know," Jon said. "Call it a feeling. I think it has something to do with a car. Maybe I'm going to die in a car wreck."

Jon began telling Sandra and others that Meyers was following him. Hollywood said what most adults would have said.

"Why would a cop do that?"

Jon was working as a teaching assistant at the daycare center that Sandra managed. He usually worked from eight in the morning until six in the evening. He began changing his schedule to arrive at unpredictable times. Sometimes he arrived as early as six-thirty in the morning. One morning he gave Anne Beck, Sandra's assistant, a license number he had written down. He told Anne the number was for a brown pickup that had been following him, and had followed him again that morning. "It's Meyers," Jon said. "Meyers is following me." Anne gave the license number to Sandra, and Sandra stored it away.

Sandra called Internal Affairs again and told Graham she wanted to talk to the Chief of Police. She wanted Meyers to stay away from Jon. Graham made a note of the phone call and filed it.

Mickey cleaned the daycare center in the evenings after nine o'clock. Mickey had an old Honda that Jim had bought cheap and fixed up for him, and Mickey always drove himself to work. One night Mickey called home and asked Jim to come get him. "There are two guys hiding outside behind the dumpster," Mickey said. "I don't want to go out there. It's like they're stalking me." Jim came to get Mickey and looked around outside, but Jim didn't see anyone.

Anne Beck lived near the daycare center and, on several evenings, Mickey called Anne's husband, Richard, and asked Richard to come and escort him out of the daycare center. Mickey told Richard that he kept seeing the same two men outside. Richard came each time Mickey called, but Richard never saw the two men.

At two in the morning on Monday, April 30, Jon came into his mother's second story bedroom and shook her awake.

"Meyers is in the back yard," Jon said excitedly. "Come see."

Sandra followed Jon across the hall to his bedroom. Henry, their curly-haired, black terrier, ran in front of them, barking and jumping about. Henry jumped at the window sill and Sandra whispered loudly, "Henry, hush." As Sandra got to the window she was certain she heard someone running. She looked out onto the tiny back yard and couldn't see anyone. The gate to their tall privacy fence was always kept closed. On this night, the gate was open.

On Wednesday, May 2, Jon woke Sandra again between two and three in the morning.

"He's out there, Mom."

Sandra followed Jon into the bedroom again and looked out the window into the back yard. She couldn't see anyone, and, this time, she didn't hear anything. She did see, however, that the screen to Jon's second story window had been cut and pushed inward.

On Thursday, May 3, at around six in the morning, Jon went into Mickey's bedroom and woke him.

"Meyers is in the back yard," Jon told Mickey.

"Meyers is not in the back yard," Mickey grumbled. "It's just your imagination. Go back to sleep."

Jon drove his silver Mercury Topaz to the daycare center. He made sandwiches for the children's lunch. He joked around with several of the children, making them laugh. Then he took off work early and spent the better part of the day helping two brothers and their family move to a house a few blocks from where Jon and Mickey lived.

At around five-thirty in the afternoon, Jennifer Hollywood called Jon from Florida, where she attended college. They talked small talk. Jon and several friends were planning a trip to Delaware that week-end, and they talked about that. A friend, Danny, who was in school in Virginia called Jennifer while she and Jon were talking, and Jennifer answered the over-ring. She had been trying to get in touch with Danny to talk about the upcoming summer vacation, so she switched back to Jon and told him that Danny was on the other line and she would call Jon back in a few minutes. When Jennifer called back a few minutes later, she told Jon that Danny had talked about his plans for going home and about the upcoming trip to Delaware. Danny was hoping he could get home for the week-end so he could go to Delaware with the others. Jon and Jennifer drifted into one subject after another for about fifteen minutes. Jennifer had seen a movie, and she told Jon about it. Jon was in a good mood. He said that Vernon Gray on the County Council was helping him get a restraining order to keep Meyers away from him, and he wouldn't have to worry about that anymore. As the conversation wound down, Jennifer said she hoped he had a good time in Delaware. He laughed and said he expected he would. Then he told Jennifer he loved her, and she said she loved him, too. They said goodbye.

After Sandra came home from work, Eddie Vickers came over from next door several times. Each time, Eddie asked Jon if he was going to a bar called Chicago's later that evening. Each time, Jon said no, he had changed his mind. Each time, Eddie hung around for a few minutes and then left.

Sandra went up to her bedroom while Jon was in the shower. She heard the water turn off, and, soon afterward, the phone rang. Jon had taken a portable phone in the bathroom with him, and he came out with a towel around his waist and the receiver to his ear.

"What?" he said so loudly that it startled Sandra. She stepped to her bedroom door just as he went into his bedroom. "Fuck that!" he shouted as he slammed the door behind him with his foot.

This was not the way Jon usually talked around the house. Sandra went back in her bedroom and sat on the side of her bed. She brushed her hair slowly in front of the dressing table mirror and wondered about the call. A few minutes later, Jon came into her bedroom. He was dressed in stone-washed blue jeans and a dark blue polo shirt that belonged to Mickey. Jon had been exercising for weeks so he would feel confident in swimming trunks when Jennifer got home from college, and his jeans were a little loose at the waist. He fidgeted with his belt, tightening it until the jeans wrinkled beneath it.

"Is this too tight?"

"A little," Sandra answered. "Maybe a notch less."

"I feel like my pants are falling down," Jon said in the semi-gruff way he had of laughing at himself. He loosened the belt a notch, hitched his jeans for feel and lay down across the end of the bed.

Sandra had been a mother too long to jump straight into a subject that concerned her. She brushed her hair for another half minute or so and then asked in a tone of casual disinterest, "Who was on the phone?"

"Forget it, Mom."

The tone of Jon's voice said it was a closed subject. Sandra laid down the brush and turned and sat cross-legged on the bed facing Jon. He headed her off with a new subject. "If I buy Jennifer a diamond, should I charge it on VISA or take out a loan?" They discussed it, and Sandra agreed to co-sign a loan if Jon needed it. Jon got up from the bed and hitched his jeans again.

"I'm off to Keith's."

Jon started out of the bedroom and Sandra said, "Seriously, Jon. Who was on the phone?"

It bothered Sandra that Jon wouldn't discuss the phone call with her. He had always told her practically anything. When Jon was fourteen he had surprised Sandra one morning in the kitchen with, "Mom, I tried marijuana last night." Before Sandra could come up with a response, he had added, "I hated it. It made my eyes burn and my head hurt. I felt like I couldn't breath. I'm not going to do that anymore."

Sandra called after Jon as he started out of the room, but he ignored her. She followed him down the stairs to the front door. "Jon Bowie, you tell me what that phone call was about."

Jon turned and, with a calm and certainty that chilled her, said, "Look, Mom, all I'm going to say is that Monday I'm dropping the charges against those police officers. Now, drop it."

"I won't drop it," Sandra said. "I'm calling the police department first thing in the morning. I'm going to find out what's going on here."

"Don't call them, Mom," Jon said. "Every time you talk to them, everything just gets worse."

"Well, I am going to call them. I intend to find out what's happening."

"At least wait until Monday," Jon said.

"All right," Sandra said. "Monday. I'm going to have some answers by then or I'm calling the police."

Jon turned to leave and Sandra reached out and touched his arm. He turned halfway around and looked down at her, and his eyes danced again with their usual confidence.

"It'll be fine, Mom. Trust me."

Sandra closed the door behind him and, in her mind, she was somewhere else. She saw two men standing in darkness at the rear of a car. The men were putting something in the trunk of the car. Sandra strained to see what the men were putting in the trunk. Then, aloud in her mind, she said, "Oh, no. It's Jon. They're putting Jon in the trunk."

Sandra jerked open the door and ran out onto the stoop and across the tiny front yard into the parking lot, but Jon's car already was out of sight.

Not much would be learned about Jon's activities after he left home that night. Jon stopped by his friend Keith's and they got together with several friends at the home of a friend named Scott.

Later, when the police seemed intent on demonstrating that this was just another beer drinking party, one young woman called everyone who had been there to learn how much each person had to drink that night. She did the necessary math and learned that there would have been no more than four beers left over, so she figured that Jon could have drunk four beers, at most. The police also made much over a beer drinking game that was supposed to have been played by some of the people at Scott's. This was the kind of thing that seemed to interest the police.

Several of the kids were going later to a nightclub in College park called Chicago's. Chicago's had a dress code and one kid had not dressed accordingly, so those who were going to Chicago's decided, instead, to go to a bar called The Cellar. Four young men left together at a little before ten o'clock. Jon had indicated earlier that he might go, but he apparently had changed his mind. As the others were leaving, Jon and Keith also went outside. Keith either was going to drive Jon's car to The Cellar, or he was going to drive Jon home. I never got that particular detail fully sorted out. Either way, Jon told Keith that he'd been drinking and he didn't want to drive, and Jon gave Keith his keys. Keith either laid the keys on another car and the car pulled away, or Keith threw the keys at the car, trying to get the attention of those leaving. Either way, Jon's keys got lost. Somebody ran the car down and the guys in the car came back and helped search for Jon's keys. Some of those in the house also came out to join the search. One young woman said later that she helped until it started raining hard, and she went back inside. Jon's keys weren't found, and he started walking home. Keith offered to drive him, but Jon said he'd rather walk. He left his car at Scott's.

A woman who lived in the end unit, a few doors down from Jim and Sandra, saw Jon at a little after ten as she was driving home. Soon after, she left home to go to the baby-sitter's house. At around ten-twenty she was returning home again, and she saw Jon a second time. He was rounding the last corner onto the street where he lived. The police tried to get her to add to her statement that Jon was swinging his arms angrily as he walked, but she refused to do that. She said he was just walking.

In a nutshell, that's what was known, or said, about Jon's activities that night.

Sandra paced the house. She went into the kitchen, looked at the wall clock, sat at the table by the window, and got up and paced again.

For as long as she could remember, Sandra had experienced what she thought of as *people on her eyelids*. When she was younger, she thought everyone saw them. After repeated blank stares, jeers and scoldings in response to her "overactive imagination," she began to keep the things she saw to herself.

Sandra had been born in a Catholic hospital in a condition that was referred to as *under the veil*. That meant a portion of the placenta still lay across her face. Some people believed this was some sort of sign. There was a story in Sandra's family that, when the nuns first saw her, they crossed themselves.

After her divorce, Sandra and her two sons lived for a while in a cabin on the wooded grounds of a state park just outside of her mountainside hometown of Wardensville, West Virginia. Her father had a friend who had a friend and a rental agreement was arranged. The boys spent more time in the woods than in the house and she couldn't imagine that life could be more peaceful. A job search, however, resulted in a Sandra taking a teaching job in Burtonsville, Maryland, on Route 29 between Washington and Baltimore. One afternoon, after they had moved there, an older teacher took Sandra aside and admonished her because Jon and Mickey had what the older teacher thought were too many black friends. It was not the kind of thing that seemed important to Sandra, and she laughed.

Sandra decided that Burtonsville was not where she wanted to raise her sons. She moved five or ten miles up Route 29 to Columbia. She soon discovered that she couldn't find a teaching job in Columbia without first taking college courses for six months, and she didn't have six months. She answered an advertisement and took a job as director of a daycare center. She rented an apartment and, as her sons grew older, they played baseball and football and survived the encumbrances of academic schooling, which did not interest them particularly despite their naturally quick minds. When Jon and

Mickey were old enough, Sandra hired them to do the occasional jobs at the daycare center that she would have had to pay someone else to do if not them.

Sandra still saw people on her eyelids, but, by and large, she ignored them. Sometimes she knew something that couldn't be explained, but she kept such things to herself unless she slipped up. A friend who was dating a married man told her the man was going to leave his wife and marry her as soon as he found a way to tell his wife. Before she thought to catch herself, Sandra said, "Don't waste your time with him. His wife is pregnant, and he'll never leave her." Sandra didn't know the man or his wife, and she didn't know how she knew the woman was pregnant. The words just came out of her mouth. When the friend asked how Sandra knew, Sandra scrambled for an explanation and finally said she had heard it somewhere. The friend met the man that week-end, and he broke the news to her.

During their freshman year in high school, Jon and Mickey were watching the Superbowl in the basement with Jim and Sandra. Jon was pulling for one team and Mickey was pulling for the other. The boys were sitting on the floor, and, when things went well for one team or the other, they scuffled and teased each other. Then whichever team Mickey was pulling for scored a touchdown. Jon took a swipe at Mickey and missed and struck his hand against the edge of the coffee table. Jon writhed on the floor with pain, and Jim and Sandra and Mickey weren't sure how much he was hurt and how much he was just clowning around because his team had been scored on.

The next morning Jon's hand was blue and swollen, and Sandra took him to the doctor. The x-ray showed that the hand was broken, and the doctor put a cast on it and said that Jon wouldn't be starting baseball practice in March, and he definitely wouldn't be catching that year.

When they got home, Jon was distraught at the possibility of not playing baseball. Sandra told him to rub his hand gently and to picture tiny butterflies and angels flying around the bone, repairing the fracture with magic thread. Sandra didn't know where the idea came from, but Jon did it. He told Sandra, "Don't tell Mickey about this." Jon spent hours each day alone in his room, rubbing his hand.

Two weeks later, Sandra took Jon back to the doctor. The doctor did a second x-ray and said he couldn't find the fracture. The doctor became angry and accused Sandra of bringing Mickey instead of Jon. The doctor said it was a misguided attempt by Sandra to get approval for Jon to play baseball. The doctor accused Sandra of being a bad mother for attempting such a thing. He didn't say how he thought Mickey had gotten the cast off Jon's hand and onto his own.

The doctor took the cast off anyway, but when Jon and Sandra got home Jon was worried. He couldn't squeeze his hand into a fist. Sandra heard the words, and, as she heard them, she repeated them to Jon.

"Drink milk. Hold your hand in cold water. When you take it out, squeeze a rubber ball one hundred times. Then put your hand back in the water and start all over again."

Sandra told Jon she was hearing a voice and she didn't know where it was coming from. She said she thought she was repeating something someone else was telling Jon. Jon didn't blink an eye. "Definitely don't tell Mickey this," he said.

Jon followed the instructions, and, in the spring, he was ready when baseball practice started.

Because of such things, there was a real possibility in Sandra's mind that someone might try to put Jon in the trunk of a car, but she didn't know what she could do about it. It was Jim's bowling night, and, by a little before ten-thirty, Jim still wasn't home. Sandra tried Keith's phone number one last time, listened to a message saying the phone had been temporarily disconnected, and then went upstairs to get ready for bed. Her bedroom window was opened a small amount for air, and she heard someone outside call out what sounded like, "Eddie," and then, "Mickey." There were shuffling noises, as if some kids had decided to play a late-night game of touch football. Then a car door slammed.

The voice had sounded to her like Mickey's. Mickey was supposed to be in his room studying, and Sandra could just imagine that Mickey had snuck outside to get into something. She thought, "That stinking Mickey. I'll give him what for." She went across the hall to Mickey's bedroom and knocked on the door and opened it almost simultaneously. Mickey was lying on his bed with a textbook, and he looked up, startled. "What?"

"I thought I heard you outside," Sandra said. "I thought you had snuck out."

"Mom," Mickey said, complaining at the interruption. "It was probably Jon. It's almost ten-thirty."

Sandra went to her bedroom and looked out the window. She saw nothing unusual, and she went back to Mickey's bedroom.

"There's nobody out there. What do you suppose that was?"

"Well, if you thought it was me, then it probably was Jon. Maybe somebody picked him up to go somewhere. Quit worrying."

Sandra returned to her bedroom and looked out over the parking lot again. No one was there. She put on her pajamas and then knelt at her bedroom window and peered out. Every half hour or so a car turned in and parked. People got out and fumbled for their keys in front of their townhouse doors and then went inside. Jim came home in the burgundy van that he kept so meticulously polished and cleaned. She watched as he came inside and then she heard him knocking about in the kitchen. He came upstairs to the bedroom, stopped at the door, and said, "Oh, you're in one of those moods," and went down to the basement to fall asleep in the recliner in front of the television.

Light showers fell intermittently. An occasional breeze blew rain in through the screen. Moisture accumulated in Sandra's hair, matting her hair against her forehead, and she ignored it. Droplets formed and ran down her face. There was a sudden downpour and she squinted to see through it. At around one in the morning, she realized that her pajamas were soaking wet. She got another pair from a dresser drawer and went into the bathroom to dry off and change. She came back to the bedroom window and knelt before it again. The rain had stopped and she looked outside, waiting. On her eyelids she saw someone leading Jon into the edge of the woods.

The crack of lightening came only an instant before an explosion of thunder. I sat up in bed, wide-eyed and still half asleep. When the thunder had rolled and then disappeared, I lowered my head back into my pillow. There was a moment of still silence; then rain came down straight and hard, as if God had opened a wide door in Heaven. The hard rain lasted only for a minute or so. It was followed by a another silent pause and then by a light, windless shower. The bedroom window was opened slightly for air, and the pattering of rain drops on the roof and on the grass gradually blended with Jane's deep, soft breathing, and then with my own.

The next morning I sat at the kitchen table smoking a cigarette and pulling on my shoes. I asked Jane if she had heard the thunder and the rain, and she said that she hadn't. I said I was amazed that it hadn't awakened her.

At least a week had gone by, maybe more, before Jane found the occasion to share her own experience of that night. She said that once during the night she had sat bolt upright in bed for no apparent reason. It was such an uncharacteristic experience for her that she found herself sitting in the darkness wondering what might be wrong. I asked her if it was raining when she woke, and she said she was all but certain it was not. She said that, in fact, if I had not told her I had heard the rain, she would have assumed it had not rained at all that night.

We agreed it was odd that each of us had experienced an unordinary awakening well past the middle of that night, of all nights.

7 I'll try to be brief.

At around six o'clock on the morning of May 4, 1990, the body of Carl Jonathan "Jon" Bowie was found hanging from the back of a softball field backstop. The backstop was behind the high school that Jon and his identical twin brother, Mickey, had attended until two years earlier. At that time of morning at that time of year in Maryland, the sun is not yet up, although the sky would have been growing increasingly light.

A backstop, for those not versed in baseball terminology, is a chained-link, wire fence supported by long pipes. It stands behind home plate to stop foul balls. The better ones have vertical wire sides that angle out and away from the back and a wire roof that inclines upward toward the playing field. This was one of the better ones.

A tiny oriental woman was out jogging along the asphalt bike path that ran alongside the school, and she saw the body. She thought at first it was some sort of effigy. The prom was scheduled for that night, and she thought there might have been some sort of sporting event planned, or maybe some students had hung something there as some sort of gesture. As she approached the backstop from the rear, she saw it was a person up there and she was looking at his back. His legs and most of his body dangled over the back side of the backstop. His shoulders were just above the horizontal pipe that separated the back from the forwardly inclined roof.

She ran around to the front of the backstop. It had rained off and on during the night, sometimes hard and more often not, but the ground was hard packed and her jogging shoes left no noticeable impressions in the infield dirt. She looked up at the young man through the wire. His head was turned to one side and one cheek rested against the wire just above a horizontal pipe that supported the roof. The base of his right palm was propped against the pipe. A foot or so up the roof, the thumb and fingers of his left hand were bent through the wire, clutching it in a tight grip.

As she stood there looking up, the thought occurred to her that he was looking down at her through the wire. It was as if he was asking her with his eyes to help him in some way. Later, after the story had been in the Washington and Baltimore and local papers, she would tell a friend that she didn't want it to be known that she thought he had been looking at her. She wouldn't want his mother or close friends and family members to hear that, and she couldn't be sure.

She ran across the first base line, across the bike path and up a short path that passed through a row of tall, bushy evergreen trees. A short, residential street less than a normal block long and with a row of townhouses on each side led away from her. She had no way of knowing that until the night before, Jon Bowie had lived six doors up on the right in a townhouse that was empty at the moment except for Mickey, who was upstairs asleep, or that his mother was hardly out of sight on her way to work. The oriental woman knocked on several doors and finally, across the parking lot and a few doors down from the Bowie-Keyser home, a slender and stately woman answered. The woman didn't want to call the police unless she could be sure it was needed, and she walked down to the evergreens and looked through. Then she hurried back to her house to make the call.

A second woman walked past the backstop on the bike path. She saw the body and she saw the oriental woman run off through the evergreens. The first reaction of this second woman, who was some sort of clinical social worker with a private practice, was that someone was doing some odd calisthenic on the backstop. Other people stopped from their jogging and early morning walks with their dogs and watched with her. The oriental woman came back through the evergreens and joined them. There were whispers and hands to the mouth and then everyone there knew.

A neighbor who lived next door to the woman who had called the police joined the group. This man walked up to the backstop, looked at the body and said, "My God, he's dead." He returned to his house beyond the evergreens.

A jogger, a tall man in his twenties, ran past. He looked over at the body on the backstop and continued on along the bike path.

The Oakland Mills section of Columbia was in Officer Tim Burns' patrol area, and Burns was the first police officer to arrive. Burns was the fiercely muscular officer who, at the motel, had led Jon to his car and later had given Pamela a ride home. Burns also was a close friend and drinking buddy of Officer Meyers. Burns' car came slowly around the school with blue lights flashing and no siren. Burns parked at the end of the asphalt parking lot near the backstop and got out of his car. He walked to the backstop, inspected the body from the ground and then returned to his car.

More police cars came. Some officers, especially the plain clothed ones, stayed in the rear of the school. Others went around to the front to deal with traffic. Later, as people gathered in small groups around the neighborhood, waving hands and noting to each other such things as how the police had not thoroughly inspected the scene and how there had been no efforts at resuscitating Jon, it also would be said that it would have been better all around if those police officers who brought dough-nuts had left them in their cars.

The second woman stood with the crowd on a small, grass-covered slope between the bike path and the backstop. She thought what a nice young man the person on the backstop seemed to be. He looked so neatly groomed in his stone-washed blue jeans and dark blue polo shirt and heavy, round-toed boots. His sandy, almost blonde hair was trimmed short in a style that could only be neat. She couldn't help thinking that somewhere a mother was waiting anxiously, futilely, for him to come home. She also thought that something about the scene - the odd position of the body, perhaps - was ominous. It was as if the body had been arranged as a warning of some sort. In her mind she associated it with an old movie about a godfather.

An officer stood beneath the wire overhang, and, looking up, began photographing the body. As with the jogger who had stood there before him, his shoes left no noticeable impressions in the dirt of the playing field despite the rain of the night before.

A red and white rescue truck arrived. Men got out and took a ladder from the truck and leaned it against the backstop. A detective dressed in plain clothes climbed the backstop and inspected the body. He climbed down and talked with some of the others. He climbed back up and tugged at the cable but could not loosen it. Uniformed policemen and plain clothed officers agreed aloud that something had to be done fast. School would open soon, and children would be arriving.

A length of blue, vinyl-clad cable a quarter-inch in diameter was clamped permanently to the backstop roof, near the upper edge. The cable, pulled tight, continued down the roof to Jon's neck, where it was fastened in a loop. The short, looped end of the cable was connected to the longer upper section by a turnbuckle. The loop was tight around the neck and the police and rescue squad workers could not remove it. Someone finally cut the cable, or unfastened the turnbuckle - it's not clear which.

A rescue squad worker climbed the ladder and, leaning out and reaching, looped a thick rope around Jon's stomach. He tied the rope in a large knot at the middle of Jon's back. Another rope was draped across the roof to the front of the backstop. A rescue worker stood on the ground in front of the backstop holding the rope and slowly lowering the body. The weight of Jon's body pulled down against the ropes. The knot at his back pulled the thick rope away from his back near the armpits. When his feet were near the ground, rescue workers took hold of the body. They removed the rope and laid the body face up on the grass behind the backstop.

Onlookers began looking at their watches and discussing among themselves whether they should approach the officers and give their names and addresses. Some agreed to do it. Others said they had to leave to get ready for work.

The principal had been called at home and she arrived. She looked at the body and said she knew it was one of the Bowie twins, but she couldn't be certain which one. They were virtually identical. The varsity baseball assistant coach had also joined the group. He leaned over the body and then stood up.

"It's Jon Bowie," he said, and he pointed out a small scar that was all but hidden by an eyebrow.

A deputy medical examiner for the county arrived. Soon after, the detective who would be given responsibility for investigating the case also arrived. I'll call him Detective Lampest. The body had already been lowered when the deputy medical examiner and Lampest arrived, and, together, they inspected the body as it lay on the ground. They determined between themselves that the death was a suicide. The detective would insist later that it was the deputy medical examiner who had made the decision.

The school's athletic director arrived. I'll call her Wanda Truce. She explained to the police that the cable apparatus had been attached to the backstop several years earlier, and that Jon Bowie had been one of several athletes who had helped attach it. Once a year, for a field day event, the cable was lowered and a tire connected to it. Students crawled through the tire as one of the field day events. Sometimes, also, the cable was lowered so baseball pitchers could attach the tire and pitch baseballs through it.

When the cable had first been installed, it was tossed on top of the backstop when it wasn't it use. Parents had complained that it was dangerous to have a cable lying on the backstop where it could fall off and do Lord knows what. The athletic director had bought a lock so the loose end of the cable could be locked to the backstop roof. She had bought a combination lock that also had a key slot in the rear. Since she never could remember the combination, she always used the key to unlock it. The next field day was scheduled for the upcoming week, and she had inspected the cable the week before. If it had not been locked down at that time, she told the officers, she would have noticed. The police looked around in the grass and in a nearby garbage can, but they could not find the lock.

The athletic director had wrapped grey duct tape around the turnbuckle so students crawling through the tire would not scratch themselves. She pointed out the tape and a plain clothed investigator, I'll call him Dayton Arnold, inspected it. Half of the tape had been removed, and, by the freshness of the exposed adhesive, Arnold observed that the tape must have been removed recently. He looked around in the grass for fragments of the removed tape, but he could not find any.

Jon carried a house key on a red key tag. His car keys had been lost, but the house key was separate.

It was close to eight o'clock when, almost three hundred feet away from the backstop, beyond the row of evergreens, someone entered the home where Mickey Bowie lay upstairs asleep. The intruder's noises woke Mickey, who listened as the footsteps came up the stairs and went into Jon's bedroom. The telephone rang, and the intruder ran down the stairs and out of the house. After several rings Mickey answered the phone in a sleepy voice. It was Sandra.

"Has Jon come home?" Her voice was panicked. "He hasn't come to work yet."

"I heard him come in a few minutes ago," Mickey told his mother. "He came upstairs and went in his bedroom. When the phone started ringing, he ran downstairs and went out. He should be there any minute."

I'll call Meyers' attorney Stephen Kent. Kent was representing Meyers against the Bowie twins' charges of excessive force. According to official records, Kent got a phone call at approximately the same time that the intruder would have been leaving the Bowie-Keyser residence. I say it that way because, if this is correct, it essentially rules out the possibility that it was Meyers who broke into the Bowie-Keyser residence that morning.

Kent was a past county police officer who often defended officers accused of various things. Official records do not name the officer who made the call to Kent. A less than official source says that the officer was calling to inform Kent of Jon's death, and to ask for instructions. Official records say that, when the call had ended, Kent called Meyers.

Meyers then called the woman with whom he later claimed to have spent the better part of the previous evening. The woman didn't answer right away, and Meyers got the answering machine. He shouted over the recorded voice of the woman, "Pick up the phone. Jon Bowie's dead."

8 When Mickey Bowie played baseball, he had what is called *field sense*. People who have it can focus their attention on a matter at hand without missing much that's going on around them, or getting rattled by any of it. The ball comes hard at you on the ground and you field it. Maybe you glance at third so the runner there doesn't try for home. Maybe you slow your step a bit so the runner at second knows you haven't forgotten him. Then, as smoothly as if all you had done was field the ball, you throw out the batter. It would be unusual for a person with such an awareness to be caught off guard. It would not be unusual for a person without it to see it in action and not recognize it.

Mickey also was seldom at a loss for words. He wasn't a chatter-mouth, but he didn't mince his words, either. When the kids were sixteen or so, Mickey was playing shortstop in a night game. The batter hit a hard ground ball up the middle and the ball crossed second base a few inches off the ground. Mickey moved quickly backward and to his left and reached down with his glove. At the last instant he stood up and let the ball roll into center field.

The groans from the sidelines showed that not everyone there knew that it was the right play. The batter stopped at first base, which he would have reached anyway if Mickey had dove belly out and come up with the ball instead of trusting the center fielder to do his job.

When the inning was over, Mickey came off the field and was walking in front of the bench. A nice kid who didn't get as much playing time as some other players couldn't resist tossing out a dig.

"Good range," he said.

Mickey looked at him, grinned, and kept walking.

"Good bench."

A year later the team was playing in another night game. By the last inning the team was so far behind that it couldn't have caught up if everyone on the other team but the pitcher had quit and gone home. It was late, and getting foggy to the point that the outfielders had crept in a few steps to try to see home plate. As Mickey, who was one of the best hitters in the county, took his position in the batter's box, the umpire said, "You'd better swing at everything. I have to get home."

The next day was a Saturday and the team had an afternoon game. The same umpire was behind the plate. This was the game in which the Great Potato Play occurred. This had already happened in the earlier innings, and the umpire was pretty steamed at Jon, as if he thought Jon had tried to show him up. A few innings later, Jon reached third base and I signaled for him to steal home. As the pitcher began the last half of his motion, Jon started running full out. He caught the pitcher, the catcher and, unfortunately, the umpire completely off guard. He slid head first on the pitcher's side of home plate and, in a cloud of dust, he reached out his right hand and dragged it across the plate. The ball bounced in the dirt in front of the catcher and then against the catcher's chest protector. The catcher trapped the ball against his chest and fell forward. Jon had started to get up as the catcher fell against him and knocked him back to the ground. The umpire looked down, jerked a thumb in the sky and called, "Out." Jon jumped up and stared at the umpire. Then he shook his head and laughed, looked down at home plate, and started for the bench. The umpire lost his cool and chased after him, shouting. Jon had almost reached the dugout when the umpire shouted at his back, "You're out of the game."

Mickey was waiting for a turn at bat. He was standing with his fingers through the protective wire fence that ran between the backstop and the dugout. The umpire turned back toward home plate and, seeing Mickey through the fence, looked back at Jon and then back at Mickey. The umpire shouted at Mickey, "If you say one word, you're gone, too." Mickey looked at him and grinned.

"What's the matter?" Mickey asked. "'You have to get home?"

The umpire tossed Mickey, too. Without going into all the laborious details, suffice it to say that it was the only game I ever was thrown out of, as a player or a coach. I made sure that part took about five minutes.

Two years later, on that morning in May, Mickey was caught off guard. It was almost nine o'clock, and the two men at the front door showed him badges and said they were detectives. The one I'm calling Lampest was tall and thin with slumped shoulders and a long, concave face. The other, the one I'm calling Dayton Arnold, was even taller and more athletically built. They showed Mickey the fake ID that Jon used to buy beer. Mickey took the ID and looked at it and handed it back. He waited.

"Is this your brother?" Lampest asked.

"Yes, sir, it is," Mickey said.

Lampest, in a tone that he might have used if he'd just handed Mickey the morning paper off the stoop, said, "Then he's dead."

Mickey tried to take it in, incorporate it, fit it into a slot in his mind where it made the kind of sense that he could act on. In an instant he knew he couldn't do it.

"You'd better call my mom," he said. He showed them in, gave them the number and pointed to the phone on the kitchen wall. Then he quietly sank into a fog of despair that would not begin to lift for many months.

Except for the industrial-grade-glass front door, the daycare center Sandra managed looked like a small, one-story brown barn. It sat up a short, sloping asphalt driveway and was surrounded by a scattering of tall pines.

At precisely six-thirty in the morning, Sandra parked her economy-sized white pickup with the wide, red stripe down each side in front of the school. She got out and unlocked the school door and went into the large front room to begin her day's work. Teachers and group leaders began arriving soon afterward. They scattered throughout the three large classrooms, opening cabinets and laying out toys and work sheets and pausing to greet those children who came early.

By eight o'clock, when Jon still hadn't arrived, Sandra called home. Mickey assured her that Jon had just left the house and was on his way, but then eight-thirty came, and then eight-forty-five.

Anne Beck, Sandra's assistant, arrived at ten till nine. Sandra was standing at the high reception counter by the front door, and her face was pale and tense. She gripped the edge of the counter as if she might fall.

Anne was a genuine mountain woman. She came from generations of mountain women and was a direct descendent of the McCoys of the infamous Hatfields and McCoys. She was blonde and in her middle forties and, at five-two, was the same height as Sandra. She had weathered features and blue eyes that held more than a hint of the suspicion and readiness of a cat. In another time it would have been said that she had spit.

"Jon's not here," Sandra said. "He didn't come home last night."

"Quit worrying," Anne said. "He'll be here."

There was an edge to Anne's reassurance. Jon had changed his arrival times frequently for the past two weeks so they couldn't be predicted, but he had let Anne and Sandra know beforehand each time, and he had arrived when he said he would.

Ordinarily Sandra wouldn't have said it, but it just came out of her.

"They took him in the woods, Anne. He's dead."

Anne looked as if she had been slapped.

"Who? What are you talking about?"

"I don't know," Sandra said. "I just know it."

"Shut up," Anne said. "You're talking crazy."

"I mean it, Anne. We're going to get a phone call."

"I'm not listening to this," Anne said, and she walked away, jerking off her jacket. The phone rang at nine o'clock and Sandra grabbed it. She stood listening quietly for a moment and then, in a voice so intensely calm it all but trembled, she said, "Okay," and hung up the phone. She looked at Anne.

"That was the police. They asked me to come home. I don't think I can drive."

Anne drove and Sandra sat on the passenger side and squeezed her hands together. "The police said there was a little problem," Sandra said, and she laughed a laugh of controlled hysteria. "They said there's nothing to worry about, that I just need to come home." She sat quietly a moment and then added, "They're lying."

"Well, we don't know yet," Anne said. "Just wait."

"He's dead, Anne. I know it. I think they put him in the trunk of a car. His car is parked in somebody's driveway. He's not with his car."

"Stop it," Anne shouted. "I'm not listening to that kind of talk."

The trip across town normally took fifteen minutes, but Anne made it in closer to ten. Anne parked in front of the townhouse and the car still was moving as Sandra slung open her door and jumped out. The image that burned itself indelibly into Sandra's future memories was Mickey standing inside the storm door looking out, his shoulders shaking and tears streaming down his face and dropping from his face onto the inside of the glass, and trickling down it.

Sandra stopped a few steps from the door and said, "No."

Mickey saw her standing there and he nodded his head as if to say, "Yes."

Sandra opened the door and they held each other in a long hug. Mickey's sobbing stopped, and he said, "Don't believe them, Mom. Don't believe them."

Lampest and Arnold were in the kitchen. Lampest asked Sandra to sit down.

Sandra said, "No. Just tell me what you have to say."

"Well, it's about your son. Jon." He waited, as if he wanted her to say something, to help him somehow, but she waited, too. Finally, Lampest said, "He's dead. He committed suicide."

Sandra stood a moment as if the blow had knocked her out but she hadn't yet fallen. Then she turned and ran stumbling out of the kitchen into the living room. She fell to her knees and looked down at the carpet. Then she looked up at the ceiling and screamed.

"No."

When Sandra returned to the kitchen her face had changed. The color was gone from her skin and long, dark lines ran down her cheeks. Her eyes looked more steel black than brown.

"There's no way in hell he killed himself," she said to Lampest. She was talking through her teeth in as close to a normal tone as she could manage when she started, but her voice kept getting louder until she was shouting. "If you want to know what happened to him, ask Meyers. He's been harassing Jon for weeks. If Jon's dead, Meyers killed him."

Lampest's face flashed red, and he shouted back, "He hung himself at the school. I was there. I saw him. He was hanging eight feet off the ground. Do you want to come down to the station and see the rope?"

Anne watched with a stunned expression. She asked Lampest, "Where is the... where is Jon?" Lampest looked at her and didn't answer. "Sandra should identify the body," Anne said.

"It's not necessary," Lampest said. "We have a positive identification from the teachers. The body is at Slack's Funeral Home in Ellicott City."

Sandra went to the phone and called Jo Glasco, and Jo said she would be right there. Then Sandra phoned Jennifer Hollywood in Florida.

"Who are you calling?" Lampest asked.

"Jon's girlfriend," Sandra said in a tone that suggested it was none of his business.

"Let me talk with her," Lampest said.

When Sandra had told Jennifer, and had given her some time, she handed Lampest the phone. Lampest asked Jennifer if she and Jon had argued, or if he was depressed. When Lampest hung up, Sandra shouted at him, "This is no suicide. Somebody's going to have to investigate this, and I can't see that you're investigating anything. You've already made up your mind."

Still red faced, Lampest asked where Jon's room was. He went upstairs and Anne followed him. He looked around for a suicide note but there wasn't one. He took an address book off the dresser and put it in his coat pocket.

Arnold asked Mickey where Jon had been the night before. Mickey answered mechanically that he thought Jon had visited friends in Arbutus. They left together, and, as they were leaving, Arnold said, "When we get there, let me do all the talking. I want to see how they react."

A woman named Barbara, Sandra's employer, arrived. When Lampest and Anne returned to the kitchen, Sandra was telling Barbara that Jon was at Slack's funeral home.

"What about an autopsy?" Barbara asked Sandra.

Anne answered the question. "Detective Lampest here says it's not necessary."

Barbara looked at Lampest and went to the phone. She called information for the number and then she called the funeral home. After a brief conversation, Barbara said into the phone, "The family will be requesting an autopsy." Then she hung up. She said to Sandra, "The woman at the funeral home says this is highly unusual. She says there's almost always an autopsy in cases like this, even if it might be a suicide."

Sandra flinched. "It's not a suicide."

Lampest still was angry. "Listen," he said to Sandra. "This is my investigation, and it's no movie. Your son committed suicide, and I'll decide if there's an autopsy."

"We'll see about that," Sandra shouted at him.

Jo Glasco arrived and close behind her was the Reverend John Wright. Wright was a stocky black man whose confident demeanor made him look taller than his five feet eight inches or so. His belly out, chest back and chin in stance dared anyone to affront him.

"What's this about an autopsy?" he asked in the demanding, bellowing voice of a man accustomed to fiercely assessing mountains and then ordering them to move.

Anne and Barbara and Sandra shouted versions of Lampest's decision. Lampest shouted that it wasn't his decision but that it was the decision of the county medical examiner. Wright finally held up a hand for the shouting to stop, and, when it did, he turned to Lampest.

"On behalf of the N-Double-A-C-P, I am insisting that there be an autopsy on this child."

Lampest started to speak and Wright interrupted him. "Please do not misunderstand me. I am not asking. If you ascertain in your official capacity that there might not be a necessity, then please be advised in the presence of these people that, if necessary, I am willing to pay for it myself."

By mid-day, Detective Walter Lampest was accompanying Jon Bowie's body from Slack's Funeral Home in Ellicott City to the offices of the State Medical Examiner in Baltimore.

9 My sons were approaching school age in the early 1970's when I found myself in the Washington, DC, area looking for a house. I sat in a musty chair in a ratty motel and read a long article in the real estate section of the Washington Post about the new community of Columbia, Maryland. It was halfway to Baltimore up Interstate 95 and had the advertised nickname of *New America*. On a hot morning in July in what was reported on the radio as the thickest smog to cover Washington in twenty-five years, I drove up to check it out. By the time I took the two-lane exit off the interstate the smog had all but disappeared behind me.

There didn't seem to be a straight road or street in the town. I immediately got lost and wandered for miles past lakes and trees and asphalt paths for bicycles. The houses were a little on the underbuilt side and shaded mostly by four-foot-high saplings, but I was looking for something more than a house. Trees grow.

I eventually found myself in the town's central section, which consisted mostly of a large lake, a tall motel, a waterside restaurant, a two-screen movie theater, some recently built office buildings and a large mall, all in earth tones. Except for the movie theater marquis, there were no billboards or lighted outdoor signs and only a few traffic lights. I parked across from the movie theater and went into a small exhibit hall. One or two other people stood with me in front of a large screen that took up a wall of the room, and we watched a fifteen minute film about this new town. When the town was completed, there would be schools in every neighborhood and families of various races living together on the same streets. Twenty percent of the land would remain undeveloped, so there always would be trees and wildlife.

I left the exhibit hall and immediately got lost again. I parked in front of a brick elementary school, and, finding the front door unlocked and no one in sight, I went inside for an unguided tour. I had no way of knowing that this was the school my children ultimately would attend, or that Jon and Mickey Bowie would soon live a short walk away. Cartoons were painted on the yellow walls of the entrance way and indoor-outdoor carpeting covered the classroom floors.

I went back to Mississippi, where Jane and I had moved from North Carolina. We crammed our belongings into a rented truck and moved to *New America*. I went through culture shock for a while. For several years I made the one-hour commute to Washington every day and worked my way up the bureaucratic ladder in a federal regulatory agency. The commute and the regulatory work became a bit much and I quit the government job. A friend helped me get into technical writing in the telecommunications industry and I faked it until I began to get it right. The pay was decent, although companies I worked for kept getting bought out and down-sized and I kept having to find other companies that at least temporarily wanted to give permanent jobs to technical writers.

On that morning in May, I drove the thirty miles to Gaithersburg to my second or third permanent job since leaving the government. I didn't know Jon's body already had been found. Toward five in the afternoon, I realized I needed to stay late to finish some work and I called Jane to tell her. I was hoping she hadn't prepared a nice dinner and I hadn't forgotten any plans I'd promised to remember. I was half into some preparatory way of saying I would have to work late when Jane interrupted me.

"I've got terrible news."

There was nothing in Jane's voice that sounded terrible, and I almost kept talking. Instead, since Jane was not one to exaggerate, I waited. She said, "Jon Bowie's dead," and she burst into uncontrolled crying before she had finished saying it.

I couldn't respond. I kept waiting to deal with it, or to have something to say, or to feel something, but I couldn't do any of those things. Jane regained control. "I was going to wait until you got home to tell you."

Words came from somewhere far back in my head and I could hear them coming out.

"What happened?"

She burst into tears again and forced herself to manage, "He killed himself."

Jane hates to cry, and, even more than that, she hates for anyone to see or hear her do it. It's a part of her personality that I've come to accept and respect. The fact that she was weeping so openly and without restraint immediately erased those normal protective thoughts about whether someone is joking or might have heard it wrong or only got a bit of it and it could be somehow less or different. Those thoughts passed through my mind in less than an instant, and I didn't raise any of them. Jane wept until she could stop herself and then added, "Paul Donovan called." Paul was a coach and baseball commissioner I knew. "Paul said that he knows how you feel about the Bowies, and he didn't want you to hear it on the radio. I didn't know what to do. I couldn't decide between having you driving home knowing it or maybe hearing it on the radio, and then you called."

"I'll be right home."

She was crying again as I started to put down the receiver, so I waited. "David, I'm so sorry," she said. It struck me then that she was crying for me. She knew that when I did feel something, it would cut deep.

The thirty mile drive from Gaithersburg to Columbia took forty-five minutes under the best of conditions. It consisted mainly of back roads that ran north and east a few miles above the nation's capital, through little crossroad towns and what remained of farm and horse country. During Friday rush hours, the best I could hope for was an hour's drive.

There's a shy or self-conscious streak in me that I keep trying to outgrow, but it still sticks its head up occasionally. I worry about things I don't like to admit, such as whether someone in a passing car might see me doing something I wouldn't want to be seen doing. I actually had to force that thought out of my mind as I tried several times without success to cry. From time to time I struck the steering wheel hard with the base of my palm and shouted such things as, "God damn it, Jon," and, "You of all people," and, "How could you do something so stupid?"

When I got home Jane and I stood in the kitchen of our small, split-level home and she told me what she knew. She had withheld the part about the backstop until she could tell it in person. As she told me there was a hitch in my thinking. Something about it didn't feel right.

"You know," I said, "That doesn't sound like something Jon would do. It's too..." I searched for a word and settled for, "...showy."

I didn't want to go to Jim's and Sandra's for all the natural reasons. I didn't know what to say, how to act, to feel. I made excuses to myself such as that I didn't want to intrude at such a time. I called a friend of Mickey's and asked what he'd heard. He had been to the house and he said lots of people, mostly Jon's and Mick's friends, still were hanging around. He thought I should go.

I hadn't been to Sandra's since the kids were younger and exchanging sleepovers. I didn't know where she and Jim had moved after they got married. The kid gave me directions and we hung up. I told Jane I wouldn't be gone long.

The drive took about fifteen minutes. Evening darkness had set in as I turned onto one side street and then another through rows of tree-sheltered townhouses. Finally, I turned onto a short, wide street that served two short rows of townhouses. All of the parking spaces facing the buildings were filled and several cars were parallel parked behind the cars in the marked spaces. The center of the street was filled with young adults and a scattering of older ones. I drove slowly through the crowd, nodding through the window when I recognized any of the kids who looked up. Few looked up. I parked at the end of the street facing the evergreens and walked back to the crowd. I grabbed the arms of kids I recognized or nodded through the crowd to them. The kids stood in small groups, either silently or engaged in half-hearted conversation. A few of them dangled beer cans at their sides and their eyes were red from the strain of too much beer and not enough drunkenness.

Sandra looked up from a group near the sidewalk and saw me coming. I had usually seen her in summertime and she always was tanned and vibrant. Now her face was deathly pale and the flesh on her cheeks sagged. She left the group and came toward me saying, "Thank you so much for coming." I'm normally more self-conscious about hugging people other than family members than I think I should be, but this was a time to forget such things. We hugged and I said, "I'm sorry." A man I didn't recognize arrived and Sandra turned and started toward him.

Jim was standing in the group Sandra had left and I went over. I had spoken to Jim once or twice at baseball games, the last time being at least a year earlier, maybe more. Jim grinned a sad-eyed grin and we shook hands without speaking.

John Hollywood and his wife, Claudia, were in the group. John had coached girls' softball in the county for years and I knew him from organizational meetings and ballfield conversations. John was about my age and his hair was still more blonde than grey. I forgot, as I still do, that his right forearm and hand were withered from some past accident or affliction he probably had explained and I also had forgotten. I reached out my hand and, rather than make an issue of it, he reached out his withered hand and we shook.

"John."

"Dave."

John introduced Claudia and I thought I might have met her before, but I didn't feel like going through the back and forth of asking. I stood quietly as they resumed their conversation. John was saying that someone had found a twenty-two caliber bullet at the backstop.

"Two bullets," Claudia said, correcting him. "One was coated with dirt and looked as if it had been there a long time. The other was new."

I asked what it had to do with anything and John interrupted Claudia to answer me.

"Well, the police couldn't have inspected the area very well if people are finding bullets after they leave. They're not taking this thing seriously."

I didn't push it. People have a hard time accepting suicide. I waited a respectful time, only half listening, until there was a pause in the conversation. I asked Jim where Mickey was and he pointed to his front door.

"Top of the stairs. Door on the right."

The stairs were just inside the front door to the left. I met two or three young people on their way down as I went up. Each of them glanced straight in my eyes without speaking and then looked away as if to acknowledge that we were there for a common purpose and didn't need to go into details or courtesies. The sound of several low voices came through Mickey's bedroom door. I knocked lightly, and although no one answered the voices stopped and I went in. Mickey was sitting stretched out on a single bed with his head leaning against a pillow propped against the wall. His eyes were swollen and distant and his face was expressionless. Several young people sat on the floor or on the foot of the bed. A television was on and no one was watching it. Mickey looked up as I came in and a flash of recognition passed across his eyes. I wove my way through the bodies and offered a hand and he took it.

"Tough, Mick," I said.

"Yeah. It is that."

I held his hand a few seconds and then released it. The odd thought that shot across my forehead before I could stop it was that I wouldn't have to worry about getting him and Jon mixed up anymore. I made my way back through the bodies and stood for a short time with my back leaning against the door. The absence of conversation indicated that the young people would be more comfortable if I left. I raised a hand to Mickey and he raised one back and I went out and closed the door behind me.

Jim, Sandra, John and Claudia were in the kitchen. The two women were sitting at the round, oak table in front of the window. Jim sat in an oak rocker in the corner behind the table. John was at the refrigerator getting a can of beer. He offered me one and I declined with a shake of my head.

"I'd better be going," I said.

"Please don't," Sandra said.

The intensity of her request made me push past my feelings of awkwardness. I took a seat at the table across from the two women. They resumed their conversation and it soon became obvious that it was a conversation that had been underway for some time. John and Claudia and Sandra were animated and angry as they recounted events of the day. Jim listened quietly, smoking cigarettes and sometimes looking at the floor and sometimes looking at whoever was speaking. If I hadn't recognized that same demeanor of calm awareness and few words that I had grown up seeing in my dad, I might have mistaken Jim's silence for disinterest.

"They wouldn't let me see him," Sandra was saying. "They took him straight to the funeral home. If Anne Beck and Reverend Wright and Barbara hadn't been here, they wouldn't have done an autopsy." She hesitated before saying *autopsy*, and then pushed quickly through the word.

They talked about the recent suicide of a teenager in a nearby neighborhood. He had shot himself in his bedroom while on the telephone with his girlfriend.

"He left a note," Sandra said. "They did an autopsy and roped off the bedroom and investigated for three weeks before they called it a suicide. They didn't even rope off the area around the backstop. What's different here?"

"I'll tell you what's different," John said.

"I'll tell you what's different," Sandra said, interrupting John. "They don't want to investigate it. They're afraid Meyers had something to do with it."

"Hold it," I said. "Who's Meyers?"

For an hour or more, they related stories about the Red Roof Inn, about Jon being followed, and about Meyers thumping the seat in the courtroom. Twice, Sandra left the room without a word but with tears flooding from her eyes. Each time, she returned after a minute or two, dry-eyed and chiming in. After the second trip out of the room, she reached on top of the refrigerator and retrieved a Polaroid photograph and handed it to me. The picture was a head-and-chest shot of Jon and Mick standing side by side. Mick had a black eye, one cheek was swollen from his eye to his chin, and his chin was raw. Jon's lip was swollen and his face looked as if he had been beaten. Both were hardly recognizable. I remembered my last conversation with Jon.

"I think I'll have that beer," I said. I handed the photograph back to Sandra, and John Hollywood went to the refrigerator for the beer.

I don't know when the young people started gathering at the kitchen door, heads and shoulders in the doorway and feet in the hall, but a half dozen or more crowded there. A young woman I didn't know apparently had been one of the people at the Red Roof Inn. She said Meyers had a reputation for being a bully, and she began relating other stories of people she had heard he had roughed up or harassed. "Everybody's heard about the kids at Wilde Lake," she said. Wilde Lake was a high school in western Columbia.

"What about them?" I asked.

"I don't know their names. One was a wrestler. The cops beat up him and his friends. I think Meyers was one of the cops."

I knew a kid who had wrestled for Wilde Lake, and I made a mental note of it.

A stocky oriental youth they called Chong said in excited and heavily accented English, "I saw them beat up Jon and Mickey. The police beat them. One stuck a billy club in my mouth and we weren't doing nothing. Just having a party. Now Jon is going to testify against the police and he committed suicide? Sure." He shook his head.

Jim got up to answer a knock at the front door. He worked his way through the young people and came back a step behind a trim black woman I would have put in her middle to late thirties, although I would learn eventually that she was a few months older than I was, which was forty-five. She was dressed in a professional, two-piece grey suit and carried a leather portfolio. Sandra stood and introduced her to me across the table. Her name was Jo Glasco, and she eyed me with suspicion.

"He's all right," Sandra said, but I could see by a clouding in Jo's eyes that she wasn't convinced. She hugged Sandra lengthily and then sat to my left at the table. She put her hand into her portfolio and hesitated as she eyed me again. She pulled out a two or three page letter and handed it to Sandra.

"I got this today."

Sandra took it and looked at it but her eyes were not focused on it.

"In essence," Jo said, "it says that we can get a restraining order."

"Against who?" I asked.

Jo gave me a who-are-you look again and Sandra said, "Meyers. To keep him away from Jon." Then she laughed a soft laugh of irony.

I stayed another half hour or less, but I heard little that was said. I was suffering from overload, and the conversation echoed around me. From time to time some bit of information caught my attention and I joined in.

"That detective," Sandra said, "that Lampest, kept saying that he knew that Jon had been depressed because Jon had an argument with his girlfriend." Jon's girlfriend, Jennifer, was John's and Claudia's daughter. "It wasn't Jon who had an argument," Sandra said. "It was Mickey. Mickey and his girlfriend broke up."

"When did this Lampest say this?" I asked.

"This morning, when he told me about Jon."

"Regardless of whether it was Mickey or Jon, how did he learn it that fast? I thought you said they came here straight from the school?"

"I don't know," Sandra said. "It's what he said."

I drifted out again. There was an animated discussion about a lock that hadn't been found and then Jo was explaining that Jon wasn't found hanging from the front of the backstop. He was practically lying on the roof at the rear, holding onto the wire mesh.

"He was what?" It just came out of me.

Jo repeated it, and we sat looking at each other. I had known Jon since he was eleven, and he was one of the most agile kids I had ever coached.

"You mean that this kid committed suicide with the means of his salvation clutched in his hands?" I held my hands in front of me as I said it, clutching the air, trying to picture it, trying to feel the wire in my hands, trying to imagine how a person could have the determination to lie there and die. Sandra winced and got up and left the room.

Jo didn't answer at first, as if she had not yet thought of it that way. Then she said, "That's what they are saying."

I don't know if I said goodbye. I just know I left. Chris, a kid I knew from past baseball teams, was in front of the house, and I took his upper arm in a greeting grip.

"'You still be here in a half hour or so?"

"Sure," he said. "I guess. What's up?"

"I don't know," I said. "I'm not sure. I mean, nothing. Just asking."

"Yeah, I'll be here."

Jane was in bed when I got home. I went straight to the basement and turned on my computer. I typed and retyped what I gradually realized was a petition of some sort. Finally, it read:

Because there is presently underway a legal matter based largely on allegations made by Jon Bowie against a member or members of the Howard County Police Department, we the undersigned citizens of Howard County, ages eighteen or older, believe that there should be an independent investigation by a police agency outside of Howard County into the circumstances surrounding Jon Bowie's death. We make no presumptions about those circumstances and believe that it would be irresponsible to do so prior to a thorough and independent investigation.

I printed twenty-five copies and returned to the Keysers'. Chris still was standing in front of the house.

Part of my reputation as a coach - a deserved part, I confess - was that, having said something once and not having anything to add, I would say it again, and again. I kept trying to get over it, and over it.

I handed the petitions to Chris and asked if he thought he could pass them around and get them signed. He read the top sheet slowly and then read it again.

"Sure, Coach," he said.

I explained that he had to keep one copy as a master in case he had to make copies.

"Okay, Coach," he said.

I told him to give one to one person and another to another and let each person make copies.

"Yeah, Coach," he said.

I told him to tell everyone to get the signed sheets back to him, or to Sandra. There had to be a plan, I said. We didn't want signed petitions sitting in somebody's living room.

"I' got it, Coach," he said.

I asked if he would be sure to keep the master copy and not give it away. He could call me and get more, but time might be lost.

"You said that, Coach," he said.

"Well, don't try to do everything yourself. Anybody you give them to, ask them to make their own copies, and tell them to do the same thing with the ones that they hand out."

He looked at me and made a determined effort at a grin.

"Coach, I' got it. Don't worry about it."

I was nearly home when I realized I hadn't gone inside to mention the petition to Jim or Sandra.

Some things have to be attended to. On Saturday, the day after Jon's body was found, Sandra walked her black terrier, Henry.

Some things have to be faced. Sandra walked Henry along the bike path that led past the backstop.

Some things are difficult to explain, or can't be explained at all. A young man whom I know and will not name was on top of the backstop, wiping it down with a red rag. Sandra was in a daze and she gave this young man no thought except to notice his presence. She stopped and watched for a moment and then continued her walk. Later, when the autopsy results came out and it was found that there were unexplained red wool fibers on most articles of Jon's clothes, Sandra discounted that part of the report. She assumed the red fibers came from the young man's rag. They couldn't have, of course, because Jon's body had been lowered from the backstop a day earlier, but Sandra was in a daze and that was what she assumed.

There was a viewing on Sunday, but I didn't go. It probably was just as well. If I had got wind that early of what happened to Sandra at the viewing, I don't know if I would have been ready to deal with it.

Sandra was sitting on a chair in the front row of the funeral parlor, near the coffin. Someone leaned over and gave her a firm hug. She looked around to offer her thanks, and no one was near her.

Sandra kept this to herself for some time, and I probably wouldn't have had to deal with it even if I had been there. Either way, I wasn't.

10 On Monday morning, Jane and I called our offices and said we wouldn't be in. The funeral home was a small, one-story brick building on a side street in northeast Columbia. From a distance it could have been mistaken for a branch office for a bank. Sandra was inside in the red-carpeted entrance area. She wandered about in a daze in her black dress and nose-length veil, desperately greeting each new arrival and seeing to any possible need.

Sandra introduced me to her brother, Jack, and said I needed to talk with him. She walked away with Jane, and Jack and I went into a side room.

Jack was a serious, dark-haired man in his early or middle thirties. He was some type of administrator for a college in western Maryland. A grey-haired man came in the room and told Jack that someone in the police department was coming with Jon's watch and some other personal items. It was clear from the conversation that there had been some sort of controversy about whether the police would release the articles in time for the funeral. The head of the county council had called the police department and angry words had been said. The grey-haired man left and Jack eyed me and I eyed him.

"Sandra says I can trust you," he said. "Something's not right about all this."

"How do you mean?"

"At the very least, it appears that the police are determined not to investigate. You heard about the bullets that were found?"

"Yeah, but I can't make anything of it." Where I was raised, twenty-two bullets were almost as common as blackberries. Jack was from West Virginia, so he was likely to have seen a few as well. When I first heard about the bullets, I automatically discounted the dirty one. It could have been lying in the grass for some time. The newer bullet seemed like a detail worth remembering.

"What do you make of it?" I asked.

"If nothing else, the police didn't exactly comb the area."

"Someone could have held a gun on Jon and made him climb the backstop. Somehow they dropped a bullet."

"Why would you think that?"

"No reason," I said. "Just speculating at the possibilities."

"Sandra told you about the tape that she found?"

"No. What tape?"

"Grey duct tape in her back yard. Several strips of grey duct tape that looked as if they had been torn off of something. The police say that grey duct tape was wrapped around the cable, and some had been torn off. If it's a coincidence, it's an odd one. Jon thought that Meyers was in his back yard."

"If the tape came from the cable, why leave it there? That would be stupid."

"Killing somebody is not exactly a sign of higher intelligence," he said. "There was some orange cord, too, like the cord from a lawn edger."

I thought it over. "I'm having a hard time putting a police officer in Jon's back yard."

"Who knows?" Jack said. "If nobody investigates, there's no way to prove he was and no way to prove he wasn't."

"What about the lock?" I asked.

"The what?"

"I heard that the cable was locked down."

"Right."

"Well, if the lock was there, and they don't find it, then it means that Jon had to climb the backstop twice. He had to climb up and remove the lock somehow, climb back down and dispose of it in a way that it couldn't be found, and then climb back up again and hang himself. It sounds more deliberate than depressed to me. If nothing else, it's a reason not to jump to the conclusion that he committed suicide."

"I'm pretty sure they didn't find it," Jack said. "I doubt that they're looking."

Jack had a reason for believing that the person who fixed the cable in place was left-handed. It had something to do with how the cable was arranged. I had trouble following it and before I could ask him more about it the grey-haired man stuck his head in the door and said it was time for the family to be seated. I took a long look at Jack as he talked with the man, and I decided that Jack looked like an intelligent and calm person.

There's no need to go on at length about the funeral. It was hard. Jane was waiting for me in the entrance hall and we started into the funeral parlor. I wouldn't have joined the line that was waiting to pass by the opened coffin, but we walked in and found ourselves in line without meaning to be there. Most of the two hundred or so card chairs that all but filled the room were already occupied, and I thought we were waiting to be seated. By the time I realized we were in line to pass by the coffin, other people had lined up behind us and it seemed disrespectful not to continue. Jane usually knows when I don't feel like talking, and she left me alone.

I find that I can get teary-eyed at the damnedest little things in movie theaters where the lights are out, but at funerals, I don't do it. I don't try to explain it. It's just the way I am. Still, as the coffin drew nearer, I found that I was bracing myself against the possibility that I might have difficulty controlling myself. I didn't want to look ahead. When there were only a few people between us and the coffin, I stared straight ahead at the coffin itself. The wood was dark and heavily lacquered and looked like cherry. The lid was in two parts and the lower part was closed to the waist. Jon's hands lay one on the other below his waist. Long-stemmed, half-bloomed roses lay in a fan arrangement on his chest, thirteen of them. His high school baseball jacket, orange letters on black, was folded neatly at his far side so his favorite number, thirteen, showed. Someone had leaned a cardboard sign against the coffin lid and a statement on the sign was written in the high school's orange and black colors. I didn't read it. Then Jane and I were first in line and I glanced at Jon's pasty face. His youthful mustache had been shaved and I wondered why the medical examiner or the funeral home would have shaved it. I wear a mustache myself but I hadn't particularly cared for Jon's, and I had expected him to grow out of it eventually. Still, it didn't seem right to me to change a person to make him somehow different when he no longer had a say in the matter. I paused for a brief, respectful time and then moved on. I immediately regretted that I hadn't lingered more.

There weren't many seats left and Jane and I sat off to one side, which was fine with me. As everyone waited, a black youngster who looked little more than five years old got out of his seat a few rows from the front. He marched up the aisle to the coffin and stood for a few seconds at stiff attention, looking up at the coffin. Then he snapped a military salute, turned, and marched back down the aisle. He climbed up in his seat next to his startled parents.

Sandra was sitting with Mickey and Carlen and other family members on the front row. Jim sat in the second row, immediately behind Sandra. I assumed that the blonde, muscular man next to Sandra was her first husband, Jon's father. I wondered at the gesture that relinquishing his seat to Jon's natural father represented on Jim's part. As I got to know Jim better, I would realize that it was the kind of seemingly small thing he was inclined to do naturally.

A stocky, black minister spoke first. Jane leaned over and whispered to me that he was Reverend Wright of the local NAACP. Given the way that Jane whispers, she also told anyone sitting within several rows of us. Wright talked compassionately about someone named Carl and I leaned over to Jane and whispered that Carl was Jon's first name. Then Jo Glasco came to the lectern and read a psalm that had to do with justice and with evil eventually getting it's reward. There was a heavy silence in the room when she had finished.

A large, white minister with a dark-blonde mustache that matched his wavy hair spoke next. He looked like a football player fifteen years after the playing field. I asked Jane who he was but she didn't know him. He got Jon's name right. When I thought he was winding down, he said, "I know that many of you are not convinced that Jon Bowie took his own life, but, whether he did or he didn't, it is a serious issue that must be addressed." Then he went on for five minutes about why any who were in despair should not succumb to such a drastic action. I knew that with so many young people present it needed to be said, but it irritated me anyway. I leaned over to Jane and whispered, "There's not a young person in this room who thinks that Jon committed suicide."

The preacher talked on and I shut him out until flashes of memories from baseball fields were too much to deal with and I had to stop myself from letting them rise up in my mind. Then the preacher really was winding down and he said, "If Jon Bowie did not commit suicide, we have to stand together, hold hands together, and demand the truth together. Only the truth can set us free." He sat down and I decided that maybe I had judged him too harshly.

When the service was over a long line formed and people filed past the coffin for a last farewell, but I couldn't do that again. I looked about for any young people I knew who might be having a hard time and spoke to a few. Then Jane and I left.

There's a special feeling that comes when you walk into your own empty house. There's an underlying order to it, and it's either never as cluttered as you thought you left it or it doesn't seem to matter as much as you might have thought it did. Jane and I hung our coats in the closet by the front door and then wandered into the kitchen. I tried to explain something about Jon that I couldn't seem to get into the right words.

"He was who he was," I said. "That's a wonderful thing, and not as common as some might think. It's not that I saw him and Mickey that often, but there was a part of my mind that always looked forward to the next time I'd bump into them at the mall or some other place. He was a part of my life that, without necessarily even thinking about it, I always expected to be there."

Then I was crying and shaking as if I never would be able to stop, and Jane held me.

11　　In the days following Jon's funeral there was a whirlwind of television and newspaper stories. The reports kept referring to Jon as Carl, and they kept saying that he was twenty instead of nineteen. I found that the least of errors in these reports offended me. They usually referred to Jon as a man, and I began to feel that the choice of that word was intended to make it seem that the police had been required to deal with a lot in taking care of the motel incident. I also noticed that the newspaper articles often were on the same page as an article about an officer of the year or some detective who had pulled a cat out of a tree.

The Baltimore Sun reported that friends and family did not believe Jon's death was a suicide. The story said the twins and Steve Ko (the article spelled it C-O-E) had been arrested for possession of drug paraphernalia and resisting arrest. John Hollywood was quoted as saying Jon had no reason to kill himself and an officer had been harassing him. The FBI had been asked to intervene and a spokesman for the FBI said it was not likely the FBI would get involved.

I was reasonably certain neither Jon nor Mickey used drugs and neither had been charged with anything involving drugs. I called Sandra to ask but she wasn't home. I had forgotten that the family was traveling to West Virginia for the burial ceremony.

The Washington Post reported that the county state's attorney, which is what the county prosecutor is called in Maryland, was confident in local police but was open to having an outside investigator assigned to his office. Over 500 people had signed a petition asking for an outside investigation. The Chief of Police said Jon had a .18 blood alcohol level at the time he died. A level of .10 gets you charged for drunk driving in Maryland.

The county insert to the Baltimore Sun said the Police Chief, I'll call him Elvin Hickory, was moving to dispel rumors that foul play was involved in the hanging death of the twenty-year-old Columbia man. The autopsy showed that Jon died of asphyxiation. Detective Lampest said the body had not been moved after the death. He mentioned that, ironically, Jon had helped to construct the cable apparatus two years earlier as a student. Lampest said there were no grass stains or dirt on the clothing or any other signs to indicate a struggle. The story ended by stating that, in the motel incident, Jon had been charged with assault, resisting arrest and possession of drug paraphernalia.

It struck me as odd as I read the articles that the police were revealing autopsy results, pounding away at charges against Jon and Mick, and emphasizing such things as Jon helping put the cable on the backstop. It seemed they were defending a position rather than conducting an investigation.

The details were repeated on all seven of the local Baltimore and Washington television news shows. There were morning stories, noon stories and evening stories at six and eleven. One station showed Officer Meyers taking out his garbage. Most stations showed shots of the Red Roof Inn and of the backstop laden with flowers and cardboard signs left there by friends.

Ginny Thomas called. At the time, Ginny was a State Delegate to the Maryland State House of Delegates. She represented the voting district in which both Sandra's family and mine lived. I had known Ginny through mutual friends for a dozen years or so and had done some campaigning for her among my friends. Ginny knew I coached baseball and she was calling to ask if I knew the Bowies. I said I did. Ginny thought there should be a meeting between the police and people in the community who were concerned about the investigation of Jon's death. She wondered if I would mention it to Sandra's family and try to persuade them to attend.

I hate meetings. People talk differently and act differently and sit uncomfortably in their too-tight clothes and usually come out of meetings pleased or displeased because the opinions they had when they went in either were or weren't approved. The only things of significance I've ever seen accomplished in meetings occurred after someone said, "Adjourned," and I've been to a few. Meetings are too much like churches. Still, Ginny was *bona fide* good people, a grassroots politician who took the job for the simple purpose of providing a service, and things were getting hot. In one of those little stories that go on behind the scenes and don't make the news, police had tried to break up a group of teenagers having a beer-drinking field party at the field where Jon had been found. The teenagers refused to leave and threw beer bottles at the police and shouted, "Murderers." In other incidents people had broken out headlights of parked police cars. Police were retaliating by increasing patrols in the neighborhood around the school. They followed on the bumpers of teenage drivers until the drivers got nervous and made mistakes. They charged kids for the least of real and feigned offenses such as missing tail lights, and the encounters often ended in shouting matches.

I agreed to talk with Sandra. In a flurry of phone calls and short visits after Sandra and her family returned from West Virginia, Sandra agreed to attend the meeting, changed her mind after talking with her attorney, was going anyway in spite of her attorney's opinion, and then wasn't certain she should. It went back and forth and I finally called Ginny and said we would just have to wait to see if Sandra came.

In preparation for the meeting, I spoke with several of Jon's friends on the phone or at Sandra's. I also attended a gathering of a sizable group of Jon's friends at John and Claudia Hollywood's home. Several of the young people who came to that meeting had been interviewed by police regarding Jon's death, and most of them had found the interviews to be unsatisfactory. They were convinced that no real investigation was taking place. Several said they had been shown photographs during their interviews and had been asked such things as, "Doesn't this look like a suicide to you?" Lampest, the detective in charge of the investigation, told one young man during a taped interview that he was convinced Jon had committed suicide.

I compiled a list of concerns and sent the list to Ginny, who said she would forward the list to the Chief of Police so there would be ample time to prepare responses. The list was tough and obvious. The kids wanted to know about the lock, where Jon got enough beer to have a .18 blood alcohol level at six in the morning when he hadn't been home and the stores were closed, where he had been between 10:20 at night and the time he was found, why the police were insisting on an eleven p.m. time of death when someone who had walked past the backstop around 2:00 a.m. insisted no one was there, where Meyers had been that night, and on and on. It was agreed that anyone who wanted to could attend the meeting, but, to keep things orderly,

I would present the list of concerns.

My mother can see things.

Mama's psychic abilities were not a central part of my childhood. It was more like in the Old Testament, where a miracle of some sort might happen every hundred or every thousand years or so; in the telling of it, though, it can seem they were everyday occurrences. If you pressed Mama about it she would say she had a gift from God, but she preferred not to talk about it. She didn't want people to think she was crazy.

There were times when Mama was going about her house cleaning, and, hardly looking up, she would say so-and-so was dead. Then we got a phone call from some relative or friend saying they wanted to tell us about so-and-so, and when the funeral would be. There were other times when she would say, "I wonder who that is?" or, "Oh, it's so-and-so," and then the phone would ring.

There is a family story I learned in bits and pieces over time. The way I tell the story to myself, Daddy was in Europe in the war and Mama and my oldest brother Ronnie and I were living with Daddy's brother and his wife in Raleigh. Ronnie was a toddler and I was a home-on-leave baby and too young to remember any of this. The war was nearly over and some troops were being sent home, but, for security reasons, the army didn't want word to leak out that troops were being moved. Daddy wanted to send Mama a letter and say he was getting on a ship to come home, but the army wouldn't let him do it. When the ship got to New York City, the troops were put on a train to South Carolina where they were to be processed out of the army. Mama would have been about twenty-one or so at the time since she and Daddy were married when he was nineteen and she was eighteen. Either it snowed uncharacteristically deep for North Carolina that night or I just remember the story that way. Mama didn't want to say anything at first and have Daddy's brother and his wife think she was crazy, but finally she had to say something.

"Terry's in Raleigh," she said. "We have to go to the train station."

There was some fuming and complaining, but Daddy's brother drove us there. The train had stopped for only an hour or so. The soldiers were allowed to mill around on the wooden platform and stretch their legs. They weren't allowed to use the phone. Mama hurried onto the platform with Ronnie in tow and me in her arms and she found Daddy in the crowd of soldiers. She and Daddy hugged and she told him how she had just known he would be there. Then Daddy got back on the train with the rest of the soldiers and went to South Carolina.

There are many other stories about what I once thought of as my mother's unusual ability. This is enough, though, to provide some understanding of why, when I began to suspect that there might be something about Jon Bowie's death that was terribly wrong, I did what seemed to me to be the natural thing.

I called Mama.

Jane was at a meeting, Mike was away at school and Dan was out with friends. I paced between the kitchen and the living room for a while and then I picked up the wall phone in the kitchen and called my mother.

"I know you don't like to do this," I said to her, "and I know that it's hard when it has to do with family, but there's something I need you to, you know, to look at."

"Well, don't tell me too much," she said. Her voice was resigned and weary, as if she was not feeling all that well and was accepting only because she knew I hated to ask.

"Somebody I know died. The son of a friend of mine."

"I'm so sorry," she said.

"Thank you. There's something about it that troubles me, and I wondered if you could try to get a sense of it."

"Okay," she said. "Just tell me his name and how old he was. Don't tell me anything else."

"His name is Jon, for Jonathan. It's spelled J-O-N. He's... he was nineteen."

"Okay. I don't know how long it will take, but I'll call you one way or the other."

I hung up and went into the basement family room to watch television, but I couldn't concentrate. I turned off the television and paced back and forth for about fifteen minutes. Our family room's not large, and I was a bit like a tiger in a cage. The phone rang and I jumped up the short flight of steps and dashed into the kitchen and jerked the receiver from its cradle. It was Mama.

"Tell me," Mama said, and she sounded upset, "was he found hanging from a goal post?"

The near accuracy of it surprised me and I talked to make room to think. "Sometimes there's a portable soccer goal near there. It looks kind of like a goal post. It might have been set up."

"What was he hanging from?"

"It was a backstop, the wire thing that stops foul balls behind the batter on a baseball field."

"Is it a tall, fence-like thing?"

"Yes."

"Oh. I didn't know what it was called. I thought it was a goal post."

"Mama, did I tell you he was found hanging?"

"He was, wasn't he?"

"Yes, ma'am, he was."

"Well, I wanted to be sure I was seeing the right place. I'll call you back."

She hung up and I went back down to the basement to pace. After ten minutes the phone rang again and I dashed up the steps to answer it.

"Do they know who killed him?" Mama asked.

"They say it was suicide. They say he did it himself."

"Oh, no," she said. "I don't think so. I'll call you back."

I didn't bother returning to the basement. I paced back and forth between the kitchen and the living room. I was near the wall phone when she called again and I answered on the first ring.

"Mama?"

"Yes." I waited a moment and she continued. "This is hard. I'm not sure exactly what it is that I'm seeing, but there's something wrong here. Something terribly, terribly wrong."

"What do you mean?"

"I don't know. It's as much a feeling as anything else, and it scares me. I've never been so frightened. It's," and she searched for a word, "it's *evil*. It's something very evil. It really scares me."

"What should I do?"

"I don't know. I'm very tired. I don't think I can do anymore tonight. I'll try again tomorrow. Maybe I'll draw you some pictures."

"Okay, thanks." I gave her more specifics about what I had heard and I told her how I knew Jim and Sandra and Jon and Mickey.

"David?"

"Yes."

"I don't think this was a suicide."

"An accident maybe?"

"No, I don't think so. It was worse than that. They meant to do it."

"They?"

"I think so. And David?"

"Yes."

"Be careful."

"About what?"

"About... everything. I mean it, David. Be careful."

I knew it was difficult for her to separate motherly concern from whatever it was she had seen, so I tried to get her to clarify.

"Is this Mama talking, or is it..." I didn't know how to end the question, so I just let it dangle.

"I don't know," she said. "I wish I did. Maybe both."

12 One concern that came up when I talked with the kids at John's and Claudia's about the upcoming meeting was that the kids wanted a police officer present whom they knew and trusted.

They gave me a name. It seemed like a reasonable request, so I took a few hours off from work one afternoon and went to the local police department. It was what a salesman would call a cold call.

I'd never been to the county police department before and I had to look up the address. It was in Ellicott City, an old mill town whose main street had evolved toward gift shops and restaurants. Ellicott City also served as the county seat. It was a few miles north of Columbia.

The police department was in an attractive, modern, low-standing brick building that sat up a long hill from the town's main street. It shared a large parking lot with two larger government office buildings. I told the officer behind the glass partition why I was there and found his reaction to be surprisingly cool. He went away and soon returned with several higher ranking officers. The one who seemed to be in charge was younger than I, maybe in his late thirties or early forties, and average in height, which put me looking straight in his eyes. The word *smug* comes to mind. I explained my mission and he said, "You suffer from a misconception, Mr. Parrish. There will be no meeting."

It's a personal encumbrance of mine that I have one of those faces that often reflects what I am thinking, and this is sometimes accompanied by blushing. I have noticed that people who have done something to generate this reaction often misinterpret my facial responses as a sign of weakness on my part, not realizing that one of the emotions that leads to this is sudden and unexpected anger. Of necessity, I have developed a habit of measuring my words under such circumstances so I do not lose the floor by default. "I didn't come to discuss whether there would be a meeting," I said as calmly as I could and in measured words. "State Delegate Virginia Thomas tells me that she has already arranged the meeting with the Chief of Police. Perhaps you were not informed. I came simply to request that someone the young people are comfortable with be present at the meeting." His face reddened slightly and I decided not to press the point. I gave him the name.

"That gentleman is no longer employed here as an officer," he said.

This surprised me, and I went into tap-dance mode. I suggested an officer I knew who umpired softball games and had what I had observed to be a firm but fair attitude. At least I could represent him comfortably to the kids.

"Why him?" he wanted to know, so I told him what I was thinking. "He works in my office," he said, "but just because a man is a good umpire doesn't mean he should be doing the other."

"Who would you suggest?"

"I don't think we have to get into that," he said. "We'll decide who represents us at the meeting."

It was clear that he was seeing our conversation as some sort of power struggle, and I wasn't exactly helping matters by getting angry. I didn't want to jeopardize the meeting by coming away empty-handed, so I tried again. "If you look at it from their point of view, you can see why the kids would want someone there they know. It seems to me that it gives the meeting a better chance for success. What can we work out?"

"There's nothing to work out," he said. "Now, if you'll excuse me," and he and his entourage turned and left me standing in the lobby.

Dan was at an age when he was out at dinner time as often as he was home, and, that night, Jane and I ate alone. Even in my own home I'm not that comfortable with out-loud prayers, so I always do a short grace and then we eat. We were passing peas and potatoes and I told Jane about the visit to the police station. "You know, I said, "I don't want to form any hasty opinions, but these boys are starting to piss me off."

The Columbia Flier is a company newspaper. The company is *New America*. The paper is free to Columbia residents and it's tossed onto driveways and apartment stoops each Thursday. It's about half the height of a regular newspaper and usually runs around a hundred and a few pages long. Every week several pages are devoted to current local issues and the rest are filled with advertising and such things as local sports, local arts, movie reviews and calendars of upcoming events and meetings.

On the Thursday after Jon's funeral, the Flier had two long articles related to Jon's death. There also was an editorial titled *Cops and kids should not be mortal enemies*. I caught the clever insinuation behind the word *mortal*, but nothing I had heard yet demonstrated that a police officer had been responsible for Jon's death. At most, there were things that warranted checking out. I had written a letter to the editors of the Flier that week saying, in essence, that as a community we should start listening to our young people and watching to see if they in fact were being harassed by the police, and the editorial alluded to the letter. Both articles re-hashed the events to date and one quoted a police officer as saying the police would continue to investigate despite the medical examiner's ruling of suicide. The other article quoted Reverend Wright of the NAACP saying he was not at all satisfied that Jon had committed suicide. Both articles quoted Sandra expressing disbelief that Jon's death was being called a suicide.

I know two of the county's medical examiners. Actually, the county doesn't have a medical examiner. It has several deputy medical examiners. One of the deputy medical examiners I know is a nurse. The other is a construction worker with no extensive medical training. To be a deputy medical examiner, you take a class. Both of the deputy medical examiners I know are very bright people, but it would be a bit of a stretch to ask either of them to make a scientific ruling of suicide. The articles didn't go into that; I just thought I'd mention it.

Anyway, I pulled the related pages from the paper and took them downstairs to add them to the growing stack on the table in the storage room. I had come back upstairs when Mama called.

"Write this down," she said. "You have to tell it to Sandra."

I found a pencil in the junk drawer in the kitchen and a small pad of blue paper on the counter.

"Okay."

"Tell it to her just like I tell it to you."

"Okay."

"Sandra has to be careful. The person responsible for Jon's death knows that Sandra provides the intensity that keeps the story alive. That puts her in danger."

"Do you mean someone might try to hurt her?"

"Just write," she said. "Yes, that's what I mean. There is a person who knows what happened, maybe who did it, but he would never talk. He has no conscience. I can't see his face, but I can feel his evil. It's very frightening. She must not go back to work. She works, doesn't she?"

"Yes, ma'am. She manages a daycare center."

"It's important that she not go back to work. If something is going to happen to her, that's where it will happen."

"She'll have to go back eventually," I said.

Mama paused. "If she insists, then she has to be watched all the time. Somebody has to follow her to work and somebody has to follow her home. Anytime she's outside, there has to be someone with her. All the time. Is there going to be a trial?"

"Mama, there are more trials scheduled than I can keep track of. There's a grand jury hearing getting ready to start, there could be a trial from the charges that Jon and Mickey made against the police officers, and Mickey is supposed to go on trial in June for the charges against him."

"That one," she said. "The one in June. I think it will all come out then."

She stopped talking and I waited in case there was more. I looked with more than a smattering of disbelief at what I had written.

"Mama, I can't tell Sandra all this. She's in grief, and, besides, I don't know her that well. This would be like adding to her trouble. You know better than I do things like this are not always one hundred percent reliable, or things don't always mean what we think they mean."

It wouldn't be accurate to say my mother never swears or curses, but she very seldom does, and it's usually with a self-conscious little giggle. This time she didn't giggle. She exploded.

"Then what the hell do you think I'm doing this for?"

"Okay, Mama," I said. "I'll tell her."

People were constantly in and out of Jim's and Sandra's house in the days after Jon died. I was there often myself. There were so many rumors, and friends came to Sandra and told what they had heard. When the police interviewed a person, that person often came by to tell what had been said. After Ginny called and asked me to help set up a meeting, I stopped by several times to learn whether Sandra currently planned to attend. Usually we sat at her kitchen table with whoever else was there at the time.

On this Saturday, a week and a day after Jon's death, I didn't want to sit at the table with anyone else present. I didn't want to be there at all, but I had promised my mother. Sandra answered my knock and her face was drawn and pale. I asked her through the screen door if she would mind coming outside on the sidewalk. She went to get a windbreaker and then came outside.

I walked a few paces down the sidewalk and she followed until we were between her townhouse and the next. It was as if I stopped there instinctively to ensure that no one overheard me. I crammed my hands deep into the pockets of my blue jeans and hunched over, looking down at the sidewalk.

"I'm not sure how to go about this," I said. "I really don't want to add to your grief." I looked up and could see she wasn't inclined to say anything. I couldn't believe I was doing this, and I wanted to turn and run off. "My mother has what I guess you would have to say is some sort of gift. I've been talking to her about Jon, and she says there are some things I should tell you." Sandra still didn't say anything. I had summarized the notes so I wouldn't forget anything, and I took a sheet of paper out of my pocket and referred to it as I talked. When I had finished I said, "I really didn't want to come and tell you. These things are not always completely accurate, you know, and at such a time. My mother insisted, though. She said it was important. I hope you don't think I'm crazy, but she really does have a gift. I don't want to go into it right now, but I could tell you stories."

Sandra looked straight at me and there was a calm behind the trouble in her eyes. I felt as if somehow she was reassuring me. "I don't think you're crazy," she said. "I don't think you're crazy at all. I'm glad you told me. If she sees anything else, please tell me."

I promised I would. I was returning to my car and Sandra said, "Wait." I turned around and she came up to me and spoke in a low tone, as if, now, she was the one who didn't want to be overheard. "When you talk to your mother again, tell her I said thank you. And tell her I said hello. Tell her that I feel like I know her."

I drove home feeling relieved, and more than a little puzzled. Sandra had seemed to know more about what I had told her than I did.

Between the day of the funeral and the day of Jon's burial, Mickey had a dream. Mickey and Sandra were so much alike, independent and hard-headed, that they didn't talk to each other a lot. It wasn't that they didn't like each other; it was that they were so much alike. And Mickey was a private person. He didn't have much to say about what he did. If he decided he would do a thing, he did it. Before the funeral, when the family still was not being allowed to see Jon's body, Mickey went to the funeral home alone. He found the funeral home director and told him, "I'm Jon Bowie's brother, and I've come to see him. Where is he?" Mickey had a private farewell visit with Jon and saw no reason later to discuss it with anyone. So, Mickey didn't tell Sandra about his dream for a while. It was later, as they began to open up to each other, that he told her.

In Mickey's dream, Jon was crying.

Mickey asked, "Jon, why are you crying?"

"Everyone thinks I committed suicide," Jon said.

Mickey said, "No one thinks you committed suicide."

Jon stopped crying, and he laughed.

"Good," he said, "because I didn't."

13 At around seven-thirty on Friday, May 11, the Reverend David Rogers was barbecuing chicken on the raised deck behind his two-story, wood-sided house. The house was located on a heavily shaded side street in east Columbia. Rogers was six-feet-two and weighed in at about two-hundred-forty pounds. His two young sons and his near-teen daughter were entertaining themselves somewhere in the house. His wife was in the kitchen helping with the dinner preparations.

From the deck, Rogers could look out over the small back yard and beyond into a forested area that was the type of land referred to in Columbia as *open space*, space that would be left essentially in its natural state. Rogers tried to arrange his Fridays so he had no evening clients at his Wellspring Counseling Services, but the business almost always was on his mind or in the back of it. Wellspring was his compromise between the social expectations of what a minister should be and the inner stirrings of his heart. He had been a regular minister of a regular church, and, when he wasn't quietly suffocating, he had in his best efforts at a humble opinion done a fairly good job of it.

The first thirty-five years of his life had been good, all in all. He had grown up in a small town in Kansas and had married his high school sweetheart, the daughter of a Presbyterian minister. He had two young sons and a pre-teen daughter. After seminary in Dayton, Ohio, he had worked for almost five years as director of the Criminal Justice Program for the Cincinnati Council of Churches. He had worked in back streets and jails and prisons and had trained police officers in crisis intervention.

When funding started running out for the Criminal Justice Program, Rogers accepted an appointment as the pastor of a United Church of Christ congregation in Columbia, Maryland. That had lasted another five years. At first he had thrown himself into the job. The congregation met in an interfaith center, a Columbia-concept type of building in which the congregations of several churches met in different sanctuaries in the same building. He had told the search committee that interviewed him that he was a born activist. He believed a church should get involved in the social needs of its community. The committee members had agreed at the time that this fit the concept of the place known as *New America*.

Rogers was on more boards of directors and committees in Columbia than he could name off the top of his head. Columbia had grown rapidly and still had many vestiges of the earlier rural government, including a sizable good-old-boy network. In meeting after meeting, Rogers had been struck by the incestuous nature of government in the county. The same dozen or so representatives of government agencies kept showing up at every meeting, loading the committees and vetoing anything they disapproved. Rogers had suggested at one meeting that, in the interest of time, they just get together once a week and call themselves by all of the committee names. This led some people in local government to begin eyeing him with suspicion.

In a year in which the county had a budget surplus of twenty million dollars, Rogers had supported a recommendation for a program that would develop a national model for dealing with the homeless. Since the state would provide matching funds of up to two million dollars, Rogers recommended a two million dollar program. Existing county services were turning away two-hundred-fifty homeless a year in a county with one of the highest *per capita* incomes in the nation. The County Executive, who was Howard County's version of a mayor, disapproved the recommendation and supported, instead, county funding of two hundred and fifty thousand. That resulted in twenty-one new beds. Rogers was quoted in the Flier as saying the county could have had a new Cadillac and had settled for a used VW bug. This didn't make him any friends in local government. When such disapproval didn't make him tired, he loved it.

Rogers' congregation merged with a more conservative church. New members began loading committees and they quickly pulled off something of a coup. Members who had supported his programs began seeing the writing on the wall and started leaving the church. It had been something of a final straw when the president of the church's board of directors stopped by Rogers' office one afternoon and asked if they could talk a minute.

"We're tired of hearing sermons about South Africa and the homeless and things like that," the president said. "We come to church to feel good."

Excluding a few words that wouldn't be found in any religious text,

David said something that closely approximated, "When you become the pastor of this church, you can decide what the sermon topics will be." The conversation went downhill from there. Eventually, after a few hard weeks of heated meetings and sleepless nights, David resigned.

Wellspring Counseling Services hadn't exactly taken off from the beginning, but it was growing. Sometimes his wife had tried to be supportive. Other times, she had suggested that Rogers might be succumbing to obsessive idealism. The finances bothered his wife, too, David knew. She had a good job as assistant to a representative on the local County Council, but they needed two full incomes and the promise of a future. Besides, he was beginning to be viewed as something of a radical in government circles, and that was becoming an increasing embarrassment to his wife. She had to work with those people every day. David didn't have to give up his ideals, she kept trying to explain; he just had to learn to work better within the system. David turned the chicken and let out a sigh. He loved his wife, and she loved him, but they couldn't seem to come to terms with his ways of doing things.

The Bowie thing was eating at him, too. Something about it wasn't right. He kept searching his mind for an *it* he could put a finger on. He had left his beeper at home that day so, just once, he could drive from Columbia to Baltimore and back without it going off. One meeting in peace. He had no more than returned and walked through the front door of his home when the phone rang. It was his wife.

"The police department has been calling you all morning. They want you to help with a suicide."

In his role as one of the voluntary chaplains for the Howard County Police Department, which was another of the many things David was involved in, he had frequently insisted that a chaplain always be the first to notify the family of a death. Officer training simply wasn't adequate in that regard. Of all days to leave his beeper. When David had finally caught up with Sergeant Dayton Arnold, David's friend and neighbor, Arnold had been uncharacteristically upset. The death of any young person was upsetting, but this was different. Again, David couldn't put a finger on exactly what it was about Arnold's reaction that had bothered him. Arnold's upset had seemed more than... David just couldn't pin it down.

David turned the chicken again. He had never met Jon Bowie. John Wright knew the family and had called and asked David to assist with the funeral, which, of course, he did. By the time of the funeral there was considerable controversy in the community about whether a police officer might actually have been involved in the Bowie kid's death. David had seen enough of the inner workings of police departments to know that it definitely was possible. Still, he had felt it was his responsibility to mention suicide at the funeral in as compassionate a way as possible. There were so many young people there, and a young person could get upset and do something drastic in reaction to the death of a friend. Rogers thought he had handled it as well as it could be handled. There always was the danger of a copy-cat attempt, and certain things had to be said. Young people had streamed into his office after the funeral, wanting to talk about Jon Bowie. They were so upset, and so convinced that this young man could not have committed suicide. David was trained in suicidology, and he had explained to each of them that there was always a period of disbelief, of an unwillingness to accept, but they were so convinced. It troubled him.

The phone rang in the kitchen. His wife came out through the sliding glass door, handed him the receiver and took over the chicken. David pictured several clients who might be calling, and, as he took the phone, he shifted his mind into business mode. He didn't recognize the trembling voice of the woman on the phone. She obviously had been crying.

The woman blurted, "I know who killed Jon Bowie."

"Excuse me?" David said.

"I know who killed Jon Bowie," the woman said again, and she began sobbing.

David stepped quickly from the deck into the kitchen. He pulled open an under-counter drawer in which he always kept a note pad and pencils.

At the time, Columbia was divided into seven villages, and the villages were further divided into neighborhoods. Most of the villages had shopping and office areas called village centers. There might be a grocery store, liquor store, barber shop and such inside a small, mall-like building. By design, most of these village centers were situated off the street so they would be hardly noticeable.

The meeting between the community and the police was on again and off again. It finally came about on a week-day evening eleven days after Jon's death. It was held at The Other Barn, which was a building that once was a real barn with a real hayloft and had been converted into village offices at the Oakland Mills Village Center. Sandra didn't come.

Large, green, formica-topped tables were pushed together in the center of the board-walled room where the meeting was held. The tables filled most of the room. Two or three dozen people easily could have sat around the tables. Instead, only five of us sat there. The rest sat in card chairs away from the tables, nearer the walls. Claudia Hollywood and I sat one end, across from Ginny. Police Chief Elvin Hickory and the county's State's Attorney, I'll call him Arthur Boudreaux, sat side by side at the other end, fifteen feet or so away. A large group of plain-clothed and uniformed officers sat behind Ginny and a few more sat behind the Chief. An equally large group of young people and a few adults sat behind Claudia and me. To an overhead camera the arrangement would have looked like some sort of standoff.

Ginny thanked everyone for coming, expressed concern at the serious events occurring in the community, and assured the group that anyone who wanted to speak would be heard. She asked for decorum. Then she deferred to Chief Hickory for any opening remarks. Sandra's absence hung like a dark cloud.

Hickory was tall and thin and appeared to be in his early fifties. He had senatorially grey hair and wore wire-rimmed glasses that gave him a scholarly look. He remained seated and said expected things. He was concerned and intent on getting to the bottom of things. The community had to remain calm. Then he said he had no particular agenda and was open to questions. Ginny looked at me and I took a few folded papers from my inside coat pocket. I was nervous, so I began to read from the remarks I already had forwarded to Chief Hickory.

I said we were there because we were concerned that a premature ruling of suicide had prejudiced the investigation of Jon's death. We also were concerned about stories that were surfacing about police harassment and abuse of young people in the community. I asked that the ruling of suicide be changed until an independent investigation could be completed. I said Jon's family hadn't been treated very well since his death. When I was finished you could have cut the silence with a knife, so I moved to the specific questions.

The meeting fell into a pattern. I would ask a question and Hickory would have an answer. It soon became apparent to me that no progress would come of the meeting, and I found myself simply going through the motions. Even now I don't care to relate the things that were said in any great detail, although I suppose a summary is necessary.

I asked Hickory what, in his professional opinion, was the statistical likelihood that an identical twin would commit suicide, and he laughed.

"I'm not a psychologist," he said. "I'm a professional police officer. I don't have anything to go on but facts."

I asked why the body was taken straight to a funeral home with no autopsy. He answered that the county medical examiner had ruled that it was a clear case of suicide, and the police had no reason to disagree. It was a school day, he said, and the police had worked quickly to avoid upsetting the children, who would be arriving soon at the school.

I asked why the scene had not been searched thoroughly and the area had not been roped off. He said Detective Lampest had searched through the garbage cans and around the vicinity and had located nothing of significance. He said the area was clean and there had been no signs of a struggle and no indications of foul play.

I asked why Jon's death had not been treated similarly to a recent instance when a student had shot himself while on the phone with his girlfriend and had left a suicide note and the police had roped off the area and had not made a ruling of suicide for several days. He said every case was different.

I asked a few more questions, all along the same lines, and there was an answer for each.

State's Attorney Arthur Boudreaux cleared his throat and introduced himself. He was about five-eight and looked like an aging bulldog. "I just wanted to inject," Boudreaux said, "that, in response to the petition I have received, and the considerable public interest generated by this case, my office has made the determination that Carl Jonathan Bowie's death is to be officially considered as *unattended* rather than as a suicide."

I asked what he meant and he gave a long explanation of the difference between "manner of death" and "cause of death." Several officers got involved in the discussion and offered excited clarifications. It seemed to matter to them, so I waited. One could be called suicide and the other could be called hanging. I forget which was which.

Chief Hickory cleared his throat. "I just want to point out," he said, "that we have an honest difference of opinion here. Mr. Boudreaux sees the death as unattended. My department still believes it was a suicide, and will continue to do so until such time as evidence is presented to the contrary."

"With all due respect," I said, "if the Chief of Police thinks it's a suicide, and the officers investigating the case are sitting here listening to you say it, then it doesn't seem very likely that we're going to get anywhere other than a conclusion that it's a suicide, whether it is or not."

Hickory's face reddened almost imperceptibly. "We are quite capable, Mr. Parrish," Hickory said, spitting my name at me, "of conducting an objective investigation."

"But the investigator in charge of the case told a young man during a taped interview that he thinks Jon committed suicide. It seems to me that he's not leaving the door open for other possibilities."

A tall, thin man with leaning posture and a wearied, concave face practically jumped from his seat in the first row behind Ginny.

"I'm Detective Lampest," he said, "and I want to ask you something. Don't you have an opinion about what happened to Jon Bowie?"

"No, sir. I don't." I said. "I don't think there's enough information yet for anyone to have an opinion."

"There's nothing wrong with having an opinion," he said.

I could feel myself getting angry and I measured my words in an effort not to let my emotions show. "There is if you're investigating what happened. Do you think there's anything wrong with asking the mother of a dead child if she wants to come down to the station and look at the rope?"

Lampest stepped forward, closer to the table.

"There was no rope. There was a cable."

"I'm aware of that," I said. "I was repeating what I was told you said. Did you also say that this was your investigation, and that you would decide if there was going to be an autopsy? That this wasn't a movie?"

"Ms. Keyser was excited and angry. I don't think I would have said that."

A young man I didn't know stood behind me and interrupted with a polite, "Excuse me." He was slightly built and had short, neatly combed dark hair.

"I have a question," he said. Eyes turned to him and no one responded, so he continued. "If I had been Jon Bowie's only known enemy, and if Jon had told people that I had been stalking him the week before he died, and if he was supposed to testify against me in a few days, would you interview me?"

Lampest's face flashed red. He leaned forward and pointed a shaking finger across the table at the young man. In a startlingly loud voice he shouted, "Listen, young man..." Then he swallowed hard and was silent for several seconds. The sudden outburst left the room uncomfortably silent, and no one spoke or even seemed to move as Lampest composed himself. Then, in a calmer but still shaking voice, he said, "I can assure you that no police officer had anything to do with Jon Bowie's death."

The young man stood silent for a moment, as if it seemed important that he at least give an impression that he was considering the answer. Then he asked calmly, "Based on what? Have you interviewed him? Do you know where he was that night? Who can back it up?"

Lampest didn't answer him. Boudreaux and Hickory started making other points and the young man sat down. I wrote *Who is that?* on a scrap of paper and pushed it over to Claudia Hollywood. She wrote *Sean Stewart* beneath my question and pushed the paper back. I folded it and put it in my coat pocket.

We went through the motions of asking and answering the remaining questions on my list. Hickory doubted there ever had been a lock on the cable. He didn't know where Jon had been between ten-thirty on Thursday and six the next morning. He thought Jon could have climbed the backstop with a .18 blood alcohol level.

There was a final question I had promised Sandra I would ask.

"Has Jon Bowie ever been charged by the Howard County Police Department with any drug related offense, including possession of drug paraphernalia?"

Hickory turned to the officers behind him and whispered with them for almost thirty seconds. Then he turned back around.

"I am not able to determine at this time that he has."

"Would you mind checking that out and providing Ms. Keyser with an answer? I keep seeing in the newspapers that Jon was charged with possession of drug paraphernalia. I don't know any place except the police department where they would have gotten that information."

Hickory turned and whispered again with the officers and then turned back around.

"No, he has not."

"Am I correct in assuming that means there never have been any charges against Jon Bowie that are in any way related to drugs?"

"That is correct."

I looked at Ginny and nodded that I was finished.

Arthur Boudreaux stood. He looked to his left and asked three men to stand. He introduced the men as investigators from the Maryland State Police.

"The state police have assigned these men to my office to conduct an independent investigation. While I have complete confidence in our police department, I believe the citizens of this community have a right to an investigation with which they can feel comfortable."

A tall, grey-haired man I'll call Captain Deane was introduced as being in charge of the investigation. If I had known at the time that he was a long-time personal friend of Chief Hickory's, I would have been less impressed, but I didn't know. Deane introduced a man I'll call Sergeant Simpson. Simpson was tall, black, and athletically trim. He had a firm, intelligent air that immediately impressed me. The third man was a white guy, fortiesh, medium height and dark hair. I'll say his name was Wilkinson. Simpson addressed the group.

"I will be investigating and reporting to Captain Deane. When I have completed my investigation, I will report the results to Mr. Boudreaux." He made a few more crisp remarks that increased my favorable impression, and then he sat down. I was thinking that I couldn't wait to tell Sandra how professional the state police investigators seemed.

I had prepared a closing statement and had given it to Ginny beforehand. It lay on the table in front of me. Ginny looked at me and raised her eyebrows as if to ask if there was anything else. I looked down at the statement.

A young man in our community stands accused by rumor and innuendo of committing a serious crime. He and his family, and the family of Jon Bowie, deserve a complete and impartial investigation of the circumstances surrounding Jon's death.

I folded the statement without reading it aloud and put it in my inside coat pocket. I looked at Ginny and indicated with a slight negative nod that I had nothing to add. I was hopeful, but the police still had not convinced me that they were willing to do their jobs.

The meeting ended and people got up and formed into small groups. There was hand shaking and quiet conversation. I was leaving when Arthur Boudreaux and his assistant, a tall and wiry-haired man I'll call Calvin Delight, cornered me. Boudreaux asked if I knew any of the young people who had been at the Red Roof Inn, and I said I did.

"The grand jury is supposed to hear this case in a few weeks," Boudreaux said. "If I had to present the case today, I'd have only one witness. Do you think you could persuade more young people to talk to me about it?" Delight repeated that it was important that he and Boudreaux talk with the young people who had been at the motel. I said I would see what I could do.

Boudreaux and Delight thanked me in that distantly exuberant way politicians thank everyone and they walked off. I looked around the room and everyone else seemed engaged in conversation, so I left. I was standing on the sidewalk in front of The Other Barn smoking a cigarette when a man in street clothes came up to me and introduced himself as a police officer.

"Mr. Parrish," he said. "There are some of us who understand what you are trying to do. There's only so much that we can do officially. We have pressures that you wouldn't know about, but we do understand. We'll continue to do what we can. You have to do the rest."

He offered his hand and his palm was warm and his grip was firm. We shared a long and mutually unblinking moment of eye contact. I wasn't too sure what it was he thought he understood that I was trying to do, but I was comforted that he thought he did, and that he had found it important to say it.

If anyone were to ask me the name of the police officer who spoke to me that night after the meeting, I'd have to plead what I've come to think of as the *President's Defense*. It's what several people who were President of the United States during my generation have said when they found themselves in potentially sticky situations.

I don't remember.

On the Sunday following the meeting, the county insert to the Baltimore Sun carried a short, boxed correction on page three. The correction stated that the Associated Press had provided incorrect information about the charges against Jon, and the correct charges against him in connection with the motel incident were disorderly conduct, resisting arrest and obstruction. There was no other clarification.

14 There was something about Sergeant Simpson of the Maryland State Police that reminded me of a childhood friend of mine named Bucky.

One afternoon when Bucky was home from Thailand where he had worked for Air Force Intelligence during the Vietnam War, and I was finishing up at the University of North Carolina, Bucky told me he wanted to be a police officer. We were sitting on the front stoop overlooking the large front yard where we had played neighborhood football as kids. Bucky was recently married, and his wife, Molly, and his mom and dad and Molly's mom and dad were very much against his choice of careers. They had their natural concerns, Bucky explained. They were afraid he would get killed, and, if not, everyone knew that being a police officer could put terrible strains on a marriage. Bucky could make more money with any of a number of other offers.

"I know in my heart that I'm a police officer," Bucky said. I can feel it. It's who I am."

Bucky was about as naturally inclined to talk about his innermost feelings as he was to get naked at a funeral, so I knew he already had made up his mind. He was just building up the courage to tell Molly and both families.

Bucky became a police officer and Jane and I got married and moved into a little cabin in the woods until I could finish school. Sometimes Jane and I went over to Bucky's and Molly's for dinner and board games or whatever and sometimes they came to our place. We were sitting in their living room watching television on the night of the first moon landing.

One evening in a time when a popular term for a police officer was *pig*, I was sitting at Bucky's kitchen table and he told me how a woman had walked past him on the sidewalk of the main street in Chapel Hill and had spit on his badge and shouted, "Pig," at him. He didn't know her, and she didn't know him. He had just walked on. Chapel Hill was a college town, and you would have expected a higher than normal education level, but Bucky said she had done it so I believed it. There was hurt and bewilderment in his eyes as he told it, and he said, "Why would someone do that?" He said it in a way that showed he wasn't looking for a response so much as he was trying to figure it out for himself.

When Bucky and Molly and Jane and I got together, Bucky and I usually would have a few beers. To be more exact, I'd have at least a few and Bucky would have only a couple. Bucky and I had put down some beers over the years and this new restraint of his surprised me at first, and I mentioned it. It wouldn't look right, Bucky explained, for a police officer to be staggering around drunk. What if he got called out? It was just a little price that went with the job. If not that many people were looking up to police officers at the time, he said, then he had to conduct himself in a way that they could if they ever decided to. He wanted his kids to be proud of him, and he wanted to be proud of himself. Everyone else would just have to think what they thought.

I had been living in Maryland a year or two when a mutual friend called from North Carolina to tell me Bucky was in trouble. He said it was in the local paper in Chapel Hill and even in the Durham and Raleigh papers and on the television stations all around that Bucky had been charged with some sort of sexual harassment, which was a hot, new topic at the time. By then Bucky had risen to the rank of Captain in the police department and was being groomed to be the next Chief of Police. I called Bucky and he sounded about as close to cracking as I could imagine him getting, which is to say that he had been caught completely off guard by the charge and was dealing with it as best he could. I asked him what had happened and he said, "I don't really know." He said a female officer had resigned to take a job in Durham. During her exit interview she was asked as a matter of form if she had any problems with the department. She said Bucky had offended her in some way. I asked him in what way and he said, "I don't know. They haven't told me. Maybe I told a joke she didn't like. She was in some of my training classes, and you know me, I don't watch every word that comes out of my mouth. I've thought it over a thousand times, and I just can't come up with anything."

Over the next several weeks I spoke on the phone with either Bucky or Molly every few nights. A group of people marched through town with signs demanding that Bucky be fired. Bucky got an attorney and the attorney told him not to talk to the press. I asked Bucky if that was smart and he said, "It is for me. I'm not that good with words, and the press would just chew me up and spit me out. I intend to come out of this still being a police officer, and with my family intact. That's all. The rest is something I can't do anything about."

The Chief of Police eventually asked Bucky to resign. I asked Bucky how it felt to have the man who was grooming him for his job ask him. Bucky said the Chief was only doing what he had to do. Bucky felt sorry for his Chief for being put in that position. I asked Bucky if he was considering resigning and, without hesitation, he said, "No, I couldn't do that."

Considerable political finagling followed involving the Chief of Police and the mayor and numerous local politicians and activists groups. The Chief of Police eventually told Bucky that if he wouldn't resign then he would have to take a demotion to Lieutenant. I asked Bucky what he said when the Chief of Police told him that. His voice cracked at first and then became firm again.

"I said I was the best Captain in the department, and the Chief knew it. I said that if I was busted to Lieutenant then I was going to be the best Lieutenant in the department. I said they weren't going to run me out just because I'm suddenly some sort of embarrassment. I said that I'm a police officer. It's who I am. And if they want to take it away from me, then they'll have to fire me and find out then what I'll do about it."

Bucky didn't get fired but he did get busted to Lieutenant, and he stuck with the job. The department insisted for political reasons that he undergo psychiatric counseling. He resisted vehemently for a while and eventually relented and said he was damned if it hadn't actually helped him some. After a year or so the furor died down. It was not the kind of thing Bucky and Molly could forget, but they found out who their friends were, and they survived it.

I can't put a finger on exactly what it was about Sergeant Simpson of the Maryland State Police that reminded me of Bucky. Maybe it was his proud, soft-spoken, confident manner. Maybe it was something I thought I saw in his eyes, or heard between the words he used. I don't know. All I know for sure is that I had so much hope.

Mama called.

"Is there a tunnel near where Jon was found?"

"There are tunnels all over Columbia. Columbia has bike paths that go all over the place. There hardly ever are any bicycles on them, but people walk on them and they're called bike paths. They go through tunnels under the street. There are probably a few near where Jon was found."

"Are they more square than round?"

"Yes. I think most of them are sort of square. Maybe all of them."

"I see a tunnel. There are what look like steps off to one side, and a rocky front. There's some kind of structure nearby that's like most of a rectangle, like a carport. I don't know if it's a carport, but that's the shape of it. If you're facing the tunnel, it's like the tunnel is up to the left and the carport, or whatever that is, is down in the right corner."

"That sounds like a lot. I suppose I could find that. What does it mean?"

"I don't know. It's what I see. And there's another thing. Inside the tunnel it's light and then dark."

"You mean like..."

"I don't know what it's like. It's light and then it's dark. And wheels turning. I don't know if it means that it's near a road, or maybe it's the wheels of justice turning. I see a wheel with spokes inside and it's spinning. There's also a mechanical thing of some sort that I see sometimes. It has a round part in the center and teeth around the round part."

"You mean like some sort of mechanical lift?"

"David," she said, as if to remind me that mechanical things were not a strength of hers.

"Sorry."

I asked if there was anything else and she said, "No." I started saying goodbye, which anyone raised in the South knows takes more than a sentence to accomplish, and Mama interrupted me. "Sandra didn't go back to work yet, did she?"

"No, Ma'am," I said. "But she's thinking about it. She can't stay home forever."

There are dreams, and there are dreams. Some are grainy and vague and you wake in the morning trying to recall them, if you remember them at all. Others are vivid and startlingly clear. You sit up in the middle of the night with your heart pounding, knowing you'll never forget.

I was coming out of a building I had never seen before, but which I knew to be a courthouse. It was large and made of red brick and had white, fluted columns. Twenty or more wide steps led down to a spacious, brick-surfaced courtyard. I came down the steps alongside Sergeant Simpson of the state police. Several of Jon's and Mickey's friends also were leaving the courthouse in small groups. Something had been decided inside, and the kids and I were not satisfied with the decision. Only Sergeant Simpson seemed satisfied. It was as if he had done his job and the outcome was not his concern.

The backstop stood to one side in a small dirt area beyond a far corner of the courtyard. I didn't want to leave, so I climbed the backstop to rest and wait. I lay chest down on the top with my arms stretched out. I felt self-conscious about being on the backstop. It seemed somehow inappropriate, disrespectful, but I was there and I looked down through the wire roof at the others.

Sergeant Simpson walked past the front of the backstop. He stopped and looked up at me through the wire. In a matter-of-fact tone, he said, "Jon will call you."

With a sense of unhesitating calm and certainty, I said, "I know."

I was immediately awake and sitting upright and my heart was pounding so fiercely I could hardly breathe. I tried to shake the dream from my thoughts, but it wouldn't leave. I sank my head back into the pillow and stared through the darkness at the ceiling.

I half-expected the phone to ring.

15 As good a parent-coach as I ever had the misfortune of coaching against was a fellow by the name of Charlie Brown. I'm not making that up. That was his real name.

It seemed that Charlie always had good players, and they just kept getting better. Charlie was a gruff, good-hearted sort with a thick shock of premature white hair and a hoarse way of talking that was somewhere between a growl and a friendly whisper of a secret he was going to share only with you and the next few counties. Charlie had two sons, Andy and Howie, who were close enough in age to play together on the same team and who were legitimate all-stars every year. If memory serves me correctly, we actually defeated Charlie's team once in the playoffs at the end of a season. That left a lot of other games we lost. Kids loved playing for Charlie, and you had to admire him even from the other side of the field.

Charlie's son, Andy, was a real scrapper. Andy, who was a little on the small side, wore a constant grin. Andy eventually gave up organized ball to devote his attention to wrestling. He became a county wrestling champion for Wilde Lake High School. When he graduated from high school he went off to college in Cleveland, on a wrestling scholarship, I think.

The night after Jon died, the kids at Sandra's had mentioned a Wilde Lake wrestler. I figured that, if they had their information straight, Andy would know about it. I called Charlie to get Andy's number in Cleveland. As luck would have it, Andy was home and answered the phone. I asked if he had heard the story.

"Yeah, you could say that," Andy said. "I was one of them. I was there."

Charlie lived in the village called Town Center, near the mall. Town Center was the smallest of Columbia's villages and the residences were mostly townhouses and apartment buildings. I drove over one evening after work. The house was on a side street and was one of several connected townhouses arranged in a *U* around a large asphalt parking lot. Charlie was in the parking lot underneath a car. He got up wiping grease off his hands and extended a mostly-clean hand, and we shook. We exchanged pleasantries and he pointed me to the correct door. He told me that, if I was intent on pursuing the Bowie thing, I should watch my back. I asked him what he meant and he said, "I didn't know about the police around here until this thing happened to Andy. I'm serious. Watch your back."

Andy answered the door and suggested that we talk in the back yard. He led me through the house and out a sliding glass door into a small yard enclosed by a high hedge. We sat on a metal glider and he went over his story in detail.

Andy is a kid whom I trust without reservation. If he says something, I believe it. Still, I questioned him extensively to be certain I had the details right. We talked for well over two hours and I interrupted him frequently, sometimes asking him to stand and demonstrate where this person stood, how that person held his hands and things such as that.

I went home and wrote it up on the computer and took Andy a copy a couple of days later. We got together again a few days after that and he had written a lot of notes and corrections in the margins. We talked for a while at his kitchen table and I went home and made the corrections.

Summer had come and gone by the time I finally got the statement right to Andy's satisfaction. I added a few comments Andy made toward the end of the summer and faxed a copy to Cleveland. Andy signed it and got it notarized and faxed the signed copy back and then mailed the original. Some of it is getting a little ahead of the story, but, except for leaving out kids' last names and changing the names of the police officers and government officials, here is the entire statement of Andy Brown, a kid I trust.

I attended a party at a friend's house; the party, to the best of my recollection, was held December 4, 1988. At that time I was 17 years old and a student at Wilde Lake High School in Columbia, Maryland. I was 5'6" tall and weighed 129 pounds.

I arrived at the party around 9 p.m. and left around 1 a.m. Approximately 20 people attended the party. Most of the people at the party were drinking beer. I was not drinking because it was my turn to serve as designated driver.

*Shortly before I left the party I was looking around for *Andrzej <last name>. He had drunk a lot and had become very intoxicated. Someone said that he had already left so I left with Willie <last name>, Daryl <last name>, and Andy <last name>. I was driving. The others had each had several beers at the party although none of them was noticeably intoxicated.*

Almost immediately after leaving the party I was driving down Governor Warfield Road away from Little Patuxent Parkway at a point where Columbia Mall is off to the left. I had just passed the intersection of Governor Warfield and Windstream, at the traffic light, and started down the hill when I noticed a police car pulled to the side of Governor Warfield and Andrzej was sitting on the curb beside the police car.

Friends told me later that two girls who were at the party had seen Andrzej earlier as he was walking along the road. They stopped and offered to take him home. The police car arrived while the girls were talking to Andrzej. The police instructed the girls to leave. The girls had left when I saw Andrzej sitting on the curb by the police car.

I knew that I could get cited for driving after 1 a.m. because I was 17 so I parked out of sight on a side street and Andy, Daryl, Willie and I walked up the grass to the police car. A second police car got there at about the same time that we got to the first police car. Officers present at that time were Bragg, Burns, and Loveless. Officer Bragg was seated in a police car. I walked up to him and said that I knew Andrzej and that Andrzej lived nearby. I asked if I could take Andrzej home and Officer Bragg said that I could. I walked over to Andrzej and said, "Come on."

Officer Burns said, "What the hell are you doing?" Officer Bragg was coming over and I looked at him and said, "He said I could take him home." Officer Bragg then said, "I didn't say you could take him anywhere." I had helped Andrzej up from the curb and when Officer Bragg said that I helped Andrzej back down onto the curb. Andrzej was very drunk and didn't seem to know what was going on.

Andy <last name> started arguing with Officers Bragg and Burns. Andy said, "You said he could take him home." While Andy and the police were arguing Andrzej got up and started walking off. Either Officer Loveless or Burns, I forget which one, threw Andrzej to the ground and handcuffed his hands behind his back. He leaned Andrzej against the police car with Andrzej' back to the car. Then Andrzej said, "Take these handcuffs off me, you fucking pig."

---

* *It's pronounced AHN-dray*

When Andrzej said that the same officer (Loveless or Burns) put an arm around the back of Andrzej' shoulders and his foot in front of Andrzej' feet. He pushed Andrzej forward and at the same time swept Andrzej' feet out from under him with his (the officer's) feet. This threw Andrzej face down onto the ground and the ground cut a long gash along the upper right side of his head. The officers all looked at each other as if they were stunned that Andrzej had hit the ground so hard.

Andy <last name> stepped up to one of the officers and shouted with his face right up against the officer's face, "What the hell are you doing? You said we could take him home and then you said we can't. Then you throw him down." The officer said, "Oh, you want to be a tough guy?" and he threw Andy against the police car. At this point Daryl was yelling and I was trying to see if Andrzej was all right and Willie was watching without really doing anything.

Officer Burns threw Andy against the police car two times or more. Then he grabbed Andy from behind and tried to handcuff him. Andy struggled and pulled his hands away so he couldn't be handcuffed. He leaned forward away from Officer Burns and put his hands over his face. Officer Loveless hit him in the face and ribs with his elbow, forearm, and fists as Officer Burns held him from behind. They finally got him stomach-down on the ground with his face turned to one side. Bragg pressed the side of Andy's face against the ground and Loveless pressed his knee in Andy's back and handcuffed Andy's hands behind him.

Daryl was standing off to one side yelling while the officers handcuffed Andy. After Andy was handcuffed Officer Burns stood up and went over to Daryl and shouted, "Shut up." He and Daryl started arguing and then struggling and then Burns was trying to handcuff Daryl and saying, "You're going to jail." Willie and I were still trying to see if Andrzej was all right. Officer Bragg came over to where we were and said, "Leave unless you want the same thing to happen to you." Willie ran and hid in the bushes where he could watch. I started walking off on the grass beside the road.

Officer Meyers arrived in a police car as I was walking off. His car skidded to a stop and he jumped out of the car and shouted, "Freeze." It startled me. I stopped walking and raised my hands up over my shoulders. As I was standing there I couldn't see behind me but I was hit in the back between the shoulder blades and knocked to the ground. It felt like I had been hit by someone's upper body or forearm in a tackle. Then Officer Meyers was on top of me with his knee in my back. He jerked my hands back and handcuffed them behind me.

A paddy wagon had arrived, and 8 or 9 police cars, and there were a lot of people standing around watching. Officer Meyers yanked me to my feet and walked me to the paddy wagon. I fell several times while we were going to the paddy wagon. Officer Meyers threw me into the paddy wagon and my head struck the paddy wagon door and the door cut my eye.

Andy <last name> and Daryl were already in the paddy wagon with their hands handcuffed behind them. Andrzej was lying on the ground. An ambulance came for Andrzej. They took him to Howard County General Hospital and treated him for the gash in his head and for internal injuries. He went into a coma twice during the night. The police said later that the comas were alcohol induced. I heard that Chief Hickory went to the hospital but I'm not sure. Andrzej told me that he doesn't remember anything about that night after he left the party.

One police car followed the paddy wagon to the police station in Ellicott City. The paddy wagon parked about 30 feet from the police station. Six officers gathered in a semi-circle behind the rear door of the paddy wagon. I could look out the rear door window and see them. Two of the officers had been at Governor Warfield Road. I suppose the other officers were already at the police station but I'm not sure where they came from. I would recognize most of them if I saw them again but I don't know their names. One was a large, stocky black man. The rest were white.

Officer Loveless was one of those in the semi-circle. He pointed through the rear window of the paddy wagon at Andy <last name> and said, "That's him." Someone opened the rear door and I stepped forward to get out. I was stooped over and about to step down three feet or so onto the asphalt parking lot. One of the officers, I don't know which one, grabbed my ankle and jerked me out of the paddy wagon. He jerked me straight out so that I was parallel to the ground and I landed on my back on the parking lot. I landed on my hands where they were handcuffed behind me and the parking lot jammed my hands into my back just above the left hip.

They jerked Andy <last name> out of the paddy wagon the same way, by his ankle. No one held me or even watched me as they were taking Andy out of the paddy wagon. I just lay on the parking lot and they jerked him out by the ankle. I don't remember how Daryl got out. I think he just stepped down.

A slender, dark-haired officer led me from the paddy wagon to the police station. He pushed me and dragged me along and kept shoving me to the ground and saying, "Get up." When I got up he would push me down again and say, "Get up," again. The officers taking Andy and Daryl to the police station kept pushing them down, too, and telling them to get up. When we got to the police station door the officer leading Daryl threw him against the door.

There were two halls inside the door. One went off to the left and the other went straight ahead. Two officers took Andy <last name> down the hallway to the left. One officer took Daryl and another took me down the hall that went straight ahead. They kept pushing us down and telling us to get up. They kicked us several times when we were down. There were other officers present, walking by and watching. They might have kicked us, too, but it was hard to tell who was kicking when I was on the floor. I would know several of them if I saw them again. While they were kicking us they were saying things like, "Don't fuck with us," and "Shut up. Don't mess with us."

An officer jerked me to my feet by my sweatshirt and nearly tore the sweatshirt off of me. They took Daryl and me down the hall through a door. The cells were in a room to the left beyond the door. They put me in one cell and Daryl in another with our hands still handcuffed behind us. We kept asking, "What did we do?" and "Why are we here?" No one ever answered us and they never told us that we were under arrest or why we were there.

By now it was about 3:30 a.m. We had been in the cells about 5 minutes when an officer brought Andy <last name> in without the handcuffs on. He locked Andy in a separate cell and left. Andy's eyes were puffed up and his face looked raw. There was a piece of skin hanging down from his chin and his chin was bleeding. He said that the officers had taken him into a room and taken the handcuffs off of him and beat him up.

They left us alone in the cells for a long time. We started shouting things like, "Take these handcuffs off," and "What the hell is going on?" An officer came in and shook his keys at Daryl and threatened to come in the cell. He said, "Shut up. 'You want some more?" Then he left.

A small, slender officer came in and said that we should be quiet if we didn't want it to happen again. He left. I started shouting that I had to go to the bathroom and if they didn't take the handcuffs off me I was going to piss on the floor. The small officer came back and took the handcuffs off of us through the bars. This was between 5 a.m. and 6 a.m.

About an hour later they finger-printed us and took mug shots. My dad came and asked Officer Bragg if he (my dad) could get a copy of the police report. My dad says that Officer Bragg was drunk and couldn't seem to understand anything that was being said to him. Sergeant Winstead interrupted and said that we couldn't have a copy of the report. When we left the police station I still hadn't been told why I was arrested or what I was charged with.

I got a letter about a week later saying that I was charged with disorderly conduct and hindering a police officer. About a month later I got a second letter saying that I was charged with these two things plus disorderly intoxication, resisting arrest and assault with intent to maim.

My dad called the FBI and an agent came and talked with me. I told him everything that happened in pretty full detail. The FBI agent called later and said that there was not enough evidence to press charges against the police.

My dad got an attorney and the attorney said that the police were willing to drop the charges but my dad wouldn't do it. There was a hearing scheduled in juvenile court and the hearing got postponed about 6 times. It finally took place in September, 1989. Andrzej' case and my case were heard together and the hearing lasted about 7 hours. The judge was a grey haired man. My dad says that he wasn't a judge, he was a commissioner.

When I was on the witness stand I kept trying to tell what had happened but the state's attorney, a tall man with glasses and a mustache (I'm pretty sure that his name was Talbott) kept objecting and saying that it wasn't relevant. The state's attorney said that I was a vigilante and tried to take the law in my own hands. When I said that Officer Meyers said, "Freeze," the state's attorney said, "He didn't say that."

When Officer Meyers was on the stand he said that I had a stick in my hand and that was why he tackled me. That's not true. I didn't have anything in my hands. I just held them up and stopped walking when he shouted, "Freeze."

When Officer Burns was on the witness stand he said that Andrzej got hurt accidentally because he (Officer Burns) pushed Andrzej aside so Andrzej wouldn't get hurt while he (Officer Burns) was dealing with Andy, who Officer Burns said was hindering. That's not true, either. They threw Andrzej down while he was handcuffed and so drunk he could hardly stand up, and they did it because Andrzej called one of them a "fucking pig." Andrzej shouldn't have said that, but that was no reason to throw him down while he was drunk and handcuffed.

My lawyer objected that the police were allowed to say things that were not in their police reports. He said that they couldn't change their stories. The judge or commissioner said that they could. My attorney said, "This trial is a mockery," and the judge or commissioner told him to be quiet.

A man named Langston from Juvenile Service said that I should get 2 years probation, be assigned to participate in an alcohol assessment program and be required to visit a shock trauma unit under another program.

In his summation the state's attorney said that, "A bunch of drunks got wasted and decided to take the law in their own hands. The police were doing their jobs and along come these punks." The judge or commissioner said, "These kids need to grow up." He said to me, "You're a small guy, but you've got to learn to control your temper. You're a cannon waiting to be unloaded. Learn to respect police officers. You can't take the law in your own hands and you can't get in the way of police business."

I got all the penalties that the man from Juvenile Services recommended plus one hundred hours of community service. My dad says that he should have just taken the police's offer to drop the charges. He thought that I would get a fair hearing but now he says that he was wrong. He also says that it was a mistake to hire a black attorney in Howard County. The attorney tried to do all right, I guess, but he couldn't get a word in edgewise. It was obvious.

My dad sued the police department but I don't really expect anything to come of it. My friends in Cleveland, Ohio, where I go to college, say that they've never heard of such a thing. They say that they thought that the police in Cleveland were bad, but nothing like that. All I know is that I'm going back to Cleveland in a few days and I'll just be glad to get out of Howard County.

I've been to a few parties in Columbia this summer and there usually are 20 or 30 people at a party. The police almost always show up even if we're not making any noise and are just inside the house talking. It's like they know where the parties are or are riding around looking for them. As soon as the police arrive I always run out the back door. If I go to a party I know I'll end up running out the back door to get away from the police. I just plan on it and watch out for them. There are some bad police in Howard County, and I mean really bad. I don't know if that's how it is in other places but that's how it is here, and I don't want anything to do with them.

I wanted to tell all of this to the grand jury that investigated whether the police beat up Jon and Mickey Bowie. I went to the court house to testify but I never got called to be a witness.

This statement was written for me by David Parrish. He came to my home and we talked about it for about two and a half hours. Then he wrote it up and I proof read it and made corrections and it is a true and accurate statement of what I said to him.

Andrew Wayne Brown

16 In June, a notice in the newspaper said there would be a public meeting to discuss whether the police department should be accredited by a national group. Sandra thought someone should go to the meeting and say something about the investigation of Jon's death, and about young people who said they were harassed by police officers.

I wasn't in favor of it. I thought the accreditation process, as it was called, was a good idea. You tried to set high standards and good policies and live up to them. I told Sandra I wouldn't do it. I didn't confess that another part of my reluctance had to do with stage fright.

I suppose that, at least in part, I changed my mind because I was so afraid of doing it. I figured if I didn't see it through then I wouldn't be able to look at myself straight in the mirror. Charlie Brown went with me to give me some moral support. We sat with a sizable audience in card chairs in a conference room in a county government building. Police officials of various ranks stood around the room in dress uniform, some with yellow braids on their shoulders. The Chief of Police, Hickory, was cordial to me even though he had to know the kinds of things I was intent on saying. Several members of the national commission, including some Chiefs of Police from various parts of the country, sat at a table in the front of the room. Reporters and camera men were scattered throughout the audience, and the camera and related wires for the local cable station took up a good portion of the center aisle.

People who wanted to say something signed a list and then waited their turns. I sat remembering something I'd read about how you recognize stage fright. The mouth goes dry and the heart pounds almost uncontrollably. My mouth wasn't dry, so I figured I had at least an even chance of not fainting. A parade of local politicians, agency heads, ministers and relatives of police officers went up front to the podium and described the many merits of the local department. A man named Reverend David Rogers took a turn and I leaned over and told Charlie I was pretty sure he was the man who had spoken at Jon's funeral. I told Charlie maybe things would start getting interesting, now. Rogers had a long list of good things to say about the department and Charlie finally leaned over and whispered for half the county to hear, "I don't know. He sounds pretty kiss-ass to me." Then it was my turn, and that's when my mouth went dry.

The only thought I could hold onto as I approached the podium was that, if I didn't stop shaking, I might fall over something. Then I was at the podium and I said, "Gentlemen," and it came out in about three different octaves in rapid succession. I grabbed the podium and held on tight. My legs were shaking, my hands were shaking, and my voice was shaking. If my feet had been screwed down, I might have lost a few body parts. The thought actually went through my mind to keep one hand on my notes and the other on the microphone so, if I fell to the floor, I still could keep talking.

I said, as intelligibly as I could get it out in a quivering voice, I didn't appreciate it when young people I knew and trusted told me they were being harassed by the police. I said I didn't appreciate it when they said they had been kicked and pushed around inside the police department with other officers looking on. I also said I didn't think the Bowie investigation had been handled very well so far, and I gave a few examples. Finally, I said the national organization would discredit its own reputation if it found these things acceptable and accredited the county police department. If the police department straightened up its act, I said, then I'd be first in line to support them.

It was pretty quiet as I tried to work my way back to my seat without stumbling over something. I didn't see any reason to believe I'd made any friends.

Claudia Hollywood spoke and did a better job of it than I had. She said she was a nurse and police officers regularly bragged in the emergency room about hitting people and pushing them around. Andy Brown's attorney spoke, saying he'd seen too many cases of young people who'd been beaten up by police officers, and he couldn't support the accreditation until some unsatisfactory practices were dealt with.

Subsequent articles in the papers said the police department had received overwhelming support from the community, and there had been a few complainers. The local cable station played a tape of the meeting every few hours for the next several days, but I couldn't bring myself to watch it.

I had started keeping articles about the Bowie case and, after the accreditation hearing, there were several. I was thumbing through the papers looking for related articles when another article caught my eye. I couldn't say why. It just did.

A young man, I'll call him Doug Iglesia, had escaped from a drug treatment program and the police were looking for him. The article described him as a cat burglar. It said the police thought he was responsible for a rash of burglaries that had occurred since his escape.

For the life of me I couldn't see why there was anything about the article that interested me enough to keep it. As I put it with the other articles on the growing stack on a table in the basement back room, I wondered to myself why I was doing it. It made no sense, but I had already started to lay it on the pile with the rest so I continued the motion. As I walked away, still feeling puzzled, I told myself I could take it off the stack later.

If it wasn't so sad it would be funny, or maybe it's the other way around.

On the night I did my nervous-quiver dance at the police accreditation hearing, I had a brief conversation with Chief of Police Hickory. I was leaving the county office building as quickly and inconspicuously as I could and Hickory was sitting on a vinyl bench just across the wide hall from the exit. Several officers were standing around him in a small group.

"Mr. Parrish?" Hickory called out. I turned around and he motioned for me to join him. As I've suggested, Hickory's physical appearance was impressive - scholarly and father-like. I walked over and sat beside him on the bench. The tone of his voice suggested he was concerned about my welfare and wanted to explain something he didn't think I understood. "These young people," he said, "are not as innocent as you think. They have a group, you know, and they get together in each other's basements and wear togas and drink. You should look into it."

I didn't know anything about a group of young people. He told me the name of the group and I wasn't sure I had heard him right. I asked him to give me the name again and, again, it sounded as if he had said, "The Fidos."

I said I would look into the group, and I left. A day or two later I stopped by Jim's and Sandra's. Sandra came outside on the sidewalk and I asked if Jon and Mickey had been members of some group.

"What group?" she asked, and her eyes were clouded with confusion.

"I think it was called something like The Fidos. Hickory said they wear togas."

"Oh, for goodness sake," Sandra said.

When Jon and Mickey were juniors in high school, they had a friend whose brother was in a college fraternity. The friend, who had something like a 4.0 grade point average and eventually graduated from West Point, decided to start a fraternity of high school kids. There were about thirty kids in the fraternity and they called themselves the Phi Sigma Epsilon. Underclassmen had to carry seniors' books in the halls and all that stuff. They had sweatshirts made with the fraternity name on them and wore the sweatshirts to school. School administrators got upset and called the kids' parents and said fraternities weren't allowed in high school and the kids couldn't wear the sweatshirts. Parents got upset and said it wasn't a school group and the kids had as much right to wear their sweatshirts as other kids had to wear things with writing on them. A group of kids who couldn't get in Phi Sigma Epsilon started a rival group called the High Fives, and lots of kids wanted to get in one group or the other.

I asked Sandra, "What's the business about the togas?"

"That was the night of the initiation," she said. "They wrapped bedsheets around themselves and paraded up the street." She pointed to the end of the street in the direction of the evergreens. "Jim looked out the window and thought it was a Klan rally or something until he saw that about half the kids were black."

After the kids paraded up the street, they gathered in Eddie Vicker's

basement.
    Fidos.

From time to time, seemingly little things popped up that were so far beyond my ability to do anything about them that all I could do was take note of them, maybe get a little terrified a while at the possibilities, and finally calm down and move on to other things.

Sandra told Mickey he had to get out of the house more, and Mickey attended a party a friend's house. There, he met another friend who was home on leave from the army. This friend, no doubt after a few beers, told Mickey he had been sitting in an office at a nearby base, waiting to get orders, when he overheard several officers in an adjoining room talking about Jon's death. One of the officers looked up, saw him in the next room, and came to the door and closed it. The friend said he didn't want to go into a lot of details with Mickey at the party, but he promised to come by Mickey's house the next day and tell him in more detail what he had overheard. He also said he would bring Mickey a pistol, because he thought Mickey was in danger.

Mickey told Sandra, Sandra told me, and somewhere in the telling or the re-telling the door wasn't just closed, it was slammed; and the officers were not just officers, they were high-ranking officers.

The friend didn't come by Mickey's house the next day. The friend was expected to be home on leave for a couple of weeks, so Mickey tried to get in touch with him. Mickey learned that his friend had gotten a call the morning after the party telling him he had to ship out early. He no longer was in town. In fact, Mickey never heard from him again.

A split-rail fence enclosed a small play area in front of the daycare center where Sandra worked. The fence was connected to the wall to the left of the front door and ran along the front of the building and joined the wall again at the end of the building nearest the street. Sandra was leaning against the fence with her back to the parking lot.

Sandra had worried about coming back to work. The warning from my mother had more than frightened her. It had shaken her at the core of her confidence. Still, she couldn't stay home forever. Each morning Jim watched as she left in her truck. She took a different route each day and, as she drove, she constantly looked about and in her rear view mirror. She parked in front of the door and waited to get out until a parent drove up or someone inside looked out and saw her. During the day she would go outside only when someone went with her. Even now, Anne was kneeling in front of her planting flowers inside the fence although, to someone approaching from behind, it would have looked as if she was standing alone at the fence.

The man came up the wooded hill and through the pines beyond the parking lot. He walked at a brisk, confident pace, not looking to either side. He stepped onto the asphalt and strode across it. He was six feet from Sandra when Anne jumped to her feet.

"What do you want?"

Sandra turned and locked eyes with the man. He stopped abruptly four feet from her. He was well over six feet tall and in his late forties. His hair was a mixture of grey and something like strawberry blonde that seemed to have faded from what might once have been red. He was dressed in a khaki brown shirt and slacks and stood in a stiff, military posture. In his right hand he carried a three foot length of rope. He stared at Sandra a moment, jerked his eyes toward Anne, and then pivoted heel-and-toe and walked briskly back across the asphalt and into the woods. Sandra and Anne watched in stunned silence until he had disappeared. Anne broke the silence.

"That man was going to kill you."

Sandra turned to her friend.

"I know." She shook her head violently back and forth to regain her composure. "You have to promise me that you won't tell anyone about this."

"You're crazy," Anne said. "You have to tell the police."

"No. They'll think I'm just being hysterical. Then they won't believe anything, and we'll never know what happened to Jon. Swear it."

"Sandra," Anne said, objecting.

"Swear it," Sandra said. "I mean it."

"Okay," Anne said. "I swear it."

A few days went by before Sandra told me about the man with the rope. We still were sorting out the nature of our increasing friendship, and, as she explained later, she hadn't decided whether to trust me with the story. When she did tell me, I insisted that she tell the state police. She insisted that she couldn't do it.

"Who are you going to trust if you can't trust the police?" I practically shouted at her. "How can they do their jobs if you hold things back?"

"They won't listen," she said. "They'll think I'm hysterical, and they won't take the investigation seriously."

Sandra was at home alone a few nights later and, at around eight o'clock, she picked up the phone to call Captain Deane, Simpson's boss. She was hoping to get an answering machine. That way, she could tell herself she had tried but it hadn't worked out. Maybe by the next day, she told herself, she would have the courage to stick to her own determination not to go through with it. As fortune would have it, Deane was working late, and he answered the phone.

"I have something to tell you," Sandra said.

She told Deane how the man had come up behind her from out of the woods with a rope in his hand, how Anne had jumped up and confronted him, how he had pivoted and walked off, back into the woods, and why she hadn't told Deane or Simpson before.

When she had finished, Deane asked, "Why are you telling me this? If this really happened, you should be talking to Chief Hickory. It's not really our jurisdiction."

"I don't trust Hickory," Sandra said. "That's why we asked for an independent investigation. He won't do anything."

"Hickory's a fine person," Deane said. "He and I have been friends for years. You should talk to him."

Deane told Sandra a long story about a police officer in his home town in West Virginia. People made up stories about this officer, Deane said. People said he was a bad officer. "He was just a big old boy," Deane said. "Just like Meyers. You're on the wrong track with Meyers. He's just a big old boy himself. Howard County has one of the finest police departments in the country, and the community is treating Meyers bad."

When Sandra hung up she stood with her hand on the receiver, asking herself, "Why did I put myself through that? He didn't believe a word I said."

A few days went by before I saw Sandra again. The man with the rope was on my mind and I asked her if she had told the state police about it.

"Don't talk to me about the state police," she said. "You don't know anything."

———

An acquaintance of Jon's and Mick's showed up one afternoon at Sandra's. She let him in and they went into the kitchen and Mickey joined them. They talked in snippets of memories about Jon and about people's reactions to Jon's death.

"I could have Meyers killed," the young man said.

Sandra brushed the remark aside. "Get out of here with that foolishness," she said.

"I could do it," he insisted. "I know about such things."

"Get out of here," Sandra said again. She saw him to the door and waved as he left. Then she returned to the kitchen.

Mickey said, "He wasn't joking, Mom."

"Well, I'm not having that kind of talk," Sandra said.

17 When Sandra finally thought to tell me Eddie Vickers had walked past the backstop at almost two o'clock in the morning, and Jon's body had not been there at that time, I walked next door from Jim's and Sandra's to talk with Eddie and his mother about it. The county police and the state medical examiner's office were saying Jon had died at around eleven o'clock, and Eddie's story conflicted with their claims. I know now that when a medical examiner's office says something official, you never know for sure if it's a scientific observation or if it's just a repetition of what the police want said, but I didn't know that at the time. All I knew was that eleven o'clock was the official time of death and, if Jon died then, and he wasn't at the backstop three hours after that, then he had to have died somewhere else. That would have made it pretty difficult to call his death a suicide.

Eddie wasn't home and I talked with Katy Vickers, Eddie's mother. Katy worked the night shift, and Katy said that she had been outdoors chasing after her dog and a sock when Eddie came through the evergreens at a little before two in the morning. Eddie was visiting a friend and Katy told me how to get there. I drove over and Eddie and I sat on the friend's front steps and he told me himself. Eddie said he was out with a friend, a young woman, and she dropped him off at the backstop. It was a short walk through the evergreens to his home and dropping him off there saved his friend a few turns on her way back home. It was something they apparently had done several times before.

Eddie and his mother told me Eddie wanted to talk with the county police about his late night walk past the backstop, but the county police wouldn't talk with him. Then word went around that the state police would be investigating and the county police became interested in talking with Eddie, but he refused. He said he would wait to talk with the state police since maybe they were more interested in doing a real investigation.

On several occasions when I stopped by Jim's and Sandra's and I had seen Eddie and knew he was at home, one or two county police cars showed up in front of Eddie's house, and officers got out and knocked on the door. I watched through Sandra's kitchen curtains and the officers always eventually turned and walked away. As I said, I knew Eddie was home, but he wouldn't come to the door.

Then the state police got involved. Sandra told me Eddie talked with them about it.

———————

Even though Deane had rebuffed Sandra about the man with the rope, Sandra still was excited, at first, that the state police were investigating.

Every few days, when I stopped by, she would tell me the latest news about the investigation. Simpson, it seemed, was stopping by her house on a regular basis. It impressed Sandra that Simpson, sitting at her kitchen table, had said, "I'm a Christian, Ms. Keyser, and I intend to find out what happened to your son."

I told Sandra I didn't find his remark particularly comforting. What if she had been Jewish, or Muslim? Would that have made a difference? She scolded me, saying, "You know what he meant."

The state police removed a large section of wire from the backstop and sent it to a laboratory for analysis. This created a stir of conversation in the neighborhood. Two county detectives stayed up all night one night approaching anyone who walked past the backstop, asking if they knew anything about Jon's death. This also created a stir and, in the rumor mill, the state police got credit for the effort.

For several weeks, Sandra talked excitedly about different people the state police had interviewed and about how she just knew the state police would turn up something. Then there was the business with the beeper, and Sandra began to sour on the state police.

Simpson, Sandra told me, stopped by her house one afternoon and asked if Jon owned a beeper. Simpson said he had blown up a photograph of Jon on the backstop and there was a beeper attached to the waist of Jon's jeans. Sandra told Simpson Jon didn't own a beeper, but the county police used them. Maybe, Sandra suggested, Jon had taken the beeper from someone without the person knowing it. Maybe it was a clue as to who had killed Jon. Sandra still was of the opinion Meyers could be involved in some way, and she suggested Simpson find out if Meyers or any of his friends had lost a beeper. Simpson didn't take to this idea. He accused Sandra of destroying the beeper to protect Jon's reputation. Drug dealers used beepers, and Simpson thought the presence of a beeper indicated Jon somehow might have been involved with drugs. Sandra didn't take to this idea at all.

Sandra contacted the funeral home and asked the owner to check the receipt for the items returned for the funeral by the police. She asked if a beeper was listed, and it wasn't.

Simpson and Sandra began having an ongoing argument about the beeper. Simpson wanted to know if Sandra had done something with it, hidden it, or destroyed it. Sandra wanted to know why it hadn't occurred to Simpson to call the funeral home, as she had done. Since when, Sandra asked Simpson, did the police just hand over evidence to family members?

The relationship between Sandra and the state police began getting increasingly testy, to say the least. Finally, Simpson said to Sandra, "Don't talk to me about the beeper." After that, he wouldn't discuss it.

There was less contact between Sandra and Sergeant Simpson of the state police after the beeper business. I kept telling Sandra she had to trust the police. After Simpson accused her of destroying the beeper she invariably refused each time at first, but she eventually relented and told Simpson most things. My trump card in these conversations was that the police were her only hope of finding out what had happened to Jon. I had to keep finding new and increasingly subtle ways to use it.

There's a condition with a name I've forgotten again that involves the repression of memories after a tragedy. Details are blocked out and then come back later, one now and one another time, if at all. Sandra seemed to me to be suffering from it and, judging from the reactions of the police that she told me about, the police had no understanding of it. Sometimes she was afraid they thought she was inventing things.

Gradually, Sandra became aware that several items were missing from Jon's belongings. As she remembered them, she refused at first to tell Simpson about them. Over time, however, she relented and told him. There were Jon's missing car keys, which Simpson already knew about, and the red key tag with Jon's house key on it. And Jon's wallet. Jon had two wallets. A brown one he no longer used was found in the trunk of his car. The burgundy cloth one he did use never turned up. Jon's belt also was missing. It was a reversible brown and black belt with a designer buckle. Sandra distinctly recalled, when the memory eventually returned to her, that Jon had made a point of not fastening his belt too tightly before leaving home, and, when he was found, he was not wearing a belt.

"And his shoelaces were untied," Sandra told me. We were sitting at her kitchen table and she was recounting another conversation she'd had with Simpson. "Jon wouldn't even walk around the house with his shoelaces untied. Why would his shoelaces be untied? It's the kind of thing a mother would notice."

"You told Simpson about this?"

"He didn't think it was important."

One such forgotten and then remembered detail had to do with the break-in of her home the morning that Jon died. She finally told Simpson about that, but, as she was telling me she had done it, she mentioned things that were missing from Jon's room after he died. One was a camera she had loaned him. Another was the tape to his answering machine. When I asked if she had told Simpson about these missing items, she looked at me as if from inside a fog and said, "I only just now remembered them myself."

I asked Sandra once why she no longer trusted Simpson. He was only doing his job the best he could, I said.

She said, "He can't be trusted. My friends told me."

I wanted to know, "What friends?" and she looked at me across the table and didn't answer.

———————————

On the Fourth of July, Jon had been dead for two months. There was an evening vigil at the backstop. Sandra insists adamantly that there were well over a hundred people there. I counted sixty-four, including myself. There were several dozen kids and a dozen or so adults. They stood around talking in small groups as TV reporters and camera operators hung around near news vans in the parking lot, waiting for things to get underway. Word had come second-hand from the police that they would stay away, which I took as both an intelligent move and a good faith gesture. A half dozen or so kids dangled beer cans in their hands. Sandra shoo-ed them back to their cars to return without the cans.

My mother had said she thought the June trial, the one in which Mickey was to be tried for his involvement in the motel incident, was the one in which everything would come out. Mickey's trial had been postponed and June had come and gone. Now the trial was scheduled to begin the next day and there were buzzing undertones of interest and tension.

Sandra's face still was an almost uncontrollable boiling of hope and despair. She darted about from group to group thanking people for coming and worrying that the choir from her church had not yet arrived. She must have said a dozen times to one person or another that someone from the choir had promised and she was sure they would come.

The choir never came. It was nearly dark when the crowd spread out around the baselines. A young, stout black woman from Sandra's church made a few consoling remarks and led the group in a prayer for justice and comfort. The news teams took video shots and left.

By the time the group began to disperse a larger group was forming a hundred yards away, on the upper field, to watch the annual fireworks display. The fireworks display was a few miles away at the center of town. Large groups of people who didn't want to fight the traffic traditionally gathered at various good vantage points around town. The high school baseball field was one of those gathering places. People spread out blankets and unfolded lawn chairs and waited for the fireworks to start exploding above the tree line.

A large group of kids, some local and some who had come from out of town for the vigil, left the field and gathered at Sandra's. They came and went throughout the evening, going to different locations to see the fireworks and then returning. At around eleven, Sandra began to worry that Mickey was not in the house, and she went back to the field. Mickey was there with several friends, standing around at the backstop.

"You kids get back to the house," Sandra scolded. "Are you crazy? You can't be hanging around here this late." In telling it later, Sandra said she had some sort of premonition, an intensely strong feeling the kids were not safe at the backstop, but she didn't see that she could explain this to them at the time.

"Mom," Mickey said, complaining.

"I'm serious," Sandra said. "You get away from this backstop. It's not safe here."

They grumbled, but Sandra insisted and they returned with her to the house.

At around one in the morning, Sandra was feeding snacks to those kids who were staying over. The sandwiches and chips were almost gone and Sandra had made a large plate of deviled eggs. There was a loud knock at the front door and Sandra set the plate of deviled eggs on the kitchen table and answered the knock. The young woman who had led the prayer at the vigil, I'll say her name was Amanda Garvey, was at the door. Amanda was a plump, fairly short black woman in her early twenties. She had pleasant, smooth-skinned facial features and an outgoing personality. She wore an almost ever-present smile. I've seen people with smiles like that in churches that teach people are different, Christianity is a crusade, and love is a sword for fighting it. Amanda was visibly upset and excited.

"Somebody's got Mickey," Amanda said.

Mickey had gone upstairs to bed, and Sandra said, "What are you talking about? He's asleep."

"He can't be," Amanda said, pointing down the street toward the backstop. "I was just down there. Someone came up behind him and grabbed him. It was two men, a really tall man and another man. I saw it. You have to come with me."

"I'm not going anywhere," Sandra said. "Mickey is upstairs. Go see for yourself."

Amanda pushed past Sandra and went up the stairs. She came back down with a mystified look on her face.

"I saw it," she said.

Amanda was so upset that Sandra finally relented and went with her to the backstop. The field was dark and empty.

"I saw it," Amanda kept saying. "I saw it."

Amanda's white Mercury was parked near the end of the street. When Sandra told me this part of the story, I asked why Amanda's car would have been parked at the end of Sandra's street at one o'clock in the morning; Amanda lived several miles away, and this struck me as odd. Sandra said she had asked Amanda that herself. Amanda said she was talking religion with the woman named Vanessa who lived in the end unit, the woman the police had tried to get to say Jon was swinging his arms angrily when he was last seen alive.

Anyway, Sandra and Amanda walked back through the evergreens and when Amanda got in her car to leave she still was looking puzzled and disturbed.

18 I might have been in the courthouse before to check legal records or some such thing, but someone had to direct me from the lobby to the courtrooms. On the far wall of a large anteroom, evenly spaced doors led into the courtrooms. An excited crowd was gathered at one end of the anteroom. I didn't know that the woman standing in the middle of all of the excitement was a widely known and respected attorney from Baltimore named Christina Gutierrez. I took one look at her and decided that, whoever she was, she could catch bullets in her teeth and spit them out faster than they had come in. Young people were shouting frantic questions at her and she was sorting out the questions and answering them calmly, one at a time. She was a large, round-figured Latino woman with hair that looked fiercely combed and largely uncooperative. Her eyes pierced straight through a person to eviscerate any issue. She was a force. Whatever was going on in the anteroom, she definitely was in charge of dealing with it. Sandra spotted me and came over. Sandra's eyes were intense and red, and she clearly was upset.

"Whose the woman?" I asked.

"That's Tina, the attorney from Baltimore. I thought I told you about her. She's taking care of the criminal part of Mickey's case. Jo brought her in."

"What's all the fuss about?"

"Haven't you heard? Eddie Vickers was strangled last night at the backstop."

"What?"

"I called Katy and she says that he's at the hospital now. He'll try to get here in time to testify."

"So he's all right?"

"I suppose. Tina says the county's playing games. The judge who was supposed to hear the case called in sick. They've brought in a man from Prince George's county who's supposed to be some sort of hanging judge."

I turned toward the circle of young people and reached into it and pulled at the attorney's sleeve to get her attention. When she looked at me, I introduced myself.

"It seems that you could use a gopher. What do you need to have done?"

She looked at me as if she was trying to size me up. Then she looked at Sandra and Sandra gave her an affirmative nod. Gutierrez' eyes glazed over for an instant and then returned to their fierce brightness. "Court is in recess because of what happened to Eddie. When it reconvenes, I really need Eddie to take the stand. Go to the hospital. If Eddie can leave, bring him here. If he can't, come back and tell me."

The drive took about fifteen minutes. I parked in the emergency room lot of the large, palomino brick building and went in through the automatic glass doors. There were no patients in the small waiting area. I approached a white-uniformed woman who was sitting in a reception booth.

"I understand that you have a patient named Eddie Vickers?"

She gave me a guarded look and asked the nature of my interest. I explained that Eddie was scheduled to testify in a court case and I had come to offer him a ride if he could be discharged.

"Wait here," she said, and she hurried away.

An authoritative black woman in a nurse's uniform came into the waiting room.

"You were asking about Eddie Vickers?" she said to me.

I explained again and she said, "Listen, that is a very terrified young man. If I discussed it with you, I could lose my job. In fact, I'd rather not give you my name." As she said it she raised one shoulder and stuck out one side of her chest so her name tag stood out. She was Yvonne Last, the same woman who had seen Jon when he was treated for the injuries he got at the motel. "I will tell you this," she said, returning to a normal posture. "The attorneys in this case should subpoena his medical records."

"I'll tell them," I said. "Where is Eddie?"

"Two friends of his picked him up a few minutes ago. It was my understanding that they were going to take him to the courthouse."

I thanked her and left. I was pulling into the courthouse drive when I met John Hollywood driving out of the parking lot with a carload of kids. We stopped beside each other and rolled down our car windows.

"The trial is postponed," John said. "Everybody's meeting at Jo Glasco's office. Follow me."

I wasn't sure I was invited to the attorney's office, but I wanted to know what had happened. I made a u-turn and followed John to an office park in north Columbia. The buildings were one-story and each office had a separate entrance. About a dozen young people and Sandra and John and Claudia and Jo Glasco and I crowded into Jo's reception area. Sandra and some of the kids sat on the small sofa or in chairs. The rest of us stood. Jo explained to the young people that they were involved in a serious matter, and it was absolutely essential that they behave themselves and not get so much as a parking ticket. The county was, in her opinion, not taking the situation seriously and had indicated, in fact, that it would do anything it could to discredit the kids who had been at the motel. As she was explaining, Christina Gutierrez arrived in a flurry. Gutierrez brushed through the crowd and began making telephone calls at the most distant of two secretarial desks.

Eddie arrived in the company of two guys. One was a kid, Donnie, who was a friend of Jon's and Mick's. The other was the young man, Sean Stewart, who had stood up at the meeting with the police and asked if he would have been investigated if he was Jon's only known enemy. All conversation immediately stopped. Gutierrez hung up the phone.

Eddie was about five-eight and had a medium, muscular build. He wore his reddish-brown hair short. His face was flushed and he held his chin close to his chest, as if he was shy about all the attention focused on him. The kids looked at him for a moment without speaking. Then they began questioning him excitedly about what had happened. The initial burst of questioning died down and Eddie talked about it in a low, even voice. He had stopped at the backstop the night before on his way home. He was nervous about testifying in Mickey's trial the next day and he had gone there to calm down and to, he hesitated and turned slightly aside, to say goodnight to Jon. Anyway, he had no more than sat down on the little bench near the backstop when there was some kind of cord or rope tight around his neck. It was so tight he couldn't breathe. As the cord tightened and pulled up from behind him, he had no choice but to stand. He was marched across the grass beside the school, across the street, and along a bike path through the woods. He tried several times to turn, to see who was holding the cord so tightly around his neck, but each time he tried to turn the cord was pulled tighter still and his knees went limp and he thought he would faint. Something sharp kept poking in his back, urging him forward. He tried to stagger off the bike path, to leave a footprint, but he couldn't. He thought he was going to die and he wanted to leave a trace. After several minutes he did faint. When he woke he was alone and lying on his back in the dirt under a wooden bridge in the woods where a bike path crossed a creek. He crawled out from under the bridge and ran to a friend's house and woke the friend, who called the police and an ambulance. The police escorted Eddie to the hospital and he was examined. They released him and he went home, but in the morning he began hyper-ventilating and returned to the hospital. Friends drove him from the hospital to the courthouse, and here he was.

When Eddie had finished telling it, he raised his chin and pointed to the marks on his neck. It looked as if something had been pulled tight around the center of his neck, in two loops. Perhaps, I thought, there had been only one loop and it had been so tight it had left a center mark and two red streaks at the outside of the mark, one above and one below. I couldn't be sure, but two loops seemed more likely.

Eddie pulled his shirt out of his pants and lifted it. The entire upper half of his back was covered with large welts that crossed each other in a fiddlestick pattern. They looked to me like large welts caused by someone rolling, or being rolled, in grass that had very large blades. Again, I couldn't be sure, and I kept my opinion to myself.

"They poked me in the back with something sharp," he said.

I said, "They?"

"I don't really know," he said. "The thing around my neck was so tight, and there was something poking me in my back. I thought there had to be at least two of them. I didn't see anybody."

He lowered his socks and the area above each ankle was encircled with red scratches that looked like more grass cuts.

"What caused that?" I asked him.

"I don't know. I noticed it later."

His dress shirt had short sleeves, and, as he turned away from me, I saw he had a bruise the size of a thumbprint in the rear-center of each upper arm. I took an arm and half turned it.

"What's this?"

He strained his head backward to look.

"I don't know. I hadn't noticed that."

"Well, there's one on each arm."

I turned him around and gripped his upper arms from the rear. When my fingers wrapped around his biceps my thumbs rested naturally on the bruises.

"Were you grabbed like this?"

"No," he said. "Not while I was awake."

"Are you sure?"

"Yes. I'm sure."

The attorneys discussed getting Eddie to a professional photographer. Gutierrez had called a friend of hers, another attorney from Baltimore, to ask him to represent Eddie.

"This is getting too complicated," Gutierrez said. "Eddie needs his own attorney."

I told Jo what the nurse had said at the emergency room. Jo responded with a mechanical, "Okay," and I was concerned that the morning's events were beginning to wear on her. I wrote the nurse's name and her message on a slip of paper and took it into Jo's office and laid it on her desk. I told her I had done it and started to leave.

"Come by the house," Sandra said. She looked tired, dazed, so I told her I would.

I stopped for a fast food sandwich, and, when I got to Sandra's, her red and white pickup already was parked in front of the house. Kids, Mickey's friends, were letting themselves in and out the front door so I knocked and went in. Sandra was sitting at the kitchen table drinking a glass of water. I sat and loosened my tie and she filled me in on what had happened in court while I was at the hospital looking for Eddie. Although she looked even more tired than she had at Jo's office, she was animated and excited as she spoke.

"Tina wanted to go ahead with the trial but the state made a motion to postpone. Tina said that, under the circumstances, she would not object. Everyone was so upset."

"Did Eddie ever get there?"

"Yes. He was going to testify."

"What was he going to testify about? I thought he got into an argument with his girlfriend at the motel and left early."

"Didn't I tell you? He saw the officers arrive and hid behind the dumpster at the Red Roof Inn. He saw everything."

"Where did you hear that?"

"Eddie told me, and Katy. I don't think anyone knew it until a couple of weeks ago. I thought I told you. Jo got him to give a statement to the state's attorney."

"Why did he wait so long to let anyone know he was a witness?"

"Katy said he didn't want to testify, but then Jon died and he felt bad about not coming forward before."

"Did you notice anything about the way he was talking today?"

Sandra got a pensive look, with her lips pursed off to one side.

"What do you mean?"

"I don't know. It just struck me as a little odd that he could speak with no particular difficulty after being strangled so hard he fainted. Did that occur to you?"

"No."

"And those marks on his back looked to me like grass cuts."

"Like what?"

"You were a country girl. Remember how sometimes when you were a little kid if you rolled around in the grass with bare skin you got large welts all over? They stung like hell the next time you took a bath. Of course, it would have taken some pretty large blades of grass to make those welts on Eddie's back. They were huge. I never saw grass cuts that big, but that's what they looked like. Lots of little scratches, big scratches, and red, swollen welts. Grass cuts."

"I don't know," Sandra said. "I don't guess I ever rolled around in the grass like that."

Two kids, guys, came running into the house and up the stairs. They were talking excitedly in loud, course whispers. I didn't catch what they were saying but Sandra sat up straight and stiff. She jumped from her chair and whispered, "Wait." She half ran out of the kitchen and up the steps. After less than a minute she hurried back down.

"They've found something," she said. "I listened through Mickey's door and heard them telling him."

The two guys came running back down the stairs. One was Sean Stewart. Since the night he spoke up at the meeting with the police, I had intended to get to know him at the first opportunity. There had been no chance for it earlier that morning when he brought Eddie to Jo Glasco's office. Now he was charging down the stairs and heading for the front door. The other guy was an athletic, muscular kid called A.J. He was a good baseball pitcher my teams sometimes had played against.

"Whoa," I shouted and they slowed and came into the kitchen. "What's going on?"

Sean talked fast. "I've been talking to Eddie," he said. "He told us where he woke up and we went there. We found some stuff that I guess the police didn't see."

"You didn't move it, did you?" I asked, and he ducked his head.

"Shit. I didn't think."

"All right, where is it?"

He led us outside and opened the trunk of his sporty black compact. He took a large plastic sandwich bag from the trunk and removed the twist tie.

"How much did you have to touch it to get it in the bag?" I asked.

"Only at the edges," Sean said. He lifted a green, weathered snuff can from the bag by its edges. There were several cigarette butts and several frayed and faded pieces of orange nylon rope. The longest scrap of rope was between a foot and two feet long.

"There's lots of this rope around there," Sean said. "I just brought some of it."

Sandra was eyeing the snuff can. In an intensely controlled tone she said, "Jon carried a snuff can. We have to go there."

Sandra went back in the house to call Jo Glasco. She came back out saying, "I asked her to call the state police."

Sean and A.J. rode together and Sandra and I followed in my car. Sean and A.J. led us around several turns toward the front of the high school and down a side street that ended in a cul-de-sac. Sean parked near the end of the street where an asphalt bike path led into the woods. We parked behind him and he led us down the path through thick trees a hundred feet or so into the woods. We rounded a bend and Sean pointed ahead to a bridge that crossed a small creek. "There," he said.

"Wait," Sandra said. She pointed to a large patch of wild grass to the left of the path. The grass was large-bladed and waist high. In the center of it, a circle fifteen feet or so across was flattened to the ground. "This grass looks like it has just been crushed," she said.

We searched the grass and the area around it, looking for anything. There was only the usual array of woods trash: a broken bottle here, a shattered tail light cover there. Several pieces of the orange nylon rope were scattered about, some up to about three feet in length. The rope fragments were faded and frayed, indicating they had been lying in the woods for some time. I couldn't make heads or tails of the whole scene.

After several minutes of searching futilely through the crushed grass, we went to inspect the bridge.

"He woke up under there," Sean said, and we squatted and looked underneath. Sean crawled under the bridge. He pointed to a place in the center where Eddie had said he woke up.

"He was lying on his back," Sean said. "His feet were dangling in the water when he woke up."

We followed the bike path back out of the woods. Sean recognized a neighbor, a tall, slender man in his middle forties who was wearing a jogging suit. Sean mentioned the matted grass to the man and the man said, "I can tell you that the grass wasn't matted down like that last night at eleven o'clock. I walked through there at about that time, and it wasn't matted down then."

Sean and A.J. decided to go to a friend's house and borrow a camera. Sandra and I left to go to Jo Glasco's office.

Jo was in the parking lot in front of her office. Sergeant Simpson of the state police and a detective, I'll call him Detective Olfine, from the Howard County Police Department were waiting with her.

"This is their case," Simpson was saying as we walked up. "We are investigating Jon Bowie's death. Anything recovered would be related to Eddie Vickers' case and would have to be turned over to Howard County."

This seemed hasty to me and I found myself wondering just how independent the two investigations really were. "I don't understand," I said. "If Eddie was strangled at the same backstop, wouldn't that suggest some connection?"

"It's their case," Simpson said coldly.

"What if there were some evidence that related to Jon's case but not necessarily to Eddie's?"

"Like what?" Simpson asked.

"Jon usually carried a snuff can, and there wasn't one on him when his body was found. The boys found a snuff can where Eddie woke up. Two people are strangled at the same place, one wakes up in a place where there's a snuff can, and the first one usually carried a snuff can. It seems at least worth looking into."

"Mr. Bowie has been dead for two months," Simpson said. "The snuff can could have come from anywhere."

"I know that," I said, "but you have to look at it to find out. The reason we asked for an independent investigation was..." Discomfort filled the air and was in danger of bringing the conversation to a halt, so I backed off. Everyone there knew why we had asked for an independent investigation. "The snuff can was closed," I said. "It would seem possible that there could be a fingerprint on the inside cover. Then we'd know something, like whether it was Jon's or not."

Simpson ignored me and asked Jo Glasco, "Where are the items?"

We got back in our cars and led them to the location. Sean and A.J. were already there and Sean opened his trunk, took out the bag and handed it to them. As they tugged at the bag to look through the clear plastic, Sean lifted a thumb to me behind their backs and winked. Then he pantomimed the motion of taking a photograph.

"We can't take possession of these items," Simpson said, and he handed the bag to Olfine, the Howard County detective. Simpson and Olfine talked with Jo Glasco. Then they left.

Sean said, "You can kiss that evidence goodbye."

"What do you mean?" I asked.

"Get real," he said. "How old are you, anyway? The reason Eddie went back to the hospital was that he got a threatening phone call. It upset him and he couldn't breathe. It was a man's voice. All the man said was, 'I see that you're still alive' and then he hung up."

I couldn't think of anything to say to that, so I just said, "Damn."

"It's not the first one," Sean said. "He was getting them before he was strangled."

"Like what?"

"One was, 'If you testify, you die,' and then the guy hung up. Another one was just, 'It's three o'clock.'"

"When was that?"

"I don't know. A week or so ago, I think."

"Did he tell that to the police?"

Sean shook his head with some disgust and said, "Shit," dragging the word out into at least three syllables. "For all he knows, that's who's making the phone calls."

19 The Fourth of July was on a Wednesday that year. After Mickey's court date fell through, and after the unusual business with Eddie, Jim and Sandra went to West Virginia to visit relatives and get away from *New America* for a while. Sandra lived with the constant and desperate hope that at any moment an explanation for Jon's death might appear. Before she left, she gave me her parents' phone number in case I learned anything.

On Friday evening at around nine o'clock, Jane and I were talking in the kitchen and I was telling Jane what Sean Stewart had said about Eddie getting threatening phone calls. Jane told me about a call-tracing service the telephone company provided. You hung up after a call, picked up the receiver and got a dial tone, and then pressed the star button and a certain two numbers. The last incoming call in the phone company's records was marked. Each marked call cost a dollar and the police department could get information on the call. With some effort, a person's attorney might also be able to get the marked number.

"I should let Katy Vickers know about that," I said. I called Katy and before I could explain why I had called she interrupted me.

"I need somebody to go to the hospital," Katy said in a panicked and almost screaming voice. "Eddie has been at the police station for several hours, and they took him to the hospital. They're trying to discredit him by saying that he's emotionally unstable."

"Katy, slow down," I said. "Why was Eddie at the police station?"

"They've been wanting to talk to him about walking by the backstop, but he told them that he would only talk with the state police. He's afraid of the local police."

"How long has he been down there?"

"Since before five o'clock," she said. "He didn't want to go, but they sent a Detective Olfine. He knows Eddie. He took Eddie under his wing when Eddie got in trouble as a teenager. He talked Eddie into going."

"So, why is he at the hospital?"

"They're trying to say he made up the story about getting strangled. Now they've got him in the hospital and they're trying to get him committed. He called me from the hospital. He said I had to get him out of there. He said they took him in a room at the police station and kept him there for hours. He said they accused him of killing Jon. He panicked and started acting crazy just to get out of there. Can you go to the hospital and get him out?"

"I'll try, but I'm not a family member. I don't know if they'll listen to me."

"Somebody's got to go," she said.

"Isn't there a family member who can go with me?"

"I'll call Eddie's brother. He's a police officer in Baltimore."

"Fine. Tell him to meet me at your house. I'm leaving now."

Jane had gone upstairs and I called up the steps to say I was leaving. A thought struck me and I went back in the kitchen and phoned Barbara Stewart. I had met Barbara around Sandra's kitchen table, and at the vigil. I had not yet made the connection that she was the mother of Sean Stewart, the young man who spoke up at the public meeting with the police. Like a lot of people, Barbara had offered to do anything she could to help. She had taken on the job of keeping a list of phone numbers of local television stations and reporters who had been involved with the story. When Barbara answered the phone I said, "I don't have time to explain in detail, but Katy says the police have taken Eddie to the hospital. They're using some sort of special procedure to say he's emotionally unstable. Katy thinks they want to discredit him. Call John Hollywood and see if he can come. Then call as many television stations as you can and meet me there."

All she said was, "Done." I hung up and hurried out feeling grateful for people who know they can ask later.

At five feet nine inches or so Eddie's older brother, I'll call him Wayne, was no taller than I am. He was younger, though, and in better physical condition. We sat in my car in front of his mother's house and discussed how to proceed. We decided that, since he was a family member and a police officer, it would be best if he did the talking. I would just be a witness and provide moral support.

As we drove to the hospital I asked about the special procedure that permitted an officer to commit someone. He told me the name of the form but I forgot it almost as soon as he had said it.

"Basically," he said, "an officer can admit someone for a psychiatric examination if the officer thinks the person presents a physical danger to himself or to someone else."

I said, "So, if an officer abuses the procedure, it's his word against the word of the person the officer wants to discredit."

Wayne shot me a look.

John Hollywood and Barbara were waiting outside the door to the emergency room. Barbara was slender and had long, wavy black hair and fair skin. Black Irish, Jane has told me, is the term for Barbara's looks. Jon and Mickey had spent a lot of time at Barbara's house visiting her sons. Barbara said several television stations were sending camera crews.

There were a few people in the emergency room waiting area. Wayne identified himself to the receptionist and she immediately led him through the glass doors to the treatment area. I wanted to call Christina Gutierrez but didn't her phone number. I had the number for Sandra's parents in West Virginia, so I called from a pay phone and told Sandra the little I knew and asked for Gutierrez' home number.

"You want her office number, too," Sandra said. "She works late."

"Even this late on Friday night?"

Sandra insisted and I took both numbers. Sure enough, Gutierrez was at her office. I explained as best I could what Katy had said about Eddie.

"You're at the hospital now?"

"Yes, and reporters from several television stations are on the way. Eddie's brother has gone in to see him. He's a police officer."

"I can't come," Gutierrez said, "so listen to me. If it looks like they are going to keep him, make as much noise as you can. Get him out of there."

"There are quite a few police officers here," I said. "I could get arrested." I was pretty sure I heard her sigh over the phone.

"The police can't tell you what you can say in a hospital," she said. "Eddie can't stay there. Do what you have to."

I hung up knowing that Gutierrez had more natural brass than I did.

The door to the treatment area was open. A police officer about my age, shorter, and past the pudgy stage of being out of shape, was standing just inside the door. I crossed the waiting room to the door, stepped one foot through it and stopped, looking around. I didn't have the slightest idea where Eddie would be.

"Step back," the officer barked up at me.

"Excuse me?" I hadn't even thought about him except to notice that he was there.

"Step back into the waiting room." His voice had an pushy edge to it that was something besides authoritative. It was the voice of a cocky kid who has a large bully for a friend.

"I was looking for Eddie Vickers," I said. "His mother asked me to make sure he got home."

"You can't come in here," the officer commanded. "Step back. Now."

We locked eyes for a long time and a flood of possibilities occurred to me. Despite what Gutierrez had said, he could use his badge to do about anything he wanted and arrange an explanation to his advantage later. I wasn't about to confront him. It did occur to me for an instant, though, as we stood exchanging stares, that he didn't look very physical. The passing thought went through my mind that I probably could deck him without even bracing myself. I had no intention of doing anything rash, but I held the eye contact a bit longer just to let him wonder. Then I stepped back through the door.

A nurse came to the door and I asked her if she could tell me anything about Eddie. I repeated the part about his mother just to give it a touch of authenticity.

"I told you to step back," the officer repeated loudly.

"I did step back," I said. "I'm just trying to get some information for this kid's mother."

The nurse turned away and shouted, "Security! Somebody call security!"

I hadn't raised my voice since entering the hospital, and I was startled by her reaction. Now I *knew* I could be thrown out. I took another step backward and shouted, almost screamed, after her, "Eddie Vickers is not spending the night in this hospital." I wasn't accustomed to confronting authority, and my legs were starting to tremble a bit. I couldn't think of anything else to say so I raised the volume a notch and shouted it again. The cocky little police officer took a step toward me and I turned and walked away from him. Gutierrez undoubtedly would have done it better, I thought, but at least it was a little noise. People in the waiting room were staring, so the hospital had to be aware of its liabilities, whatever they were. I didn't have the slightest idea myself.

Barbara and John and I went outside and waited by the glass doors. I told them what Katy had told me, and John and I smoked a few cigarettes. Everyone compared details on what they had heard about Eddie being strangled. Wayne finally came out.

"They're releasing Eddie to me," Wayne said. "A doctor examined him and said there's nothing wrong with him except that he's very frightened."

Barbara told Wayne about the reporters and Wayne said, "We'll have to leave before they get here. I don't think it would be good for Eddie to face that. One of the officers is going to drive Eddie to my apartment and Eddie will stay with me for a few days."

I was surprised. I said, "One of the police officers is driving him? Do you think that's a good idea?"

"Eddie suggested it," Wayne said.

"Katy, your mom, said he was terrified of them."

"He says he knows one of the officers and he wants the officer to take him home."

"Fine," I said. "I guess we'll be going."

118

Wayne went back inside and the rest of us walked to our cars together.

"That seems strange to me," I said to John and Barbara. "First Eddie's telling his mom to save him from the police, and then he's asking to ride home with them. I hope we've got this story straight."

"I feel bad about the reporters," Barbara said. "I don't like crying wolf."

We all agreed that we regretted that part of it. Then we went home.

I left the hall light on so the light wouldn't be too harsh. As I was undressing in partial darkness Jane rolled over in bed and half sat up. She raised a hand to shield her eyes from the light. Then she lay back on the pillow and draped an arm across her face. I went into the hall and turned off the light and groped my way back to the bed and crawled in.

"What happened?" Jane asked in a sleepy voice.

I clasped my hands behind my head and stared through the darkness in the direction of the ceiling.

"I'm not sure I know."

20 In the middle of July, a county grand jury began meeting to consider the Bowie case. The grand jury considered two things: whether the officers charged with beating Jon and Mick at the motel should be tried in court, and whether there was any evidence of foul play in Jon's death. Christina Gutierrez objected vigorously against both issues being considered together, but the grand jury considered both things. State's Attorney Arthur Boudreaux and his assistant, Calvin Delight, presented the information to the grand jurors, who had been selected for jury duty off a list of registered voters.

Two particularly interesting things happened on the first day the grand jury met. One made the papers. The other didn't.

The one that didn't make the papers happened at a sandwich shop on Route 40 a mile or so north of the courthouse in Ellicott City. Boudreaux, who was responsible for running the grand jury, had lunch at the sandwich shop with two high-ranking police officers. As luck would have it, a person I know was having lunch there at the same time. It's not a very big sandwich shop. Most customers sit on bar stools at a small counter. You could stand at one side of the room and whisper and someone on the other side of the room could hear you. If you laughed right out loud, well, you'd have to know it would be heard. So, when Boudreaux laughed right out loud and told these two officers, and this is pretty close to an exact quote, "I'll guarantee you that no police officer will be indicted for anything in the Bowie case," it got overheard.

Although this particular statement wasn't the kind of thing that tended to show up in newspaper articles about the Bowie case, it got a lot of attention behind the scenes. Some argued that there might have been nothing unethical in Boudreaux' comment, that he simply could have been expressing his professional opinion based on his assessment of the evidence. Since a major reason for having a grand jury is supposed to be so private citizens, you and I, have the opportunity to decide such things ourselves, and since Boudreaux would decide what the grand jury would hear over the next several days, I think the door is open for a different opinion.

The other interesting thing that happened that day was that an article appeared in the local paper saying Eddie Vickers had been charged with throwing a rock through a man's car window. The incident referred to in the article had occurred a year earlier. The charge had been filed a few minutes before midnight, just before the statute of limitations ran out on that particular misdemeanor. The headline read *Man says Bowie witness assaulted him.*

The man filing the charge, a fellow I'll call Hobart, was quoted in the article as saying he didn't have the slightest idea that Eddie Vickers was involved in the Bowie case. Hobart said he picked up a complaint form earlier but procrastinated and didn't get around to filing the charge until time had almost run out. As I laid aside the article, I found myself wondering what the likelihood would be that I would be standing in a courthouse at a few minutes before midnight filing a complaint against someone who threw a rock through my car window a year earlier.

I talked to a lot of kids about the rock throwing story. Although it's getting a little ahead of the story, I'll tell it all in one place. Several of the kids I talked with said it wouldn't surprise them if Eddie had thrown the rock through the man's car window; it was the kind of thing they thought he might do, but they hadn't seen it and couldn't say. They said the incident had happened on Eddie's birthday, a year before. Two other kids and Eddie bought some beer and drove to a cul-de-sac to sit and drink and talk. Some other kids showed up and these other kids were planning to have a pool party, which was what the kids called it when they climbed over a pool fence after closing and went swimming. Some girls drove away in a car and the car Eddie was in followed the girls one street over to another cul-de-sac. They parked beside the girls and, a minute or so later, another car pulled up behind them. One of the guys in the car Eddie was in got out and started talking to the driver in the car that had pulled up behind them. Then the car behind them started backing up fast. Eddie got out of the car and ran up the street after the backing car.

After the county grand jury that was meeting to consider the Bowie case had ended, Eddie was tried for the rock throwing incident and I went to the trial. Hobart said at the trial that he lived in the neighborhood where the kids were having the pool party. He got angry because someone drove across a corner of his yard. He called the police and then followed in his car to find out who had done it. It was Hobart who had pulled up behind the car Eddie was in. On the witness stand, Hobart sounded believable to me. He struck me as the sort of person most people would want to have as a neighbor. Somebody making a turn had cut across the corner of his yard and he didn't like it; and when he tried to locate the car, someone threw a rock through his car window.

For some reason Eddie's case was continued and I couldn't go to court on the second date. What I was told was that after Hobart filed the charge against Eddie, Hobart borrowed a high school yearbook from a girl who was a lifeguard at the pool. He asked the lifeguard to point out Eddie Vickers to him so he would be able to recognize him. This made Hobart's story less than credible and, as I was told, contributed significantly to the case being thrown out of court.

All of this I heard later. What I knew at the time was that it was the day the grand jury started hearing witnesses. Two articles written by the same reporter appeared in the local paper. One said the grand jury was starting to hear witnesses. The other said a Bowie witness had been charged with throwing a rock through a man's car window.

Just as you could say there was nothing to be made of Boudreaux telling two high-ranking officers before the grand jury got underway that no officer would be charged, you also could say the timing of the those two articles was coincidental, I suppose.

A grand jury is a secret process, so I didn't learn a lot about what went on inside the grand jury room. I took off a few hours each day and hung around the courthouse, picking up whatever I could.

There was a lot of arguing in the halls between Christina Gutierrez and Jo Glasco on one side and Arthur Boudreaux and Calvin Delight on the other. They argued about who would be called as witnesses and who wouldn't. Gutierrez and Glasco wanted to call people who claimed to have suffered different sorts of abuses from Meyers in the past. Boudreaux and Delight didn't want any of these people to testify; they wanted the grand jury to hear only those kids who had been at the motel. There also was arguing about the order in which witnesses would be called. It was a major battle that involved a considerable amount of shouting. Gutierrez and Glasco wanted the kids to be heard last and Boudreaux and Delight wanted the police officers to be heard last. Boudreaux got to decide and he won the point. The officers would be heard last and there was supposed to be some tactical advantage to that.

Different kids who had been at the motel testified, and Sandra and I waited with other kids who were waiting to be called. Sandra and I had engaged in a few awkward conversations during the previous several weeks about things my mother had seen. I had opened up and told her a few childhood stories, and she had told me a few about herself. When no one else was within hearing, we talked about some of these things as we waited. It was something of a time filler.

I sensed that Gutierrez and Glasco sometimes wondered why I was hanging around. I couldn't think of any succinct way to explain that, so I didn't. Still, I hung around so often that eventually we eased into a first name basis. I was in the courthouse basement getting a soda from a vending machine when Gutierrez, Tina, hung up a public telephone nearby and said, "That was somebody saying that he's an orderly at the county hospital. He says a red-haired woman he knows of saw a police car pull into the school parking lot before dawn on the morning that Jon's body was found."

"Before dawn?"

"That's what he says, but he won't give his name and he doesn't know hers. He won't come forward. He says he's recovering from cocaine addiction and he knows he wouldn't make a credible witness."

On another occasion, I said something to Tina about how I couldn't believe twenty-three ordinary people could hear the same stories I had heard and not let the case go to court. Tina looked at me and said, "You're so naive," and she walked off.

I was hanging around in the basement at around eight p.m. on the third day of the grand jury proceeding. Sandra was sitting with several kids at a table near the vending machines and I joined them. Word started going around that the grand jury had recessed for a week and we were talking about whether we might as well go home. A large group of people was led by a guard out a stairway door and past us.

"That's them," Sandra whispered with her mouth behind her hand. "That's the grand jury."

"How do you know?" I asked her.

"That's them," she said. "I know it."

Something about the people filing past bothered me. There was nothing out of the ordinary about them, but there was a cloudiness like anger in the faces of several of them. A few looked at us out of the corners of their eyes and walked hurriedly on with their heads ducked down. I didn't want to mention these observations, but I looked at Sandra as she watched the people file past and I could see in her face that she had noticed, too.

―――――――――――――――

Sergeant Simpson of the Maryland State Police was one of the people who testified before the county grand jury. In a conversation Sandra had with Simpson at her kitchen table before Simpson testified, the conversation in which Simpson told Sandra he was a Christian, Simpson suggested to Sandra that she leave the investigative testimony to him. He was a professional, he told Sandra, and it would be better if he did it. Sandra gave this suggestion no particular thought, and agreed. She assumed Simpson would tell the things she had told him, things such as that her house had been broken into as Jon lay on the backstop, that Jon had said he was being followed, that Jon believed Meyers had been in his back yard, and that Sandra had found cord and grey duct tape in her back yard, and that several things that belonged to Jon had been found to be missing.

It doesn't matter how I know Simpson didn't tell the grand jury about those things. From what I've learned about how these things are handled, at least in this county, having too much to say about something like that would be far more likely to get me charged with something for knowing than to lead to any sort of serious investigation about whether it's true.

Regardless, Sandra testified before the grand jury recessed and Boudreaux and Calvin Delight asked her a few questions. They didn't get into any of the things Simpson had said were best left to him. When they were finished questioning her, Boudreaux asked if there was anything she wanted to add. Since she didn't want to interfere with Simpson, she said there was nothing. Despite her differences with Simpson, especially about the beeper, she trusted Simpson to do what he had said he would do.

He didn't.

On Saturday, about a week after the grand jury recessed, Amanda Garvey showed up on Sandra's doorstep again.

Originally, Sandra had met Amanda at church. Since coming to Columbia Sandra had attended various churches. I once asked Sandra how it was that she kept finding herself attending churches with mostly black congregations. She said she didn't know, she went where she felt comfortable. Sandra wasn't attending any particular church at the time Jon died. She began to feel soon after Jon's death that she had to start again in the hope of finding some sort of sanity in her life.

The church where Sandra and Amanda went had a preacher I'll call Reverend Billy Bob something or other. I don't know much about him except that he had been a chaplain at the police department for a long time, he drove a gold Mercedes, and his church was in a brick building next to some commercial property. When the church was being built, village administrators got upset with him, saying the church was being built partly over the property line, and he wasn't very cooperative about dealing with that.

It was Amanda who had promised to have the church choir come to the vigil at the backstop. When the choir didn't show up, Amanda led the gathering in a prayer. It also was Amanda who had told Sandra she had seen a very tall man and a shorter man abduct Mickey at the backstop on the night Eddie Vickers said he was strangled there. After the vigil, and after Reverend Wright arranged a sign-toting demonstration in front of a county office building, Amanda's picture had been on the evening television news. This was the logic Amanda gave Sandra for why this thing might have happened to her. Amanda said maybe she was seen as some sort of organizer who was responsible for some of the public furor.

It was at about eleven on that Saturday morning when Sandra answered the knock at her door. Amanda was standing there and she was visibly upset. Sandra invited her in and led her into the kitchen.

Amanda told Sandra in an hysterical barrage of details that, earlier that morning, she had been followed by a police car. She was traveling on Route 175 headed for the Oakland Mills Interfaith Center to do some work for her church. The police car followed her with its bumper very close to her bumper. She turned and the police car behind her turned. Another police car with radar was pulled to the side of the road, monitoring traffic. The police car behind her dropped back until they were out of sight of the other police car. Then the police car behind her came up close to her bumper again. Amanda said she got scared and she set her cruise control to 20 mph. When I heard this it struck me that I didn't know if a cruise control could be set to that low a speed, but that was what she said. Amanda drove slowly to Oakland Mills Interfaith Center. The police car stayed on her bumper so close she couldn't see its head lights, and it followed her into the parking lot. Amanda parked as close as she could to the Interfaith Center and the police car parked farther away in the same parking lot. Amanda went inside the Interfaith Center and completed her work for her church, which took about twenty minutes. When she had finished she went back into the parking lot. The police car still was there and a man in street clothes was leaning against Amanda's car. Amanda told Sandra the man was about 6'6" to 6'7" and large in stature. He was wearing a plaid shirt, blue jeans, a baseball cap pulled low over his face, and sunglasses, and he had a short haircut. When Amanda told it, Sandra, of course, immediately thought of Meyers. Amanda said she was sure that was who it was. Amanda said she went back into the church to find someone to go out into the parking lot with her. She saw only older women inside, so she went back outside alone and walked to her car. As she approached the car, the man stood up straight and spoke to her.

"Did you know Jon Bowie?"

"I might." Amanda said. "Do you want to sign my petition?" The petition signing had ended by then, but Amanda told Sandra there still were some petition forms on her back seat and the man was looking at them through the car window, so that was what she said.

The man shouted, "Fuck that," in an agitated voice. He turned and walked quickly to the police car and got in and drove out of the lot. Amanda tried to get the number off the side of the police car, but she wasn't wearing her glasses and couldn't make it out. When the police car was gone, Amanda got in her car and drove the half mile or so to Sandra's.

Jim came into the kitchen as Amanda was telling her story. When Amanda had finished, Jim offered to follow her home. Sandra rode with Amanda, and Jim followed them in the his van. Jim and Sandra watched

Amanda go into her house and then they returned home.

Jim and Sandra had been home about fifteen minutes when the phone rang. It was Amanda. She said that soon after Jim and Sandra dropped her off, she got a phone call from a man who didn't identify himself. The voice was that of the man in the parking lot, and he said, "I asked you, 'Did you know Jon Bowie?'"

Amanda told Sandra she answered, "Yes, I did. Why do you want to know?"

The man, Amanda told Sandra, then said, "If you don't back off, I'll do the same thing to you that I did to Jon Bowie." Then he hung up.

Amanda finished telling Sandra the story and they hung up. About thirty minutes later Amanda called Sandra again. "We have to end our friendship," Amanda said, "and I can't have any more contact with you, but my family and I will pray for you."

On Sunday, Sandra saw Amanda in church. Amanda approached Sandra and said, "Sandra, I haven't gone away. I still want to help. My father forced me to make the phone call. He has great fear for me and for the rest of the family." Sandra said she understood.

On Tuesday, Amanda called Sandra at work. Amanda said she had decided to go against her father's wishes, and she wanted to give Jo Glasco a statement about the incident, and the phone call.

That was the last contact Sandra would have with Amanda for more than a month. Sandra tried several times to telephone Amanda at her condominium or at her father's home. Sometimes Amanda's father answered the phone and said no one named Amanda lived there. Sometimes Sandra called Amanda's sister to see if Amanda was there. Sometimes Amanda's sister said she would try to intervene with her father. Sometimes she told Sandra no one named Amanda lived there, and hung up.

21 The office of the Chief of Police was small with white, sheetrocked walls decorated with an occasional framed certificate. The floor was covered with plush, subdued-aqua carpeting. A dark cherry desk and the empty chair behind it filled a good part of the room. Most of the rest was filled by a round, cherry table surrounded by four upholstered chairs. Add the flags of Maryland and the United States on tall, brass standards, a closed door, the considerable frame of the Reverend

David Rogers in one of the upholstered chairs and the tall, stiffly uniformed Chief in another and there was little room for anything else and no place to hide.

After receiving the anonymous phone call a few days after Jon Bowie's death, David had felt compelled to do something. The woman hadn't given her name, but there were enough details in what she had said that David assumed she could be located with some effort. With all that had been written in the papers, David had been reluctant to give the information to the police. If the woman was telling the truth, telling the police might be dangerous for her. Telling the papers was out of the question. The woman might not have been able to claim legally that she was a counseling client of David's, but David did feel a duty to honor her confidence.

David struggled with the issue for a few days and then he gave a copy of his notes of the conversation to Jo Glasco, the attorney for the Bowie family. He reasoned that Glasco was close to the investigation of Jon Bowie's death and to the recently announced investigation by the state police. Glasco would be in a better position than David to decide when and whether, and to whom, to offer the information confidentially for investigation. David asked Glasco to keep the notes in her safe and not to share them with anyone just yet.

Then a few weeks had gone by. The subpoena to testify before the grand jury had been a bolt from the blue. David knew immediately why he had been subpoenaed, and he was furious. He called Glasco and spoke with her at length and in most unpreacherly terms. Glasco said she had a duty to do what was in the best interest of her client. She had consulted with Tina Gutierrez and Tina had shared the information with Arthur Boudreaux. Tina had demanded that David be subpoenaed. David hung up after saying things to Glasco that would be hard to take back.

In the grand jury room, David had repeatedly invoked ministerial privilege and had refused to provide details of the call. It was clear, though, that Boudreaux knew, and if the Chief had called David to his office then the Chief also knew. Clerical privilege was out the door.

The conversation didn't take long. The Chief said, "I'm very disappointed that you chose to share this information with someone other than the Department."

"Under the circumstances, I did what I thought was best," David said.

"Well, I can view it only as a serious breach of loyalty."

David was high on decorum but low on pussy-footing.

"A breach of loyalty? What about the phone call? What if the woman is telling the truth?"

"Reverend Rogers," the Chief said in a convincingly weary and yet irritated tone, "I have had this thoroughly investigated. I can tell you for a fact that Sandra Keyser placed that call. You've been had."

David sagged. "I suppose you want my resignation."

"I think that would be best," the Chief said.

David stood and pulled his police chaplain's credentials from his coat pocket and laid them on the table. Then he left.

When Rogers had returned home, he called Sergeant Simpson of the Maryland State Police. Rogers wanted Simpson to hear the story straight from him. Later that afternoon, Rogers handed Simpson his notes from the call. Then he told Simpson everything he knew.

A long article in the *News Briefs* section of the Flier reported that the Bowie grand jury had taken a recess. It had met until at least 9 p.m. on Thursday and Friday and then again on Monday. The article said the jurors had to get on with their lives and would reconvene in a week to hear witnesses. Tina Gutierrez had filed a motion saying that information in the supposedly secret proceedings was being leaked to the police department. The judge in the case was on vacation and wouldn't hear the motion for a week. Tina wouldn't comment on the details.

Sandra heard that at least some of the kids on the list of witnesses Jo Glasco had given Boudreaux were getting threatening phone calls. Months would go by before I talked to two of these kids, but, since it was happening at the time and it was only later that I learned the details, I'll go into it now.

One of the kids is a state trooper now, and I don't want to do him a disservice by dragging his name around. He was a wiry, muscular white kid. On an evening two years earlier, when the kid was sixteen, a woman who lived near this kid reported a prowler. Meyers responded to the call and the kid walked with Meyers through the neighborhood yards as Meyers searched the area. The woman was sitting on her porch and, according to the kid, Meyers said something like, "I could shoot her from right here and nobody could prove it or do anything about it." When Sandra heard the story she passed it on to Jo Glasco, who put the kid's name on her list.

The kid was eighteen now and both he and his parents were out of town on separate trips when his name was added to Jo's list. He returned home a day earlier than expected at a little before seven in the evening. Forty-five minutes later he got a phone call. When he answered the phone there was a long pause before the caller spoke.

"Is your father there?"

It sounded like a man in his middle thirties. The kid said his father wasn't home and asked if he could take a message.

"Yeah, just tell him that Jesus called."

The caller hung up. The kid thought maybe the caller had not expected anyone to be home and he had said the part about Jesus because he had been caught off guard. The kid was upset and didn't want to be in the house alone. He called two friends and asked them to come over. One friend was twenty and the other was twenty-two and they came and one brought a shotgun, which he kept in its case. By a little after midnight they had discounted the call as a prank, and the two friends went home. The kid was nervous, so he went to spend the night with his girlfriend and her parents.

The next day his parents returned and his mother called his girlfriend's house, looking for him. He took the phone and his mother asked him what had happened to the basement door. This was news to the kid, and he went home to see for himself. A kitchen door that closed on ten or twelve stairs coming up from the basement was kicked in from the basement side. The lock had been knocked through the strike-plate and molding was splintered in toward the kitchen. The kids had been horsing around the night before and the kid called his friends and asked if maybe the three of them could have broken the door without realizing it. They agreed that it wasn't likely.

The next day, a Monday, the kid called the police. An officer came out and looked at the door and took some fingerprints from a basement window. The officer said he had seen break-ins like that before.

"Someone wants you to know that they can get to you anytime they want," the officer said. "They want you to know you're vulnerable. Do you know anyone who would want to get to you?"

The kid said he didn't, and having the officer tell him that upset him.

The police started calling the kid two and three times a day over the next several days. One officer said he heard through the grapevine that the kid had a problem with the police a couple of years earlier. The officer who was investigating the break-in called and said he didn't have a suspect and was forwarding the information to someone else for further investigation. Another officer called and said he was with the Internal Affairs Division. He wanted to know about the incident two years ago and about any other incidents the kid had heard about in which officers might not have acted properly. The kid told the officer from Internal Affairs what he knew. The kid also said that he planned to be a police officer himself, but not in Howard County after all he had heard. He said he was going to testify to the grand jury, and the officer from Internal Affairs said he was calling from the courthouse right then.

The other kid who got an unusual call after his name was added to Glasco's list was a seventeen year old high school student. He was a black kid, average sized and seemingly athletic despite lingering baby fat. A year earlier he had been stopped by Meyers at night as he was driving home from a friend's house. He was charged with driving with a learner's permit with no adult in the car, driving an unregistered vehicle, and driving a car with a broken side mirror or something like that. Each of the offenses cost him over $250 and his mother thought the officer had stopped him without probable cause and had piled up charges because he was a teenager. When I discussed it with Sandra I said it didn't sound particularly offensive to me. A kid driving on a permit should have an adult in the car, and cars should be registered and properly maintained, I said. Sandra said the kid was holding back because he didn't know me, and what she had been told was that Meyers jumped on the hood of the kid's car and kicked out his windshield. I told her all I could deal with was what *I* was told, not what somebody said they had heard.

Jo Glasco called the kid and asked if he would testify to the grand jury and he said he would. A few days later, while the grand jury was in recess, the kid got a phone call from a man who said, "If you know what's good for your black ass, you won't testify." The kid motioned to his mother to pick up the kitchen phone but all she heard as she picked it up was someone on the other end hanging up. The kid decided not to testify if he was called. He wasn't.

22 While the grand jury was in recess, Jo Glasco and Sergeant Simpson took a trip to West Virginia to meet with the State Medical Examiner. It had to do with the second autopsy.

Soon after the funeral, a caravan of cars left Columbia for the mountainside town of Wardensville, West Virginia, to attend the burial. It was a long trip of well over two hours and somewhere along the way Sandra decided there had to be a second autopsy. At her insistence the burial was delayed and family members made the arrangements. Jon's body was taken first to the coroner's office in Wardensville. Sandra's brother, Danny, went to the coroner's officer and returned to the family home saying there was a sticky substance on Jon's hands, as if they had been taped together. When the arrangements had been made, the body was transported to the offices of the West Virginia State Medical Examiner.

A little irony about what was to become known as the second autopsy was that the family had the results of the second autopsy a month before the results from the first autopsy were released. The second autopsy was completed on the fifth day after Jon's death. The first autopsy, which was done on the day of Jon's death, wasn't signed by the Maryland State Medical Examiner until exactly a month after Jon's death due to the political wrangling going on behind the scene, and it wasn't released until several weeks after that. So, the family had to wait over a month before the second autopsy could be compared to the first.

Jo Glasco learned from Sergeant Simpson that Boudreaux had called the State Medical Examiner's office to insist that Jon's death be ruled a suicide. Jo dropped everything and drove to the appropriate state office in Baltimore and asked a clerk for a copy. The clerk obviously didn't know about the politics involved and gave Jo a copy for the normal fee. Stamped diagonally across the front page in one-inch-high letters were the words **DO NOT**

DUPLICATE.
Word of the second autopsy had gone around for some time, but without specifics. The second autopsy hung like a threat over any decision that might be released by the grand jury. Sergeant Simpson had seen the second autopsy report and wanted to talk with the doctor who had done the examination. Jo Glasco was of the opinion that Sergeant Simpson wanted to get the report softened, or even changed, and she insisted on going along. They went, they argued, and the doctor wrote an addendum to his first report.

Sandra knew little of the details of the two autopsies. She couldn't bring herself to read either of them. When she heard bits and pieces she seized on anything that might demonstrate that Jon's death was a homicide. She clung to an intensely held belief that the second autopsy held the information necessary to prove her right. I knew even less, since I got only Sandra's filtered version, so there was little I could do but listen and sympathize. I finally asked Sandra to get me copies of the two autopsies. Sandra couldn't deal with that, so he told Jim where they were and he got them for me.

I didn't understand a lot of the terminology in the autopsy reports and, even without that, reading them was a hard thing to do. I had to read them several times, setting them aside and then going back and trying again. I kept telling myself I was just reading words but I kept seeing this kid on a baseball field laughing and throwing baseballs around.

The first autopsy, the one done in Maryland, said Jon died of asphyxiation, which is not the same as strangulation. Asphyxiation is caused by a shortage of oxygen and results in death or unconsciousness. Strangulation is only one of the many things that can lead to asphyxiation; it is an obstructing or compressing of the throat, as with a jawbreaker, or a rope, and it tends to leave certain physical signs. In the autopsy report there was no indication that Jon had strangled himself or been strangled; there was no bursting of the tiny capillaries in the eyes and no significant internal damage to the throat.

The cable left a bruise high on the neck under the chin, and the medical examiner saw in the bruise reason to believe that the main point of pressure was from the rear and to the right. There were slight abrasions and bruises, particularly on the chest and abdomen, that seemed likely to have come from the wire on the backstop.

The report said there were no signs of struggle and, because of the examination, and because of investigative details that had been supplied, the death was ruled a suicide.

What the first autopsy suggests is that Jon put the cable around his neck, took hold of the roof of the backstop and quietly went to sleep.

This seems like a good point to include an observation about the detective who was in charge of investigating Jon's death, and who escorted

Jon's body to the medical examiner's offices. This detective no doubt had much to do with the investigative details that the medical examiner said helped him make a ruling of suicide. The observation I want to make is that this detective did not see Jon's body on the backstop. He arrived at the scene after Jon's body had been lowered to the ground. When Sandra took this man to task for calling Jon's death a suicide from the outset, he defended himself by saying his opinion was based on the decision at the scene by the county medical examiner. The county medical examiner did not see the body on the backstop, either; he, too, arrived at the scene after the body was lowered. These details come from the police report.

Although the second autopsy, the one done in West Virginia, was done after the first, and after embalming, the doctor performing the second autopsy did not see this as a significant hinderance. He didn't have the cable, he knew little about how the body had been found, and he didn't have a police officer standing nearby to provide investigative details. He did a physical examination, but he did not do any sort of chemical testing or other laboratory analysis.

The doctor performing the second autopsy agreed that death was due to asphyxiation that, in all likelihood, was caused by the cable.

The cable caused only one furrow. This meant it was highly unlikely that Jon could have been hanged at another location and then moved to the backstop and been hanged again; this would have required that marks on the neck caused from two separate hangings overlap exactly, and that was virtually impossible. Therefore, whatever happened involving hanging happened only at the backstop.

It also would have been extremely difficult, the second report concludes, for one or more persons to have stood behind Jon on the backstop and to have held the cable, physically doing the hanging and then leaving Jon there. Jon could have been taken unconscious to the backstop, raised onto the backstop and the cable put around his neck, the report says, but nothing about the physical examination indicated that he had been unconscious. The doctor saw no signs of a struggle. It would have to be demonstrated that Jon was unconscious for such a conclusion to be reached and, without the results of toxicological tests that presumably were done during the first autopsy, nothing further could be said about that possibility.

It wasn't likely that Jon simply became entangled in the cable and fell; there would have been greater damage to the neck.

The second autopsy noted a bruise that was not mentioned in the first autopsy. There was a faint, two-and-three-quarters inch bruise rising vertically from underneath the right armpit and up the front of the right shoulder. What the autopsy report didn't mention, because the examiner didn't have this information, was the this bruise, which looked like a mark caused by a thin rope or cord, could not have been caused by the rope used to lower Jon's body from the backstop. That rope was very thick, and police photos show that it was tied at Jon's back; so, if it had ridden up underneath the armpit, it would have ridden up the back of the armpit, and not the front.

The second autopsy also noted a second, large bruise that was not mentioned in the first autopsy. This bruise was low on the right side of the lower neck. It was too low on the neck to have been caused by the cable. It was four-and-a-half-inches long, and shaped like an inverted-y that opened horizontally in the direction of the front of the neck. The trunk and both branches of this y-shaped bruise were each about a half inch wide. The upper trunk of the y, and the point where the two forks met, were red, suggesting to the examiner that they were caused before death; the lower fork was yellowish, suggesting that it had become visible after death.

In order to help the reader picture the location of this second bruise, let me provide an example: Put the thumb of your right hand at the very base of the right side of your throat, above but resting on the collar bone; put your index finger on the other side of the throat at the same height and resting on the left-side collar bone. Now, squeeze gently; don't squeeze too hard, because I'm told this is a martial arts maneuver that's used to asphyxiate a person without leaving any outward sign. Anyway, the point at which the two forks of the inverted-y bruise meet is at the strongest pressure point beneath your thumb; the upper fork runs along the thumb toward the center of the throat, and the lower fork runs downward toward the chest.

The bottom line in the second autopsy was that the doctor performing the autopsy didn't have enough information to form a scientific opinion about how Jon had come to be asphyxiated, perhaps by a cable, or how he had come to be on the backstop. He couldn't say it was suicide, and he couldn't say it wasn't.

In the addendum to the second autopsy, which the doctor wrote after talking with Jo Glasco and Sergeant Simpson, the doctor said he was now convinced that Jon could not have slipped and fallen and somehow become tangled in the cable. Either he put the cable around his neck himself, voluntarily or involuntarily, or someone else put it around his neck. If someone else did it, then it would have been difficult for one person to have done it alone; two or more people would have had to do it. Jon would have had to be subdued in some way that he could not resist, or he would have had to be unconscious or nearly unconscious. Although Jon's blood alcohol level was quite high, it was not high enough to convince the doctor that Jon could not have climbed the backstop. It could not be scientifically answered, the addendum says, whether Jon put the cable around his own neck in some sort of gesture and then, being inebriated, unexpectedly lost consciousness and slumped with the full weight of his body putting pressure on his neck. It could not be answered, either, if he had succumbed to some sort of suicidal impulse while intoxicated. The final statement in the one-and-a-quarter page addendum, above the doctor's signature, reads, "I cannot exclude that this might possibly be a homicide."

One of the more interesting aspects of living near the nation's capital was that there was always the possibility you'd bump into some person or situation that otherwise you never would have expected to encounter. Being in this area, I suppose it was not such an odd thing that Sandra would have a friend who had a friend who knew somebody who was some sort of homicide expert for the CIA. This person in the CIA took a look at the two autopsies and sent word back that something about the results of the blood-alcohol tests was out of order. There were four blood-alcohol tests, which was standard procedure. A sample was taken from the heart at the scene and was labeled *County*. During the autopsy another specimen was taken from the heart and labeled *State*. Specimens also were taken of the fluid of the eye and from the urine. The results were: state heart: .25; county heart: .18; eye: .27; urine: .37. One of these results supposedly was higher than another when it should have been lower. I used to know which but I no longer remember. It was all a foreign language to me and I called Bucky in North Carolina and asked what he could tell me.

Bucky couldn't tell me anything, but he knew someone who was a forensics expert and he would ask. After a few days during which Sandra and I engaged in considerable speculation, Bucky called back. If I had my information right, he said, then one of the results was out of order, but that didn't necessarily mean anything. Tests could vary for all kinds of reasons. I gave him a few details about Jon's death and he offered the opinion that I was going off the deep end in my thinking. "Young people have more violent, more unpredictable reactions to alcohol than adults," he said. "A kid who would never consider suicide might have a few drinks, get depressed and do it on an impulse." I told him a bit about the motel incident and he said, "You've told me more than you might have meant to. You told me he was a good athlete. Athletes can be pretty cocky. They might bring something on themselves and not even understand what they've done. A police officer has to take charge of a situation. He doesn't always have time to explain every little thing."

I was angry at Bucky for a few days because he had not said what I wanted to hear.

One evening during the grand jury recess I was lying in bed trying to get to sleep and I found myself wondering what it must feel like to be Sandra. Suddenly, and for only an instant, I felt a rush of anger and fear and hope and despair and terror so intense I had to drop it from my mind the way a person immediately drops a package he had no idea was so heavy. I was startled. It seemed that what I had felt was completely outside of myself. It was as if I had asked without even knowing I was asking to feel what Sandra felt, and, for a moment, I had felt it. It was too heavy for me to carry. I had to drop it.

When the grand jury had been in recess for a week, the Baltimore Sun reported that the Howard County Police Department had become the 152nd police department in the nation to be certified by the Commission on Accreditation for Law Enforcement Agencies. The Commission's report said the department had a good system. The report mentioned the Commission's awareness that the state police were investigating Jon's death.

The next day the grand jury was scheduled to resume its investigation and I took off from work again. Tina argued before the judge that she wanted an open court hearing of charges that information was leaking out of the grand jury and witnesses were being intimidated. She wanted to call Boudreaux as a witness and put him on the stand. A group of us sat on the rear seat in a large courtroom as the legal arguments went on for about an hour out of hearing at the judge's bench. The father of a friend of Mickey's came. His name was Alan Zindell and, aside from having what he would describe himself as a generally pushy and abrasive personality, he also was a very bright and articulate person. At one point the assistant state's attorney, Calvin Delight, left the judge's bench and came back down the aisle shaking his head in what I took to be an effort to draw attention to himself. There was a group of people I didn't know sitting across the aisle to our right. They were young and had note pads and pens and I gathered that they might be younger assistants in the state's attorney's office. As Delight came down the aisle he looked at them and said something that made them laugh.

"What did he say?" I asked Zindell, who was sitting next to the aisle.

"He said, 'I wish that Spic would shut up.'"

"I don't get it," I said.

"He means Tina."

The conference ended and we went into the hall and waited for Tina. When she joined us her face was dark with anger and she spoke with controlled intensity. "Denied," she said. "It's over. It was all a charade. They let me stand there and present a motion knowing all the time that the grand jury reached a decision this morning. They came in, voted and went home." We stood there a moment, taking it in, and then someone asked for details.

Earlier that morning the grand jury had voted that there was insufficient evidence to rule that any officers had acted improperly in the motel incident. They would reach a decision regarding Jon's death when the state police investigation was completed.

There were more articles in the newspapers, more stories on television.

23 On a Sunday in the middle of August, an article in the newspaper said the grand jury would meet in the middle of the week to complete the second half of its charge. It would decide whether to indict anyone for Jon's death. I was flabbergasted. I had kept as close track of the investigation as I could, and I hadn't heard of anything that warranted indicting anybody. Reading between the lines, it was pretty clear that the state police investigation was over and the grand jury was piggy-backing the state police investigation. We weren't going find out what had happened to Jon.

Sandra was furious. Sergeant Simpson had promised her he would meet with her before presenting any conclusions in public. Sandra immediately called Jo Glasco and reminded Jo of the promise. Jo called the state police to try to set up a meeting. She got an agreement that there would be a meeting after the grand jury had ended.

The grand jury met on Wednesday, and a press conference was scheduled immediately afterward. The grand jury didn't meet for long. The press conference was held in a large, theater-in-the-round type meeting room in a county government office building. Alan Zindell and I sat together a few rows from the center-room raised platform. There were reporters scattered throughout the audience. A large contingency of attorneys from Boudreaux' office sat far back in the room scribbling on yellow legal pads. A group of police officers sat a couple of rows behind Alan and me and off to one side. I caught the eye of one of the officers Boudreaux had told at the sandwich shop on the day the grand jury started that no officer would be indicted for anything. Alan and I and a few others had done a pretty good job of spreading that story around behind the scenes. The officer's face reddened and he looked away.

Arthur Boudreaux and Calvin Delight and Sergeant Simpson sat at a folding table on the raised platform in the center of the room. Boudreaux leaned into the wide bank of microphones and read a brief report from the grand jury. After a few meaningless introductory sentences the report concluded:

> *There is presently no physical evidence or any other evidence that Carl Jonathan Bowie met his death through the intervention of any other individual.*

Then Sergeant Simpson read a brief report summarizing the state police investigation. The state police's conclusions were that Jon had climbed the backstop himself, that he had put the cable around his own neck, and that his death was determined, and not accidental. However, there was no note and there were no witnesses. It could not be determined what was on Jon's mind at the time. Simpson concluded:

Considering the absence of these factors, our findings
reveal no evidence of foul play and the manner of death
was undetermined.

Reporters scratched their heads and looked at each other. They asked a few questions and scribbled notes. Photographers and video camera operators walked around the platform trying to get good shots. Alan Zindell stood and asked, "What about the beeper?" Boudreaux made a good show of not understanding the question. Alan, whom I doubt has ever been intimidated in his life, elaborated. "Sergeant Simpson said there was a beeper on Jon's body when he was found. Jon didn't own a beeper, and there is no beeper listed in the evidence. Where is the beeper?"

Boudreaux leaned into the microphone and said, as if it had been common knowledge, "Sergeant Simpson misinterpreted a blown-up photograph of the deceased on the backstop. What Sergeant Simpson thought was a beeper turned out, upon examination of the blue jeans, to be a leather object that was sewn into the fabric and that had a brass D-ring connected to it."

I don't suppose I was the only one in the room who was stunned. A cameraman laughed and said, "Yeah. Right." I tried to think of something I could ask, but all I could think was that they must have known this for weeks. To announce it in a press conference without first telling Sandra, and only after being asked specifically, was malicious.

The press conference was over and reporters hung around getting individual interviews. Alan was good on camera, and he made statements that appeared in the news on several stations that night. He said the decision was confusing.

After the press conference I drove to Sandra's to give her copies of the reports and tell her what had taken place. That night, a newspaper reporter called me at home and said he had found the decision carefully worded and confusing. He asked what I thought and I said the first thing that came off the top of my head, which was, "It sounded negotiated to me." He quoted me.

When the grand jury had reached its decision and the press conference was over, Calvin Delight, Boudreaux' assistant, called the home of a young woman named Jennifer. It was Jennifer or her sister, Becky, who had taken a camera to the motel. Delight told Jennifer he had to have all the photos that had been taken at the Red Roof Inn, and all the negatives of the photos.

Sandra and I talked with several attorneys about any legal justification Delight might have had for requesting the photos after the grand jury was over. All of them said there wasn't any. He must have wanted to make sure something didn't come out.

Sandra thought that perhaps the photos showed a lot of beer cans lying around and maybe they could somehow make the kids look bad. There was, of course, the other possibility, that things looked pretty orderly and the photos could make the county look bad. It was another one of those details in the pile of too many to check out.

Jennifer turned out not to be quite the naive child of eighteen that Delight must have hoped she was. She said, "Fine. I have them."

Delight said he would send a car for the photographs, and Jennifer said she would be home. When Delight hung up, Jennifer called John Hollywood. John came for the photographs and took them to the law office of Tina Gutierrez in Baltimore.

Then Jennifer went for a ride. If the car ever came to get the photographs for the county, she wasn't home.

Sandra and I began looking for something we could do ourselves, a way to get a handle on what had happened to Jon. We had no idea how to go about it, so we simply looked into anything we learned about and had time to deal with. One afternoon Sandra handed me a scrap of paper with a license number written on it in purple crayon.

"This is the license number of the brown pickup that Jon said was following him the week before he died."

"Jon gave this number to you?"

"He gave it to Anne Beck. She gave it to me and I stuffed it away and couldn't find it. The other day it turned up. When I told Lampest a brown pickup was following Jon, Lampest said Meyers had gotten rid of his brown pickup, that he didn't drive one anymore. Then someone told me that Meyers' truck was just in the shop for repairs and that Meyers never sold it. I think Lampest was just trying to throw me off, trying to make me believe that it couldn't have been Meyers following Jon."

Jim learned from a fellow mail carrier that Meyers had moved to an apartment complex outside of Columbia. Jim offered to check out the truck himself, but I said I wanted to do it. I drove up Route 1 a few miles and onto the side street Jim had said I would find. I was in a huge complex of townhouses. There were hundreds of connected dwellings, each with its own front entrance. I drove around until I located the address Jim had given me. A dark, copper-colored pickup truck sat in the drive. I pulled behind it and took the scrap of paper from my jacket pocket. I looked at the number on the paper and compared it to the license number on the rear of the truck. The numbers matched.

I had no idea what to do with the information. I backed up, turned around and drove back to Jim's and Sandra's.

Katy Vickers came up with the idea for a plaque. She wanted some sort of remembrance of Jon put in the ground beside the bike path that passed alongside the backstop. She wrote someone in local government and that person passed it to someone else.

Jane worked as the village manager for one of the several villages in Columbia. Jane told me there was a program underway to renovate the large lake-front in the center of town. There were several offices and a few restaurants there and a pier where you could fish and rent boats. There was an outdoor bandstand and a grassy hill where people sat and listened to concerts on summer nights. Every June the city fair was held there. A wide, brick courtyard provided walkways and surfaced areas overlooking the lake.

Jane explained that anyone could pay twenty-five dollars and have something called a *paver* put in the renovated bricked surface. It took me some back and forth before I understood that a paver was a brick with an inscription on it. Jane brought home an application form and I filled it out and sent it in with a note requesting that the town pay for a paver for Jon. I attached the correspondence between Katy and the various officials and said that if there was any confusion then I would pay for the paver myself. I had to request specific wording on the application and, in the space provided, I wrote:

Jon
Bowie

I soon got a response asking that I appear at a Columbia Council meeting to present the request in person. Public speaking made me nervous, but I called the man who had signed the letter and I said I would be at the meeting.

On the evening when the meeting was to take place, a woman called and told me I didn't have to appear. The decision had been made to install the paver and the town would pay for it. I hung up the phone and asked Jane if she thought I was being told I didn't have to come to the meeting because I was becoming some sort of local embarrassment.

"I think so," Jane said. "It's easier for them just to put in the paver. People are beginning to wonder if you're a little nuts. For all they know you could create some sort of disturbance."

The fact that I might be viewed as some sort of crackpot troubled me, but at least I had accomplished what I had set out to do. The paver would be installed in the spring in the brick courtyard by the lake in the center of town. It was a nice setting for a memorial.

John Hollywood set up a memorial fund and bought tee-shirts with *Jon Bowie* and the number *13* written on them. There was talk of maybe having a fund raiser. I can't say I was all that supportive. I wanted to know what happened to Jon, and I thought our efforts should be focused only on that, although I didn't have any clear ideas about how to accomplish it. I worried about making some sort of circus event out of Jon's death.

The newspaper articles and television accounts that kept appearing seemed to lean heavily toward an official version that showed a county that had done all it could to find out what had happened. I didn't believe that to be true. It seemed to me that the county could use a boost, some sort of attention grabber.

Jane had been the campaign manager several years earlier for a friend of hers who ran for the Board of Education. Jane's an intuitively organized person, and she invested a lot of time and thought and ran a successful campaign. Her friend won even though the local political organizations supported other candidates, and Jane picked up a reputation. She even got a call the next year from a man in Baltimore who wanted to run for some state office, and the man asked Jane to run his campaign. After some soul searching, Jane turned the man down because she didn't know him well enough to know if he would make a good public official. What she had done for her friend had been done because she believed in her friend. It wasn't for sale.

During that campaign, Jane's friend had the local cable company flash a sign every few minutes asking people to vote for her. It was a service provided by the cable company to anyone who paid two dollars and came up with the words. Jane learned that the cable company believed the most effective colors were white letters on alternating rows of blue and red.

Barbara Stewart contacted the local cable company and made the arrangements. The sign had to be in white letters on blue and red bands, she told them. She had to deliver the words in person, and the person who took the information told her, "We've been wondering when you guys would get around to us."

The sign began flashing every few minutes on the local cable channel soon after the grand jury recessed. It continued for several weeks.

> *Please help us investigate*
> *the death of*
> *Jon Bowie*

Smaller letters mentioned the support fund that John Hollywood had set up and gave a phone number and an address. Very little money came from it. An editorial in the local paper suggested that the sign demonstrated a lack of confidence in the police department.

I did some research at the library on other reported suicides in

Columbia. One in particular bothered me more than the others. It was reported as the first suicide in the new town of Columbia. A female high school student, an article said, had climbed a high construction sight for a new bank building and had jumped to her death in the night.

I mentioned it to Sandra one day in her kitchen. "This one really bothers me," I said. "I can't put my finger on why, but it does."

Sandra was becoming more open about her ability to see things other people couldn't see. She said she would try to get a sense of it. I stopped by a few days later and Sandra said, "I have to tell you about this. I was trying to feel what the girl you told me about might have felt that night. I was standing high on the building looking down in the night, and it was very exciting. Then I felt a push from behind, and I was falling, falling."

"Somebody pushed you?"

"I'm sure of it," she said.

A newspaper reporter got the police report on the investigation of Jon's death by submitting an official request under Maryland's Public Information Act, and the reporter gave Jo Glasco a copy. Until then, none of us had seen the police report. There was plenty about it that was conflicting, but I don't plan to do a blow by blow analysis.

One thing that caught my eye was a statement about a neighbor of Sandra's, a fellow named John Sinelli. The report said that at around 2:45 a.m. on May 4 Sinelli heard banging and rattling sounds coming from the direction of the backstop. At around 3:00 to 3:15, Sinelli had seen a dark, late-model, full-sized car back out of a cul-de-sac that overlooked the backstop. The car pulled away and turned on its lights. Sinelli couldn't see who was driving. The report suggested that Sinelli might have seen the car of the morning paper carrier, who drove a dark green 1981 Ford.

Sandra introduced me to Sinelli. He was a stocky man of about thirty-five with wavy, brownish-red hair. He lived in the end unit a couple of doors up from Sandra. We stood on the sidewalk in front of his house and he told me that he'd been a police officer in Michigan and that he had an eye for detail. He said that at around two in the morning a phone call woke him up. He answered the phone but the caller had hung up. The phone rang again and he answered it, but the caller hung up again. He was recovering from knee surgery at the time, and having trouble sleeping anyway, and at around 2:45 he heard banging and rattling sounds coming from the direction of the backstop. Because of the arrangement of the townhouses and the location of the trees, sound from the direction of the high school was channeled to the back of his house. The sounds lasted for about 10 to 15 minutes. He came downstairs, looked outside, and didn't see anything. He opened the sliding doors for air, turned on the television and watched the cable news channel.

At around 3:15 a.m., a dark car, probably black, backed out of the cul-de-sac at the end of the street. The cul-de-sac overlooked the backstop. Sinelli said the car's parking lights were on and he could tell by the shape of the tail lights that the car was a Chrysler LeBaron or a similar Chrysler model. The car started down the street and its headlights came on. Sinelli could not tell who was driving or riding in the car. It struck him at the time that he had not heard a door slamming to indicate that someone had gotten in the car. Sinelli said he told the police there was no way the car he saw was the paper carrier's car.

Actually, there were three paper carriers, Sinelli said. The one who delivered the morning Baltimore paper drove a mid-size Chrysler K-Car-type station wagon. "I can tell the difference between a full-sized car and a station wagon," Sinelli said. This carrier usually delivered the paper at around 4:00 a.m. This carrier's brother, who usually delivered the evening Baltimore paper, drove a dark Ford LTD. "The report is just wrong about that," Sinelli said. "The morning carrier doesn't drive a Ford. His brother, the evening carrier, does." The carrier for the Washington Post drove a pickup and usually came at around 5:00 a.m. Shortly after seeing the car at about 3:15, Sinelli went to his front door to see if his morning paper had been delivered, and it hadn't.

Two days later, on Sunday, at around 1:00 or 2:00 p.m., Sinelli saw what he believed was the same car driving past his house, coming from the direction of the cul-de-sac that overlooked the backstop. It was driven by a tall and large, but not overweight, white male with dark hair. Sinelli didn't recognize the driver, who was alone in the car.

So, if you took Sinelli at his word, there was a lot of banging and rattling at the backstop at about 2:45 early Friday morning. It lasted until about 3:00. At around 3:15, a car pulled away from the cul-de-sac overlooking the backstop. A couple of days later, on Sunday, the car was driving past Sinelli's again from the direction of the cul-de-sac that overlooked the backstop.

"And there's no way it could have been the paper carrier's car?" I asked Sinelli.

"No way," he said. "That's what I told the police."

24 A little over two weeks after the grand jury ended, the state police met with Sandra in a conference room in Arthur Boudreaux' suite of offices.

A few days before the meeting, Alan Zindell called me and said he was going to call Simpson and give him a list of questions Alan wanted answered at the meeting. I asked Alan to put the missing lock on his list. Alan called me back the next day and said Simpson had forgotten about the lock. Simpson, Alan said, had seemed not to recall anything about it. Alan said he had asked Simpson to look into the lock and Simpson agreed to do it before the meeting. Simpson's forgetting about the lock and offering to look into it after the case was closed did nothing to raise my confidence in the investigation.

Boudreaux, Simpson and the other investigator, Wilkinson, were at the meeting. Alan Zindell, Sandra, Mickey, Carlen, John and Claudia Hollywood, Jo Glasco, Jon's and Mickey's natural father, I and several of Mickey's friends were present.

The meeting consisted almost entirely of Simpson reading from a seventeen page report, which he handed out to each of us. Everyone thumbed along as he read the entire seventeen pages out loud. The details get a little tedious, so I'll summarize as succinctly as I can.

The state police had found no fingerprints, including Jon's, on the vinyl cable. Two sets of fingerprints in Jon's car had not been identified. The state police had not learned where Jon was from the time he left his friend's house until he was found at the backstop. Jon had not drunk enough beer at his friend's house to account for his high blood-alcohol level. Red wool fibers had been on virtually all articles of Jon's clothing, including his underwear, and the origin of the fibers was not determined. Simpson noted that such fibers were common. I didn't think of wool as being all that common in this day of synthetics and would have thought the source would have been pretty easy to track down, but that was what he said. One blue wool fiber also was found and no source was identified. Rust stains on the bottoms of Jon's boots, and on his clothing, probably came from the backstop wire, which was rusted. Laboratory analysis could not identify a source for grease-like stains on the calf area of the rear of both of Jon's pants legs. There was a small smudge of white paint on Jon's shirt. A spray can of white paint, the kind of paint used to mark base lines, had been found at the scene. Laboratory analysis showed that the paint on Jon's shirt did not come from the spray can. A twenty-two caliber bullet that was found at the backstop was not seen as being of an evidentiary nature.

It struck me as casual, at best, that Simpson hadn't interviewed three of the young people who had gotten together the night Jon died. One was a college quarterback whose father was a local court commissioner, so he shouldn't have been difficult to locate. It wasn't the kind of omission a person would make in a serious homicide investigation.

Simpson passed around several enlarged photographs showing Jon on the backstop. Most of us until then had not seen photographs of Jon on the backstop, and there was considerable concern in the room about looking at them. Tears began streaming down Carlen's cheeks and she got up and left the room. Sandra said, "I can't look," and there was acknowledgement in different eyes that the photographs would be passed around her.

I left the room to smoke a cigarette and to see if Carlen was all right, and she wasn't. Carlen had a slender build and long, blonde hair and contrasting dark brown eyebrows that gave her an exotic look. A couple of reporters noticed her and asked who she was. I said the meeting was hard and they should leave her alone. I finished my cigarette and went back in the room, and the passing of photographs was over.

Simpson repeated the State Medical Examiner's conclusions that Jon was not unconscious just before his death, that a drug screening test was negative, and that Jon had been highly intoxicated at the time of death.

Simpson had interviewed Meyers, and Meyers had said that on the evening before Jon's body was found he had dinner with his parents and left there at six-thirty and went home. At eleven-thirty he called a local bar and talked to a young woman he knew who worked there. He went to the young woman's apartment after she got off work and they watched videos. The young woman's room mate showed up at around three in the morning, and at around four Meyers went home. On the way home he passed an officer who had pulled over a vehicle, and Meyers stopped to see if the officer needed assistance. I found myself thinking it sounded damned convenient that Meyers had happened across this officer at four in the morning and had stopped to help. It made me wonder just how often in the past Meyers or any other off-duty officer had happened across a fellow officer making a routine traffic stop in the wee hours of the morning and had stopped to help out, but I kept this thought to myself. Simpson said Meyers then went home and Meyers' attorney had called Meyers the next morning to tell him about Jon's death.

Lenny Hamilton, Simpson said, had been at home watching television that night and couldn't remember if anyone had called him or stopped by during the evening.

There were few interruptions as Simpson read his report. Then Simpson turned a page and began reading a summary of several interviews of unidentified people. He said Jon had started drinking at fifteen, that between the ages of fifteen and seventeen Jon was usually intoxicated, and that Jon drank between twelve and eighteen cans of beer each day on the week-ends and between three to six beers each week day. I looked at Sandra and her face had reddened and her eyes were fiercely intent.

Sandra said, "That's simply not true. Who told you these things?" Sandra and Simpson argued heatedly and Simpson never revealed his sources.

Simpson said Jon was aggressive in high school and had suffered a broken hand and finger and a black eye as the result of various altercations.

"It's not true," Sandra said. "He broke his hand scuffling with his brother, and he broke his finger playing baseball. I've explained all of this to you. Why are you doing this?"

Simpson ignored her and continued. "He was known to have provided the names of drug users to a known drug peddler."

This was completely unexpected. To say that Sandra broke into a one-sided shouting fit would be to understate the fusillade that followed. Simpson sat mostly expressionless as Sandra tore into him. Sandra didn't so much wind down as just take a breath, and I asked, "Where did you get this information?"

At the time I didn't recall the article about the cat burglar I had cut out of the paper two months earlier. It was as if Simpson was explaining it for the first time. He told of a young man named Iglesia who had violated parole and fled to California. California police had arrested Iglesia and planned to extradite him to Maryland, but Iglesia told the California police he couldn't go back to Maryland. Iglesia told the California police that the police in Maryland had killed his friend Jon Bowie and would kill him, too, if he was extradited. That, Iglesia said, was why he had fled.

I was dumbfounded. I looked at Sandra and there was complete confusion on her face. I leaned over and whispered, "Have you ever heard of this Iglesia person?"

"No," she mouthed.

So far as I remembered, neither had I.

The other investigator, the one we're calling Wilkinson, said that this Iglesia had been returned to Maryland and interviewed. It appeared that Iglesia was simply making up his story, but it had to be further investigated. "It is a serious matter," Wilkinson said. "when two police officers are alleged to be involved in illegal drug activity. We have to take it seriously."

"Why is it in the report?" I asked, "if it's still not verified? Why are we meeting? Why has the grand jury already reached a decision? Is this investigation over or not?"

"It's what we know to date," Simpson said. "It's a part of the information that was gathered during my investigation."

"But that's not what the report says." I put a finger on the sentence that applied. "It says *known to provide names of drug users to a known drug peddler.*"

"That's what was said," Simpson said.

"And you believe it?"

"It's what was said," he repeated.

"Let me get this straight. You believe this guy Iglesia when he says Jon gave him names of drug users, but you don't believe him when he says the police had something to do with drugs, and with Jon's death. It sounds like

you're being pretty selective about what you choose to believe."

"We're still looking into that," Wilkinson said.

The conversation didn't seem to be going anywhere beyond what was in the report, so I changed the subject.

"What about the lock?"

Simpson gave me a blank look and Alan Zindell said, "Dave's thinking on that is that, if the cable was locked down and the lock wasn't found, Jon had to climb the backstop twice. He had to climb it once to go up and get the lock. Then he had to come back down and dispose of the lock in a way that it couldn't be found. Then he had to climb the backstop a second time to put the cable around his neck. If that's not the kind of thing an inebriated person intent on suicide is likely to do, and I don't think it is, then you have to consider the possibility that someone else was involved, and that whoever it was got sloppy and disposed of the lock, not realizing at the moment that the missing lock would discredit the theory that Jon killed himself."

"I spoke with the baseball coach," Simpson said. I'll say the name he used was Cantrell. "Cantrell, I believe was his name. He said he didn't have any reason to believe the cable was locked down."

"Cantrell," Sandra said, "plays and practices on the varsity field. He doesn't have any responsibility for the field where Jon was found, which is the field where they play girl's softball and little league baseball. Did you talk to Wanda Truce, the athletic director? She's the one who told the police that the cable was locked down. That field is her responsibility. She said she had checked the cable the week before and it was locked down."

"I contacted Ms. Truce," Simpson said, "and she was too upset to discuss it."

So that was it. The state police had forgotten about the lock. When Alan had asked them about it, they had checked with someone who didn't spend much time if any at the field and who wasn't sure if the cable was locked down. The person who had originally said it was locked down no longer felt like talking about it, four months after Jon's death. End of subject.

The meeting by this time had gone on for a couple of hours, and I was beginning to feel worn down. Simpson completed the list of things he said his investigation had revealed about Jon's character with, "Known to utilize false identification to gain access to bars and purchase alcoholic beverages." I thought *who cares* and didn't join in the argument that followed. I knew a woman who had manufactured fake ID's at the University of Maryland in the sixties and who eventually became President of a local PTA. It was becoming increasingly apparent to me that the state police investigation had been held at a third grade level and with a total absence of motivation at finding out what had really taken place.

"I knew this kid a long time," I said, "and you have not described the kid I knew. Even if you were describing him accurately, I don't understand what all of this alcohol business has to do with how he died. Why did you spend so much time on this instead of pursuing the possibility of homicide?"

Simpson began looking backward through his notes and seemed about to repeat something he had said earlier, and Wilkinson interrupted him. "You have to understand," Wilkinson said, directing his remarks to me, "that this report was put together for Mr. Boudreaux' purposes. This is not a normal investigation report."

"I don't know what to say to that," I said. "Why would Mr. Boudreaux' purposes be anything other than finding out what happened to this young man, and why would he need anything other than a normal investigation report?"

People argued and again the question didn't get answered. The meeting ended and I didn't feel like talking with anyone. I just drifted out. Camera crews and reporters were waiting outside the courthouse. Sandra and Alan and the kids and I walked up the sidewalk more or less together and reporters walked along with us, asking questions. Boudreaux came jogging out of the building and up the sidewalk and caught up with us. He had copies of the report tucked under his arm and he gave a copy to each reporter.

Later, in Sandra's kitchen, I said, "Simpson looks like such an honest and sincere person."

She laughed a bitter laugh. "He was gift wrapped," she said, "and he had a ribbon around his forehead. Boudreaux tied it there."

———————————

An article in the Flier mentioned the state police claim that Jon had been in a constant state of intoxication between the ages of fifteen and seventeen. When Sandra read it she was like a wounded tiger guarding her cubs. I tried to explain to her that these unfounded claims had nothing to do with finding out what happened to Jon, that we would only get sidetracked by spending time countering them. She didn't listen. In only a few days she had gathered about six dozen notarized statements from Jon's friends, coaches, teachers and past employers, all saying Jon was one of the more admirable people they had ever met. No one recalled his ever being intoxicated in school or on the playing field or at work. Gathering the statements was a mission for Sandra, and she wouldn't be sidetracked. I wrote one myself. I even typed a few handwritten ones from various people and delivered them to Sandra for signing and notarizing.

One evening after work I had dropped off some statements I had typed and I asked Sandra, "What are you going to do with them?"

"I don't know," she said. "I just know that we have to do it. I'll give them to Jo Glasco to file. When we need them, they'll be there."

"I still don't see what it has to do with finding out what happened to Jon," I said again.

Sandra gave me a disgusted look. She said, just as she had after I had talked her into telling the state police about the man with a rope, "Sometimes, you don't understand anything."

After the article that repeated the state police claims about Jon being in a constant state of intoxication, Jo Glasco called the Flier and said she would sue unless the Flier gave Sandra as much time as it had given the state police report. Jo didn't really want Sandra talking to the Flier or to anyone in the media, but Sandra had told Jo in loud language that she would have her say on this and Jo could either help or get out of the way.

A reporter came to the daycare center and met with Sandra and a group of Jon's friends. The reporter told Sandra that, under the circumstances, and given the way things were in the county, there was only so much he could get printed. He would do what he could, though, to write as favorable an article as he could get past his editors. The article was titled *Bowie kin, friends snub investigations* and it was decent enough. The reporter eventually won an award for his coverage of the Bowie case and then he left the paper and reporting as a career for reasons that weren't clear to me even after I talked with him a few times.

There were stories that didn't get in the article. Sandra told me three of them. She sat at her kitchen table and explained that there were stories that people who really wanted to know Jon should hear.

When Jon was in high school he heard from friends that a friend of his, a girl, was telling people she was thinking about killing herself. Jon went to her house and asked her if it was true, and she said it was. He sat up all night with her, listening to her and telling her that she shouldn't do it. That was one of the stories that didn't get into the papers.

Another was that Jon came home one afternoon from high school, pulled an old pair of jeans from his closet and started cutting slits across the knees with scissors. Sandra came into his bedroom and asked him what in the world he was doing. He told her that kids at school had laughed at a kid who had holes in the knees of his blue jeans. Jon said, "I told him that holes in the knees were in style. I told him I had several pairs just like that at home. I said I would wear some tomorrow to show him. I told some of the guys and they said they would do it, too." Jon came home from school the next day laughing about how well it had worked. "All the guys wore blue jeans with holes in the knees. Anybody who asked, we just told them it was the thing."

And there was a Christmas story. One of the youngsters at the daycare center told Jon he didn't expect much of a Christmas because his family couldn't afford it. Jon spent his entire holiday paycheck buying gifts for the kid.

There was a pleading in Sandra's eyes as she told me these stories that hadn't made it into the papers, or into any of the investigation reports. When she had finished she leaned over the table, looking down and tightly squeezing a rolled copy of the latest article that had said as much as could be gotten past the editors. If the paper had been glass, her fingers would have bled.

On the Sunday following the grand jury's decision not to indict anyone in Jon's death, the county insert to the Baltimore Sun ran a story under the headline *Hanging victim's family seeks Justice Department probe*. Tina and Jo were behind that. They were doing whatever paperwork and making whatever phone calls and pulling whatever strings were required to get the United States Department of Justice to investigate Jon's death. You would think it wouldn't be necessary to pull strings to get this thing called justice, but that's a different story. I just wanted it. I didn't have a very good understanding of what it was I wanted, but there was no doubt in my mind that I wanted it. If the county couldn't provide it, and the state couldn't provide it, and if Tina and Jo could get the United States Department of Justice to take a shot at it, great. Since the word was in the name, it sounded like the kind of thing that people in that agency were at least likely to care about.

I was hopeful again.

25 Sandra had been trying for over a month to get in touch with Amanda, and Amanda had dropped out of sight. At first Sandra thought Amanda should provide a statement to the state police. They came and went and then Sandra thought Amanda should provide a statement for the Justice Department. She was convinced a statement from Amanda could help persuade the Justice Department to take an interest in Jon's death.

I went to Amanda's parents' house and talked with her parents and her sister. Amanda's dad told me Amanda didn't have anything to say to me or to anybody else about the Bowie case, and he showed me the door.

Then I called Mama.

"I'll do what I can," Mama said, "but it's not really up to me. All I can do is ask."

The next day Amanda walked into the daycare center where Sandra worked. Amanda apologized to Sandra for hiding.

"I was scared," Amanda said.

Sandra arranged for Amanda to meet me at Jane's office. At Amanda's insistence I had to be real cloak-and-dagger about it, arranging for Amanda to come when no one else would be around and taking her into Jane's office and closing the door so no one could see her. She told me her story and it was the same as Sandra had told me. A very tall man had followed her in a police car and then confronted her in the parking lot of the Oakland Mills Interfaith Center. She was certain the same man had called her later and said that if she didn't back off then he would do the same thing to her he had done to Jon Bowie. Amanda also said she had been running into a lot of police officers lately. One had parked outside her house on several occasions and had just sat in his car. A female officer had stopped her several times for no apparent reason and the officer had said she was keeping an eye on Amanda. Amanda also wondered if her phone was tapped. She kept hearing odd sounds on the line.

I wrote it all down on Jane's computer and printed it out. Amanda signed it and Jane notarized it and I took the notarized statement to Jo Glasco's office.

"How did you get this?" Jo asked me.

"How religious are you?" I asked her. "Not in the ordinary way. I'm not talking about churches and such, but in a real way."

She studied me a moment and said, "Very."

"Then, when this is all over, I'll tell you."

I suppose it was only natural for Jo to think I actually had done something myself to get Amanda to come out of hiding and provide a statement. I couldn't think of any way to explain in a professional atmosphere that Mama had taken care of it, so I didn't go into that. Jo asked if I thought I could persuade a woman I'll call Patsy Wyman to come to her office. Patsy and several other people Jo knew about had told people that, on the night Jon died, they were in a local restaurant called Clyde's. These people said Meyers came into Clyde's that night dressed in uniform even though he was off duty, and he had made a loud show of being there. This restaurant stop was not part of Meyers' official alibi. One of the women who was supposed to have seen Meyers there couldn't be a witness because she and her family had died in a small plane crash. A man who was supposed to have seen Meyers at Clyde's was refusing to talk about it; he had a professional reputation around town and he was afraid of getting involved. Patsy Wyman was the only person Jo knew about who might provide a statement. Patsy had told Jo some weeks before that she would provide a statement, but she hadn't followed through. With Amanda going into hiding, Jo was concerned that Patsy also was becoming reluctant. I told Jo I would try, and I went home and called Mama again.

"How did you get Amanda to come in?" I asked Mama.

"It wasn't up to me whether she came in," Mama said. "I don't give God instructions. After I talked with you, I tried to visit Amanda. It was like going to the moon. She was in bed, and I could tell that she was very frightened. She's also a religious person, so I told her that she didn't know what fear was until she turned her back on something that God wanted her to do. Then I rolled her around in her bed a little. I hope I didn't overdo it. I didn't want to hurt her."

"From what I can tell, she seems all right to me."

"Good."

"Do you think you can do it again? I don't mean go to the moon or anything like that. Just a gentle reminder that someone should give a statement to Sandra's attorney."

"This is pretty tiring," Mama said, "and I have to be honest with you. I'm getting frustrated with it not leading to anything."

"It's important," I said. "Maybe wait a day or two."

Mama agreed somewhat reluctantly. A couple of days later Patsy Wyman stopped by Jo Glasco's office and provided a statement.

You don't just drive up to the window at the Department of Justice and order some to go. It takes time, which you might as well fill doing something else.

There was a county election coming up in November, and a primary before that in September. Alan Zindell and I met with a candidate for the county state's attorney's job. Alan would ask a nun if she ever diddled with herself and be startled if the question offended her. The meeting was his idea, and he did most of the talking for the two of us.

The candidate and his campaign treasurer met us in the candidate's office in an old, renovated house near the courthouse. The candidate was a decent enough fellow, but his ideas about justice were vicious. He was tall and thin and was running on the Republican ticket. He sat reared back at his desk in a swivel chair pulling at his red suspenders and putting his feet on his desk from time to time so we could see his red socks. Alan and I sat in old, stuffed-vinyl chairs and Alan asked the candidate his position on various things.

"I take pride in my conviction record," the man said. He described how he snuck up to people's houses and went through their trash cans, looking for anything that could be used against them. He said if he was elected the members of his staff would have to have a ninety-five percent conviction record to get promoted. Then he twirled in his chair and took an old book off a credenza behind him; he twirled back around and started reading quotes to us from Abraham Lincoln. I finally couldn't take it anymore.

"I've got a problem," I said. "On the one hand, I've got kids I trust telling me that the police are making false charges against them. On the other hand, I've got you saying that you're proud of your conviction record. That seems to leave the kids caught in the middle."

He had an answer for that, but I don't remember it. We shook hands, and Alan and I left.

Alan and I met frequently at Alan's home or mine and talked about election strategies. Sandra sometimes came, and she was beginning to display more energy. We discussed going directly after the County Executive. The County Executive was the one responsible for hiring the Chief of Police. We figured that if we influenced the election then a new County Executive, and the Chief of Police, might find it politically advisable to take Jon's death more seriously. The County Executive, a woman I'll call Stella Waters, had a reputation for being a strong leader, but she also was picking up a reputation for being a bit on the arrogant side, liking her job and the politics a little too much, and that wasn't helping her any. We finally decided it was too risky since Waters was a Democrat, which was the dominant party locally, and she was expected to win in a landslide. Going after her directly could leave us in a precarious position in the future. We decided, instead, to learn more about her and hold that option open. There was still the primary election before the main one, so we had time to get a better feel for things.

The axe fell at work. The employees had held up their end by meeting the letter of the contract, so the severance pay and benefits were good. A large office was set up with computers and printers and telephones for setting up job interviews and fax machines for sending out resumes. Counselors were hired to offer advice. I'd go in every day for a while just to stay busy. I was pretty distressed about my job situation, but I was feeling what I was expected to feel more than what I really felt. I had the oddest feeling that, when I needed a job, one would turn up.

One day toward the beginning of that odd and stressful time, I sat down during lunch at the computer and cranked out the draft text for a pamphlet. Using clip art, I made a cover that showed two footprints standing in front of a ballot box. There was a small map of the United States going into the box. I titled the pamphlet *Jon Bowie Still Votes*. Although I was rushed, I couldn't help but notice how well the draft of the pamphlet came together.

Alan and I met and played with the words in the pamphlet and came up with a list of candidates we would support. As a place-holder, I put in the name of the candidate who had not exactly impressed me with his ideas, and Alan and I agreed not to distribute the draft until we had talked with more candidates.

Ginny Thomas was running for re-election and was quite likely to win, and I called her for one reason or another. I told her about the pamphlet and said I didn't intend to put her name in it since any direct association with us could damage her campaign. She brushed that off and said she wanted her name in the pamphlet, so I re-wrote it and added her name and put in a statement saying the candidates listed had not asked for our support.

Ginny said the loosely formed group that was becoming known as *Friends of Jon Bowie* would have to register with the Board of Elections if we intended to distribute literature supporting candidates. It was a law, she said, so we registered at the county and state election offices. John Hollywood agreed to be the chairman of what had to be called a Political Action Committee and Barbara Stewart agreed to be the Treasurer and keep track of all the necessary records.

There was an evening when I got home late from Zindell's or some other election-type thing and no one else was home. I was sitting in the kitchen with my legs stretched out and my tie dangling and wondering again what I had gotten myself into. I was seriously considering giving it up. Even though I had this odd sense that a job would be there when I needed it, I couldn't help feeling pangs of guilt when I was working on campaign issues rather than actively looking for a job. I also couldn't see spending time working to replace one unsatisfactory candidate with another.

As I sat mulling these things over and sinking further into an almost abject weariness, the phone rang. It was Mama.

"What does it mean," Mama said, "'Jon Bowie votes?'"

"It's an idea I came up with for a pamphlet," I said. "Some of us are not too happy with how things are done around here, and we'd like to do something about it."

"I just wondered," she said. "I kept hearing it, and I didn't know what it meant. I knew it had something to do with you."

"I was just sitting here wondering if it was a mistake," I said.

"I don't think so," she said. "I like it."

Jon Bowie

Still Votes ☑

26 Richard Kinlein was different, which was a shame. We could use more like him. Alan heard that Kinlein had thrown his hat into the ring for the state's attorney's job, and Alan called Kinlein and set up an appointment. I took an afternoon off from resume mailing and Alan and I met with Kinlein at his office.

Kinlein's office also was in an old, renovated house near the courthouse. Alan announced us to the secretary and Kinlein overheard him and came out of his office to greet us. He was a large, affable man with grey-streaked, dark hair combed close to his head and thick, round glasses that gave his eyes a look of amused surprise. Kinlein ushered us down the hall to a small conference room. Again, Alan did most of the questioning.

Kinlein, it soon became apparent, was a natural born story teller. Any subject took him off on a personal journey into the past. He supposed he was the only person still practicing law in the county who had actually read for the law. He thought capital punishment was ethically wrong, and his best legal argument against it was that he had seen too many innocent people convicted of crimes they hadn't committed. He had been the county's state's attorney before and had worked in the office with Boudreaux. Boudreaux had done as much good as bad, Kinlein said, but he was a dinosaur, and an opportunist, who was more interested in winning cases than in seeing justice done; a *bone fide* good-old-boy.

One of Kinlein's favorite cases to recall - I forget the question that led to his telling it, and maybe he did, too - had to do with his defense of H. Rap Brown. Brown was a civil rights activist back when a lot of us white people were afraid the civil rights movement had more to do with taking something away from us than with giving other people their rightful due. Brown had said at a rally nearby that somebody ought to burn the schools and, that night, somebody burned one. Brown was charged with inciting someone to burn the school. Kinlein went on about how there is such a thing as freedom of speech. Burning a school down was a different matter, but Brown hadn't done that. Brown was found innocent due largely to Kinlein's efforts, and I got the impression as Kinlein told it that this ethical stand had cost him some friends.

Alan asked Kinlein what he thought about the local police. Kinlein told of one of his sons who had struggled with a drug problem. The son had been in and out of trouble and rehabilitation and Kinlein was doing what he could to help his son get his life straightened out. One night circumstances were such that Kinlein thought he had to call the police to get them to assist him in getting his son to a hospital. His son became aware that the police were coming. He ran outside to escape them and met them instead. Kinlein came running out as an officer grabbed his son in a choke hold and wrestled him to the ground.

"For God's sake," Kinlein said he cried out to them, "I only wanted you to help him. Don't kill him."

Kinlein told us stories of officers who charged people falsely and took some sort of twisted pride in it, of officers who had lied so often in court they had become an embarrassment and were no longer permitted to testify, of officers who took undue advantage of money allocated for undercover drug buys.

"Boudreaux drives a car confiscated from an alleged drug dealer," Kinlein said. "A car can be a dangerous incentive. If you can find an excuse to arrest someone, the police department gets to keep the car. There's a police officer who works in the county right now who drives a Mercedes with a ten thousand dollar stereo system in it."

Alan looked at me and we nodded at each other and Alan reached across the table and shook hands with Kinlein.

"I think we have our candidate," Alan said.

Kinlein stood and we stood with him.

"One last question," Alan said. "Why do you want to be the state's attorney?"

Kinlein smiled an almost shy smile with just a hint of devilment in it.

"I don't," Kinlein said. "If I thought I had any chance of winning, I wouldn't run. It's just that I don't think the people running have any particular desire to do a good job. They just want bigger salaries and their pictures in the paper. I decided that if I run it might shake things up a bit, maybe do some good."

"But you could win," Alan said.

"No, I couldn't," Kinlein said. "Boudreaux has the system behind him, and he'll win. It's funny," he said, and his eyes went to some place in the past that he didn't describe. "I'm older now, and I could do a better job than I did the first time. I wouldn't say things anymore just to get votes, though. I'd have to say what I think, and that alone would keep me out. Besides, what would I tell my secretary? She's been with me for years. I have responsibilities. The best we can hope for is maybe to get a few thousand votes and do a little good in the process."

A brief article in the Baltimore paper said Meyers had stopped a motorist who admitted to having had two beers. The motorist passed a breath test but Meyers still told him that if he came into the county again in the next thirty days then he would be charged with driving while intoxicated. The motorist got upset and filed a complaint against Meyers.

Several more brief articles followed the story. The police department found Meyers guilty of misconduct. Meyers' attorney, Stephen Kent, appealed, saying Meyers' rights had been violated. Meyers' case was heard again and, the second time, the police department found him innocent of any wrongdoing. The final articles on the matter said this was one of at least six pending charges against Meyers, most of them related to rudeness. The head of the local police union said Meyers was being targeted because of the Bowie case, and the Chief of Police was responsible for it.

A local County Councilman, Vernon Gray, was running unopposed for re-election in his district. Before Jon died, Gray had done what he could to help Sandra and Jon get a restraining order to keep Meyers away from Jon. Although the order never was actually obtained, Sandra was grateful and said we should put Gray's name in the pamphlet. I objected that Gray was running unopposed and it didn't really matter, but Sandra insisted. I put Gray's name in the pamphlet.

Tina Gutierrez knew a young attorney, a black woman named Branche, who was running for Judge in the county. Tina said the woman was a good person with not much chance of winning. By then, at least two judges had called in sick when Mickey had court dates scheduled, and, each time, the county had brought in someone from another county. Mickey's case was rescheduled each time, Tina saw to that, but I figured the county could use an honest judge. Tina's word was all I had to go on, and I couldn't ask for better. We added Branche's name to the pamphlet.

I erased the name of the first candidate for state's attorney and added Kinlein. I photocopied so many copies after hours at a friend's office that on more than one occasion the machine overheated and shut down and had to be left to sit overnight to cool off. I gave copies to Sandra and she distributed them among her friends, who made more copies. Soon we had literally tens of thousands of photocopies of the pamphlet.

The pamphlet was a tri-fold of an 8.5x11 sheet of paper, and each pamphlet had to be folded twice. Several of us met at different people's houses and had folding parties. Jim was the best at it. He figured out how to fold almost a dozen at one time without making them look homemade. Anne Beck took a stack home to fold and her husband came home from work and asked what she was doing. She told him and he reminded her that in his business he sold office equipment. He brought home an automatic paper folder and the process really began to roll.

One friend told another and, by the time the primary came around, we had people sticking pamphlets in screen doors and under windshield wipers throughout most of Columbia. I went out on several occasions with Alan or Sandra to pass out the pamphlets at malls and such. Sometimes Jim came along. Jim and I were not inclined to walk up to people and carry on conversations as we handed out pamphlets, but Alan and Sandra would do it in a heartbeat. A man and woman in a shopping center parking lot approached Sandra one Saturday and said they were teachers and they supported the police. Sandra said she also was a teacher, and she supported all of the police except those who hit people without justification. Another woman approached Sandra on a bike path one afternoon and said she happened to know Jon Bowie's mother and she knew for a fact that the things the police were saying about him were true. Sandra listened and the woman finally introduced herself and asked for Sandra's name. Sandra told her and the woman went white in the face and hurried off.

I wore out a pair of tennis shoes but didn't do much talking. The only specific encounter I recall involved a young woman who took the pamphlet off her windshield where I had placed it in a shopping center parking lot. She read the pamphlet and then walked over to where I was putting pamphlets on more windshields. "Did you know Jon Bowie?" she asked me. I said, "Yes," and she said, "So did I," and she walked off. She had tears in her eyes.

I bought some tomato stakes from a lumber yard for a quarter each and some cardboard and ink markers from a school supply company. Sandra and I sat at her kitchen table and made posters in dark blue and red letters on white cardboard. The posters said *Jon Bowie Still Votes* and listed the four candidates. Even with our best efforts the posters looked pretty amateurish and would definitely attract attention, which was fine.

On the morning of the primary election, I picked up Sandra before sunrise at her house and we went to each polling place in the county. There were a few over eighty polling places, and it took a while. We drove the stakes in the ground with the blunt side of an axe and the posters stood out among the other nicely printed campaign signs.

Kinlein came over to Sandra's that night and Jim and Sandra and Alan and Kinlein and I and maybe a few more people watched the election results in Jim's and Sandra's basement. Kinlein beat the other candidate handily and was eligible for the November election. Ginny and Vernon Gray also won. JoAnne Branche, the political unknown who was running for a judgeship, got forty percent of the vote, but she lost.

Over the next few days, people neither Sandra nor I knew began calling and saying they were running for this office or that and they would support us if they got elected, but they couldn't say it publicly until they got elected. Most of them we just ignored.

———————

When all was said and done, what I remembered most about the primary election was an afternoon stop at a hamburger place. Some nights when I went home after distributing pamphlets, I was so tired I fell straight into bed without showering. It was a dumb thing to do and, as a consequence, I came down with a nasty case of athlete's foot between the little and next toe of my left foot. I tried various over-the-counter remedies and none of them worked. It got worse and was beginning to get infected. I was shy about it and mentioned it only to Jane.

One afternoon Sandra and I were sitting in a local fast food store eating a hamburger and Sandra said out of the blue, "Soak your foot in Clorox."

I was startled because I had not told her about the infection, and I said, "What?"

"I don't know why I said that," she said. "It just came out of my mouth. Is there something wrong with your foot?"

I told her about the problem and her face turned pale.

"I prayed for a sign," she said. "I know it's not good to test God, but I was desperate. I prayed that if God wanted me to know what happened to Jon, He would give me a sign."

Such things still were pretty new to me, out in the open anyway. I said, "Did you ask for anything in particular?"

"I had to know if it was what I had asked for," she said, as if she were apologizing. "I asked if maybe someone I knew could have a minor injury to the left foot. Nothing serious. Just something to let me know."

I sat staring at her a moment. Then I laughed.

"Damn," I said, long and slow. "Maybe you should meet my mother."

27 I was self-conscious about being at Tina's house. It was a delightful house, an old, two-story farmhouse that sat in a secluded lawn between a Baltimore park and a somewhat run-down neighborhood. Tina did nothing to make me feel self-conscious; it was just this intimidation thing I had that involved attorneys and other people of some social status. Being there seemed like an intrusion. Still, Tina was cordial and we sat on high stools around a center-floor counter in her kitchen drinking soft drinks.

Mickey's trial had been postponed until after the November elections, which I didn't see as an accident. I thought I knew what Tina would have to say if I asked her outright, so I put what was on my mind in hypothetical terms.

"It's my belief that Mickey cannot risk spending a single night in the Howard County jail. Let's say that I was writing a book." At the time I wasn't writing a book, but that was the way I put it to Tina. Tina's eyebrows went up and she didn't respond. "Let's say that in this book there was a kid in court, and there was his attorney who suddenly realized that he was going to jail. I know that an attorney could not participate in such a thing, but let's say that I had suggested beforehand that if, in fact, the attorney realized that he was going to jail, she would say her client's middle name, which he never uses, as a sort of tip-off, a code. Then, even though she has already said she can't do it, let's say that, in the surprise of the moment, she slips up and does it anyway by accident. Then Mickey and anyone else who knew the code would suddenly believe, even though she hadn't intended to convey it, that he was definitely going to jail. What they did after that would be none of her concern. She wouldn't have intended it and wouldn't even know what it was."

Tina didn't smile and she didn't frown.

"I'm going to assume that you're upset and talking crazy, and this conversation is over," she said.

"Fine," I said. "Just remember that Mickey's middle name is *Carlton*." I said Mickey's middle name slowly. "I've never heard him use it."

The plan was devised by a friend of mine who was - how can I say this? - from a large family in New Jersey. I'm not talking just about blood relatives here. To be just a bit more specific, which is as specific as I have any intention of getting on this subject, an uncle of this particular friend of mine was Al Capone's chauffeur for quite a while. This friend of mine from the large family in New Jersey didn't know Sandra personally, but only knew about her from things I had said. This friend said Sandra had to know about the plan.

So Sandra and I sat alone at Sandra's kitchen table and I said, "Don't talk. Just listen. Mickey has to write a letter to you saying that he is afraid of what could happen to him if he is put in jail in Howard County, and that he is not suicidal. Then, if he's found guilty and goes to jail, and if this doesn't work, you'll have to give the letter to the press. That way you know he's protected. It'll make too big a splash for anyone to try anything. It would be better, though, if we don't risk his going to jail. Just before the trial, I'll tell him a code and how he will hear it. If he hears the code, then he has to pick his time and run like hell. It would probably be better if he gets up and starts running as soon as he hears it. He's fast, and he would have surprise on his side. I'll talk to some of the other kids and ask them to stick out their feet or get up and look confused and get in the way and such until Mickey's out of the court room. He'll run through the woods behind the courthouse to the river. He should wear a second set of clothes underneath so he can strip as he runs. If he follows the river to the left, he'll come to the bridge where Route 40 crosses the river. I'll leave a two-liter soda bottle and a stick by the guardrail at the bridge. I'll keep driving by until I see the soda bottle leaned up against the guard rail on the stick. That's how I'll know he's there. I'll use a neighbor's car and drive him south of Washington. Someone else will meet me and take him to Richmond. Someone else will get him from Richmond to a fishing cabin that's several hundred miles from here. After a few weeks I'll get him into Canada. It's already arranged. It'll work. If it doesn't, you start waving the letter around and make a big fuss about how he had to do it."

Sandra looked at me with her lips pursed off to one side. She finally said, "I can't believe we're talking about this."

"We're not," I said. "I am, and neither can I. God willing, it'll never be necessary."

I called my dad and said I needed him to let someone stay at his place at the Pamlico River, maybe for several weeks. I said it would be best if no one knew who this person was or why he was there. I said I didn't want to drag him into anything by saying more than that.

My dad said, "I'll have to go down and explain about the pump, and how to turn on the water. Is he strong?"

"Yeah, he's pretty strong."

"And smart?"

When my dad asked if someone was smart, he wasn't talking about the person's IQ. He was talking about whether the person could walk and chew gum at the same time.

"Yeah, he's smart," I said.

"Good," he said. "Maybe he can help me shingle the roof."

"I've got him taken care of as far as Richmond," I said. "I might need somebody to pick him up in Richmond."

"Give me some notice," he said. "If you can."

That's what family is for.

28 Sandra told me Jo Glasco had been to the Justice Department and there was some attorney there, a woman, who had all of the newspaper clippings on the Bowie case on her desk and a file of other related documents. Sandra was too excited to sit at the kitchen table and we walked down to the ball field past the backstop and on behind the school.

"We can't talk about it," Sandra said.

"Why not?"

"I don't know. Jo said if word gets out the Justice Department is interested, they'll just fold their tents and go away."

"It doesn't make sense," I said. "They're either interested or they're not. Maybe word getting out could hurt their investigation in some way."

"Who knows?" Sandra said. "It's what Jo told me."

We turned and walked back toward the house. When we were behind the backstop Sandra stopped and looked at the ground.

"This is where they would have laid him that morning," she said.

"I suppose."

"Sometimes I see that night in my mind and I can almost make out what happened. There was a flashlight, I think, and some sort of crank thing. I see more than one person, but I can't see the faces."

"I told you my mother saw some sort of mechanical device, maybe like a lift."

"It could be that I'm making it up," Sandra said. "Maybe I think I see it because your mother saw it, and it's planted in my mind."

"Maybe," I said.

Mickey's twentieth birthday was in September. It was not an easy day for him. Sandra planned the day out for him and kept him busy. A friend told her that would make the day easier for him, so that was what she did.

I wanted to buy Mickey a present. I'd never bought him a present before but I wanted to do it, to let him know that people were thinking of him. A friend suggested I make certain the present was something that eventually would be discarded, or worn out, or used up. I never would have thought of that by myself. I probably would have bought some schmaltzy memento he would have come to hate and would have felt guilty about throwing away. My friend said it was important for the present not to serve as some lingering reminder of that particular difficult day.

I bought Mickey some gift certificates for home movies at a local video store. He and Sandra were off somewhere when I stopped by, so I left them with Jim.

I had never seriously considered the possibility that Mickey might be lying. I had wondered about it, even worried about it, but that was only because I was trying so hard to stay honest with myself that I went through all of the scenarios I could imagine. It was not that I thought Mickey had become some sort of saint by the age of twenty and was beyond the convenient arrangement of details to which all of us are occasionally susceptible. Even in this time of his extended grief, Mickey had enough humor, watchfulness and devilment in his eyes to keep you on your toes. It was just that his personality simply didn't require lying. Jon and Mickey were very much alike in that way. To them, the sky was blue and the grass was green and most days were good days; if you didn't want to hear it, you shouldn't ask.

Tina came up with the idea for a lie detector test. Lie detector tests, Tina explained, were almost never admissible in court, but they did have advantages, not the least of which was that they got people's attention. Tina knew an expert with a considerable national reputation, a man named Brisentine, and Tina made the arrangements. Brisentine was expensive and Sandra worried about where the money for his fee would come from, but she came up with it anyway. When Sandra called and said Jim was having trouble getting off work to take her, and she was afraid of getting lost in Baltimore, I jumped at the opportunity to be there.

Tina's office was in a spacious, three-story, renovated Victorian townhouse in north Baltimore. We parked in a graveled parking lot off an alley behind the building and took a long, narrow wrought iron staircase up one long flight to the rear door. An assistant let us in and escorted us to a large, high-ceiling waiting room. The assistant informed Sandra that Tina had been called to court but that the polygraph expert knew what to do. We waited, talking about anything but the upcoming test.

After a half hour Brisentine finally came into the waiting room. He was a tall, grey-haired man with an air of calm self-assurance. He looked like a man born to fish and smoke a pipe and wear flannel shirts. He extended a hand to Sandra and she stood to greet him. Sandra's head came up to about his lower chest.

"Ms. Keyser," he said in the most courteous of mellow tones, "before we do this, before you give me a check, there is something that you must understand. I am here to determine if this young man is telling the truth. My reputation depends on that. If what you want to know is the truth, then fine. If what you want is to hear what you want to hear, then I must suggest that we stop now. Do you understand?"

"I understand," Sandra said.

Brisentine motioned to Mickey and smiled a welcoming smile, and he and Mickey disappeared down the hall.

Sandra thumbed hurriedly through magazines without taking the time to read them. From time to time she got up and paced the waiting room. I finally said, "You're so nervous, you're making me nervous. Mickey's telling the truth. Please relax."

"I know," Sandra said. "But those lie detectors can show all kinds of things. Maybe Mickey's nervous and the test can't tell the difference."

"Tina says this man is the best. He should be able to tell the difference. I really don't think there's anything to worry about."

Sandra finally paced and sat down and got up again and paced so much I had to go outside to smoke. I walked up and down the sidewalk a few times and then went back into the waiting room. Mickey came back in followed by Brisentine. Mickey was a little red-cheeked and looking more or less down at the floor. Brisentine had a wide grin on his face and he stepped over to

Sandra, who got up from her seat. Brisentine extended a hand and Sandra took it and Brisentine said, "Ms. Keyser, this young man is telling the truth."

Brisentine and Sandra talked and I punched Mickey in the arm and he gave me a self-conscious grin.

Sandra and I took Mickey down the street to a small Italian restaurant for hamburgers and fries and we pumped him for details.

"What did you tell him?" I asked Mickey.

"I told him the truth," Mickey said in that disarming way of his of getting right to the point.

"Come on," Sandra said. "Tell us what happened. What questions did he ask you?"

"Only one," Mickey said. "We talked a while. You know, he asked me about the motel and what had happened, and I told him. Then he told me I didn't have to take the test if I didn't want to. He said if I did, though, that it would come out like it came out. He said he had his reputation to look out for. I told him I wanted to take it. He put some things on my arm and asked me if the things I had told him about getting hit at the motel and in the police car were true, and I said yes. That was it."

The FBI acts as the investigating arm of the Department of Justice. It was by way of two almost simultaneous coincidences on a day in October, five months after Jon's death, that Sandra learned the FBI was investigating.

In the first coincidence, Jim Keyser saw several men dressed in drab suits get out of a plain car in the parking lot in front of KoKo's convenience store. Sometimes after work, Jim and several other postal carriers stopped at a bar called Classics Pub, which shared a parking lot with KoKo's and several other new stores in a recently developed business park. For one reason or another the postal workers no longer played darts at The Last Chance Saloon. Instead, every few days they met after work and played darts and had a few beers at Classics. Jim often called Sandra before leaving and asked if she wanted him to bring home pizza.

Jim was a quiet sort of fellow. He didn't have a lot to say and, at the same time, he didn't miss many details. It was not at all unlike him to wander off by himself for a while, to get away from whatever hustle and bustle was going on about him, and then simply to return and rejoin the group. He went out to his van to sit and smoke a cigarette. He could smoke in the bar, and did, but going out to the van for a quiet, private smoke was the kind of thing he naturally would do. He sat in the van and watched as the drab-suited men arrived in a black Ford and one of the men got out and went into KoKo's. The man came back outside with Chong Ko, whose family owned the store. The other men got out of the car and Chong and the men had a long and often animated conversation. Then the men got in the car and left and Chong got into his 4-wheel drive red Toyota and drove away. Jim put two and two together, added the many details he had picked up listening to Sandra go on about the Justice Department, and realized that at last the FBI actually was doing something. He went back into the bar to call Sandra, but she wasn't home.

Sandra was at a membership-type discount warehouse in Laurel, a town a few miles south of Columbia. Shopping was one of the things she did with a passion when there was nothing else to fill the time between missions that might give her a clue as to how Jon had died. She often wandered through a store buying a dollar item here or there for the house or a present to store away for some upcoming birthday or holiday. The store where Sandra was filling time happened to be where Chong Ko headed after talking to the men from the FBI. Sandra was wandering the aisles when she and Chong spotted each other. Chong told her in excited whispers that he had just been interviewed by the FBI.

"They told me not to tell anyone," he said, "but as soon as I saw you I knew I had to tell you."

Sandra promised not to repeat it and then hurried home to tell Jim. As she rushed into the kitchen, Jim said, "I have something to tell you."

"First I have to tell you something," Sandra said, and she was practically jumping up and down. "The FBI is investigating. I just talked to Chong Ko and he told me."

"Damn," Jim said. "That's what I was going to tell you."

I didn't get around to meeting the Reverend David Rogers until toward the end of that first summer, although his name kept coming up and I had begun looking for a way to meet him.

One afternoon, before I met Rogers, Sandra and I were in Tina's cluttered, third-floor office for some case-related reason. Sandra and I were tossing around the subject of the upcoming elections and things that might be done to improve how the county dealt with people. Tina was very careful in such conversations, I suppose because there are things attorneys can and can't advise their clients to do. Tina did mention that she had heard that Reverend Wright and Reverend Rogers and some candidates might go about the county doing some sort of dog and pony show for truth and justice and politics. I thought she might be implying that I should join this caravan, and I recall exactly what I said to her. I said, "If you think I'm getting on a platform with a bunch of goddamned preachers and politicians, then you don't know me very well." Tina changed the subject so abruptly that it left me wondering that maybe that wasn't at all what she had intended. Anyway, I didn't do it and I didn't meet Rogers.

Sandra had a conversation with Rogers at some occasion that didn't involve me, and during that conversation she expressed concern about the effect of Jon's death on Mickey. Rogers offered to meet with Mickey as a counselor if Sandra thought that would be of help. I didn't know anything about this and I stopped by one evening to look in on Mickey. Sandra told me he was meeting with Rogers. I said, "Who the hell is this Rogers guy, anyway, and what does he want to talk to Mickey about?"

"He's a preacher," Sandra said. "He says that he's concerned about Mickey and wants to help him."

I guess I was in a protective mood. I said, "I've been wanting to ask. Just how is it this man who works with the police department and who is off talking to Mickey about God knows what came to take part in Jon's funeral?"

The answer was that Rogers was a friend of Reverend Wright's, and Wright had invited him to participate. Rogers had even spoken with Sandra before the funeral and offered, and Sandra had agreed. Sandra often was in a fog during those days and she didn't remember Rogers asking and I didn't know about it. "I don't really know," Sandra said, answering my question.

"Well, I think we have to learn more about him. You don't want some goofball messing with Mickey's head. And if he's with the police department, there's no telling what he's up to, or who put him up to it."

Sandra told me later that the meeting between Mickey and Rogers went well, and she thought it had been helpful for Mickey, but I wasn't convinced. Rogers was on my mind along with a lot of other things when Jo Glasco sent word through Sandra that she wanted to talk to me. I stopped by Jo's office one afternoon and she told me the Justice Department wanted to talk to Rogers. She wondered if I could set up an interview. Rogers was angry with Jo about something and she didn't think she was the one to arrange it. I said, "Sure." I didn't mention that I'd been wanting to talk with him myself.

Rogers' office was in a brown, batten-board, barn-like extension off the main buildings of the Oakland Mills Village Center. It wasn't one-hundred-percent bullshit when I stopped by one afternoon, shuffled in with a dumb country boy slide that I'd grown up knowing how to pull off, added a touch to my natural drawl, took his outstretched hand and said, "I've been wanting to meet you." He led me into a large inner office, waved to a chair opposite his desk and lowered his large frame into a black burlap chair behind the desk. When we were seated he asked what he could do for me.

"There comes a time," I said, "when a person has to trust somebody, and I've decided to trust you. I like your face."

He put his fingers together under his chin in a church steeple arrangement and looked at me as if he couldn't decide if he had just heard a joke or a battle-cry. I decided to back off the accent a bit.

"Well, thank you," he said. "Go on."

"It's not supposed to be known," I said, "and I'd appreciate it if you'd honor that, but the Justice Department is investigating Jon Bowie's death." Rogers didn't say a word, but he looked as if about ten pounds of air had just left his body. "They want to talk to you. Jo Glasco asked me to see if you would agree to that."

I know from experience that preachers tend to be expressive, but I wasn't prepared for Rogers' reaction. He leaned back in his chair and then leaned forward over his desk. He leaned back again and then half forward and threw his hands out in a wide, air-sweeping gesture and said, "Agree to it? Agree to it?" His voice kept getting louder and he said, "Hell, I've been praying for it." I don't think I'd ever heard a preacher say, "Hell," in any context other than to tell me to watch out for it. I could feel walls falling down around me and I had to remind myself not to be too trusting too fast. I was starting to like this boy and I still didn't know him. He was talking pretty loud when he asked, "Do you know what they want to talk to me about?"

I said, "Tell me."

He did. It took a lot more leaning backward and forward on his part, and some hand waving and a few marches around his desk, but this is essentially the story he told me. I've changed a few details because there are lawyers who say I have to, but I haven't changed the essence of it. In fact, I've changed more than some lawyers say is necessary, just to be on the safe side.

A few days after Jon died, Rogers got a phone call. "I've counseled a lot of people," he said. "I'm trained in suicidology and crisis intervention and marriage counseling..." He mentioned some other things he was trained in and I wanted to wave my finger in a circle the way television people do to signal that someone should get on with it, but I waited. "I'm not just using the word lightly," he said, "when I tell you that this woman was *terrified*. She didn't want to call me but she thought that she had a moral imperative to do it." Preachers talk like that, but I got his point. This was not a casual phone call.

The woman had experienced a professional encounter with the police. I'll say that the woman's house was broken into and that the police came to investigate the break-in. It was something similar to that. After the police business was over, one police officer and this woman struck up a friendship. It wasn't a romantic thing, but she liked having a police officer as a friend. This police officer began stopping by every few days, first to check on her and then because they were becoming friends. The woman was divorced and had children, and having a police officer for a friend made her feel safe. This woman told Rogers that one evening she invited the police officer over for dinner. During dinner she threw into the conversation how happy she was that her boyfriend had asked her to marry him. The police officer apparently didn't see the relationship in the same way the woman saw it.

"She said, 'He raped me,'" Rogers said. "Her voice was trembling when she said it. He raped her and he sodomized her because she was getting married and he was angry." Rogers eyes started getting red around the edges.

I said, "Are you sure you should be telling me about this? I mean, you're a preacher and this woman must have known that when she called you. Isn't there something that says you can't talk about some things?"

"Clerical privilege?" he said. "Hah. That went out the window when Jo Glasco gave my notes to Arthur Boudreaux. Boudreaux gave them to the grand jury and Chief Hickory and God knows who else."

I followed Rogers to a small adjoining room. He retrieved his notes from a four-foot-high, elaborately locked two-door safe with a horizontal pipe across the front and a padlock holding the pipe against the doors. He re-locked the safe and we went back into his office. He told me about the grand jury and about leaving the police department. I wouldn't say he sounded bitter when he said Hickory had told him he had showed a lack of loyalty by passing on the story. He sounded *intent*.

"Do you know what she said to me when I picked up the phone? She said, 'I know who killed Jon Bowie.' I grabbed a pencil and said, 'Who?' and she told me. She said, 'He raped me,' and then she burst into tears and told me all this.'"

This police officer and several of his police officer friends, it seemed, sometimes visited this woman. They would have a few beers and sit around shooting the breeze. She said the officers liked to brag about people they had beaten up.

"She said she knew killing Jon was the kind of thing he would do," Rogers said.

I almost didn't say out loud the thought that went across my forehead, but I caught myself and said it.

"That's not evidence," I said.

Rogers looked hurt, and puzzled, and angry. He said, "Did you hear what I just said to you?"

"I heard it," I said, "and I can tell that this woman believes this police officer did a bad thing. Maybe he did. And if he did one bad thing then she thinks he's the kind of person who could have done another, who could have killed Jon. But what she believes is not evidence. She could be wrong. Did she actually say that he told her he killed Jon?"

"She didn't say it like that," he said, "but, Christ Almighty."

How can you dislike a preacher who says, "Christ Almighty," like that? If you do then you'd better reconsider your outlook. As if to give his argument more weight, he said, "She told me that she was sitting at a traffic light and he pulled up beside her in his police car and grinned at her and pointed his pistol at her. Doesn't that say something?"

I thought about it. "I suppose it does," I said. "If she's telling the truth, then it says that he's an asshole, and he doesn't want her to tell anyone that he raped her. He's trying to intimidate her. I don't mean to be callous, but if she's been raped then she needs to press charges. I'm just a little wrapped up in what happened to this kid I coached in baseball, this kid who died and nobody wants to do anything about it, and nothing you've said has told me anything about that."

"I tried to get her to press charges," Rogers said. "I pleaded with her. She said that as long as he is walking around in uniform, carrying a gun, she can't do it. Who knows what he might do? And I can't really blame her. The police department has my notes, thanks to Boudreaux, and I can't see that they've done anything about it."

"When will you talk with her again?" I asked.

"I don't know if I will. She didn't give her name. She did mention a lot of details, without meaning to. She could be found. I've tried to find her myself, but I don't have the resources of the police department."

Rogers and I wrapped up our conversation and we were at his door shaking hands and making small talk when it came up somehow that he played football in high school. He said he had been a linebacker. My first thought was that linebackers, who are noted for being more than a little crazy and for not letting anybody spend a lot of time standing between them and the other team's quarterback, were a lot bigger than they used to be.

What I said was, "That fits."

29 Anne Beck came up with the idea for a fund-raiser. Sandra saw Anne every work day, and Anne knew Sandra's and Jim's expenses were piling up. Anne bought a large roll of tickets, visited local merchants and got door prizes, and made dozens of flower arrangements for the tables.

Sandra saw the fund-raiser as a way to keep Jon's death in people's minds. She and I called some candidates and invited them. Ginny Thomas came, and a woman who was running for the Board of Education. We were supporting a write-in campaign for JoAnne Branche's bid for a judgeship, and she came. JoAnne was getting some behind-the-scenes pressure not to pursue election any further since she had lost in the primary. She had received a phone call telling her she would make a lot of political enemies if she insisted on letting her name be used in a write-in campaign, and the phone call aggravated her and persuaded her to attend the fund-raiser. A few politicians sent literature but didn't show up.

Several hundred people came to the fund-raiser. It was held in the vast loft of The Other Barn, the renovated barn where the meeting between the police and a few community representatives had been held. Most of those who came to the fund-raiser were young people who had known Jon and the music was too loud and I couldn't do any of the dances except the slow ones. When time was made for the politicians to speak, a few people got angry and said that if they had known it was going to be that kind of thing then they wouldn't have come.

The fund-raiser brought in a several thousand dollars, and Sandra gave it to John Hollywood to deposit.

Zindell and Rogers and a few more people and I met with Stella Waters, the County Executive. The Chief of Police, Elvin Hickory, was there, and several people from Hickory's staff. During the meeting Rogers argued that the county needed a civilian review board to monitor the police. Waters said she could live with that. Hickory said it could cause problems for the police but, if the people wanted it, he could live with it. All of this was a side issue to me, and I didn't have much to say.

After the meeting Rogers decided to lock Waters in, and he wrote a letter to the Flier saying that he admired her for taking a stand in favor of a review board.

A few days after the fund-raiser, I got a phone call from someone who had not attended and who was running for something. I'll say it was a man. He had been at some political gathering and was standing with a group of people that included Arthur Boudreaux and Stella Waters. Waters, this man said, told Boudreaux that she had said she would support a review board only to keep us quiet. After the election, she intended to come out against it.

Between Jane's choir work and her job as a village manager, and her naturally out-going personality, she had met a lot of people in *New America*. I asked Jane to learn what she could about the man who had called me. Jane asked a few questions of a few friends and told me the man had a reputation for being a good person who was not likely to lie. I called Sandra and said, "Put the word out. We're supporting Scarsy." Sandra had struggled with whether to support Scarsy or Waters for County Executive the same as I had, and we had finally decided not to address the issue without a reason. I told Sandra about the phone call and she said, "It's done." Sandra also knew a lot of people, and those people knew more.

Kinlein lost, which was what he wanted, but it was a close enough race to give him a scare. He was expected to get four or five thousand votes and he got well over twenty-thousand and lost to Boudreaux by only about four thousand. I'm told his showing still is talked about in county offices and up and down the courthouse steps. Shortly before election day, a brilliant young reporter who had disappointed me more than once visited Kinlein at his office and - on an impulse of integrity, I suppose - told Kinlein he had been sent by an editor of the Baltimore Sun to, "do a job," on Kinlein. They talked for hours and the reporter wrote a story about how Kinlein had once shot a kid. The kid had broken up with Kinlein's daughter and had showed up with a can of gasoline one night saying he was going to burn Kinlein's house.

"I had to shoot him," Kinlein said when he told me the story. "He was going to burn my house. I didn't try to seriously injure him, kill him or anything like that, but I had to stop him."

The article didn't get into all the details, and it didn't help Kinlein any. The Flier had endorsed Boudreaux, which also was a major blow to Kinlein.

I called Kinlein after the election and asked how he felt about losing. He said he was glad he didn't have to figure out what to do about the secretary who had worked for him for years.

JoAnne Branche got fifteen hundred or so write-in votes and she also lost. She rented office space from Jo Glasco and set up a private law practice. She sent word that she wanted two Jon Bowie tee shirts and would pay. She wasn't in when I went by with the tee shirts so I just left them on her desk.

Ginny Thomas and Vernon Gray won and would have without us.

The County Executive lost. A newspaper article suggested that the neighborhood where Sandra lived had turned the election.

30 Chong Ko was not happy about being charged with possession of a pipe that wasn't his. For a while he would tell anyone who would listen. Then he became disgusted with the whole business and didn't want to talk about it anymore.

On the Monday after the Red Roof Inn incident, Chong visited a doctor and got a drug test. It came back negative, as he had known it would. He didn't know what that officer, that big guy named Meyers, was thinking by charging him with having possession of the pipe that was found in the motel room, but he wasn't having any of it. He didn't know why Eddie's girlfriend, Pamela, had said he had brought the pipe into the room, and he didn't care. Early on, when he was talking to anyone who would listen, he would say that his family didn't come to America to be treated like this.

Chong told Meyers at the police station that he was going to get the drug test. A day or so after the results came back, Meyers called Chong at home. Meyers wanted to know the results and Chong told him. Meyers said he might be able to get the charge of possession of drug paraphernalia dropped against Chong, and Chong said, "Sure."

Jon and Mick told Reverend Wright about Chong and Chong talked with Wright. Wright told Chong it was outrageous for Meyers to call him at home and to offer to drop the charges. Wright said Meyers was interfering with the courts, and that was illegal. Meyers called Chong again and said he had arranged for Chong to meet with the state's attorney. Chong told Meyers that

Reverend Wright had said Meyers shouldn't be calling him.

Chong's case was heard in court in the early spring. Meyers called Chong again before the court date and said Chong should meet with Meyers and the state's attorney before Chong went into court. Chong agreed this time, and met with them. He didn't really understand all that was said. They told him he had to do his part, or something like that, whatever that meant.

In court, Chong told the judge that Meyers had called him at home and the judge said a police officer wouldn't do that. The judge asked the state's attorney for the test results on the pipe, and the state's attorney told the judge the test results were not back yet. The judge put the case on the *stet docket*, which meant it was set aside and would be dismissed if Chong stayed out of trouble for a year.

Then Jon died and there were all those rumors about things Meyers was supposed to have done to other people and about how Meyers was the only enemy of Jon's that anybody knew anything about who might have done such a thing. An officer from the Internal Affairs Division of the police department started calling Chong and asking him to come in for an interview. Internal Affairs, it seemed, wanted to file a complaint against Meyers on Chong's behalf. Chong had already taken off several days from work at his family's combination convenience story and deli and he didn't want to have any more to do with the police department. He suspected that the police department was filing the complaint just so they could find Meyers innocent and clear the record. Chong had his problems with English, but he wasn't stupid. He had already been interviewed by the same officer in Internal Affairs after the motel incident and he had met with the state's attorney and he had appeared in court. Everyone official he had talked with still acted as if he had done something wrong and they had done him some sort of favor. He told the officer from Internal Affairs he'd already said all he had to say and if the police department wanted to do something about Meyers they already would have done it.

Sooner or later everything got back to Sandra. When she learned that Chong didn't want to talk with the police, she asked me to try to persuade him. I went by the his family's store a few times and he finally agreed to cooperate with the police. Internal Affairs must have found Meyers guilty of whatever it was he was charged with in Chong's behalf because there was police trail board hearing, which is an appeal process for officers who have been found guilty by Internal Affairs. Or, since Chong had some trouble with English and it was Chong who told me this, maybe there was a meeting at the police department for some other reason. Either way, Reverend Wright went with Chong to the meeting or police trial board or whatever it was. There were several police officers in the room. Chong told me the only thing he remembered for certain about it was that, when he told about being charged with a pipe that wasn't his and about his conversations with Meyers, the officers in the room laughed at him.

"They laughed at me," Chong said. "This is America, and they just laughed at me. 'You think I can forget that?"

During the summer Chong attended a party and met a girl I'll call Allison. Allison told Chong about a friend of hers, I'll call her Courtney, who was from Chicago. Courtney worked for a national weight-loss chain and was in Columbia on business the day Jon died. Courtney asked the motel clerk for a good jogging route, and, on the morning Jon's body was found, she jogged past the backstop. The way Chong had the story, Courtney jogged past the backstop at about daybreak, and she saw three men. Two were arguing and the third was leaning against the backstop. The two men who were arguing looked at her and she leaned down to pet a dog and continued on with her jogging. She went back to the motel and attended a meeting that morning. During lunch she saw Jon's picture on the television news and recognized him as the person she had seen leaning against the backstop. She called a friend in Chicago who was an attorney and the attorney told her not to get involved. He said Maryland was so far from Chicago that it could get messy for her, so she took a plane back to Chicago. Before leaving, she told her friend Allison what she had seen.

During the week-end after Thanksgiving, Chong called Sandra and told her about Allison and Courtney. Sandra asked why he had waited so long and he said the FBI had told him not to talk about it. He said he had decided to wait until Thanksgiving to give the FBI time to do something about Jon's death. If they hadn't taken care of it by then, Chong said, then he had made up his mind to tell Sandra.

Sandra asked me to try get the story straight from Chong, so I drove out one evening to meet with him. He repeated the story he had told Sandra and added that Courtney's friend, Allison, had moved to Baltimore to live with a friend. Chong didn't know the friend or how to locate her, but he remembered the directions to the apartment where Allison had lived until recently.

The next day, Sandra and I followed Chong's directions and found the apartment where Allison had lived. We got out of the car and walked up to the apartment to be certain of the address. Then we returned to the car and Sandra wrote the address on a scrap of paper.

"Now we give this to Jo to give to the FBI," I said. Sandra wanted to find out more about Allison and the friend Allison had moved in with. "What's the point?" I said. "The FBI probably doesn't even need this address. This Courtney in Chicago is the one who's supposed to have seen something. There can't be that many people named Courtney who work for that chain of stores in Chicago. Hell, I could find her with a phone book. Let the FBI handle it."

We drove off feeling very optimistic. We had a witness, or, at least, the hope of one, and an eyewitness at that, someone who could place Jon with other people at the backstop. The FBI would put two and two together and realize they weren't dealing with a suicide, and it would be over. This was, after all, the FBI we were talking about.

Sandra said, "I have a feeling that eventually we'll have to go the Chicago ourselves to find Courtney."

"Why would we do that?"

"I don't know," she said. "The thought just came into my head."

"That's crazy," I said. "You and me going to Chicago? That's nuts."

I was so excited about the possibility there was a witness that it didn't even occur to me that it was the FBI who had told Chong not to talk about Courtney, or that the FBI already had known about Courtney for over a month.

I can be so damned dense.

After the county elections, Scarsy, the new County Executive, immediately appointed a transition team to look into county needs and to recommend changes. A retired FBI agent would review the police department and the fire department. Officer Meyers' mother was appointed to look at local social services. A reporter called me and said he wanted to know how I felt about Meyers' mother being appointed. The reporter said it looked like some sort of political signal to him. All I knew about Meyers' mother was that Jane had told me she was a good person and had a reputation around town as an active volunteer in various worthwhile causes, so that was what I said. It was not the kind of statement that got in the papers, though, and it didn't.

About a week after the election, the police department charged three officers with what a newspaper article referred to as *procedural violations* in the motel incident. The officers were Meyers, Hamilton and Long. I don't know how Long got back into things, but he was named. The article named Meyers attorney, Steve Kent, as the source who had said the charges against the officers included the use of excessive force. Kent criticized Hickory for releasing the report of the Internal Affairs investigation to the public, and said Hickory was only trying to bolster his credibility in the community. A police spokesman said the report was released because every television station and newspaper in the area was asking. Hickory said the report was released at that particular time because the investigation had taken a long time and couldn't begin until the county grand jury, which had ended almost five months earlier, had finished its job. Regardless, the election was over and suddenly the police department was charging the officers. The charges would automatically be appealed to a panel of three police officers appointed by the Chief of Police. If the panel agreed with the Internal Affairs Division that the officers were guilty, the officers could be suspended, demoted, transferred, terminated, or charged a day's pay. Mickey was quoted in the article as saying that he was surprised; he mentioned that with witnesses, photographs, and a lie detector test, it had taken almost a year for the officers to be charged. Jo Glasco was quoted as saying it was too early to celebrate.

Article followed article for several days. Hickory was quoted as saying he was confident that the new County Executive would keep him on as Chief of Police.

A newspaper story three weeks before Christmas said a man was trying to get the courts to release Officer Meyers' personnel files. The man had been charged with assaulting Meyers and another officer during a traffic stop, and the man said he was the one who had been assaulted. The police department said Meyers' personnel files were confidential and couldn't be released. The judge would decide in about a month whether to release the files.

More articles on the subject followed. Boudreaux was quoted in one as saying the man was an informant for the police. Because of some previous problem with the law, the charges against him could put him in jail.

Jane was in the kitchen preparing dinner and I wandered in with the paper in my hand. I read aloud the part about the man being an informant.

"People around here really don't like to get complaints against the police," I said. "Either this guy cops a plea, or Boudreaux just wrote his death warrant. Can you imagine going to jail after the state's attorney just announced to the world that you're an informant?"

To make that long story short, the man eventually worked out a plea bargain, Meyers was found innocent again, and the man stayed out of jail.

I almost never go out for a morning paper. I woke up early one morning, though, so I went out for the paper. I had no intention of reading it, but I thought Jane might enjoy it with her coffee. It was December and cold and I let the car warm up a minute or so and then drove around the corner to a convenience store. When I returned Jane still wasn't up, so I slumped into a living room chair and started thumbing noncommittally through the pages.

The headline of an article on the third page of the second section of the Baltimore Sun read *At sentencing for theft, man alleges he sold drugs to two Howard officers.* I was awake. A twenty-three year old young man, Doug Iglesia, had been sentenced to six-and-a-half years for stealing a pair of sunglasses, some tennis shoes, and an undisclosed amount of money. The charge was for a burglary committed three years earlier and was the result of plea bargaining and dropping charges in three other burglaries. Over the years Iglesia had been arrested ten different times. After being found guilty on May 2 (which was two days before Jon died, although the article didn't put it that way), Iglesia had been ordered to attend a drug rehabilitation program pending sentencing. On May 21 (two-and-a-half weeks after Jon died), Iglesia walked away from the facility. A rash of burglaries followed in the county, the article said, and the police suspected Iglesia. Then the Howard County police tipped off the San Diego police that Iglesia was believed to be headed for San Diego. The San Diego police arrested Iglesia and were preparing to return him to Maryland. Iglesia told the San Diego police that he and Jon Bowie had sold drugs to two Howard County police officers.

Iglesia said that if he was returned, he would be killed just as his friend Jon Bowie had been. Iglesia was returned anyway. The article said that Chief Hickory had seen a videotape of Iglesia's statement and that Hickory had said that unless he got some other solid evidence he would give no credence to Iglesia's claim. Hickory wanted to interview Iglesia, but Iglesia's attorney had asked Hickory to wait until Iglesia's criminal case was over. After the sentencing, an attorney for the county said Iglesia was just making up the story about Jon to make things easier for himself. The judge had ignored Iglesia's claims.

Jane came downstairs and I followed her into the kitchen and pointed to the article.

"Look at this, "I said. "This guy says that he and Jon were involved with some police officers in some sort of drug thing. Hickory says he doesn't believe it, but it's clear from the article that Hickory hasn't even talked with this guy yet. I thought the police were supposed to draw conclusions *after* they investigated something."

During the week before Christmas, the newspapers carried one story after another that was in some way or another related to the Bowie case.

A police trial board had found Meyers innocent of the charge that Meyers had threatened a motorist to stay out of the county for a month or be charged with driving under the influence.

There was another article about Iglesia.

Another article said Eddie Vickers had been charged with filing a false report with the police department for saying he had been strangled at the same backstop where Jon was found. The charges said Eddie made up the story so he wouldn't have to testify in Mickey's trial. I knew Eddie had showed up in court that day after leaving the hospital. He even had been shown on the television news that night standing in front of the courthouse, waiting to testify. I guess people lose track of things.

Several months earlier, Eddie's mother, Katy, had told me Eddie had been subpoenaed to appear in court. The charge at that time had been that he had filed a false report for the same reason. Katy told me she called the courthouse to find out what was going on and she was told that the charges had been dropped. She went to the courthouse and asked to see the book where such charges are listed, she told me, and she said that the page for names that begin with the letter *V* had been torn out. Katy called Eddie's attorney. Eddie's attorney called Arthur Boudreaux and asked what was going on. I later confirmed with Eddie's attorney that this call to Boudreaux took place and that Boudreaux admitted during the call that the charge had been made and then dropped. During the call Boudreaux told Eddie's attorney, "But we'll get him on something." Now a few months had gone by and, obviously, the something that Boudreaux was getting Eddie on was the same charge that had been dropped earlier.

Another article said Chief Hickory had been fired. The new County Executive said there were personality differences. Hickory said the firing was political. I actually felt a little sad about Hickory being fired. He had to make a living the same as everybody else, and getting him fired wasn't what those of us who were close to the case were after. We just wanted to know what had happened to Jon.

There was a day before the project I was working on closed down when I was driving to work and worrying about what I had gotten myself into. I didn't like being seen as coming out against the police. I hated even considering the possibility that a police officer might actually have had something to do with Jon's death. I didn't like it, either, when kids I trusted told me they had been abused by police officers. I didn't like it when friends told me to watch my back. I didn't like it that the county seemed to be turning itself upside down with what I saw as unrelated issues while I still had no idea what had happened to Jon. All of these things were going through my mind, and, about halfway to the office, I came to a decision point. I consciously chose to follow this path wherever it led, trying to stay as objective as I could without getting swept up in some over-emotional kind of thing and without backing off, either, just because some people didn't like it even to be discussed. The exact words that I said out loud to myself as I came to this decision were, "In for a penny, in for a pound." Just to bolster my resolution, I struck the steering wheel with my palm as I said it and then I said it three or four more times. I was convincing myself I meant to stick with it.

Call it a weird coincidence if it makes you feel better, but pennies started showing up. I'd find them in the car, on the floor at the office, on the sidewalk. You name it.

I knew a man once who had a very responsible management position with a large telecommunications company. This man never would pass up a penny. It was something of a joke with his co-workers, and they'd sometimes leave a penny where he could find it just to watch his reaction. Once I even left one myself on the floor outside his office door. He was a hard working, intelligent fellow and I considered this penny business of his an odd quirk in his personality that did no particular harm. So I wasn't one hundred percent thrilled that something like this seemed to be happening to me. At first I just ignored it and wrote it off as coincidence, but there were so many coincidences to write off that I couldn't help but notice. For a long time I didn't mention it to anyone. I didn't mention it even to Jane, whom I'd usually tell anything.

I finally mentioned the pennies to Jane, who surprised me again and said they probably were some sort of message, a reassurance that I had assistance in what I was trying to accomplish. I also eventually mentioned them to Sandra, who said the same thing had been happening to her. She hadn't wanted to mention it for the same reasons I hadn't wanted to. She said Jon had always had a thing about pennies. He would sit in his bedroom when he wanted to think and flip pennies against the baseboard. He had a jar of them.

Our Christmas tree always looks like the aftermath of an explosion at a flea market. It has garlands and lights and a white felt star with gold sequins that Jane made and a piece of the Berlin wall and various angels and bells and candy canes and bent-and-creased crepe paper approximations of shapes our sons made in kindergarten. Each year we buy one ornament with the numbers for the year engraved or painted on it. After one particularly bad year, we bought the ugliest ornament we could find and hung it at the back of the tree where it couldn't be seen unless you wedged yourself between the tree and the wall and looked for it. The year the pennies started showing up, I bought a frame for a penny at a collectors' shop. I fastened a blue ribbon to the frame and tied the framed penny to the Christmas tree.

There still were times when the sadness of Jon's death pressed down on me with a weight so heavy I had to sit or find a wall to lean against, but something was changing. It didn't have to do only with the various stages of grief. Something else was going on. My whole attitude about things was starting to change. I didn't understand it, but I was pretty certain it had something to do with the pennies.

31   Scarsy's transition team wrote a final report and then Scarsy created two more committees. One was supposed to look into things at the police department. The other was supposed to review applications and recommend a new Chief of Police. Scarsy would appoint members to both committees, and neither committee interested me. Sandra thought I should apply for the committee looking into the police department and Alan Zindell should apply to the committee that would interview applicants for the Chief of Police. David Rogers and I were becoming friends, and Sandra thought David also should be on one of the committees. I sat once again at Sandra's kitchen table and said I wouldn't do it. If Rogers and Zindell wanted to do it, I said, then that was up to them. I said, "It's got nothing to do with what happened to Jon."

I did agree to attend a meeting with Scarsy, although I wasn't too happy about it. A friend I had worked with on a couple of occasions in the past had called and told me he needed a writer. I had started working with him at a company that was about an hour's drive from Columbia, and I had zero leave built up. I had to work out an under-the-table arrangement to work late to make up any time I took off during the day.

Jo Glasco and Sandra and Rogers and Zindell and I went. We sat around a dark wood conference table and Rogers and Zindell explained to Scarsy their concerns about how the police sometimes handled people and about the investigations into Jon's death.

Scarsy expressed concern and Rogers and Zindell and Jo expressed concern and everyone seemed to agree there was some reason for concern, but no one could seem to bring any particular issue into focus. I took a photograph of Mickey's face out of my sportcoat pocket and passed it down to Scarsy. Although the photograph had been taken after Mickey had showered and then slept for a day following the motel incident, his face was swollen and bruised and his chin was cut. Scarsy looked at it and I said, "That is unacceptable." He studied the photo with a serious expression on his face and then passed it back without comment.

Zindell was appointed to the committee to screen applicants for the Chief of Police, and Rogers and I wound up on the one that would look into the police department.

I once asked Richard Kinlein if he knew at least one county police officer I could trust unequivocally. I'll say the name Kinlein gave me, without hesitation, was Gus Ingersoll. I didn't know Ingersoll, or many other county officers for that matter, but I took note of the name.

The committee that was screening applicants for a new Chief of Police met every week to go over applications and interview candidates. There were several articles in the paper about one candidate or another. I spoke regularly on the phone with Zindell, who was on the committee, about various candidates and issues. When the selection process was just underway, I got word from a fairly high-level person in county government, a person I don't care to name, that Ingersoll should not be considered. I asked for specifics and couldn't extract any. I passed this on to Zindell and asked him to ask Ingersoll pointed questions so Zindell could get a good sense of the man. When the committee had interviewed Ingersoll, Zindell called and said Ingersoll had impressed him immensely. "He's a tough and compassionate man," Zindell said. "He almost had me in tears, and you know how likely that is for me. I asked him if there was anything about his police career that he would change. He told a story about how he once shot and killed a man who had taken a hostage. He actually got tears in his eyes when he talked about it, and I almost did myself just hearing him tell it."

The time came for the committee to make a recommendation and Zindell called again. "It looks like Ingersoll's got the inside track. I could de-rail it if I tried. The people on the committee are looking to me because of the Bowie thing. Call this person you told me about and see what you can learn."

I did. Let's say it was a man. I told him, "Give me some specifics. I can't go after somebody without a reason." I hung up and continued sitting at the kitchen table, more or less lost in thought. Jane came in the room and I vented my frustrations at her. "Who the hell do people think I am," I said, "that I should have some say in who becomes the Chief of Police? What do I know about what it takes to be a good Chief of Police? If it was up to me Hickory would still have the job. I just want to know what happened to Jon and all this other stuff keeps coming up." Jane kissed me on the forehead and went upstairs.

I was still sitting in the kitchen about a half hour later when the man called back. "That's all you get," he said. "My sources won't provide details. They just tell me not to trust Ingersoll."

I thanked him and hung up. Then I called Zindell back. "If you think Ingersoll would make a good Chief, then vote for him."

Ingersoll's appointment was announced in the papers a few days later.

The committee Rogers and I were on was called the Citizens Advisory something or other. I just referred to it as the Whitewash Committee. It took a few weeks for the committee to get off the ground because so many people volunteered to be on it. Scarsy upped the number of members and eventually appointed twenty-six. The first meeting was held around several large, folding tables pushed together in the center of a conference room in a county office building. To start the meeting, we went around the table introducing ourselves. There were a half dozen present or retired law enforcement officers of one sort or another, a handful of attorneys in private practice, and Calvin Delight, the assistant state's attorney who had been in the grand jury room assisting Boudreaux in the grand jury investigation of the Bowie case. There also were some teachers and preachers and social workers and a couple of high school students, but not enough. It was well known behind the scenes that Jo Glasco soon would be filing a civil rights lawsuit in Mickey's behalf against the county and the police department. An attorney I'll call Thelma Tasselton, who was from the Office of Law and would be defending the county in Mickey's civil suit, was there. I could see right off I was going to have to spend a lot of time trying to keep my mouth shut. I wasn't about to spill my guts to a group half made up of people who had charged Mickey with various things, who had conducted the investigation of Jon's death, who had steamrolled the grand jury investigation, or who would be defending the county against Mickey's lawsuit. I would have felt more comfortable videotaping a Klan rally.

The committee chair person, a past County Executive himself, handed out instructions for setting up seven subcommittees. There was a subcommittee on computers and one on training and another on community relations and so on and so on. There was a subcommittee on the policy on use of force, and I got myself placed on that one, so that particular committee consisted of three past or present law enforcement officers and me. Call me a pessimist. I knew divide and conquer when I saw it, but this splitting up of the committee into subcommittees to study everything except what the public wanted to know was more like quarter and dress. I silently vowed to attend all the meetings for whatever good might come of it, and because my presence would help keep the story of Jon's death in the public eye, but I didn't expect anything significant to come of the meetings. Rogers got himself placed on the training subcommittee, which at least he was qualified for.

The chair person asked if anyone had anything to say and a retired military police officer, who just happened to live across the street from Scarsy, looked across the table at me and said without once looking away, "If anyone on this committee tries to say anything bad about the police, he'll have to answer to me."

I don't intend to spend a lot of time going into the things we did on the Whitewash Committee. All I can associate it with is a fellow I knew once who could sleep sitting up with his eyes open. We had meetings every Wednesday and wrote reports and brought in speakers and talked to reporters who wrote articles about whether it was a good thing or a bad thing. The new Chief of Police attended most meetings to observe, in uniform. He was a heavy-set, athletic man with a firm and likeable manner. He didn't strike me as the sort to intentionally intimidate people. I took it as genuine interest on his part that led him to attend the meetings. Just the same, his presence in uniform was intimidating. Even those members who didn't work for him clearly wanted to be liked by him and spoke carefully around him, apologizing profusely in advance for any upcoming remark that might be taken as even mildly critical.

A reporter asked me after a meeting for my opinion of the committee. I said the whole process could be shortened considerably if we would just get ourselves some little short skirts and pom poms, meet in the center of town and lead the whole goddamned county in a cheer. It wasn't a concise enough statement for a good sound byte, but the reporter shortened it some and more or less quoted me.

32 At about two o'clock one morning, Jim's and Sandra's little curly black terrier, Henry, came yipping into the bedroom tugging at the bed covers with his teeth and running back and forth between the door and the foot of the bed. Sandra couldn't quiet him and she finally got up and pulled on a housecoat and followed him downstairs into the living room. When she was a few steps from the sliding glass door that led onto their rear patio, she heard a dog let out a sharp yelp. Venetian blinds covered the sliding door, and, in a unified motion, Sandra flipped on the patio light with one hand and, with the other hand, she raised a few rows of blinds.

The man in her back yard had climbed halfway over the eight-foot-high privacy fence and his chest was pressed down on top of the fence. He struck Sandra as being tall and maybe in his thirties. He either was white or he was a very light-skinned black man. Sandra couldn't be sure. She froze in place and, for a moment, he also remained frozen, looking at the door. Then he pushed himself backward off the fence and dropped out of sight onto the ground. Sandra heard one person behind the fence shout something in a coarse whisper. Then she heard what sounded like the running, shuffling steps of at least two people hurrying away behind the row of townhouses.

Jim came downstairs. He went out back with a flashlight and inspected the fence. He came back inside and Sandra said she wanted all the windows screwed shut and she wanted safety bars put on the sliding glass door. He promised to take care of it. They finally went back upstairs to the bedroom. Sandra couldn't sleep and she sat on the edge of the bed and stared out the bedroom window onto the parking lot.

The morning paper carrier parked his economy-sized pickup truck on the street and got out. Eddie Vickers' Doberman, Max, snarled at the paper carrier and cornered him against the front of a townhouse across the street. It still was in the wee hours of the morning and the paper carrier screamed out for someone to come get the dog. Eddie came running barefoot out of his front door into the parking lot. Eddie shouted something like, "What have you done to my dog?" and the paper carrier shouted something like, "I didn't touch him. Just get him away from me."

Eddie grabbed up Max in his arms and hurried back inside as blood streamed from the dog's neck down the front of Eddie's clothes. Soon afterward Eddie came back outside carrying Max. Eddie shoved the dog onto the front seat of his car and left.

I stopped by Jim's and Sandra's the next evening on the way to a meeting of the Whitewash Committee. There were large splashes of blood on the sidewalk and on the street in front of their house. Eddie's car was parked in front of his house, and the dashboard looked as if someone had slaughtered a pig on it. Jim and Sandra came outside and walked with me around the row of townhouses to the back of their house. The blood splattering began behind their house and continued around the end of the row of townhouses and on around to the front. Sandra explained what had happened the night before. She said Eddie had taken Max to a vet, which explained the blood in the car.

"Max's throat was cut," Sandra said. "It's a wonder he didn't bleed to death."

It seemed apparent that Max had encountered someone trying to break into Jim's and Sandra's house and the person had cut the dog. That was the reason for the yelp Sandra heard just before she lifted the slats to the blinds and saw someone climbing over the privacy fence. Eddie came out of the house and saw the paper carrier and saw Max covered with blood and Eddie thought the paper carrier had cut Max.

We went into the kitchen and I asked Sandra, "Did you call the police?"

"They won't do anything," she said. "What can they do?"

"Still, I think you should call them. With everything else that's going on, it needs to be on the record that somebody tried to break into your house in the middle of the night when they had to know you were likely to be home."

Sandra said she would think about it. I went to the meeting and when it was over I stopped again at Jim's and Sandra's. A police car was sitting in the front of the house. Sandra answered the door and I followed her into the kitchen. Two uniformed officers, a woman and a man, were asking Sandra about the man she had seen behind her house. The woman, a tall, athletic and slender brunette, sat at the kitchen table with Sandra. This female officer did most of the questioning. The man, a stumpy, grey-haired man with sergeant's stripes, mostly listened. I got the impression he was some sort of supervisor. I assumed the police department wasn't going to send an officer alone to Sandra's. If I had been with the police department, I wouldn't have.

The female officer seemed very thorough in her questioning. I stood by the kitchen counter listening and reminding myself not to interfere. There didn't seem to be any reason to get involved until Sandra asked the stumpy sergeant what he thought had happened.

"I think it's obvious," the sergeant said, "that somebody was trying to get into Eddie Vickers' house and you surprised him."

So much for not interfering. I said, "What? Sandra sees a man on the far side of her privacy fence, about as far away from Eddie's house as you can get and still be in Sandra's back yard, and you think he was after Eddie?"

The sergeant's face got red and I immediately regretted that I hadn't taken a beat first to find a more civil way to say it. I wouldn't have said anything else but the sergeant asked in a puffed up, arrogant way, "What do you think I should do?" That's a question I hate to hear from professionals, and, once again, my tongue started moving before my brain engaged. I said, "I think I'd go around back and look around before I made up my mind that Ms. Keyser here surprised someone climbing over the wrong fence to get to the house next door."

The sergeant and the female officer actually did leave to go around back, and the sergeant was muttering as they went out the front door. I stomped back and forth in Sandra's kitchen saying something about how the woman seemed pretty sharp but the sergeant had the IQ of a creek pebble.

Sandra said, "They already looked around back before you got here. I think they only went back again because you said to do it. I think they're a little nervous about being here."

"Great," I said. "Now I've got two more friends in the police department."

The next day a neighbor, Patti, spoke with Sandra on the sidewalk between their townhouses. Patti was an excitable, quick-talking brunette in her middle to late thirties. Sandra told Patti about the attempted break-in, and Patti said she had something to tell Sandra. Patti had seen a man driving slowly in front of Sandra's house on the afternoon before the attempted break-in. The man was in a grey, squared-off car that looked like a Buick or a Monte Carlo or maybe even a Grenada. Patti wasn't good at identifying cars. The driver was white, dark-haired and tall. He turned onto Patti's and Sandra's street, drove to the evergreens at the end, and turned around. Patti was in the living room doing her ironing and she watched through the window as the man drove slowly back up the street and stopped in front of Sandra's door. He sat looking at Sandra's front door for a few seconds, raised an arm to look at his watch, and then pulled slowly away.

I stopped by Sandra's that afternoon and Sandra asked me to talk with Patti. I walked up the street and knocked on Patti's door and she came outside onto the sidewalk. Patti was a person who used her hands when she talked, and, when she told the part about the man raising his arm to check his watch, she mimicked the motion.

"So he was left-handed?" I asked. Patti gave me a confused look and I said, "You raised your right arm. Is that what he did?" She thought about it and raised her hand a few more times, looking into her mind as she did.

"It was this hand," she said.

"I've never really thought about it," I said, "but I would think a left-handed person would wear his watch on his right arm."

Patti called the police and, a day or two later, two investigators visited her. She told the investigators she was pretty certain she could identify the driver. They took her to the police department so she could give a description to a police artist. As the investigators led her into the police department, she saw the man she had come to describe. He was sitting at the front desk in a police officer's uniform. She panicked and gave the artist a slightly varied picture. She had the artist draw the nose a little too large and she threw in a few other such variations.

Patti's husband, John, was the man who had been a police officer in Michigan and who had told the police he heard rattling and banging sounds coming from the area of the backstop the night Jon died. Patti went home from the police station and told John she had seen the man at the police department. John suggested that she ask the investigators to visit them again at their home.

Two investigators came, a black man and a white man, and Patti told them she had become frightened and the picture was not accurate.

"You don't need a picture," she said. "The man I saw was sitting at the front desk when we went into the police department."

The black investigator said, "You mean Roland Meyers."

"I don't know," Patti said. "All I know is that the man sitting at the front desk was the man I saw in front of Sandra's house."

The two investigators agreed it was Meyers Patti had identified. The investigators taped their conversation with Patti and, at John's insistence, Patti made her own tape of the conversation.

I sat with Patti and John at their lace-covered kitchen table and listened to the tape. When it was over, John said, "Meyers was on duty that day. I checked. There would have been just enough time for him to come here straight from the police station after work."

The police circulated a flier with the picture the police artist drew based on Patti's original description. Photocopied illustrations of several mid-seventies cars were included on the flier. There was a request for anyone who recognized the man to come forward. It was a pretty typical police drawing, and anyone who thought he recognized the person should have taken aspirin and gone straight to bed.

Internal Affairs investigators interviewed Patti again and asked her not to discuss their investigation until it was completed. A few weeks went by and the investigators told Patti it was possible Meyers had been the man she saw, but there was nothing that could be done about it. Sandra lived on a public street, the investigators told Patti, and Meyers had a legal right to drive there. It's a free country.

I was sitting in Sandra's kitchen one Saturday morning when a woman named Mary knocked on Sandra's front door. I would have put her in her late thirties, but I would learn in time that she was in her middle forties, closer to my own age. She was black and had neatly cut short hair and smooth, light skin with a touch of olive in it. She was attired with the precision and taste of a professional person with a good eye for color. Sandra answered the door and Mary said to Sandra before even introducing herself, "You don't know how long I've been looking for you."

I stayed long enough to learn that Mary lived in a county south of Columbia just outside of Washington. She had a son named Keith whose body had been found hanging from a tree several years earlier, when he was sixteen. The body was found one morning in a wooded area near Mary's home. A long rope had been strung up through the limbs of the tree, across to another tree, and down the trunk of the other tree, where it was tied near the ground. Keith's body was hanging so low to the ground he was in an almost seated position. His feet and legs were stretched straight out in front of him, and his buttocks almost touched the ground. He was not wearing the clothes he had been wearing when he left home to visit friends that night. The clothes he was wearing were too large for him.

Police in Mary's county immediately concluded that Mary's son had committed suicide. Mary went into shock when she was told of her son's death, and she was given repeated doses of sedatives. Only after her son's funeral did she begin to piece things together. By the time she learned that there had been no autopsy, her son had been buried.

Mary was from a small community in North Carolina that was about as far north of Durham as the small community I grew up in was south of the same town. She and I knew some of the same people.

Sandra and Mary had an immediate basis for a relationship and began comparing notes across the table with great energy. It was a therapeutic conversation for both of them, and, as soon as I thought I had heard the core of Mary's story, I excused myself and left them together.

I drove home puzzling over two coincidences. The first was that a woman from my hometown had showed up on Sandra's doorstep with a story similar to Sandra's. The second had to do with an acquaintance of Jon's. As Mary told her story, this young man's name came up for one reason or another. Mary was certain this acquaintance had been dating a friend of Mary's daughter at the time Mary's son died.

33 February would have been difficult enough even if Amanda Garvey hadn't turned up again.

When Sandra had told Jim about someone coming into the house on the morning Jon was found, Jim had replaced the front door lock. After the break-in attempt, Jim put special locks on all the doors and windows. He put a safety bar on the rear sliding door in the living room and drilled a hole in the wall and stuck a nail in it so the door couldn't be opened without first removing the nail.

My friend from the large family in New Jersey, the friend who had devised a contingency escape plan for Mickey, told me a security trick Sandra could use. With string, you tied an empty coffee can to a doorknob or a window latch, and, in the can, you put a large handful of pennies. If anyone tried to open the door or window, the string toppled the can with a racket equivalent to dropping a tray of spoons on a library floor. Jim put a lock on the privacy fence gate and Sandra rigged a string of cans and maybe a few rakes and shovels and hoes and garbage can lids so it would all come crashing down if anyone tried to get through the gate. Anne Beck's husband, Richard, set up a security alarm and ran thread around the gate lock so the alarm would go off if anyone tried to open the gate. The day after Sandra rigged the cans and Richard set up the alarm, at two o'clock in the morning, something or someone triggered the trap and the alarm when off and the cans and such came crashing down. There was such a racket that, the next day, the neighbors complained.

Sandra bought a pistol, a twenty-two caliber Saturday night special. She said she was from West Virginia and she knew how to handle guns. Jim hid the pistol a few times but she kept finding it and scolding him and he finally resigned himself to maybe getting struck by a ricochet in his sleep. To anyone who phoned, Sandra made a point of talking about the pistol on the phone in case anyone was listening. On the phone, she said what she had bought was an Uzi and she imagined it would make a good sized hole in the front door from the other end of the hall. She didn't know what an Uzi was, but it sounded like a frightening thing so she said it.

From time to time there was one reason or another for police officers to stop by and ask questions, and two police cars showed up one day in front of the house and the officers got out. Sandra watched and listened through the kitchen window as they argued about who would knock on the front door. "I'm not knocking on that door," one said. "That woman is crazy." They got back in their cars and left.

It still was dark when Sandra left for work each morning, and the short walk to her car terrified her. When she finally confessed her fear to Jim, he started walking her the short distance to her car each morning, and he watched until she drove away. Then Jim's work schedule changed and he had to leave for work before Sandra left. I started driving over and sitting in my car in the parking lot in front of the house so there would be someone to watch as she got in her car. She was afraid someone might follow her on her way to work, so I started following her to work to see if any suspicious vehicles showed up. She sped up unexpectedly so often, and made so many sudden turns onto so many different routes, I finally persuaded her that, even if someone tried to follow her, they couldn't do it. I couldn't. Still, she worried that someone might wait for her in the parking lot at the daycare center, so I kept showing up to watch her get into her car, follow her to work, and watch her get out and go into the building.

Several of Jon's and Mickey's friends, and Jim, and John Hollywood and I and anyone else we could drag into the group started watching the house on a regular basis from around nine in the evening until sun up. The nights were freezing cold and we rotated three shifts a night, sitting in strategically located cars. We wore two and three sets of heavy clothing and brought blankets and sleeping bags and hot coffee. Sometimes it was so cold we had to crank the engines to warm the cars for a few minutes, which pretty well announced our presence, but it was that cold. I wasn't aware that anyone involved talked about these nightly watches, but someone must have; a reporter asked me after a meeting of the Whitewash Committee if I and others were watching the house. Since the objective was to keep anyone out of the house who didn't belong there, I confessed that we were. Then, toward the end of February, Amanda showed up.

It would take a lot to convince me that Amanda Garvey was acting on her own.

Until February, I didn't know a lot about Amanda. I knew she went to the same church as Sandra, that she had told Sandra the church choir would sing at the July 4 vigil and, when the choir didn't show up, she had led the gathering in a prayer. Later that same night, the night Eddie Vickers said he was strangled at the backstop, Amanda showed up on Sandra's doorstep saying she had seen a tall man and a smaller man grab somebody at the backstop. During the grand jury recess, Amanda told Sandra a tall man had followed her in a police car and, later the same day, she got a threatening phone call from someone she was sure was the same person; then she disappeared and I called Mama to try to get her to surface so I could get a statement from her. She did, and I took the statement.

One day Sandra was in the waiting room of Jo Glasco's office and Sandra overheard Jo mention to her secretary the name of the FBI agent in charge of investigating Jon's death. It was a man I'll call Arthur Bellinger. Sandra acted as if she hadn't heard anything and, when Jo had gone back into her office and closed the door, Sandra took an envelope and pencil from her purse and wrote down the name. On several occasions after that, Sandra and Amanda Garvey and the Reverend Billy Bob whatever met in some private office at the church and prayed for this Arthur Bellinger. Until February, that was about all I knew about Amanda Garvey.

Sandra answered a knock one afternoon and there was Amanda, again, on the doorstep. Amanda was holding two brown grocery sacks filled with clothes and Sunday School teacher's guides.

"Meyers is threatening me," Amanda told Sandra. "I'm afraid to go home."

Sandra took Amanda in. Meyers, Amanda told Sandra, had been calling her regularly, threatening to do terrible sexual things if Amanda testified about seeing two men at the backstop on the night Eddie Vickers said he had been strangled. Amanda said she had been contacted by the FBI, and she had told them her story. The FBI knew, Amanda said, that she was coming to live with Sandra. The FBI, in fact, encouraged it, Amanda said. At the time, neither Sandra nor anyone in her family had been contacted by the FBI. Sandra didn't know if she was supposed to know the FBI was investigating.

To have this link with the invisible investigation show up on her doorstep left her ecstatic.

Sandra made up the sleeper sofa in the basement and offered Amanda the run of the house. At night, Amanda and Sandra sat up late talking about Jon's death, about the motel incident, and about what Amanda said were her almost daily visits to the FBI offices. Amanda stayed with Sandra and her family until well into spring, and her behavior was, to put it mildly, suspicious.

Amanda told both Sandra and me that the FBI wanted Sandra to get rid of all of the cans and other noise-making contraptions put up to impede any intruder. "If Meyers finds out I'm here and he comes after me," Amanda said, "the FBI might have to come rushing into your house in the middle of the night. They don't want to be stumbling over a bunch of cans." Amanda told Sandra, "The FBI also wants Dave Parrish and his friends to stop watching the house. The FBI says that they're amateurs, and they could complicate things."

Amanda said the FBI had people all over the neighborhood. She said she wasn't really supposed to tell, but the FBI had agents staked out in a townhouse that was for sale across the street, and in a rental unit that overlooked Jim's and Sandra's back yard. She said FBI agents patrolled the area in two Columbia Cabs and a red maintenance truck.

Amanda arranged a meeting, supposedly at the FBI's request, with many of the kids who had been present at the Red Roof Inn in January. Amanda pumped the kids for details about the motel incident. Who sat where? Who saw what? Who had actually seen Jon and Mickey being hit?

It was Jim who first mentioned that Amanda never seemed tired. Jim told Sandra, "I think she's sleeping all day and keeping us up all night. And if the FBI wants to know something, why don't they just come ask us? What's all the secrecy about?"

Amanda told Sandra the FBI wanted to set up something like a sting operation. The FBI wanted Amanda and Mickey to start taking walks at the same time every evening at the field around the backstop. The theory was that there were people who were watching the house and who wanted to get to Mickey, but they couldn't do it because there always were so many people around. If Mickey and Amanda started taking a walk each evening, say, down to the field past the backstop and back, word would get out. These people who wanted to get to Mickey would know and might go after Mickey during one of these walks. The FBI, Amanda said, would be watching from various vantage points on and around the school. If anyone tried anything, agents would move in quickly to prevent any harm and to apprehend whoever was trying to do whatever it was the FBI thought might get tried.

Sandra went for it because Amanda said it was what the FBI wanted. Jim and I went for it because Sandra wanted to do it. Mickey said, "That's nuts. I'm not going to parade around down there at night like some sort of target. If the FBI wants me to do that, then let them come ask me themselves and I'll consider it."

Amanda became upset that Mickey wouldn't cooperate. She told him the FBI couldn't be publicly associated with Sandra and her family for political reasons, and that it was Meyers the FBI was after. Mickey said, "No way. It's crazy."

The first evening walk took place in early March. Mike Keyser, Jim's youngest son by his first marriage, stood in for Mickey. Mike had played on one of my baseball teams when he was sixteen or so. What I recalled most about him was that he would try anything. Every evening for close to two weeks Mike pulled on a baseball cap and a red and white sweatsuit that belonged to Mickey and walked down to the ballfield with Amanda. He carried a loaded twenty-two pistol in a sweatsuit pocket and Amanda told him the FBI said he couldn't do that. Mike said, "Like hell I can't. If you want me, you get the gun."

Amanda reported the regular appearances of a gold Toyota and a brown pickup truck. She said the FBI had told her to watch for them. The FBI, she said, ran the license plates for these vehicles and confirmed that it was Meyers and his buddies. Mike said he didn't see the vehicles, and he didn't see the FBI agents Amanda said she saw stationed on top of the school and in cars and behinds trees in various locations. Amanda said Mike wasn't very observant.

The walks were into their second week when Mickey came into the kitchen one evening wearing the sweatsuit and cap Mike had been wearing. Mike followed him into the room and held out the pistol.

"Nah," Mickey said. "I might shoot myself. I just hope the hell Meyers or whoever's down there does come after me."

When Mickey and Amanda had returned and the rest of us had gone home, and Mickey and Sandra were alone in the kitchen, Mickey said, "Mom, she's crazy. There's nobody down there." Mickey said he looked everywhere. Amanda kept pointing here and there and saying, "See? See?" and Mickey said he looked and there was nothing to see. He said, "Mom, she's making it all up."

Sandra decided that Amanda had to go. Sandra told me that Amanda had started tearing her down. It had been in the papers that Jo Glasco had filed a lawsuit on Mickey's behalf against the county for a million and a few dollars and Amanda said Sandra was just after the money. Amanda said any money that came from the suit was devil money and should be donated to Amanda's church.

When Sandra confronted Amanda about what Mickey had said, Amanda insisted that the FBI had requested the trips to the field. Amanda said Sandra didn't appreciate what Amanda was trying to do, and the trips would have worked if they had just kept at it. Amanda said the FBI was very angry with Sandra but they would think of something else to do to get Meyers because they were convinced Meyers had something to do with Jon's death and it was their job to prove it.

Amanda had told Sandra on several occasions that the FBI had Amanda's condo phone tapped and Meyers kept calling and leaving threatening messages on Amanda's answering machine, saying he was going to kill her. When Sandra told me this, I said, "That would make Meyers the stupidest person who ever put on a uniform." Amanda stuck with her stories, though. She said she stopped by her condo one evening to check her mail or something and there was a box of prophylactics on her porch. There was a phone message and Meyers was laughing and saying he was going to rape her before he killed her.

One evening Sandra had started telling Amanda that she had to find another place to stay when the conversation was interrupted. Either Amanda called her sister or her sister called Amanda. I forget. Amanda's sister supposedly had stopped by Amanda's condo to check the mail and, while she was there, she had answered the phone. Amanda had told her sister not to answer the phone, that the FBI wanted to get copies of any threatening messages left on the answering machine, but Amanda's sister had forgotten and had answered it. It was Meyers, Amanda told Sandra, and he thought Amanda's sister was Amanda and he said he was nearby and was going to kill her. Amanda had told her sister on the phone that the FBI was listening and would be there before Meyers could get there. Then Amanda left and Sandra phoned me and she kept saying, "They're going to arrest Meyers. They're going to arrest Meyers." Sandra said that as Amanda rushed off police cars started taking off all over Sandra's neighborhood. "There were tires squealing and sirens all over the neighborhood," Sandra said, and she was practically screaming.

Meyers didn't get arrested. Amanda returned to Sandra's later that night saying that when she got to her townhouse the FBI already was there and the place had been ransacked. Her sister had been too frightened to stay, and whoever had ransacked her house had already come and gone. The FBI couldn't arrest Meyers because they hadn't actually seen him do anything. They hadn't been taping her tapped line at that particular time, so they had no evidence. If only her sister hadn't answered the phone, Amanda told Sandra, it all would have been on tape.

Sandra kicked Amanda out. I never did figure out what the Amanda part of Sandra's ordeal was about, but a lot of little things led me to conclude that Amanda was not acting on her own. One of these little things was a roll of undeveloped film the kids had taken at the motel. Sandra had asked me to hold onto the film and I had stored it in some place I thought I would remember and then I had forgotten where I put it. Amanda kept after me to find the film so she could give it to the FBI. I finally found and gave it to her and she told me she gave it to the FBI. I kept asking myself later, after Sandra kicked Amanda out, even if Amanda was starved for attention or emotionally off-kilter or any of those kinds of things, why did she want the film?

34 Jane called me at work and said an FBI agent had called and wanted me to call him back. I was immediately nervous. I'd never knowingly spoken to an FBI agent and images of Elliott Ness and J. Edgar Hoover came rising up to make my heart beat a little faster than I could control. I called the number Jane gave me and the man who had spoken with Jane said he had a subpoena for me. I was being subpoenaed to appear before a federal grand jury that was meeting to consider the Bowie case. The man said he lived in Howard County and could drop off the subpoena after work. I said he didn't have to make deliveries on my account after work. If a grand jury wanted to talk to me, then he could tell me when and where and I'd be there. He insisted, so I told him the earliest I could get home would be six.

As I turned onto the side street where I lived, I saw the plain black Ford parked in front of the house and my heart started beating fast again. I went in and he was sitting at the table in the dining area of our combination living room and dining room. Jane had made coffee for him. He stood to greet me, and he had a combination of firmness and weary warmth about him that was appealing. He wore a navy blazer and grey slacks and a drab tie. I put him in his middle fifties by the streaks of grey in his otherwise dark hair. He looked like a person who was easy to talk to, like a neighbor you didn't visit often but whose mower you could borrow in a pinch. I was more relieved than disappointed to see that the fantasies born of my hero worship had dissolved into a real and normal person.

I sat across the dining room table from him and he explained the details of the subpoena, giving particular attention to my right to be reimbursed for travel and meals. I downplayed that part of it, saying it wasn't important to me since Baltimore was so nearby. That seemed to make him even more intent, and he insisted I had a right to the expense reimbursement and should apply for it.

He didn't seem to be directly involved in the investigation, and when he asked me a few details about the case I sensed it was more out of courtesy and curiosity than investigative need. I told him what I knew and could tell in brief, summary fashion, and I told him how I knew Jon. He started gathering papers into his briefcase and I stood and waited. He stood and hesitated by his chair. I thought he was going to make some courteous parting remark, but, instead, with slow intensity, he said, "I hope you get these Howard County bastards. They beat up my son, too, and there was nothing I could do about it."

He gave me a long handshake, and his face muscles twitched slightly with what I took for anger that he usually controlled better than he was doing it at the moment. I saw him to the door and shook his hand again and wished him well. I closed the door behind him and stood looking down at the floor with my hand still pressed against the door. I wondered what I could possibly accomplish that the FBI couldn't.

One benefit that came out of the Whitewash Committee was that I got to know Reverend Dave Rogers better. He and I sometimes stopped off for a beer after a meeting. After we'd started getting more comfortable with each other, which took a surprisingly short time, we'd stop off at his house or mine and save a couple of bucks on the beer. Preachers make a little more than technical writers, but not a lot more. The things we talked about pretty well fill this book so far or I'll get to them.

Aside from the fact that Rogers was pretty huge and I wasn't, and he was a preacher and I'd usually go out of my way not to be in the same room with one, there was another major difference between Rogers and me. He was more direct than I was. If I went bear hunting with a shotgun, I'd probably apologize to the bear first and then go on about the necessity for the food and maybe thank the bear for the contribution he was making to my survival until the bear finally jerked the gun away from me and shot himself. Rogers would just shoot the bear. If the bear growled at him first, he'd probably slap the bear around some and then shoot it.

Rogers also had been subpoenaed by the FBI, and after a few weeks he got a call to go to their local office. He went down and told them about the anonymous call and about getting forced out of the police department and, no doubt, about anything else that came into his mind. A few more weeks went by and I still hadn't heard anything more from the FBI. I mentioned this to Rogers one night as we were standing outside a county office building after a meeting of the Whitewash Committee. Rogers said, "I'll take care of it." I told him I didn't want that. I wasn't out to alienate the FBI. I just wondered why I hadn't heard from them. "So pick up the phone and find out," he said. I said, "Nah," and he grinned in the way he had of leaning forward and doing it with his eyes and his mouth at the same time and said, "Then I'll do it."

Rogers called me a few days later at work and said he'd spoken with this Bellinger fellow. "I told him he needs to talk to you. He said he'd asked around about you, and anything you had to say was only hearsay."

"I know that," I said. "I just want to make sure he's heard it all." I ran a few things off the top of my head that I thought Bellinger should know, and, to my surprise, I hadn't yet mentioned some of them to Rogers.

"I'll call him back and tell him again," Rogers said.

"I don't want to piss him off."

"Well, that's the difference between you and me," Rogers said. "If doing his job pisses him off, it's not my problem." He hung up.

When Bellinger called me at work a few days later it made me a little nervous, but I wasn't surprised. Bellinger had a mild, courteous voice and there was nothing in it to make a person nervous. It was that awe thing I had about the FBI. Bellinger didn't go into why he hadn't called before. He just asked if a certain date was all right and I said something like since he was with the FBI I supposed any date he wanted was all right.

"You need to understand, Mr. Parrish," he said, "that the only thing the FBI is investigating is whether any law enforcement officer was involved in Jon Bowie's death. We're not investigating the motel incident, and we're not investigating whether anyone other than a police officer might have been involved in Jon Bowie's death. If we learn anything that implicates anyone other than a law enforcement officer, we'll turn the information over to the local police."

"I understand," I said. It was, in fact, something I had not understood until that moment, but he had said it and I didn't mention my disappointment.

The place where I worked had about a thousand employees and put telecommunications satellites in space, among other things. It was a pretty sophisticated place, technically. Later that day, after I spoke with Bellinger, a repairman came into my office to check the phone. The repairman probably had at least a drawer-full of degrees, and he was responsible for a basement room filled with telephone switches and wires.

"There's something funny with your phone," he said. He tinkered with the phone and left. About an hour later he called to say he couldn't figure it out, but he had switched some things around and the problem had gone away.

Sandra had been getting strange noises on her phone. She had a friend, a state trooper whom I won't name, who gave her a phone number that was supposed to be known only to telephone repairmen. If Sandra called the number, the trooper said, and a recorded voice stated her phone number back to her, then her phone was not tapped. If she got a busy signal instead, there was a good chance it was. Sandra tried the number every few days. Sometimes she got a busy signal and sometimes she didn't.

I had tried the number a few times myself on my home phone, and I always got a recorded message telling me my phone number. I told Sandra that since she got a busy signal so often, maybe there was some technical explanation and her phone was not tapped. The day after Bellinger called, I tried the number on my home phone again and, for the first time, I got a busy signal. After that, sometimes I got a busy signal and sometimes I didn't.

I took off work on the afternoon of my appointment with the FBI. The address was in a light industrial area on the outskirts of Baltimore and only a few miles north of Columbia. I was nervous, so I arrived early and found the place. Then I went to a fast food hamburger place and went in the men's room to make sure my hair was combed and such. I sat in the car in the parking lot of the hamburger place smoking cigarettes and squeezing the palm of my right hand into a fist so my hand would be warm when it was time for shaking hands.

The FBI office building looked like a large, pebble-sided warehouse. It didn't have windows and it sat on a graveled parking lot. I parked and walked across the lot and, with my fist in my pants pocket so it wouldn't be observed, I gave my palm one last opportunity for warmth. Amanda Garvey's white Mercury Cougar was sitting in the FBI parking lot. Amanda's license plate had a memorable letter combination and I was certain it was her car. I took note of it and walked past it without making a show of having seen it.

A small sign by the front door instructed me to press a buzzer, so I did. A woman's voice asked for my name and the lock clicked and I went inside. A polite woman behind a glass wall took my name and directed me to a long row of green-vinyl chairs. I sat for a half hour or more pretending to read a magazine I had thrown in my briefcase earlier so I would have something I could pretend I was reading.

Bellinger came into the far end of the room through a heavy door with a security code lock on it. He was a tall, trim, slow moving man I'd put in his early fifties. There were streaks of grey in his dark, parted hair. He had a slow-moving weariness about him that suggested that he would follow up on a thing as long as it took, and it had taken a while. He offered a large hand and smiled a weary smile.

Bellinger led me through a gymnasium-sized room filled with rows of desks, most of which were not occupied at the time. He led me into a conference room. The largest wooden conference table I'd ever seen filled most of the room, and there were enough upholstered chairs around it for a lot of people to listen to somebody talk. Bellinger excused himself with a courteous apology and asked me to make myself comfortable while he attended to some other business. I assumed that the other business had something to do with Amanda's car being in the parking lot, but I didn't ask.

I sat a couple of chairs from one end of the huge conference table and studied the wall-full of hand-painted portraits that had no doubt been shipped *en masse* from some central office. I wondered if the room was bugged, or if there were hidden cameras in the eyes of the people in the portraits, since those were the kinds of things I had seen on television.

Bellinger returned accompanied by a young lawyer I'll call Washington. He was from the Department of Justice. Washington looked like any number of bright young lawyers I knew when I worked with the government: tight fitting suit, tasteful tie, neat hair, everything by the book until forced-to-fit had turned natural. When I was with the government, I called them robots from the future.

Washington explained that the FBI was the investigative arm of the Justice Department and that, when the Justice Department had a need, the FBI essentially ran its errands. He didn't put it like that, but that was the core of it. He said he and Bellinger would have some questions later, but first they wanted to hear anything I had to say.

"That'll take a while," I said.

"We've got time," Washington said.

Rogers and Sandra and I had spent a good part of the previous night in my basement typing out a list. There were about three dozen items on it. I gave Bellinger and Washington each a copy and started at the top. As I went down the list Bellinger penciled notes on a yellow legal pad. A retired law enforcement officer who was on the Whitewash Committee had told me he'd had considerable dealings with the FBI. This fellow had told me that if the FBI was serious about a case, they took their notes in hard-bound note books. If they weren't, they used yellow legal pads and then tossed the notes out later. I don't know about that. I just know it was what he told me.

I didn't get past the first page of the list, and the little we went into took a couple of hours. I told everything I knew about Eddie Vickers and how the county seemed to be after him for saying he'd been strangled.

I went into detail about Jon's house being broken into and his camera and answering machine tape turning up missing. I mentioned an acquaintance of Jon's who lived across town and was rumored to be heavily into drugs, and who had found his truck ransacked the morning Jon was found dead. It was the kind of thing that could mean nothing, but if I was investigating the case, I would want to know about it. I mentioned the acquaintance of Jon's who had offered to Sandra to have Meyers killed soon after Jon's death, and who had showed up snooping about Sandra's house soon after Amanda moved in. It could mean something.

I talked about the threats people were supposed to have gotten during the grand jury. There were those Eddie said he got, including one Katy Vickers had let Sandra listen to that had been left by mistake on Eddie's answering machine tape when Eddie had answered after the pre-set number of rings. I mentioned the kid who had received a threatening call after his name was put on a list of potential grand jury witnesses. I called the kid by name and said, "You already know about him." Bellinger looked up from his yellow pad.

"Now, tell me who he is again?"

"You know," I said. "I took a statement from him and then he was afraid to sign it and I sent in a statement about it myself."

"There's so much paper," Bellinger said. "Tell me again."

"You must remember," I said, feeling a little frustrated. "A man called him and said, 'If you know what's good for your black ass, you won't testify.'" When I said *black ass*, Bellinger flinched noticeably. There's something discomforting about seeing an FBI agent flinch at an obscenity, and I said in an apologetic way that I hoped hid my surprise, "It's what was said."

I was pretty worn down from talking so much and I asked if I could go outside and smoke a cigarette. Bellinger showed me out and I walked out to the parking lot. Amanda's car still was there. I smoked a cigarette and went back inside after the woman had answered the buzzer again, and Bellinger escorted me back into the conference room. We sat again and Washington said he had a few questions for me. Beyond Washington's introductory explanation of the roles of the Justice Department and the FBI, it was the first opportunity I had to get a sense of his and Bellinger's thinking, so I said, "Sure."

"Tell me, Mr. Parrish," Washington said, "is there anything in your background that would give you a reason to have any sort of vendetta against the police?"

After all I had said about the few items on the list we had gotten to so far, it wasn't the first question I expected to come out of his mouth. A red flag went up inside my head. I said, "No." He sat a few moments looking at me as if he thought I might have more to say about that, but I didn't. Bellinger finally broke the silence with his own first question.

"We've received a lot of statements that you prepared and your wife notarized. How do you explain that?" Another red flag went up, but I didn't want to see it and I tried not to show any particular emotion as I answered him.

"That's easy," I said. "Somebody had to do it. I have a computer and my wife is a notary. Some people were pretty nervous about providing statements, and using my wife to get the statements notarized made it easy to ensure confidentiality."

Bellinger cleared his throat and looked down. He doodled on his yellow pad and seemed to be thinking about something. The he looked back up.

"What is your relationship with Sandra Keyser?"

That was three red flags in a row. I didn't want to get off on a side track, and I ignored what I saw as the suggestive nature of the question.

"I coached her son in baseball since he was eleven years old, and now he's dead. She's a friend of mine."

Bellinger doodled some more with his pencil.

"What do you think about Amanda Garvey?"

This seemed like a more relevant question, and I said what had been on my mind for some time.

"I figure she's either terrified, emotionally disturbed, or a plant."

When I said *plant*, Bellinger flinched again and his face blanched. He looked legitimately startled.

"What do you mean by *plant*?"

"I assume she's been telling you the same things she's been telling Sandra and me. She says that Meyers has been threatening her with terrible things. She's also been pumping Sandra for details about the Red Roof Inn. It goes beyond idle interest. I figure that if you guys didn't put her up to living with Sandra, somebody did. It certainly would be interesting to find out who, and why."

Bellinger and Washington ignored my observation. Washington said they didn't have any other questions and he thanked me for coming. I had thought that the question and answer session was only an interlude before getting to the rest of the list, and I said, "But we hardly started on the list.

Are we going to pick this up again?"

"We'd be happy to do that," Bellinger said, as if it wasn't particularly important but he was willing to spend the time if it made me happy. He got up from his chair and the meeting was over.

Bellinger led me back through the room of desks and through the reception area to the front door. He gave me a warm hand shake and said, "We're very serious about this investigation. We intend to find out what happened to Jon Bowie."

"Good," I said. "That comforts me. So do I."

As I left the FBI building, I noticed that Amanda's car still was in the parking lot.

I'd promised Sandra I would stop by her house after the interview. The trees were starting to bud and the weather had turned to light-jacket crisp. We walked down the sidewalk and through the evergreens toward the backstop.

"I don't know," I said. "They hardly asked me anything investigative. They wanted to know if I had a vendetta against the police, why I had prepared so many statements, why Jane notarized them and what my relationship is with you. Aside from anything I could cram in, that was about it. I was a little disappointed."

We walked a short distance before Sandra said anything. Then she asked, "Can we trust them?"

"We have to," I said. "This is the FBI we're talking about, and the United States Department of Justice. Who else is there?"

I told her every detail about the meeting I could remember. I could tell she was looking for anything that might give her even a small reason for hope. I wished I had more to tell her.

We had walked past the backstop and on into the field beyond and had turned around and started back before I decided to say something that was nagging me.

"I just wish I could shake this feeling," I said, "that, instead of investigating Jon's death, they're investigating us."

Sandra told me, sitting at her kitchen table, that she had seen an angel. I studied her face and decided she wasn't lying and she didn't appear to be running a fever. She looked a little nervous, even desperate, saying it, as if she was afraid I would turn and run out the door.

I don't know what I thought about angels before then. I hardly ever thought about them. I suppose I thought they were like fairies, or elves. Sometimes you ran into some reference about them in books and you knew what was being referred to, but you didn't take it seriously. They were sort of like Santa Claus, or Jack Frost, nice ideas that made everybody feel better in some vague way.

I asked Sandra if she was awake or asleep and she said she was awake. She was in her kitchen and the angel hovered over the floor between the table and the stove. The angel smiled at her and held up three fingers.

"It was beautiful," she said. "I wish I could describe it."

"What do you think it means?" I said. "Three what? Three months? Three years?"

She said, "If it's three years, I don't know if I can stand it. I don't think I can."

"Well, whatever it means, we're not alone in this. It at least means that. Somebody's paying attention to all this."

It must have been my religious upbringing that made me say that. It was not a thought I was likely to have, much less express. It just came out of my mouth.

35　Eddie Vickers was an enigma. No one I encountered knew he was a witness to the motel incident until about six months after it happened, and about two weeks before he said he was strangled at the backstop.

Eddie was a stocky, muscular young man with a short, brown crew cut that bordered on reddish. He had a sideways, closed-mouth way of grinning, as if he didn't want to but couldn't help himself. He'd look you in the eye and talk to you and, just as often, look off to the side or down at the ground.

I didn't know Eddie before Jon died. I might have seen him around the ballfields, but he was a lacrosse player and I wouldn't have known him by name. I never did get to know the kid that some of his past friends and acquaintances described. They would say such things as, "Eddie doesn't really have any friends. Sometimes he lies, you know."

I didn't know. I knew he had a juvenile record, and I was told the things that caused it. Since he was a juvenile at the time, I won't go into what I was told. I knew that a considerable number of people once called themselves his friends and then no longer did.

Part of it had to do with his juvenile record and events surrounding that. Part of it had to do with Jon. After Jon died, friends of Jon's wondered aloud if maybe Eddie knew something about Jon's death. Why, they wondered, would Eddie get threatening phone calls before anyone knew he was a witness at the motel incident? I thought about that when I heard it and it was clear that someone did know. The best I could piece it together, the phone calls started after Eddie provided a written statement to the county state's attorney's office. A lot of people worked in that office, and that office worked closely with the police. Word would have spread fast that there was a witness who said he had seen what happened at the motel. This was not something I could prove. It simply was the only possibility I could think of based on what I knew.

It was Eddie who walked past the backstop at around two o'clock on the morning Jon's body was found, and Eddie said no one was there at that time. This conflicted with the medical examiner's conclusion that Jon had died at around eleven p.m. Others speculated that maybe Eddie was lying and that maybe he had seen something at the backstop.

Two days after the state police began investigating, at nine-thirty at night, Detective Dayton Arnold picked up the young woman who said she had dropped Eddie off at the backstop, and Arnold drove her to the backstop. I'll call the young woman Patricia. Patricia said she dropped Eddie off at the backstop that night after she and Eddie had been out together. Sandra said later that, for no reason she knew of, the street lights around the backstop were not lighted the night Jon died. Maybe Sandra got that mixed up with the fact that the police report said the lights were off the night Arnold drove Patricia to the backstop. Even with the lights out, Arnold concluded that there was no way Eddie could have walked behind the backstop, which was what Patricia said he did, without seeing someone hanging there.

Eddie said that on the night before he was to testify about what he had seen at the motel, he was strangled at the backstop. The county eventually charged Eddie with filing a false report. Then the county removed the charges and Boudreaux told Eddie's attorney he would get Eddie on something. Then the county charged Eddie again with filing a false report.

Katy Vickers showed me her photocopy of the eight or nine pages of the charging document. I read it and re-read it and it was all gobbledy-gook. It said the two investigating detectives believed Eddie claimed to have been strangled because he didn't want to testify at Mickey's trial. It said Eddie had not shown up in court that morning - which was simply wrong; he was there - because Eddie was afraid of testifying. So, the report said, he made it all up about being strangled so he wouldn't have to appear. There were claims that the wounds Eddie displayed were superficial and that they were not consistent with his story, but there was no concrete evidence that Eddie had made the story up. The charges were based on the opinions of two detectives.

Rogers and Sandra and I and several of the kids and several more of Sandra's neighbors went to Eddie's trial. It was in the same courtroom where Meyers had growled at Sandra and the kids before Jon died. The county's case consisted mostly of various detectives and officers testifying.

Officer Tim Burns was one of the officers at the Red Roof Inn. He was the first officer to arrive at the backstop, and he also was the first officer to arrive after Eddie's friend called the police. Burns testified that when he arrived on the night Eddie said he was strangled, Eddie clearly was hyper-ventilating and was very frightened. When Burns returned to his seat after testifying, the investigating detective, Olfine, the one who was supposed to be Eddie's friend, leaned over to Burns and whispered loudly, "Why did you say that?" Burns leaned back and whispered loudly, "Because it's true."

The testimony of the two investigating detectives was a repetition of the information in the charging document. One of the detectives testified that he had tried unsuccessfully to lift the other detective from behind with a cord the way Eddie claimed to have been lifted. Rogers leaned down and whispered to me, "Give me a shoestring and I'll lift both those turkeys two feet off the ground."

A doctor who had examined Eddie at the emergency room testified that the injuries did not seem severe enough to him to fit Eddie's story.

Pamela, who by this time was Eddie's ex-girlfriend, testified that Eddie had told her that he had killed Jon. I had heard that story, and had asked Eddie about it. In essence, after Eddie and Pamela broke up Eddie encountered Pamela and friends of hers at a night club in Baltimore. Pamela introduced Eddie to her friends as, "the person who killed Jon Bowie," and Eddie said, "Yeah, right," the way a person would say, "Sure," or, "Are you kidding?" The county put Pamela on the witness stand to talk about that.

And that, essentially, was the county's case.

Donnie, Eddie's friend, testified that Eddie had showed up terrified and knocking on Donnie's door in the middle of the night. Donnie called the police.

Sandra testified that Amanda had showed up at her house on the night of July 4, upset and saying she had just seen someone she thought was Mickey abducted at the backstop.

Amanda testified that she had seen two men approach a young man who was sitting on the short bench behind the backstop. Amanda said she looked away and when she looked back the two men and the young man were gone. Amanda had told Sandra and me that she saw these two men grab the person she thought was Mickey, but in her testimony she said she had looked away. Her testimony was strikingly similar, in that regard, to Jon's second interview with the Internal Affairs Division, the interview in which he said he had looked away as a night stick was pressed against his neck. Neither the county attorneys nor Eddie's attorney pressed Amanda for details.

Eddie's attorney had other information he didn't use. It's been explained to me that sometimes attorneys don't pull out their big guns until there is an appeal. That way, they get everyone on the other side on record without revealing too much of what they plan to do. One of the pieces of information Eddie's attorney didn't use was the videotape taken by a Baltimore television station at the courthouse on the morning the police had charged Eddie was too frightened to appear. On the tape, Eddie was standing with several other people just outside the front door of the courthouse.

The case was heard by a judge, not by a jury. If you're guilty of something, I'm told, go for a jury trial. Your attorney might be able to work on the emotions of the jury. If you're clearly innocent, I'm also told, lay it out before a judge. I no longer believe that.

When all the witnesses had been heard, the judge excused himself and left to consider the case. He was gone maybe a half hour. When he returned, he sat and started reading from a stack of notes. It took several minutes and there was little indication what his decision would be until he finally said something like, "This case is so bizarre that I feel I have no choice but to believe the police officers."

Eddie was found guilty and I was stunned. The judge had based his opinion on the opinions of two detectives and in the absence of any evidence. This was not the way I thought courts worked.

There were several lawyers there representing the county. When the verdict was announced, these lawyers literally jumped high in the air and waved their arms over their heads and cheered and squealed like high school cheerleaders. It was a picture I was sure I would not forget.

Someone in our group said there was an attorney from the Justice Department at the trial. I looked around for someone who might be that person, but I couldn't tell. Even if it was true, it didn't seem to have done much good.

Eddie left the room looking in a state of shock. His attorney immediately filed for an appeal.

There's a detail I forgot until now. Just after Jon died, Sandra found strips of orange cord in her back yard. She and I visited several local hardware stores in an effort to determine what the cord was used for. We eventually confirmed that it was a thick cord used in heavy duty weed cutting machinery. I told Sandra at the time that this could explain why the cord was in her back yard. Someone might have simply used it to cut around the shrubbery behind the townhouses, and it could have nothing to do with Jon's death. Sandra was not convinced, and we bought a small roll of it. Sandra cut off a length of a few feet and concealed it and went next door to find Eddie and Katy Vickers. Katy let her in, led her into the kitchen and called Eddie into the room.

"Turn around," Sandra said to Eddie. "I'm not going to hurt you, but I want you to tell me what this feels like. Close your eyes."

Sandra was shorter than Eddie, and she reached up from behind and looped the cord around Eddie's neck. As she lightly tugged on the cord to tighten it, Eddie jerked away and whirled around, and his eyes were wide and his face was white as a sheet.

"That's it," he said. "That's exactly what it felt like."

Something in the county police report that bothered me had to do with a statement attributed to a man I'll call Moore. According to the report, about six weeks after Eddie said he was strangled at the same backstop where Jon was found, the county police interviewed this fellow. What the report said was that this fellow was a writer and sometimes he worked late on his deck. He was supposed to have said he was on his deck working on the night Eddie said he was strangled and, also, on the night Jon's body was found. His house sat across the street from the same open space that ran like a channel behind John Sinelli's house from the area of the backstop. On the night Jon died, the report said, Moore was working on his deck until about three in the morning. At around midnight he heard what sounded like some kids laughing near the tennis courts, which were immediately behind the backstop. The laughter didn't last long, and he hadn't heard anything else. The report said Moore could hear anything that came from the direction of the school, "crystal clear."

When I read this statement in the police report I assumed it was put in the report to counter what Sinelli had said. I stopped by Moore's house to have a look. I knocked on his door, but he wasn't home. His porch faced away from the backstop, in the direction of a large patch of woods. Whatever he had heard would have had to come around the house.

Sandra told me she and Eddie's attorney stopped by Moore's house. Eddie's attorney wanted to know anything Moore had to say about the night Eddie said he had been strangled. Since the house was only a few doors up and across a street from Sandra's, Sandra went with Eddie's attorney to point out the address. Sandra couldn't stand there talking with the man and not mention the police report. Sandra told me later that Moore got angry, that he said he wouldn't have expected to hear anything all the way down at the backstop since his porch faced the other way. He hadn't seen the police report, and he couldn't imagine why something like that would have been in it.

36   I feel the need to change a few details in telling this, but nothing essential. Call it another one of those coincidences that kept happening. Unbeknown to either of them, Sandra and the woman who claimed to have been raped by a police officer - I'll call her Hope - had a mutual acquaintance.

For quite a long time I didn't tell Sandra the rape story. Rogers promised that he wouldn't tell Sandra, either. Whether it was true or not - and I had no way of knowing if it was - I couldn't see any detail in it that demonstrated that this police officer had anything to do with Jon's death. True enough, the woman said she thought the police officer had killed Jon, but from what she had told Rogers she had more than a little reason to be angry at this police officer. What a person believes is not evidence. So I stored the story away in my mind in case it might eventually mean something. I had made some effort at locating the woman with no success and had let it drop. The county police, the state police and the FBI knew at least as much about it as I did, and I assumed they had a much better chance of finding her.

Sandra picked up a detail here and there from overheard conversations, and, finally, she confronted me about the story. I caveated it to death, saying it hadn't been proved and might mean nothing. Then I told her what I knew about the anonymous call to Rogers and how Chief Hickory had said it was Sandra who had made the call.

It took Sandra a few days to get over her anger. She was angry because it didn't appear to have been vigorously pursued by anyone, and she was angry because Hickory had told Rogers that Sandra had made the call. Although Sandra agreed that the story might not lead to any information about what had happened to Jon, she thought the whole business showed that those investigating Jon's death were not doing it with any enthusiasm. I couldn't argue with her about that.

Even in her anger Sandra recognized that, to the extent the woman was telling the truth, there could be safety issues involved, and she agreed not to repeat the story. As I had, she stored it mentally and then several months went by. Then - and this is where I have to alter a few insignificant details - I'll say a parent of one of Sandra's daycare children called Sandra at home one evening and said they needed to talk. This parent, a woman, asked if they could meet at six the next morning at the daycare center, before anyone else arrived. Sandra met the woman the next morning and the woman immediately burst into tears and said, "A friend of mine knows who killed Jon."

It was an emotional scene. The woman cried and Sandra cried as the woman told the story. The woman said a friend had stopped by her home for a visit after church on the previous Sunday. As coincidence or whatever would have it, it was on Easter Sunday. This parent, who had known Jon well and had been severely impacted by his death, had a framed picture of Jon on a table in her living room. Hope noticed the picture and asked, "Who's that?"

The parent began telling her and, as she did, Hope burst into tears. The parent asked what was the matter and Hope began sobbing and repeating the same story she had anonymously told Reverend Rogers. The parent asked for permission to repeat the story to Sandra. Hope, perhaps under the influence of that emotional retelling, gave her permission.

The woman told Sandra that Hope had told her this police officer often came by her house, sometimes with friends, and this police officer had bragged about hitting people and even about sodomizing young offenders, male and female. Sandra didn't know what sodomizing somebody meant, but it sounded serious to her. Sandra asked the woman for Hope's name and the woman said she thought it was best that she not immediately give it. Then she left and Sandra phoned me at work.

"We should call the FBI," I said. "This is a sensitive matter. They should take care of it."

"I don't know her name," Sandra said.

"It doesn't matter. You know enough that she can be found. The FBI should handle this. It's too big for us and somebody could get hurt."

"I don't think I can call them," she said. "I've never spoken with them. I don't even know if I'm supposed to know they're investigating."

I agreed to make the call. As soon as Sandra hung up, I called Arthur Bellinger in Baltimore and told him what Sandra had told me. When I had finished, Bellinger said, "Do you think you could get more information?"

I was taken aback. "I suppose I could," I said, "but if you will excuse me for saying so, it seems that you're asking me to do your job in a sensitive and perhaps even dangerous situation."

"Not necessarily," Bellinger said. "I just think it would be good to have more information."

I reluctantly agreed to see what I could learn and hung up. I called Sandra back and repeated the conversation.

"Do you think you can learn more?"

"I don't see how," Sandra said. "I don't have the name. If I start asking a lot of questions, the whole thing could fall apart. I'll see if there's anything I can find out indirectly."

After hanging up, Sandra remembered that the parent had mentioned another person who knew this woman, and Sandra also knew this other person. Sandra called the person and, in a casual way, finagled the conversation around to Hope. Then Sandra called me back with Hope's full name and her street address.

"I played dumb and asked a few questions," Sandra said. "The person who told me didn't know what I was talking about."

I called Bellinger back and gave him the information. That evening I called Rogers and told him what had happened that day. Rogers was stunned that the woman had turned up, and for a while he didn't say anything. I could hear him breathing long, heavy breaths at his end of the line. He finally said, "That's not good enough. I'll call Bellinger tomorrow and make sure he follows up on this."

"David," I said. "This is the FBI we're talking about. He'll follow up on it. He doesn't want police officers going around raping people anymore than you and I do."

"You trust the FBI more than I do," Rogers said. "I'll call him anyway."

"Well, don't aggravate him," I said. "The man's doing his job. He doesn't need us whining after him. So don't piss him off. That's all I'm trying to say."

The Reverend Rogers called me an uncomplimentary name and hung up.

Rogers was all over Bellinger like a puppy on a pants leg. It seemed that every time I talked to Rogers he had just gotten off the phone with Bellinger, and Rogers was getting more and more aggravated. For one reason or another, Bellinger still had not contacted Hope after several days.

Rogers was not a person to wait around forever for someone to do what he had said he would do. Rogers called Hope himself. Hope was tearful and she repeated her story and said that, yes, it was she who had called Rogers originally, no, she had not heard from the FBI, and, yes, she would talk with them.

That was all Rogers wanted to hear. He made an appointment for her to talk with the FBI a day or two later in his office at ten o'clock in the morning, and then he called Bellinger to tell him about the appointment. In rather clear language, Rogers explained to Bellinger that Hope would meet either with the FBI or with the local press at the appointed time. Bellinger agreed to come.

The day for the meeting arrived and Rogers met Hope at his office. Rogers had arranged for Sandra to come a half hour before Bellinger was to arrive. Sandra came and Rogers introduced her to Hope. Sandra said to Hope, "I appreciate your being willing to talk with Reverend Rogers." Then Sandra cried and Hope cried and Hope said, "I will be there for you," and Sandra thanked her again and left.

Rogers had promised himself beforehand that he would stay out of the conversation between Bellinger and Hope as much as possible since his objective, the meeting itself, had been accomplished. Bellinger arrived and he and Hope and Rogers sat in Rogers' office. Bellinger's first question to Hope made Rogers shift uncomfortably in his chair. In the sincerest of voices, Bellinger asked, "Are you aware of the difficulties a charge such as this can bring to you and to your family?"

Bellinger explained at length the difficulties that could be expected in proving a charge of rape. The fact that so much time had passed only added to the difficulty. The fact that the charge was against a police officer made it even more difficult. It would be, after all, only her word against that of a police officer.

Hope was clearly intelligent and physically very attractive in accordance with popular standards of beauty. I'll say she was blonde and in her middle thirties. After about fifteen minutes she was trembling noticeably and on the verge of tears. Rogers forgot that he had promised himself he would not interfere. He stared at Bellinger in an intense effort at demonstrating disbelief.

"What do you think you're doing?" Rogers asked Bellinger.

"What do you mean?" Bellinger asked.

"This woman has come to you for help, and you're scaring her to death. That's what I mean. You're suppose to protect her, to offer her security, and justice. Instead, you're frightening her out of her mind."

To his credit, Bellinger apologized and his demeanor softened. "I only meant to make it clear to her what she might be getting into," he said. "She has a right to know this."

"I think you've done that well enough," Rogers said. "Can you spend a little time explaining how you can help her?"

Bellinger turned to Hope and, with a gentler voice, he said, "Tell me what happened."

There's no point in going into all the details. Hope told her story again and Bellinger listened. She told Bellinger that a police officer had raped her and sodomized her. Hope had children from a previous marriage, and, when the police officer had finished assaulting her, he put his hands around her throat and said, "See what you made me do? I arrest people for doing what I did to you. If you tell anyone, I'll kill you and your children. There is nowhere you can go that I can't find you. It will look like an accident and no one will suspect me, but you and your children will be dead."

The interview lasted four hours. Bellinger wanted to know if Hope had any other encounters with this police officer. Yes, Hope said. She said that the officer stalked her, that he showed up at restaurants and bars when she was on dates. She had looked out her kitchen window and had seen him sitting across the street in his patrol car, staring at her house. She had lived in terror. On one occasion he pulled up beside her in his patrol car at a traffic light. She looked over at him and recognized him and he pointed his gun at her through the window of his patrol car.

"Was he in uniform?" Bellinger asked her.

"Yes."

Bellinger made an appointment for Hope to come to the FBI office, and Hope left. Rogers and Bellinger walked across the courtyard from Rogers' office to The Last Chance Saloon. Over sandwiches, they talked about the interview. Rape was a state offense, Bellinger explained, not a federal offense. Anything the FBI learned about that charge would have to be turned over to the local police. Pointing a gun from a patrol car "under the color of law," however, was something that Bellinger could personally do something about.

"Do you believe her?" Rogers asked.

"I believe her," Bellinger said. "That man has no business being a police officer. He should be in prison."

Rogers called me that evening and told me about the meeting.

I said "Great. So if it turns out that there's any truth to it, it gets turned over to the people he works for. That must give Hope a real sense of comfort."

"That's one way to look at it, I suppose," Rogers said. "She said she wouldn't press charges as long as he's in uniform, and carrying a gun."

"I wish her well," I said. "It's between her and the FBI and the county now. I hate to keep beating this in the ground, but let's say for the sake of conversation that he actually did rape her. That still doesn't mean he killed Jon. It's not proof."

Rogers became genuinely angry, which, even on the phone, was an experience worth avoiding. I thought my receiver cord might melt. He shouted at me, "Don't you realize how serious this is? Don't you realize what she is saying?"

"I realize it," I said, "and maybe it's true. I'm just saying it's not proof."

A thing like Hope's story can make you edgy. A few days after Hope came forward, an older son of hers was stopped by the county police in a routine traffic stop. I wondered if there was a connection. Through their mutual friend, Sandra got a copy of the traffic report and the report looked ordinary.

Hope's toddler son fell down the basement steps. The family was outside in the yard and whoever was watching the baby was out of the room and the child fell. It wasn't clear that the child would live. Rogers got excited and called Bellinger and insisted that Hope be protected in any way that was possible. It was touch-and-go with the child for a while, and then the child was all right.

When you think those who should be doing their jobs are not doing them, for whatever reason, you begin to hate the possibilities that pass through your mind. It's hard not to get a little crazy. I can only imagine how it affected Hope.

I remember the exact date in late April when I finally acknowledged to myself that the FBI was doing less than an objective investigation. I will always think of that day as a numbing day.

Sandra called me at work and said Tina had gone to the federal courthouse in Baltimore. Tina was upset because she sensed that something was going on, and she wanted to see what she could find out. That afternoon when I got home from work, I called Tina at her office.

"The FBI's doing a tank job," Tina said.

"A what?"

"You know. This case is going in the tank. The Justice Department has sent a hatchet man from Washington to shut the case down."

"Why?"

"They don't want it investigated."

"What can you do?"

"I can let them know there'll be the devil to pay if they tank this investigation. That should at least drag things out. Maybe something will come up."

As I hung up the phone, a nerve in the little finger of my right hand popped or did whatever nerves do out of nowhere for no obvious reason. Two fingers and half of my right hand became numb. The numbness gradually subsided over a period of several months, but, even after all these years, the hand still has an odd feel about it.

37

Rogers called.

"There's a man sitting in my office who wants to talk to you."

I'll say the man was a Lieutenant Crown. I heard Rogers strike a button to put me on the speaker phone.

"Mr. Parrish?"

"Hey, Larry," I said. I'd met him before a couple of times, and I liked him. I didn't want to get bogged down with the *Mister* business.

Rogers interrupted.

"Somebody broke into my office," he said. "Lieutenant Crown is here investigating it. You were here just the other night, and now Howard County's going to get something they've wanted for a long time. He wants to fingerprint you so we can rule out your prints."

"Sure," I said. "Somebody broke in your office?"

"Last night," Rogers said. "I came in this morning and the safe where I keep all the papers for the Bowie case was open. I distinctly remember locking it last night. I didn't want some cowboy coming over and telling me I didn't know what I was talking about. That's why I called Lieutenant Crown."

Rogers and I went together to the police department and Larry Crown rolled our fingers in black ink and pressed our fingers in the designated squares on sheets of cardboard. Rogers had given Crown the names of other people who had been in the office so Crown could eliminate any prints that might legitimately have been on the safe. Rogers had given John

Hollywood's name and maybe the names of a few more people. At the time, though, only Rogers and I were there to be fingerprinted.

I wiped off my fingers the best I could with the paper towel Crown gave me. As Rogers and I were leaving, I offered a hand to Crown before I realized that he probably didn't want ink on his hands. He shook my hand anyway, and Rogers and I left.

Rogers and I went to Rogers' office and Rogers walked me around and showed me the safe and explained how someone had to have come in through the rear door.

"It had to be someone with a key," he said. "I know I locked up."

"Who has a key to your office?"

"The security guards have keys to the rear doors of all the offices. Sam Long works as a security guard here some nights. He certainly would have more than a passing interest in the Bowie case." Long was the officer Internal Affairs had persuaded Jon to say might not have pressed a night stick against Jon's neck at the motel.

"I don't know," I said. "This is all pretty weird. You're sure you didn't just forget to lock the safe?"

Rogers went over it all again.

Crown called Rogers a few days later and said one or two sets of fingerprints on the safe could not be accounted for. If the police department ever learned whose prints those were, I didn't find out about it.

Tina succeeded in getting the federal investigation strung out. The federal grand jury that was meeting to hear evidence in the case probably would come to an end soon or be suspended, but the case still was open. I called Bellinger and said I wanted to talk, and he agreed to an appointment.

Rogers was a member of more committees and organizations locally and across the country than I could keep track of. He had been making noises about getting Sandra and me to go to Chicago to meet with one of them, Sandra for obvious reasons and me because I had made a point of keeping track of the details in the case. Several activist committees across the country were meeting to join into one large umbrella committee that would be called the National Coalition on Police Accountability. I'm usually not too thrilled about committee participation, but it struck me that Sandra had seemed certain for months that she and I would be going to Chicago to look for the person who was said to be a witness at the backstop. Without explaining my reasons to Rogers, I agreed to go to Chicago with less reluctance than I normally would have exhibited. When I met with Bellinger the trip to Chicago already was scheduled, but I didn't get into that with Bellinger.

There was a sense of finality to the meeting. Bellinger sat at his desk and I sat in front of it slumped in a chair. I assumed he knew what Tina knew about the Justice Department trying to halt the investigation. I didn't see any point in wasting time talking about what had taken place behind the scenes.

"What became of Hope?" I asked him.

In his solemn, soulful way that suggested without words that he had done all he could do, he repeated that rape was a state offense and not really within the jurisdiction of the FBI unless it had been done by an officer in uniform. "Now, pointing a gun at her in the car would be a clear violation, if it could be proved," he said. I didn't care to go into that subject, so I didn't say anything.

We sat in silence a few moments and Bellinger asked, "Do you think Meyers killed Jon Bowie?"

"I don't know how to answer that," I said. "We don't live in Nazi Germany. You don't make a charge like that unless you can put the evidence on the table. What I think is not relevant."

"I think Jon died a peaceful death," Bellinger said. "I think he was inebriated and he got into a situation that he couldn't get out of, and he just relaxed and let it happen. Rust on the bottoms of his shoes indicated that he climbed the backstop himself."

I sensed that he was telling me something he wanted me to tell Sandra, regardless of whether he believed it himself. It seemed pretty obvious to me that Jon could just as easily have gotten rust on the bottoms of his shoes trying to get off the backstop, so I assumed it was just as obvious to Bellinger. I let it pass.

"I don't know," I said. "What if someone held a gun on him and told him to climb it? There were those bullets found in the grass."

I couldn't be certain if Bellinger had just forgotten or if he wanted to hear me say it in case he might learn something new. Regardless, I had to go over the bullets again and tell how they were found. It seemed he wasn't really listening attentively, so I retold it quickly. When I had finished, he said almost as if he was talking to himself, "If we could just get a break. Usually, it takes a break to solve a case like this."

"What did you ever learn about Courtney?" I asked him.

"Who?"

"You know, the woman from Chicago who was supposed to have seen people at the backstop?"

"That was all pretty third-hand information," he said. "Our experience is that such things seldom check out. We can't put thirteen people on this and check out every rumor."

So he hadn't even checked it out. I was getting more adept at continuing with a conversation after having been figuratively smacked in the forehead with a shovel, and I kept talking.

"So, if I, say, bumped into her on the street, you wouldn't see it as interfering with the FBI if I stopped and had a little chat with her?"

He studied me across the desk and didn't answer.

Sandra took the window seat and I sat in the middle. A big, Irish-looking fellow with red hair and a reddish face sat to my left. I wasn't all that good at conversing with strangers, and I had leaned over and looked out the window of the plane at a lot of patchwork countryside before I learned that he was from Chicago. When I learned that his name was either John or Jon, I didn't ask which, and that he was a police officer, and that he had a twin brother, I began to feel a little eery. I wasn't sure of the directions for getting from the airport to the conference center where we were headed, and this police officer named Jon or John who had a twin brother told me exactly how to get there and all the exits to watch out for. He even loaned me a pencil, and I made notes on the back of something. By the time we landed, I felt I could stop by his house for a beer. Striking up a plane-seat friendship with a police officer was a thought-provoking prelude to attending a conference on police accountability.

The rental car place didn't have the economy-sized car I wanted, and we had to settle for a nicer car at the reduced rate. We drove for a long time and Sandra was convinced we were lost. I kept telling her to trust me and asking her if Jane had instructed her to make me crazy. We rode through increasingly burned-out looking sections of town and Sandra asked me to lock the doors.

The conference center took up most of a city block. It was an old, grey-stone building that looked like a once-elegant bank. We parked across the street and dragged our bags inside. A woman at the front desk gave us room keys and explained how one elevator only came down for safety reasons. We took the other elevator to a high floor. Sandra stopped at her door and I went a few doors down and found my room. I let myself into a room carpeted with some semblance of indoor-outdoor carpeting on which I wouldn't walk in bare feet. Several bunk beds were crammed into the room. I picked a lower bunk and handwritten instructions taped to the bed post explained that making the bed myself would save money and help the establishment survive.

Sandra and I met a few minutes later in the hall and followed poster board signs downstairs to a gymnasium-sized meeting room. A group of two or three dozen people sat in a large circle of card chairs in the center of the room. As we joined them, they stopped discussing whatever they had been discussing. We introduced ourselves and they began asking us about Jon. Sandra explained that large groups made her nervous and that I knew most of the details of the case. I started talking and then Sandra interrupted me and hardly stopped talking until it was late.

When Sandra finally did stop talking, a large black woman talked about how she believed her son had been physically tortured by the Chicago police. Several of the people in the circle apparently were from Chicago, and there was a discussion about boxes with electric wires coming out of them and about officers putting plastic bags over peoples heads and leaning people over steam radiators until they confessed to things. I studied the faces of the people in the room to see if they looked crazed, and they didn't. They looked like ordinary people.

For one reason or another, Rogers had to back out of coming to the meeting at the last minute. It was clear from the way people asked about him, though, that he was seen as some sort of leader within the group. When the meeting was over, a woman named Mary introduced herself. She looked in her fifties and had grey hair and a square body and a face that seemed to have smiled its way through more than most people ever see. Rogers had told me about her, and I had called her before leaving Maryland to ask for her help in finding Courtney. Now she was telling Sandra and me she had found Courtney on the first phone call. "I just called and asked to speak to her and she was there," Mary said. "She said it was odd that I called her at that particular time since she had just gotten off the phone with an FBI agent from Baltimore." Sandra and I looked at each other and didn't interrupt. "I don't know if you should go see her," Mary said. "Not just yet, under the circumstances. She said that the FBI wants to fly her to Baltimore to testify before a grand jury. The agent told her to call him immediately if anyone connected with the Bowie case contacts her."

"Damn," I said. "I feel like we've just been cut off at the pass. The FBI knew about Courtney six months ago. Now they call her only a few hours before Sandra and I get off the plane? I really don't understand what's going on here. Will she call the FBI and say she talked with you?"

"I asked her that," Mary said. "She says she won't since I'm not really connected to the case. Besides, she says she doesn't know anything. She says it's all some sort of confusion. When she went past the backstop the body had already been discovered. The only people she saw were the people taking the body down, and the bystanders."

"I wish I'd talked with her first," I said. "For all I know now, she could have changed her story."

"She sounded believable," Mary said. "It wouldn't surprise me if she's telling the truth."

"It still aggravates me," I said. "All the FBI had to do was call their Chicago office six months ago and find out that she didn't have anything to say. Why all this reluctance? And why fly her to Baltimore now that they know she doesn't have anything to say? It's grandstanding. They really do want to kill this investigation."

Mary waited without commenting as I blew off steam. Then she handed me a slip of paper with Courtney's full name and her address and phone number.

"It might not be smart to call her until after she talks with the FBI," Mary said. "They could say you tried to influence her."

The next morning, Sandra and I met for breakfast. We bought greasy sandwiches at a fast food place and ate in the car as I drove and Sandra leaned over a map of Chicago. The street where Courtney lived was only a few miles from where we were staying, and we found it with little trouble.

The address was for an attractive, brick, tree-sheltered townhouse. We turned around a couple of times to drive past it again. I said, "I can't believe we've come all the way to Chicago to talk to this woman, and now we're right in front of her house and can't do it."

"We can't," Sandra said. "It would be used against us somehow."

"That's sick," I said. "That's really sick."

I drove past the house for the last time and started back for the conference center.

The gymnasium-sized room was nearly filled with people sitting in row after row of card chairs. Mary stood up front at a podium and welcomed groups from Dallas, Los Angeles, Boston, Minneapolis, New York, you name it.

An ex-officer talked about cases of police brutality he had witnessed. He said he was drummed out of police work for trying to change things. He painted a negative picture of police bureaucracy. When he paused for questions, I raised my hand from near the back of the room and asked, "What about the FBI?"

"The FBI is a joke," he said.

There was spontaneous laughter and applause. Although his answer shocked me, I actually slapped my hands together a few times. I suppose it was some sort of release.

Several groups represented different branches of a national group called The National Association of Black Police Officers. A thin, athletic, black man who was in his late forties and from one of those groups gave a calmer presentation. As a police officer, he said, he had seen officers do plenty of things he couldn't agree with. Things had to change, he said. It wasn't enough just to complain. And the changes had to be responsible.

We shuffled chairs around and broke into groups. A young Latino woman from Los Angeles talked to the group I was in about the Rodney King case, which still was an evolving story at the time. She didn't think the Justice Department wanted to deal with the King case. She explained how she and other people in Los Angeles were trying to apply pressure so the case didn't simply disappear.

We went at it all day, late into the night at a local bar, and then again for a while Sunday morning. Sandra and I had a fairly early flight, so we left before the meeting was over. We didn't talk a lot on the way home.

38   May 4 came and there was another vigil at the backstop. A couple of hundred people showed up and held candles. Rogers talked and Vernon Gray from the County Council talked and I talked too long. Barbara Stewart, who was both a professional model and a professional singer, and who had a rich, coloratura voice, ended the ceremony with a song that was popular that spring about one person being the wind beneath another person's wings.

The Whitewash Committee held public meetings. People stood up in front of committee members and said they liked the police or didn't like them or had experienced some good or bad encounter with them. Sandra came to one of the first meetings. She stood from the audience with several sheets of paper in her hand. The papers were the notarized statements from people who said that, contrary to what the police report said, they had not told the police they had seen Jon climbing the backstop in the past or drinking heavily. Sandra told the committee that she had given these statements to the previous Chief. She said she had asked that the statements be added to the police report, in accordance with the law, and the statements had not been added to the report. The new Chief, Ingersoll, was at the meeting, and Sandra gave him the reports and asked again that they be added to the police report.

Newspaper articles that followed the first public meetings suggested that a few complaints don't indicate a serious problem. The head of the committee was quoted as saying that the committee would have to demonstrate a pattern, and he didn't think that was likely. The papers quoted Chief Ingersoll as saying the community believed we had a good police department and there always would be complaints.

The committee held regular meetings in between these public meetings, and the complaints that had been voiced went almost unmentioned. It was as if these complaints were an embarrassment that was best ignored. There were committee reports and a few invited speakers and that was about it. I did press to have someone look at the official complaints against police officers, and Rogers supported me. This prompted the committee chairman and the County Executive to invite me and Rogers to meet with them in the County Executive's office.

On the day of that meeting, I went in first as requested and Rogers waited outside. The committee chairman, a tall, white-haired fellow, did most of the talking. He started the meeting by saying to me, "A few members are trying to take the committee in a direction that it's not intended to go."

If I'd had any political savvy I would have resigned on the spot and made a big public show of it, but I didn't. I went on about how we couldn't learn anything if we just talked without looking at any information. I suggested that we look at complaints and listen to police tapes the way the Christopher Commission did after the Rodney King case. The two men looked at me as if I was insane and didn't offer any comment to that. We finally just got tired of talking and I left.

Rogers was in the waiting room. Since I hadn't known what the meeting was about beforehand and had been caught off guard, I wanted to give Rogers a little advance notice. As he passed me going in, I said, "They don't won't us to look at the complaints." He nodded his understanding.

Rogers fared a little better than I had, but not much. He got the County Executive and the committee chairman to agree to having two members of the Whitewash Committee, an attorney who was an ex-officer and another retired law enforcement officer, look at the complaints. To shorten the rest of that story, these two ex-officers looked at the complaints and didn't find a problem.

When the public meetings were over, Chief Ingersoll came to a closed meeting of the Whitewash Committee and responded to specific complaints that had been raised during the public meetings. There was a lot of back and forth in the press about the meeting between Ingersoll and the Whitewash Committee being closed to the public and to the press, but I didn't blame Ingersoll for insisting on it. He would be calling specific officers by name in responding to complaints that had been raised in the public meetings, and that made it a personnel type of meeting. Ingersoll went over the cases one by one and he had an explanation for each case. He explained how each officer against whom complaints had been made in the public meetings was justified in whatever it was the officer was said to have done, or he said that the officer simply hadn't done it. When he had finished, I asked him about Chong Ko and the trial board in which Chong said he had been laughed at. Ingersoll laughed himself, as if that was all the answer I needed. I asked him about Andy Brown, and he said, "You mean that thing over on Governor Warfield Road?" and I said, "Yes," and he laughed again. Other committee members also laughed even though they didn't know anything about the case. I gave it up, which might have been a mistake, but that was what I did. At the time, I couldn't see any point in spitting in the wind.

Eventually, the committee waned to about a dozen people. One fellow who quit was some sort of counselor for teenagers in the county. He had told me, in private of course, of instances he had witnessed of kids being hassled by police officers because the kids had long hair or wore earrings. Those kinds of things didn't come up too often during the meetings. The committee reports took up most of the time. I kept going to the meetings, but, as I said a moment ago, maybe I didn't know when to quit.

Meyers was subpoenaed to go before the federal grand jury. The public still didn't know the FBI and the Justice Department were investigating Jon's death until a newspaper article said they were. The article cited Meyers' attorney as the source of the information. The article created quite a stir among the members of the Whitewash Committee. On the day the article was published, the committee members sat around a conference table for ten minutes before the start of the meeting, asking each other who had seen the article and what it could possibly mean. There was genuine shock and surprise as they questioned each other about why the FBI would be investigating Jon's death. Since, barring a miracle, I had all but given up any hope that the FBI would come up with anything, I didn't join the conversation.

I've alluded to people who signed statements saying they didn't say things attributed to them in the police report. Here's what that's about.

A friend of Jon's was cited in the police report as saying that, after Jon died, she learned from another friend that Jon often climbed the backstop, horsing around. This is call *seed-planting*. You plant the seed that Jon was so familiar with the backstop that it begins to seem quite likely he would have climbed it, again, to commit suicide. This young woman signed a notarized statement saying that she had not said this and had never known Jon to climb the backstop. The young man she supposedly learned this from also signed a notarized statement saying he had never seen Jon climb the backstop, and he had not discussed it with the young woman cited in the police report. In his notarized statement, he said the only conversation he had with anyone on the subject was when Calvin Delight asked him if he had ever seen Jon or Mickey on the backstop, and he told Calvin Delight that he had not.

Detective Lampest put a bit of information in the police report that said a friend of Jon's, a young woman, had on one occasion seen Jon drink two six-packs of beer and get "giddy" from alcohol, but not overly drunk. Lampest noted parenthetically in the police report that getting "giddy" required about the same amount of alcohol as Jon would have had before he died. The implication, of course, was that Jon could easily have climbed the backstop after drinking a lot of beer, and Lampest was putting this into the mouth of a supposed witness. Lampest also wrote in the report that this young woman had heard Jon and his friends brag about climbing the backstop and that she had heard them say such things as, "I got all the way to the top and you didn't."

Talk about seed-planting. I have to inject here that I probably was nine or ten years old the first time I climbed a backstop for the fun of it, and I got all the way to the top and never gave it a second thought. In the police report, Lampest is talking about teenagers in high school, some of whom, Jon included, were better athletes than I ever thought about being. Of course they could climb the backstop, and putting any importance on "getting all the way to the top" at the age they were at the time is ridiculous. Sometimes I think the police believe they can say anything, no matter how ridiculous it is, and the public will buy it simply because it's said by the police. Anyway, the young woman to whom this silliness was attributed wrote the Chief of Police, saying that none of the statements attributed to her in the police report were true. She also retained an attorney, a Mr. Bruce M. Plaxen of Columbia, who wrote the Columbia Flier and suggested that the Flier not include the statements attributed to his client in any articles about the case.

In another episode, a police officer wrote in the police report that he was in the local hospital emergency room while following up on an unrelated traffic accident and he had a conversation with the woman I've referred to as Yvonne Last. The officer's report says that Last said she was a physician's assistant and she knew Officer Lenny Hamilton and she knew Jon Bowie through various professional encounters. She had assisted when Jon was treated for various injuries he received in fights "and so on," and she was aware that Jon had taken drugs but was getting better in that regard. She said that she had heard that Jon owed someone money for drugs and his death probably was because someone wanted to make an example for others to see. The officer gave Last's name to Detective Lampest and suggested that Lampest contact her, which he did. In that interview, Last said, she had heard the part about drugs from a co-worker in the emergency room.

When Sandra read this in the police report, it really hit the fan. Yvonne Last, in addition to working in the local emergency room, also worked with a local medical group that saw walk-in patients. This was where Sandra took Jon after he broke his hand hitting a coffee table during the Superbowl and after he broke a finger playing baseball. These were the injuries that, according to the police report - and this is an exact quote from the report - Jon "had received in fights." Sandra had Jo Glasco call the medical group and the medical group got their own attorneys involved and I don't know if the attorneys ever got everything sorted out. I think they finally just got tired and decided to stay quiet a while in the hope that all the feathers and issues that were flying would just go away. Last told Lampest that she had heard the part about drugs from a co-worker in the emergency room. When Glasco learned this, she contacted the co-worker, who was astounded that his name had come up. He said he had stood around in a group of people talking about Jon's death the first day it was reported in the papers and they had speculated about what might have happened. He called the police department and said he wanted the police report amended to remove anything attributed to him, and he wrote the Flier and suggested they not use his name in any article related to Jon's death. He suggested that since things related to him had gotten so misconstrued and blown out of proportion, the Flier might want to cast a suspicious eye on anything that was in the police report.

As both a minister and a police chaplain, Rogers had been in and out of prisons counseling people, and he had learned the ropes of the system. When I was preparing the list of things to discuss with the FBI, Rogers made a few phone calls and learned that Doug Iglesia was being held in the state penitentiary in Jessup just outside of Columbia. Rogers also learned that Iglesia was being held under some sort of special custody of the Howard County Police, which Rogers thought was an odd arrangement for someone who supposedly was in prison for burglary.

When Rogers wasn't after Bellinger to take some action about Hope, he was after him to interview Iglesia. Bellinger, or whoever was giving him his marching orders, didn't seem to see the necessity for looking into Iglesia's claims. After a lot of phone conversations with Bellinger over several weeks, Rogers became convinced that the FBI didn't want to talk with Iglesia. Then Rogers decided to talk with Iglesia himself.

I rode with Rogers to the prison in Jessup one afternoon and waited for him in the car for over an hour. When he came back out we rode to my house, where Rogers sat on the sofa thumbing through his penciled notes.

Iglesia had told Rogers that he had been arrested for burglary. A police officer had offered to get the charges dropped if Iglesia would help the officer sell cocaine that had been confiscated during various arrests. Iglesia told Rogers he didn't know anything about selling cocaine, and he wasn't selling it fast enough to suit the officer and his other officer friends. Iglesia said he didn't know Jon Bowie all that well, but he and Jon sometimes would be at the same parties at different people's homes. Iglesia approached Jon and asked him to introduce him to friends who used cocaine. Jon wasn't a user, Iglesia said, but he knew people who were.

"It sounded like he knew what he was talking about," Rogers said. "He named kids you and I know, friends of Jon and Mickey, and he described them and the places where the parties were held."

"Did he give the officers' names?"

"Yep," Rogers said. Rogers checked his notes and ran off the names of three officers I had heard of and two I hadn't. Iglesia had said that each was either directly involved or knew about the sales. Rogers said, "He says Jon's death didn't have anything to do with the Red Roof Inn. That's just a convenient smoke screen that came up. All the attention took the heat off the people who did it."

"Who does he say did it?"

"He does a tap dance about that. He says he's sure it was the police, but he wasn't there."

"But why would the police want to kill Jon if all he did was give Iglesia some names?"

"Iglesia says Jon hid and photographed Iglesia making an illegal exchange with some police officers who were selling drugs. Jon thought that if he could prove that police officers were selling drugs, it would somehow provide credibility for his and Mickey's claims that they had been beaten. Iglesia says the police found out that Jon had photographed them."

"That could explain the camera that was missing after Jon died. Do you believe him?"

"Who knows?" Rogers said. "It seems he's holding back something, being evasive about the extent to which he was directly involved. I suppose there could be some truth in it."

"So, basically, we know this guy is saying a lot of things, but we don't have any way to prove it."

"I'll have to talk to him again," Rogers said. "Meanwhile, we can talk to Jon's and Mick's friends and see if any of them remember him."

"And the FBI still hasn't talked with him?"

"Not according to him."

"And the county?"

Rogers laughed a cynical laugh. "Two detectives," he said. "They got a release to drive Iglesia around town and show them locations that he had burglarized. Iglesia told the guard at the prison that he was afraid to leave with the detectives, and the guard said he had to go. Iglesia was terrified. He thought they were going to kill him. The detectives drove him around town showing him places that he had already told the police about. Then they drove him back to the prison and parked. One of the detectives turned to him and said, 'Now, what's this crap about police officers selling drugs?' Iglesia wasn't about to tell them anything," Rogers said. "He told them to go screw themselves. That was the county investigation."

"That's it?"

"That's it."

"So the FBI won't talk with him, and the county already has done what it calls its investigation. Why is he willing to talk with you? What's in it for him?"

"He says that he feels bad about what happened to Jon, and he feels bad for Jon's mother. He feels he has to do something about it."

"Goodness of his heart."

"That's what he says."

Sandra was in Rogers' office helping prepare a mailing to a national television show that had expressed an interest in Jon's death but never came through. The work was finished and Sandra was leaving, but Rogers came into the reception area and Sandra turned to him and said, "I want to borrow that book about people who don't die."

Roger's said, "Sure," and went back into his office to get the book off the shelf. He took it to her and she thanked him and left. It didn't occur to Rogers at the time to wonder how Sandra had known he had such a book.

Sandra called me and said she had read the book and wanted me to read it. I asked her how she found out about it.

"I don't have the slightest idea," she said. "I was at Reverend Rogers office and it just came in my head that he had it, and I asked him for it."

I read the book. It was the life story of a man who talked with dead people. He said he did it because it made their relatives feel better. He said he had not had an easy life. He had a television show in a town in Long Island. People came on the show and he talked to dead people they knew. Then the people who had known these dead people said such things as that he couldn't possibly have known some of the things he said, and they cried and believed things they hadn't really believed before, although they might have wondered.

Sandra asked me to write the author. I didn't want to do it.

"It takes two years just to get an appointment," I said. "It says so in the book. I hope to hell we're not still dealing with this in two years."

Sandra prepared a packet of information anyway and asked me to type a cover letter. I objected again.

"It says right in the book that he doesn't like to know a lot of details before he talks with somebody. He says it confuses things. He says people can say he's only repeating what he already knew."

Sandra was adamant, though, and I typed the cover letter and she sent the packet of information to the man who had claimed in a book that people don't die. We never heard from him, but, one afternoon after Sandra mailed the packet, she and I were arguing about it again at her kitchen table. In the middle of the argument she put her hands over her ears and her eyes got wide. She said, "I just heard Jon. He said, 'We don't need that man. We talk.'"

Rogers got the slides of the West Virginia autopsy from Jo Glasco. I met with him in his office and he turned off the lights and closed out the sunlight with the long, vertical blinds that covered one side of the room and the room was dark. He flicked on the projector and the white light made a large square on one wall.

"You don't have to do this," he told me.

"I'll be fine," I said. I took a deep breath and told myself it was only pictures.

Rogers flipped the slides one after the other and we questioned any unusual marks or bruises. We decided the marks on the stomach and chest could have been caused by the rope that the rescue squad had used to lower Jon from the backstop, and by the backstop wire itself. The marks around the upper neck clearly were caused by the cable.

One slide showed a bruise that had been in the West Virginia autopsy report but not in the Maryland report, the rope-burn looking bruise that came up the front of the right shoulder from underneath the armpit. The incongruity of this bruise had not fully sunk into my thinking at the time, and I didn't mention it.

There also was the large y-shaped bruise at the lower right side of the neck, just above the collar bone. I had not yet learned that there was a martial arts maneuver that, if administered too forcefully, could cause such a bruise, and I asked Rogers, "What could have caused that?"

"Don't know," Rogers said. "Let's find out." He went to his desk and picked up the phone.

"Who are you calling?"

"The State Medical Examiner in West Virginia. They're his slides."

I couldn't believe he was doing it, but do it he did. He actually got the man on the phone, and the two of them had a lengthy conversation. When Rogers hung up, he said, "That bruise worries him, too. He says that, in all likelihood, it was not caused by the cable. It's more likely that it was caused by a single, straight-on blow from some object. You heard me ask him if it could have caused death." Rogers moved a finger down his penciled notes. "His answer was, 'It was a significant enough injury to have been the cause of death.'"

I had to think about that a moment.

"Why didn't he say that in his autopsy report?"

"He said he wasn't going to get in a shouting contest with the Maryland State Medical Examiner."

"Damn. Just what the world needs, another chickenshit scientist. So, what could have caused a bruise like that?"

"He wasn't sure." Rogers said. "Maybe some sort of blunt object."

That night I had nightmares.

39 Rogers set up a meeting with Chief Ingersoll and asked Sandra and me to come. We sat around the small, round table in the office where, a few months before, the previous Chief of Police had accepted Rogers' resignation. Ingersoll came in and explained that he couldn't attend such a meeting without a witness. He wanted to know if that was acceptable, and we said it was fine. Ingersoll left and returned with his chief assistant, a man I'll call Major Walter Fletcher. The five of us sat around the little round table.

I won't go into all that we talked about. It simply would take too long. Suffice it to say that neither Rogers nor Sandra nor I knew anything that could lead to finding out what had happened to Jon. If we had, we would have beat Ingersoll's door down long before that. Ingersoll was an intelligent man, so I assumed he knew that. What I hoped to gain from the meeting was for Ingersoll to take Jon's death more seriously than Hickory had, and to follow up by doing whatever he could about it. What I didn't want to come of the meeting was for Ingersoll simply to follow up on what we had to say, point by point, and then close the case. That, as I saw it, would have been nothing more than ass-covering. The meeting wasn't publicized in any way, but things had gotten to the point where neither Rogers nor Sandra nor I could walk into the police department without it getting noticed. The meeting cost Ingersoll a lot of grief from some officers in the police department who saw it as evidence that Ingersoll didn't support his officers. Ingersoll was a man caught in the middle.

To keep it short, we talked about whether the blown up photographs of Jon on the backstop might reveal anything, whether the beeper was actually a leather object, whether certain rumors about people who knew things but wouldn't come forward were true, whether the snuff can that showed up where Eddie Vickers said he was strangled had any fingerprints on it, why laboratory results showed no rain water on Jon's clothing when it had rained that night, whether the police report could be cleared up to show that some people had provided sworn statements saying that the things attributed to them in the report were inaccurate, and on and on.

And, of course, there was Hope. Rogers insisted that we let Ingersoll in on that. The FBI, Rogers said, had messed around with it long enough. Ingersoll thanked Rogers for passing on the story. Ingersoll said that he already had tried everything he could think of to locate the woman. He even had checked a large database of some sort in another state, trying to piece together details from Rogers' statement in a way that could lead to finding the woman. I don't know if the FBI was being selective in what it shared with the police department, or if Ingersoll saw some need to be less than forthcoming about what he knew before Rogers told him, but it appeared that, until then, Ingersoll didn't know Hope by name.

Sandra wanted to make sure Ingersoll knew that Jon carried a red key tag with a house key on it, and that the house key had never been found, and that someone had broken into her home at the same time Jon's body was being lowered from the backstop, and that Jon's camera and the tape to his answering machine were missing.

Ingersoll apparently hadn't heard that before, and he brushed it off with, "We probably couldn't have found the person anyway."

When the meeting was over, everybody got up from the table and shook hands. When Ingersoll shook my hand he said, "We will do everything that can be done," and I said, "It leads where it leads."

Then Rogers and Sandra and I were in the parking lot and I said I hoped Ingersoll wouldn't just follow up on the things we had to tell him. Rogers said I should be patient, and not so cynical.

Sandra said, "I don't trust them. Nothing's coming of this. It's a waste of time."

A young man named Howard traveled from New York to Columbia to visit friends. It happened that one of the friends he visited also had been a close friend of Jon's. I'd put Howard in his middle twenties. He was well under six feet tall and had dark, wavy hair. He worked for *Vanity Fair Magazine* in some capacity I never quite figured out. Howard became intrigued with the story of Jon's death, which still was very much in the local news at the time.

After some back and forth through mutual friends, several people attended a meeting at Rogers' office in the Oakland Mills Village Center. Howard, several of Jon's and Mickey's friends, and Sandra and Rogers and I were there. Two young women who were criminal justice majors, and who were working for Rogers as interns at the time, also were there. Howard asked questions about the case and listened as we filled in various details. We discussed the motel incident, Jon's death, the woman who claimed that a police officer had raped her, and our general dissatisfaction with the various investigations, grand jury proceedings and court appearances. Howard wondered aloud, as everyone who heard the story did, at the likelihood that police officers had in some way been involved in Jon's death.

"That's an issue we can't talk about," I told him. "The investigations have been half-hearted for who knows what reason. With no real investigation, we don't know what happened anymore than anyone else does. All we know for sure is that a lot of effort has gone into not looking into Jon's death, and in trying to make Jon look like a delinquent in the process."

Howard made it clear that he could not speak for *Vanity Fair*. He did commit to writing a story on a freelance basis. He would talk to several people whose names we gave him and then write the story and offer it to the editor he worked for. If it didn't suit the present needs of *Vanity Fair*, then he would, with the assistance of his magazine, seek other publishers.

One of the names we gave Howard was Doug Iglesia. By this time Rogers had met with Iglesia several times, and Howard asked Rogers to get him into the prison. Rogers arranged it, and, on Howard's next visit to Columbia, Howard talked to Iglesia. I knew when Howard was coming, and, after work that day, I called Rogers and asked how it went.

"He was blown away," Rogers said. "He intends to follow up on the story, but he has some serious concerns about his own safety."

The phone woke me late enough at night that I immediately wondered who had died. I jumped out of bed and bounced down the stairs to answer it in the kitchen. It was Rogers, and fear and panic were in his voice.

"Come get me," he said. "I'm at my office. Hurry."

"What's going on?"

"Just come," he said. "There are several police officers outside my office. They've been banging on the door and trying to get in. I'm afraid to go out there."

"I'll be right there."

The phone woke my older son, Mike, and he came sleepy-eyed into the kitchen. Mike had graduated from Wake Forest and was home for the few weeks before he was to marry his high school sweetheart. Mike's a good-sized kid, and smart like his mother. I said, "Get dressed. Rogers needs help. I'll explain in the car." I had tried not to involve my family in the Bowie case, but my mind was racing and it just came out of my mouth. I dressed hurriedly and whispered as much of an explanation to Jane as I could manage.

I got to the car first and Mike came out carrying his tennis shoes. He got in the car and I handed him a baseball bat. I started explaining and backing out of the drive at the same time.

"There's not a lot of time to talk about this," I said, "but there's a time to react and a time to hold back. I don't know which we're about to get into." I told him what Rogers had said. "When we get there, you get behind the steering wheel and I'll get out. Keep the car running and the doors unlocked. If anything happens that you can't do anything about, just get the hell out of there." On the kitchen wall by the phone, I kept a list of people to call in case of emergencies related to the Bowie case. There were numbers for reporters, attorneys and about a dozen larger than average friends. "Call everyone on the list by the phone," I said. "Tell them what's going on and where, and tell them to get there fast."

"What about the bat?" Mike asked.

"I really don't like having this conversation with my son," I said. "It's important - and I mean really important - that you and I and everybody else come out of this still respecting the police. But you can't look at a guy doing something he's got no business doing as a police officer. He's just a guy wearing blue clothes." That was about all the time I thought I had for preliminaries. "If these guys get rough, and you size it up as something you can do something about, then make the first blow count. Don't leave yourself wishing you'd put more in it. Follow through like you have to knock a tree down. Then get the hell out of there."

Mike was quiet for a moment. "Are you sure about this?"

"I'm not sure about anything," I said. "I'm sorry as hell that we're in this car talking about this. What I'm telling you is the very last thing you should even consider, and I mean the very last. But if it has to be done, then do it right the first time."

Mike gripped the bat in both hands and sat considering his fists for the rest of the ride. There probably was better advice that could have been given. I wish I could tell this honestly and put myself in a better light, but it was the advice I gave. Fortunately, it wasn't needed.

We got to Rogers' office and, as we approached with the car lights out, it was apparent from the illumination of the street lights that Rogers' blue Subaru was the only car in the parking lot. There was no one in sight. I parked and Mike got out and came around to the driver's side. I walked across the grass to Rogers' door and knocked. It was a massive door made of large timbers and my knocks made little more than muffled thuds, but Rogers called out immediately from behind the door, "Who is it?"

"It's me," I said. "Dave."

"Who's with you?"

"Mike. He's in the car."

"Is anyone else out there?"

"No."

"Look across the street, under the street light on the other side."

I backed away from the door and looked.

"Nobody."

Rogers opened the door and his face looked as if it had been pumping sweat for an hour. His eyes were bulging-tense.

"Come in," he said.

"I can't," I said. "Mike's in the car."

Rogers was too upset to drive. When he had turned out the lights and locked up he got in the car with Mike and me and I drove Mike home. As Mike was getting out of the car I grabbed his arm and said, "We'll talk."

I drove to a school parking lot in Rogers' neighborhood. Rogers kept taking long, deep breaths. By the time I parked and turned out the lights he had started to calm down.

"My phone's tapped," he said.

"Why do you say that?"

"I was at home," he said, "and, at about eleven o'clock, a client called. He said he had to talk to me and he wanted to meet me at my office. I tried to schedule him for tomorrow, but he said he had to talk to me tonight. He'd had an argument with his girlfriend, and he was stressed out. I finally said I would meet him and I set a time. When I got to the office, the police were there. My client is heavy into drugs and I guess they had a warrant for him. When he got there they arrested him in the parking lot. I feel terrible about it. He probably thinks I turned him in."

"Maybe the police followed him there."

"No, they were there when I got there. I saw them."

"Maybe his phone's tapped. He's the one into drugs."

"He wasn't calling me from his house. He said so on the phone."

"Why did you go inside? Why didn't you just stay outside and talk with them?"

"Are you kidding? I put two and two together and figured there was no way they could have known to be there waiting for him. Then I noticed that they weren't wearing name tags. Cops who don't wear name tags are up to no good. I went inside and locked the door. I was going to stay there all night if I had to. They banged on the door and said they wanted to talk to me. I told them I didn't have anything to say. They said they thought there was a warrant out for me and I had to open the door. I told them to slip the warrant under the door and I'd read it."

"They had a warrant for you?"

"They didn't have a warrant for me. They just said that to get me to open the door. They beat on the door a while and kept saying they had to talk to me and I wouldn't let them in. That's when they went across the street and stood under the light, and I called you."

Rogers finally talked himself out and I took him home. I drove home and tiptoed in the house and, miraculously, Jane didn't wake up. I had to be ready for work in three hours, and I fell asleep trying to find a hole in Rogers' logic that would tell me his phone wasn't tapped. Unless he had some of his details wrong, I couldn't find one.

Iglesia had a brother I'll call Carlos. Carlos called Rogers and said he was coming to Rogers' office. This made Rogers uneasy. I was working over an hour's drive away, and Rogers called Sandra and asked if she knew anyone who could come to his office to be there as a witness, and maybe to help out in case there was trouble. Sandra brought Mickey and a large friend of Mickey's who played football. They were sitting in the reception area when Carlos showed up. Rogers led Carlos into his office and closed the door.

Carlos said loudly enough for Sandra and Mickey and Mickey's friend to hear through the door that, unless Rogers stopped visiting Doug in prison, Carlos would see to it that Rogers regretted it. Carlos said he knew where Rogers lived, and that Rogers couldn't stay home all the time. Carlos said he had been in the army and he had several automatic weapons. He said he had killed people before.

Rogers lost it. He said something like, "If so much as a few molecules of your breath blow into the same neighborhood where my family lives, I'll make you beg me to kill you and then I'll do it."

Sandra and Mickey and Mickey's friend looked at each other and didn't know whether to break down the door or run like hell. Then Carlos stormed out of Rogers' office and left.

Sandra said later that she thought Carlos might actually have tried to get physical with Rogers if she and the others hadn't been sitting outside in the reception area.

Rogers called me at work and said Carlos had just visited him.

"Call Ingersoll," I told him. "Maybe it'll start to dawn on him that kids who commit suicide don't often provoke people into making death threats."

Rogers called Ingersoll and Ingersoll sent an officer to ask Carlos if he had threatened Rogers. Carlos told the officer that it was Rogers who had threatened him. Ingersoll called Rogers and Rogers called me.

"Damn," I said. "Don't you think it would occur to Ingersoll that you don't just knock on somebody's door and ask them if they threatened somebody? He'll never get to the bottom of things like that. I thought maybe he'd send somebody to talk to Doug and ask him why his brother thinks he has to be so protective."

"I asked him that," Rogers said. "He said he had to take the threat seriously. Safety comes first. He had to put Carlos on notice."

"Sounds good," I said, "like everything else we hear. Think he'll have someone interview Doug now?"

Rogers laughed from all the way down in his gut. He still was laughing when I hung up.

Rogers called me at work.

"Listen to this," he said. "I'm going to play back my answering machine."

There was some clicking and popping on the line. Then a voice said, "Okay. You can disconnect now." Then there was a crackling sound, and Rogers came back on the line.

"Did you hear it?"

"What was that?"

"I was making a phone call and my phone sounded funny. When the call was over, I stayed on the phone a few minutes, listening. Another call came in on the other line and the answering machine clicked on and recorded this while I was listening."

"Run outside and see if there are any telephone people working on the lines. Then call me back."

He did, and there weren't.

Rogers had a wooden-handled .357 Magnum about the size of an elephant's leg. He visited the local target range where police officers and NRA types practiced and showed off to themselves in their spare time. Rogers didn't want to take up the sport. He had grown up around guns and he just wanted to know if he still had his aim, in case he had to use the gun. With a little luck, maybe he would shoot well and word would get around and he wouldn't have to use the gun. He ordered one target, took it to the line and set it up, and fired off a few shots. He put all the shots either inside the bull's eye or just a hair outside. He tossed the target in the trash and was pretty sure it wasn't just his imagination that a few people stared at him as he left.

Rogers asked the Whitewash Committee to recommend buying a computerized situation simulator for the police department. It would throw the police department off guard, he reasoned, if he was willing to do something for them. They might at least feel a need to act friendly toward him, which could have benefits. "Besides," he said, "maybe some of the ignoramuses can actually learn not to shoot people sometimes." A simulation was scheduled with a representative of the manufacturer. Anyone on the Whitewash Committee who wanted to was invited to participate along with selected police officers. Rogers went to the simulation and he hung around making a point of going last. A couple of police officers shot simulated old ladies and children coming out of apartments and homeless people in alleys and on the sidewalk. A few committee members shot everything from high rise windows to squad car tires. Rogers took his turn last and scored the same as the fire arms instructor from the police academy.

All of this shooting might not have accomplished much else, but Rogers felt safer as word of it got around.

40 In August of 1991, about a year and a half after the incident at the Red Roof Inn, there was a county police department hearing to determine if officers Roland Meyers and Lenny Hamilton had done anything wrong at the motel. Officer Sam Long was out of the loop again and was not charged. None of the related newspaper articles explained why.

The reason for the hearing was that the police department's own Internal Affairs Division had found Meyers and Hamilton guilty of violating department policies, and of using excessive force. The hearing was an internal appeal process called a trial board. Three police officers were appointed to hear evidence and decide if Internal Affairs had made a good decision.

I had originally planned to go on at some considerable length about that hearing, countering this point and that action and such, but it's no longer necessary. Anybody who followed the Rodney King case knows the kinds of things that can happen. Anybody who followed the O.J. Simpson trial knows how the irrelevancies can become seemingly endless. Anybody who followed the Waco business knows how some people in law enforcement like to talk about anything except what took place.

The hearing lasted for three days, recessed for a month, met again for a day or so, and ended. The attorney for the police department called several of the kids who had been at the motel, including Mickey. The attorney for the police department also called a police training instructor, who talked about different danger zones on the body and how no police officer is trained to choke a person or hit a person in the face with a night stick unless it's a life threatening situation. The attorney for the police department tried to call an investigator from the Internal Affairs Division, the police department group that brought the charges in the first place, but the three police officers running the trial board wouldn't let the investigator be called. Other people at the motel had come out of their rooms to watch as the police arrested Jon and Mickey, but none of these people were called.

The great majority of the time at the trial board was spent as Kent, Meyers' attorney, cross-examined Mickey and the other kids who had been at the motel, trying to make them look like liars. There were no corroborating details or witnesses to counter what the kids said. Just cute questions. The two police officers who were charged never took the stand. In fact, the only defense witness was Sergeant Simpson of the Maryland State Police. I'm not making that up. The thousand and some odd pages of trial board testimony are public record, and you can look it up. Simpson's testimony consisted entirely of his reading into the record those parts of the state police report that had to do with Jon having a drinking problem.

The hearing ended and a few more weeks went by. Sandra kept getting calls telling her to go to this building or that because the board of officers had reached a verdict, and she kept getting called back and told that it had been called off. Finally, in November, she got a call to go to the police department because the verdict was in. Reporters came and Meyers' and Hamilton's and Sandra's friends and family came. Mickey wouldn't go. He said, "You know what they're going to decide. I'm not wasting my time."

Hamilton and Meyers were found innocent.

What's new?

The part of Simpson's report that Simpson read into the record included the business about Jon getting into various fights and breaking bones. I've already covered that, so I won't go into it again. The attorney for the police department tried to open up the issue of Iglesia, which Simpson also read into the record, but the three police officers running the trial board wouldn't let that subject be discussed. What I want to touch on is the part Simpson read into the record about Jon drinking, which was the core of what Simpson testified about.

The state police reported that between the ages of fifteen and seventeen Jon was - and this is an exact quote from the report Simpson prepared for Boudreaux and read into the record at the police trial board - "usually in an intoxicated state." It was pure character assassination, but you don't have to take my word for it.

You could ask Jerome Johnson. The kids called him J.J., and he was Jon's high school varsity baseball coach. Simpson said, at the meeting with

Sandra after the county grand jury and also at the police trial board, that he had talked with Jon's high school baseball coach. Simpson said he talked with Jon's coach about the lock on the backstop and about whether Jon was, "usually in an intoxicated state." When Simpson thought he was talking to Jon's head coach, he actually was talking to the assistant coach. The assistant coach didn't know anything about a drinking problem, and told Simpson that. Simpson never talked to J.J. If he had, J.J. would have told him that Jon was a born leader. J.J. would have said that he had the highest regard for Jon, and that was why J.J. selected Jon as captain of the baseball team, a position of honor which requires that a person have the respect of the entire student body. So, who do you believe? Do you believe the state police, or do you believe J.J.?

And if you believe the state police, which state police do you believe? Do you believe Simpson in the report he prepared for Boudreaux' purposes, or do you believe the investigator who, a month before Jon died, conducted his own routine background investigation and reported that Jon was fit to continue working at a daycare center?

Or, do you believe the Maryland Human Resources Department? Dottie Ernst and Sandy Boyd of that agency observed the daycare center where Jon worked, and they did it on an ongoing basis from the time Jon was sixteen until he was nineteen. They sat in the classrooms where Jon worked as an assistant and they observed his performance, and they approved it. This is not the kind of thing that agency does when a person is in an intoxicated state. Are we to believe the state daycare inspectors, or are we to believe the state police? The daycare inspectors kept thorough records, which could be checked. Unfortunately, if we are to believe the state police, they didn't keep any records of their investigation of Jon. When Jo Glasco asked the state police for their records of the investigation, the state police told Glasco they hadn't kept any. So you'll have to take Ernst's and Boyd's word for it when they say the state police never talked to them about Jon, although they gladly would have talked with the state police if they had been asked.

And, are we to assume that the public school system was incompetent in not referring Jon to an alcohol treatment program, or even to a school counselor for this alleged drinking problem? Or, did the school let Jon wander the halls in an inebriated state?

If it was up to Sandra, she would include all sixty-some of the statements people wrote in support of Jon back when I was asking Sandra why she was collecting all those statements and Sandra said that sometimes I didn't understand anything. I'll just touch on a few. Jon's high school home room teacher never saw Jon in an inebriated state and asked to be contacted if any further information was needed. J.J. wrote that he was shocked anyone would say Jon had a drinking problem because, if he had, J.J. would have known about it. Jon's American Legion coach wrote that he'd never noticed any drinking problem, and Jon's recreational-league football coach wrote the same thing. Parents at the daycare center wrote that they had never seen any indication that Jon had been drinking, and the woman who owned the daycare center wrote, "Why didn't this so-called investigation team talk to anyone who really knew Jon?" She asked, "What ever happened to the real purpose of this investigation?" She said she had written Simpson and asked to be interviewed. A man wrote that he had known Jon for ten years, had employed him one summer while Jon supposedly was constantly intoxicated to supervise his children forty hours a week, and had used him as a babysitter for years. He never saw any indication of alcohol or drug use. A special assistant to the Superintendent of Schools in Annapolis, and a Special Education teacher, whose children stayed at the daycare school Sandra managed, said he had known Jon ten years, had had him in his home for sleepovers with his son, had used Jon on his softball team, and had never seen Jon under the influence of alcohol or drugs. Another parent wrote, "Quite personally, I'd like to see an investigation of what happened to Jon Bowie instead of a phoney assassination of a fine young man's character." Neighbors wrote that they had never observed any alcohol or drug use and usually saw Jon and Mickey going to or coming from some athletic event, which was how they spent most of their time. Jon's high school sociology teacher wrote that he was not aware of any alcohol problem, and also asked to be contacted if any additional information was required.

I could go on, but you get the picture. The state police said one thing, without saying where they got their information, and people who knew Jon said something else.

Actually, I happen to know where Simpson got the information that Jon usually was in an intoxicated state. Simpson got it from Officer Tim Burns, Meyers' drinking buddy, and Simpson put it in the report he prepared for Boudreaux' purposes. Simpson admitted this to Jo Glasco in a meeting with Glasco and Sandra. So, let's just cut to the chase. Do you believe Meyers' drinking buddy, or do you believe these people who knew Jon?

Before the police trial board reached it's decision, while it was in recess for a month, the Whitewash Committee continued to meet. The County Executive had appointed a perky young high school student to the committee, and she came up with the idea for a survey to determine if the community was happy with the police. There was much arguing about the lack of statistical validity of the survey, but the few of us on the committee who demonstrated any evidence of having opened the cover of a statistics book lost that argument. The survey asked such questions as, "Are you happy with the police department?" and "Do you feel safe?" Thousands of copies went out in the mail along with water bills, and about seventeen hundred came back. Most of those that came back reflected general satisfaction with the local police. This was seen by some committee members as a major milestone in the process, and it was reported in the papers. Jim, Sandra's husband, worked with the post office, and he had friends who had friends.

Sandra had a conversation with a woman who worked in the post office in a small town north of Columbia. The woman told Sandra that she had been asked to ensure that the survey was mailed to zip codes that were mostly rural, and where mostly older people lived. The woman wouldn't say it publicly for fear that it could have a negative impact on her job.

Sandra hit the streets with a petition in support of a review board made up of civilians who would oversee complaints against the police department. She pulled in twenty-four-hundred signatures in fairly short time and showed up at a meeting of the Whitewash Committee to present her petition. The perky little high school kid who designed the committee's study said that she thought Sandra's petition was not valid. Most of the rest of the committee members said nothing. A few grinned. There were a few questions, and Sandra's petition got under five minutes of committee consideration.

The committee eventually voted on whether to support a review board. My personal inclinations went against a review board unless it was an absolute last resort. Nothing's going to change how some police officers act until the other officers who work with them stop putting up with it. It has to come from inside. Still, I was irritated at how the committee didn't seem to be considering it in any serious way, and at how they had laughed off Sandra's petition. I wrote a paper in favor of the damned thing and even voted for it. That made Rogers and me and maybe two or three more people for it. So many members had quit the committee in disgust or boredom or fear or whatever by the time we voted that we actually came within a few votes of pulling it off.

There were, of course, newspaper articles about the committee's decision not to recommend a review board. Rogers said in an article that he wasn't surprised that the committee didn't want a review board, seeing how the committee was made up largely of present or retired police officers. I said it had to do with the Red Roof Inn, that voting for a review board could make the county look as if something wrong might have happened there. Other members were quoted as saying that Rogers and I were just sore losers.

One committee member, the retired military police officer who lived across the street from Scarsy, wrote a letter to the editor if the Flier. It was a predictable letter. He disagreed that committee membership was one-sided, said that lots of people had been given opportunities to speak to the board, and went on at length about Sandra's petition with twenty-four-hundred signatures on it. He said that when Sandra presented her petition there were questions from the committee that led to serious reservations. As I've said, that questioning lasted less than five minutes and consisted as much of snickers and sly grins as of words, but that was what he said. He questioned Sandra's methods in collecting the signatures. He questioned the youthfulness of some who signed, said that Sandra had a personal and an emotional interest, and that she had failed to present opposing views when she presented the petition to those who signed. He suggested that Rogers was motivated by his past friendship with Jon.

If the letter had been written by anyone other than this particular retired military officer, Sandra probably would not have responded. Since it was this particular fellow, she gave it one of her better shots.

At the public meeting, months before, when Sandra showed up to ask that notarized statements be added to the police report, she came away pretty steamed, and not just because she didn't believe the statements would get added. When that meeting ended, a couple of reporters and a few committee members were standing around talking about what the Whitewash Committee was really about, which was the Bowie case, even though that almost never got discussed in formal committee meetings. This particular retired military officer walked into the conversation when it was already in progress and, not bothering to notice that such people as reporters and people who would be sure to tell Sandra were there, said, "Who, him? They should have hung him." This caused something of a furor, and not all of it that night. A reporter went home intent on writing the story, but the story never got printed.

I'll say this fellows first name was Walter, and after that Rogers and Sandra and I referred to him as Walter They-shoulda-hung-'im. Rogers, as part of his dealings with the Whitewash Committee, suggested to Walter that he and Walter share a round of golf. Rogers and Walter and a couple of the Walter's friends did that. One of the more memorable occurrences during that round of golf occurred when Rogers and one of Walter's friends were standing next to a sand trap. Walter's friend reached into the sand trap with a club and drew a swastika in the sand. Rogers took it as some sort of message that was intended for him to see.

So, now, Walter They-shoulda-hung-'im was questioning Sandra's objectivity, methods and emotions in a public letter.

In her reply, Sandra started by saying that ninety percent of those who signed her petition were over thirty years old, although she found it odd that someone on a committee with two teenaged members appointed by the County Executive would find the opinions of teenagers irrelevant. She said that the police had no more business policing themselves than her family would have being on a jury if she was being tried for something. She said that if this retired military officer was offended that she hadn't presented opposing views, then perhaps he should revisit the concept of freedom of speech. As for her personal and emotional involvement, she asked if this fellow also was opposed to Mothers Against Drunk Drivers. She mentioned that no officer had ever been found guilty of excessive force in Howard County, even though the police department had received numerous excessive force complaints. Referring to herself and a friend who had helped her collect the signatures, she said that two grandmothers had pretty well embarrassed the committee and that the committee was squirming instead of taking action. In closing, she mentioned that Rogers never knew Jon and that at the time of Jon's death Rogers worked for the police department.

I don't know how Walter took Sandra's reply. The atmosphere was pretty chilly at the few remaining meetings of the Whitewash Committee, and the subject didn't come up.

Sandra wasn't' really a grandmother, although her daughter, Carlen, was pregnant. Sandra was stretching it a bit with the grandmother talk in her letter to the Flier. Sandra became convinced that Carlen was pregnant, but Carlen didn't believe it at first.

"Well, I'm sure of it," Sandra said. "You'll see."

After Carlen learned that she was pregnant, she began to look at her mother a bit out of the corner of her eye.

The large manila envelope lay on Sandra's kitchen table for several days. The return address read Department of Police. One afternoon I stopped by and Sandra pointed to it.

"I can't open it," she said. "I know what it says, and I don't want to read it."

I took it home and opened it. It contained a three-page letter addressed to Sandra and signed by Ingersoll. The letter said an investigator had been assigned to look into all of the items Sandra had wanted looked into when she and Rogers and I met with Ingersoll, and that the investigation had taken several weeks. There was a list of things that had been investigated and, as I started reading, I said out loud to myself, "Shit. They settled for public relations and ass covering."

Item by item, the letter addressed each thing we had presented to Ingersoll. There's no point in going into all of them. As I said before, if we had known what happened to Jon, the meeting wouldn't have been necessary in the first place. The letter ended by stating that the police department's investigation of "the incident" was concluded.

I waited a day or two before I stopped by Sandra's again. I laid the envelope on her kitchen table and said, "It's what you think." She flinched and busied herself cleaning the kitchen counter. I waited a few moments and said, "Ingersoll closed the case," and she cleaned harder. "From the way it's stated," I said, "it wouldn't surprise me if the Office of Law wrote it for him. It's all so careful and precise." Sandra brought her kitchen rag to the table and sat with it on her lap, squeezing it with both hands.

"So they didn't investigate anything." It was more of a statement than a question.

I said, "I wouldn't call it an investigation. They were just touching all the bases. Now, if we ever complain about the investigation, they can say they looked into everything we told them about."

Sandra lifted the rag and I thought she was going to strike the table with it in her hand, but she lowered her hand and rested it on the table.

"They're all a bunch of crooks," she said.

I'd had a few days to calm down after my own disappointment so, instead of fueling her anger, I said, "No. It's tougher than that. What they are is a bunch of decent people who believe in what they're doing. That's what makes it so hard."

She looked at me as if I'd asked her a riddle that made no sense. "How can you say that?" she said. "You almost sound like one of them."

Her saying it stung me some, but I didn't feel like arguing.

"I didn't mean to imply that what they're doing is right," I said. "I just meant that most of them probably find it convenient to believe that it is."

Two young female criminal justice majors worked for Rogers that winter as interns. One of these young women also worked part-time at a local ice skating rink. In a conversation with her boss at the rink, it came out that she had an interest in the Bowie case. I guess this man went into some short of shouting tirade and said he had a personal friend who was an FBI agent. This FBI agent friend of his had told him the FBI was coming out with a report that would tear Sandra and her friends up one side and down the other. This young woman mentioned this tirade to Rogers, who repeated it to Tina Gutierrez.

The long and short of it was that one afternoon two men knocked on Sandra's door and introduced themselves as FBI agents. Sandra let them in and they sat at her kitchen table and talked. It seemed that the FBI was doing an internal investigation to determine if any of its agents were leaking information or were involved in any other similar improprieties. The conversation quickly got around to Rogers and his involvement in the Bowie case. Rogers, at that time, was serving as interim pastor of a small church in Taneytown, a rural community an hour or so west of Columbia.

"Does Reverend Rogers run a cult?" one of the agents asked.

Sandra was so taken aback at the question that she laughed out loud, although the question had been asked seriously.

"Right," she said. "He certainly does. And it's filled with little purple-haired ladies from Taneytown. If I were you, I'd drive up there one Sunday and investigate it."

When the FBI completed its internal investigation of that situation, the conclusion was that a Howard County police officer, and not an FBI agent, was spreading word that the final FBI report was going to tear Sandra and her friends apart. I didn't find a lot of reason for comfort in that.

Two men showed up on Sandra's doorstep in the middle of January. Mickey was at home alone and they told him they were from the FBI. They handed him a letter and left.

The letter was from a woman named Linda Davis, whom the letter identified as the head of the Criminal Section of the Civil Rights Division of the United States Department of Justice. The letter contained only three short paragraphs, and no specifics, and one sentence in the middle said it all.

After a thorough investigation and careful review of the evidence we concluded that this matter should be closed.

A couple of weeks went by before an article in the Washington Post said the Justice Department had announced that the case was closed. In a related article, Chief Ingersoll said he was pleased that it was finally over.

41 Rogers and Hope had several conversations, on the phone or at his office or in some agreed upon private place. With the FBI and the state police no longer in the picture, it was up to the local police to follow up on Hope's allegations, and Hope was having reservations. In one conversation, Hope suggested that Rogers was trying to manipulate the situation for his own purposes. In another, Hope said she had talked with her own minister, and her minister had suggested that what had happened to her was her own fault, that she had invited it. This greatly disturbed Hope. She told Rogers her minister was trying to help her become a better person, or something like that.

Rogers called Hope's minister and invited him over for a chat. Hope's minister came to Rogers' office and Rogers explained to the man in rather heated words that perhaps the man had done less than a good thing.

Rogers called me at work and he clearly was in the linebacker frame of mind. He said he was going to call Boudreaux and press charges himself against the police officer Hope said had raped her. I told Rogers I thought it was the worst idea I had ever heard.

"I talked with Tina," he said. "She says there's no reason I can't go to Boudreaux as a citizen and file a charge of rape against him. It could be just the thing to give Hope confidence to come forward after the number the FBI did on her."

"Maybe you have the right," I said, "but my gut tells me that it's the last you'll ever hear from that woman."

"I think you're wrong," Rogers said, "and I'm doing it. I've already called Boudreaux and made an appointment."

"Then don't show up," I said. "People do it all the time. Or be a nice guy and cancel."

"My mind's made up," he said. "I wasn't calling you for permission. I just thought you'd want to know. If the police won't do it, and the FBI won't do it, then somebody has to."

"Well, if you want my opinion, I think it's stupid."

"I don't," he said.

Rogers called me after he met with Boudreaux.

"So, how'd it go?" I asked him. I tried to sound sarcastic, but if Rogers noticed he ignored it.

"I think it went really well," he said. "He thanked me and shook my hand with genuine sincerity. He said that even when others told him that Sandra had made the whole thing up, he had always believed there might be a really disturbed person out there in need of help. He thanked me for trusting him to do his job."

"And you bought that?"

"I believe him, if that's what you mean." This time, he did sound a bit offended.

"You don't think that by 'a really disturbed person' he means that the woman must be some kind of nut for saying what she did, and now that you've told him who she is he'll make sure it's never heard from again?"

There was a long silence.

"I never realized you were such a cynic," he finally said.

"Actually, I'm not," I said, "but after walking on hot coals a while, I start to notice the blisters."

"With all my heart, I believe you're wrong," he said in his sincerest of preacher voices.

I said, "With all my heart I believe that, with the best of intentions, you have done a very stupid thing. You can kiss that woman goodbye."

Let's see. How much of this do I have to leave out to keep from violating any privacy laws? To be on the safe side, I think I'll leave out a lot.

Rogers got word that Boudreaux had helped Hope obtain a $10,000 settlement in a legal claim that was not even remotely connected to her allegation that she had been raped by a police officer. It just so happened that I had also gotten the same information from a fairly reliable source. In other words, I could document it if it came to that.

So, when Rogers called me and started talking about it, I interrupted him and said, "I heard."

"What do you make of it?"

"Shit," I said to the preacher. "It's one hundred percent legal. You couldn't prove in a thousand years that Boudreaux didn't just help her get her legal due."

"You don't think it was a payoff?"

"Of course I do. Until a short time ago Boudreaux didn't know her name, and now he's suddenly zipped her through the system and come up with $10,000 that's rightfully hers? Get real. I'm just saying you couldn't prove it."

I didn't remind Rogers I had warned him. There was no point in rubbing it in.

A thousand little and not so little things brought me to the brink of giving up, throwing in the towel, walking away and never looking back. I won't go into all of them. In an otherwise innocent conversation with Gus Ingersoll after a meeting of the Whitewash Committee, Ingersoll asked me what it was like being Sandra's friend. Without so much as a preliminary thought, I said, "It's like being the dog who caught the wheel."

Suffice it to say that I had been holding the wheel in my teeth for a long time, and I thought it was time to let go. I told myself I had had it, and one evening I went to sleep muttering about how it might never be over, but it was over for me. I told myself, "I quit."

I awoke about daybreak and was coming out of that fog that is half sleep and half waking, and I heard a voice inside my head as clearly as I've ever heard anything.

"You've come too far to let it die."

Hearing a voice inside my head was a new experience for me. It was not a thing for which I was emotionally prepared. I sat up and looked around and discounted the voice as the remainder of some dream I couldn't recall. At the same time, I tried to reconcile to myself how clearly I had heard it. I shook myself mentally and tried to clarify what I thought I had heard but doubted I really had by speaking out loud to myself in an exasperated way.

"What?"

There was no denying that, eyes open and looking down at the covers, I heard it again as clearly as I had heard it the first time.

"You've come too far too let it die."

It's the kind of thing that can get a person's attention. It got mine.

I called Mama.

"I'm pretty stressed out," I said.

"I know," she said. "I was going to call you."

"Maybe it was an accident," I said. "That's possible. Maybe Jon and his girlfriend argued or something like that. Maybe he had too much to drink and climbed up on the backstop and thought he would give everyone a good scare. It *was* prom night, and he was a star athlete from a year or two earlier at that same school. Maybe he was a big fish in a small pond who had a bad night for whatever reason and wanted to make some kind of point. Maybe he got drunk and crawled up there and just fell asleep or stumbled or something and it just went all wrong."

"If it makes you feel better thinking that, then go ahead and think that for tonight," Mama said. "I'm concerned about *you*. It's not good to be this upset. I'm going to send you peace."

"You're going to do what?"

"Just go lie down," she said. "It could take me ten minutes or so, but you'll see. You need some rest."

I knew I didn't have any more reason to believe all I had said than I had to believe the opposite. Things seemed to be winding down, and I didn't know what to do next. I was exasperated, and tired. Jane was at a meeting and I went upstairs and laid across the bed without undressing.

The feeling started slowly and built for perhaps a half minute. Then I was drifting weightless in a sightless and impressionless world. *Euphoria* is not really the right word for the sensation. The right word is *peace*.

For perhaps as long as a half hour I floated in the feeling, enjoying it, looking around in my mind and seeing only a faint, pinkish cloud that enveloped me and continued on forever through nothing else to see and nothing to think.

I woke the next morning more rested than I could recall ever having been. I got ready for work and, before leaving, I called Mama.

"What did you do?" I asked her.

"Nothing, really," she said. "I just sat in the chair in the dark, except for a candle. I like to have a little candle. I pictured your face and the word *peace* all around you. I'm glad it worked."

There was no planned vigil for Jon that year on the second anniversary of his death. A few people went to the backstop, each for private reasons. Some laid flowers at the base of the backstop. Others threaded flowers by their stems through the wire.

Sandra called Mickey and suggested he not to drive up from College

Park. She thought it would be too difficult for him, and he was relieved.

I drove by toward dark when no one else was around and sat in the car in the school parking lot. I didn't stay long.

———————————

The city doesn't matter; it wasn't *New America*. The state doesn't matter; it wasn't Maryland. The bar was just another bar.

Two men sat in a dark corner at a table. One man said, "Could you use a mechanic?"

The other man returned a confused look and said, "There's nothing wrong with my car."

The first said, "I wasn't talking about cars. I was talking about the Bowie case. You said you had a problem. Could you use a mechanic?"

The other man sat looking for a while at his friend and then a light starting to come over his face.

"Oh. A mechanic. Is that what it's called?"

"This man, Meyers," the first said. "We wouldn't put up with that in..." He named a city, a major metropolitan area in another state.

The second man took a long sip of beer and thought about it. Finally, he said, "No. That wouldn't be right. I can't talk about how wrong this was, on the one hand and, on the other, turn around and do the same kind of thing. Besides, maybe Meyers had nothing to do with it. I wouldn't want to make a mistake like that."

"All I'm saying," the first said, "is that we wouldn't put up with that kind of thing in..." and he named the city again.

"No. Thank you, but no. I couldn't go along with that."

They sipped their beers in silence. Then the first said, "Okay. If that's how you feel about it. Just remember, the offer stands."

They finished their beers and left, each in his own direction.

42 Sandra and I decided to seek the services of three nationally renowned psychics. Such things were not all that popular at the time, but they were beginning to show up on television programs and in magazine articles.

Our criteria were that each psychic we chose had to have a national reputation and had to have a history of working with law enforcement agencies. We didn't want to deal with credibility issues, and we wanted people who were familiar with investigating cases such as Jon's death. We decided to use three different people so there would be ample opportunity for comparing the information.

We eventually selected Noreen Renier, Nancy Myer and Sylvia Browne. Renier, who was from Florida, made her living working with law enforcement agencies and referred to herself as a *psychic detective*. Nancy Myer - her last name was Czetli at the time - was from Pennsylvania. She also worked frequently with law enforcement agencies. Sylvia Browne was from California and had been involved in a rather famous case referred to as the Hillside Strangler Murders. All were frequently on such television shows as *48 Hours, America's Most Wanted, Sightings,* and *Unsolved Mysteries.*

This effort took up the better part of Sandra's and my spare time for three years, and I will summarize what each told us. Going into all the things we did to follow up on the things they told us would take too much time.

I first spoke with Ms. Renier on the phone in July of 1992, and Jane used an extension phone to sit in on that conversation. Ms. Renier had two assistants with her at her home in Florida, and a professional police artist. All any of the participants in Florida knew about Jon was his nickname and that his death had been ruled a suicide in 1990.

Ms Renier began by trying to get a sense of Jon. She said that he was very close to his mother, and that he had broken his arm when he was younger, which was true. She said he was a big person in the sense that he was very big about who he was. She tried to deal with the issue of suicide by sensing how he felt on the morning of the day he died and concluded that Jon's death definitely was a homicide. She said there had to have been more than one person involved, and added, "The only way anyone could get me to go where I didn't want to go would be to have me unconscious and carry me out. There's no way anyone could overwhelm me. I would have to have been either sleeping or in a position that I wasn't ready for an attack."

I hadn't mentioned anything about an autopsy, but Ms. Renier said, "I think the first autopsy really was sloppy. I feel like it went through what was so obvious instead of examining other parts of the body."

Ms. Renier described the person she felt was responsible for Jon's death and the police artist drew a picture of this person. There seemed to be several people to choose from, and she said she had to be careful to see only one.

She described a slender man of mixed nationality who had a wiry, muscular body and stood about five-ten or five-eleven. She saw the numbers 3 and 2 and said his age might be thirty-two, but he looked older. The numbers could be reversed, so he might be twenty-three. He had an obvious adam's apple. His hair was wiry and thick and either covered or almost covered his ears. He might sometimes have parted the hair more to one side, but Noreen saw it without a part. "Maybe," Noreen said, "I'm just getting him with his hair, with the struggle and all, more disarray."

Noreen seemed particularly taken with the man's eyes. They were wild eyes, she said. "I almost want to say the Charles Manson..." she said, and her voice trailed off for a moment. The eyes were round, she said, with maybe a little protrusion. There was wide, not narrow, spacing between the eyes. "They, they really scared me, and, when I saw them, I think maybe they're more into some drug, or... They don't look like normal eyes."

The eyebrows were more thin than thick and had a slight upwardness, or an affect that gave them a slight upwardness. The eyebrows were a medium-to-large distance from the eyes. The man's forehead was narrow and had deep creases. "Perhaps an old scar, or birth mark. Some imperfection on the forehead itself." He had some angle to the shape of his face, and prominent cheek bones. Noreen said she saw a shadow on his face and she took this to mean a five-o'clock shadow. She didn't see a beard. The space between his upper lip and nose seemed small to her. She saw what she believed was a small, old, pencil-thin scar near the upper lip and suspected he might have trouble growing a mustache. "Maybe something happened to his mouth at one time." The mouth had fullness to it but wasn't terribly broad. It was a medium to small mouth. The lower lip was full or perhaps more like a half moon. The upper lip was almost indistinguishable. "Maybe the scar is bigger than I'm telling you," she said, "or I think it is."

The man's nose might have been broken. It seemed to have "a broken place on it." It was not a long nose. It was more medium and with a little sharpness to it. The nostrils were somewhat flared and more oval-shaped than round.

"It doesn't look like a black person's nose to me," Noreen volunteered.

---

* The police artist Noreen Renier uses, a man named Detective Sergeant Michael Deal, clearly is a talented person. I eventually had occasion to speak with Deal, and he asked me to mention that he works for Ms. Renier as a professional, and not as an advocate for, or a detractor from, Ms. Renier's work. He views Ms. Renier as a witness in a case. At the time Deal drew the two pictures used in this book, he was thirty-three. He had been a police officer for eleven years, and a police artist for all but one or two of those years.

The chin had a crease and was short and only slightly jutting. There was some ovalness in the shape of the chin. There was nothing particularly remarkable about the ears. The earlobes would be medium sized and fleshy, but, if you weren't really looking, the ears wouldn't grab your attention. You couldn't see much of them because of the hair.

The man had a somewhat swarthy complexion and might be of the complexion that is referred to among blacks as *high yellow*. He did not have light skin.

On his lower arms he had strong, dark hair. His fingers were not long and his hands looked as if he might have worked with his hands a great deal. If he wore a watch at the time it would have been an inexpensive watch, perhaps a Timex. He wore boots that were worn and scuffed, well used. The boots might have been brown, but the scuffing made the color hard to distinguish.

Noreen thought at first that if a person watched very closely as the man walked, the slight affects of a minor upper leg injury sometime in the past might be detected. Then she wondered if, instead, there might be a scar or imperfection in the upper leg area.

This description took quite a long time. When Noreen had finished, she said her lower neck hurt on the right side, along the neck line. "It's just, really killing me," she said. Her assistant asked if I could confirm the lower-neck injury and I immediately thought of the y-shaped bruise.

"Yes," I said.

Noreen got beyond the discomfort and said that where Jon was killed was not where he was found. She thought the people involved had to know Jon well and were familiar with where he lived and his terrain. Then Noreen said, "My lower ankle seems to hurt. I don't know if I'm David or Jon." I couldn't say anything, and Jane laughed. I had torn a calf muscle playing softball the week before and I still needed crutches to walk.

Jane said Jon had been at a party that night and asked where he went when he left. Noreen thought Jon might have stopped by a friend's home or the home of someone who lived nearby. Jane asked if Jon ever got back to his own neighborhood and Noreen said, "Oh, I don't want to talk about it." Noreen thought Jon didn't want to talk about it because some promises had been broken.

Jane asked, "Did he meet up with some friends, or did he run into some people going home?"

"I could have picked up somebody there, or given somebody a ride. I don't know if I gave somebody a ride to the party, or picked up somebody that was walking away from the party. I feel like there's somebody else in the truck."

I asked, "Could it have been you who were picked up?"

"Oh, yes, yes, yes," she said. She asked if Jon could have been picked up in a truck, and I didn't know. Her assistant asked if Jon was familiar with the other people in the truck.

"He might be from the old neighborhood."

I asked, "How does Jon feel about this person?"

"I'm a little nervous. It seems like we've got some serious business going to go down, and I can feel it. I can feel it. Somebody else is in the back. I feel something going around my neck. Me struggling. Other things happening. I think I was killed in the car."

The switch from *truck* to *car* threw me, and I drew a blank.

Noreen said, "Ah, I think the reason we're killing Jon is either that he told on us, or informed on us, or, there's some way we're mad at him for something he did. It didn't have to be just yesterday. It could have been a while back, and it has to do with the old neighborhood."

We had switched from Jon's *own* neighborhood to the *old* neighborhood, and I could feel myself getting lost in the conversation.

Noreen said that, in the car or truck, she could see the man to her left that the police artist was drawing. "He's driving. There's somebody else there. Somebody else there. Somebody else there."

"How does Jon know these people?" Jo asked.

She said that one of the people present had either done some time or time had passed since whatever had happened that made these people angry at Jon.

"I'd like to know more about why these people did that," I said.

"It's, they had to get rid of me. They had to get rid of me. They didn't want it to look like murder so everybody'd be up at arms and could make the connection. So it had to look like suicide."

I asked, "Was it premeditated?"

"We knew we were going to do it. I don't know if we knew exactly that time. I think it was premeditated without, with maybe a blank in exactly when it was going to go down. It was going to go down."

Noreen's assistant asked, "They weren't just trying to scare him?"

"No," Noreen said. "It's beyond that."

"When I first got into Jon," Noreen said, "he was to me a very... giver, or doer. And a lot of kindness. But when we got into these bad guys, they hated his guts. Maybe not so much because he was nice but because... well, maybe because he was nice. And maybe he said things, or told things, or... Did he give any information to anyone, or do they think he, he squelched on a deal?"

Noreen's assistant instructed, "Jon wants to relate some clue, some lead. He wants these killers to be found. He wants this matter cleared up. Jon wants to relate to us..."

Noreen interrupted and said, "I feel really it has to come from somebody that's already in prison."

This was out of the blue and, thinking immediately of Iglesia, I said, "We might know something about that."

"Okay. I feel maybe if we can make a deal, he'll talk. I think that's the only way you're going to find him, 'cause I don't think there's any evidence, or anything that we could dig up and say, 'Aha. Gotcha.' I think it's going to be an informant. I think he's already in prison, so I'd go after that guy."

I asked her to describe the person in prison.

She said the person in prison might wear glasses, and he looked young.

"I feel like this person might have tried to commit suicide at one time in his life, or they cut themselves up on the wrist just for fun. Some inner wrist slashes."

Noreen said the man had a very distinct Southern accent and was more slow talking. In prison he might be studying or in some way be involved in schooling. He was a repeat offender who was in for a number of serious charges, and he knew he would be in prison for some time.

Jane asked, "Do you feel that this person in prison was one of those who was in the group that killed Jon?"

"Yes. I feel the person, whoever's in prison, knows about what happened. And if I can get a lesser... 'cause I think they've got him in for all sorts of stuff. Some heavy... It'd be more felony than misdemeanor. And I felt slashing to my arms. I mean, God, that's a good clue, whoever that is. Unless there's some tatoos at the wrist area that people wear."

I asked if the person in prison was someone that Jon knew, and Noreen's manner suddenly was uncharacteristically scattered.

"Pardon?" she asked.

"Is this someone that Jon knows?"

"I don't know. I, I, I... I'm sort of out of it. I just... sort of, ah... I, I'm just sort of out of it for a while. Let's just sort of, if you don't mind, just rap a little bit and let my artist finish and, ah... "

"Just relax a little bit for a moment," Noreen's assistant said.

"I just felt a little too hyper there," Noreen said. "I was getting hyper."

Sandra had mailed Noreen the clothes Jon was wearing when he died, and Noreen held the shirt, which had a small paint mark on the chest area.

Noreen said, "I feel, ah... I'm nauseated. I feel confused. I, I feel very disoriented. I feel like I'm, I'm... Like, on... I don't know if something was given to me that drugged me. I feel there might have been a, a minor ritual with my body before it was found. I feel like a rope might have hung me, but not necessarily in the place that I was found." She said the paint seemed to be more of a sealer than paint.

Jane asked, "Did it get on the shirt that night, or would it be an old stain?"

Noreen said in a gruff, almost affronted and yet somewhat joking voice, "I wouldn't go to a party with a, a stain on my shirt. That... that... that party."

"Is it significant?" Jane asked.

Noreen's voice remained gruff, like Jon's, and she said, "'As they said...' - now, I can't talk like him, but he wants to, to do a quote - 'As they said in the western, 'Yep.'"

I asked, "How do we get to what he wants to tell us about it?"

"Ah, you've got to find the guy that's going to break," Noreen said. "I seem to be seeing too many wagon wheels."

I remembered the wheels my mother had seen and asked if we could stick with that. Noreen said she was losing it and needed a better question, and I asked, "Jon, how do we deal with these guys?"

"Cautiously," Noreen said. "Ah, these guys are talkers. These guys are braggers. They're also very frightened, and scared to talk. So it's sort of easier to cut them from the herd."

"Who's the weak link?" I asked.

"Ah, you've got more than one weak link. I think the guy in the picture's going to be good."

"Will one of us recognize him?" I asked.

"Oh, yes," Noreen said. "Yes, yes."

I had more questions, but I as getting tired. I reasoned to myself that, if we would recognize the picture, then we didn't have to go over every detail. As if she was reading my mind, Noreen said, "Yeah. And, and remember, it's not an exact photo, but it's like eighty percent accurate there. I think you'll be pleased when you see the face."

Noreen's literature had said she worked particularly well with metal objects, so I asked her to hold the metal D-ring on Jon's pants.

"Yeah," Noreen said. "Ah, there was something hooked on to here." Then the gruff voice returned. "You don't think I'd just have things hanging onto my pants without a purpose."

I didn't quite pick up the words clearly and I said, "I didn't understand that."

"Ah, there's... sure... whole bunch of keys. I think only two were significant for the murderers. You're dealing with more than one person. It was a real good cover-up, because the cover-up involved, ah, a police person. You have a... Oh, God. It's..."

"Okay," I said. "I didn't want to say that before, but that's what we have suspected."

"Well, a police person," she said.

I didn't want to throw things off with a question, so I said I would prefer to follow Noreen's lead. Noreen hesitated and then seemed to be speaking directly to me.

"Oh, darn you," she said, "You know what's coming up now. You know I... what I'm seeing. And I feel more sheriff than police."

She asked if the sheriff had done the investigation and I said the police had done it.

"Why do I see sheriff?" she asked herself. "I see a star. I see a star, and my interpretation of the star, of course, was sheriff."

I asked if she had seen a number associated with the star. She said she hadn't until I asked. She gave a number, cautioning me that she might be reading my mind, and I asked if it could be a badge number.

"Possible," she said. "That could be some reason why there was a cover... I don't think it started intentionally as a cover-up. I think it started off with ignorance, and then I think other people started blocking things."

Noreen felt a change of plan. She said, "I think, like, first we're going to do one thing so he's transported one way, and then we decide a different scenario. So, maybe somebody else enters the picture and we go back, 'cause it's almost double-backing."

Jane asked, "Can you see people lifting him up onto that backstop? Do you see any pictures like that?"

"Oh, absolutely. But I feel like I was dragged up there. I don't feel like I was killed there. No, I feel I was dragged there."

I asked if her sense of it was that the police were involved in Jon's death, or if they simply came afterward and didn't follow up on it very well.

"I smell something," Noreen said. "I smell a rat. Might be a couple of them. I feel some, some bad... Oh, dear. I'm so sorry to say this. One is prominent, and there's more than one. And one is pretty powerful. And, so, it's like, oh, frantic people, frantic. Oh, this is... " She hesitated and then began speaking as if she was someone other than herself. "Look, we've got more important things to do."

"Important people?" I asked, not really hearing what she had said.

"Ah, I feel some important people involved. But I don't know why they know, or they are, but they are. So it had to be the drugs. "

"Say that again?"

"Had to be drug... or money laundering some way. What state are we?"

"Maryland," I said.

"Maryland. Yeah. Probably drugs," she said.

I ran the names of a few police officers by her and she gave me her impressions.

I gave her Roland Meyers' name.

"Ah, Roland. Sort of stands his ground. Would... would do the kind of stare at you. You know, just sort of the bull. Not moving. Ah, waiting to see what you're going to do. He just acts like a bad-ass."

"Involved?" I asked.

"He scares me," Noreen said. "Roland scares me. Now, I don't know if he's a ferocious cop or just a, a, a scary bad... He scares me."

"Get any sense," I asked, "of involvement in Jon's death as opposed to just being a bad guy?"

"He could just be a tough cop," Noreen said. "And, if I was just the average person, then he would still scare me."

This description certainly didn't come close to implicating Meyers in Jon's death. I gave her Chief of Police Ingersoll's name.

"Sort of spit and polish, "she said. "By the book. Sort of a namby-pamby."

Then I gave her the name of the previous Chief of Police.

"Hickory?"

"Hickory. I get bad vibes with Hickory."

I gave her Sam Long's name, but she didn't want to continue and she broke it off.

Personality variations aside, I couldn't see that she had told me anything incriminating about any of the officers I had asked about. The conversation had taken over two hours, and everyone involved was exhausted. We chatted a few minutes, said goodbye and hung up.

I laid the picture on Sandra's kitchen table and she picked it up and studied it.

"I have no idea who that is," she said.

She called Mickey downstairs and he looked at the picture and said, "Nope. Nobody I know."

We passed around copies of the picture and no one recognized it. A retired police officer thought he did, but we couldn't learn of any connection between Jon and the person the retired officer named except that Jon and this person had once worked together on a summer job at a drug store.

I showed the picture to two female officers at in a convenience store parking lot and asked if they had any idea who the person was.

One said, "Charles Manson?" and handed the picture back to me.

MIKE DEAL
7/23/92

I typed a transcript of the conversation and gave a copy to Rogers. He called me at work one afternoon and said he had talked with Iglesia again. I asked if he wanted to come by my house that evening to give me the long version, but he said he couldn't wait. He sounded out of breath.

"Noreen said the person we should talk to was continuing his education in prison. Right?"

"Right," I said.

"Well, I walk in and Iglesia's late for the appointment because he's studying for his high school equivalency test."

"I guess that's a fit," I said.

"And you remember how she described some slashing or cutting on his wrists for pleasure, and then said that maybe it was a tatoo?"

"I remember."

"I never noticed it before but, on the underside of Iglesia's forearm, he has a large tatoo of a dagger."

"Damn," I said. "That's really getting close. Glasses?"

"He wears them when he studies."

"Would you say that he has a southern accent."

"Thick," he said.

"Did he have anything new to add?"

"I was so blown away," Rogers said, "I could hardly think to ask him anything. He says he's still committed to seeing that justice is done in the Bowie case."

"So what do we do?"

"I'm going to call Howard and ask him to talk to Iglesia again. He already has the story, and I can't see the police doing anything about it. I think that's the way to go."

"Tattoo of a dagger, huh?" I said.

"Plain as day," he said. "I thought I would pass out."

Sandra was convinced we had to talk with Noreen again, to get more specific information about the person in the picture, and about the truck. I took off work one afternoon in August and called. I had a list of questions on the table in front of me, but Noreen and her assistant had already discussed the case before I called, and they wanted to summarize what they had covered.

Noreen said that if I was standing in front of Sandra's house and facing it, I would go a certain number in one direction. She didn't know if the number was miles or feet or what it was. Then I would take two turns she described and go down the road a short distance. At that time I would be standing in front of the killer's house, and I would be within a radius of just under three miles from Sandra's house.

Noreen said the killer's home was in an isolated location, and there was "a lot of dead stuff" around it. A big tree to the right had unusual bark to it. There might be some "dead stuff" in the tree. There was something yellow, also, "associated with the growing." It was on a rural road, and there were three numbers associated with it, which she gave. She said I should play around with the numbers, considering all possible arrangements. The numbers probably represented a mailbox number, but they could be a street address, or perhaps even a road number.

Noreen said the truck that was supposed to have picked up Jon after the party was American made and not too old. She gave the color. She saw some change in color and wasn't sure if that meant it had been painted or if it might be two-tone with different shades. She just saw "different colors" and didn't know what it meant. You had to step up to get into the truck. Since she had suggested in the first session that someone might have attacked Jon from behind in the truck, I asked if it was a truck or a van. She said it reminded her more of a pickup. Margaret asked Noreen to look at the front of the truck, and Noreen said she saw an orange and black sticker on the windshield. She also saw a "strong bumper" in the front. "There's some chrome," she said. "Not a cheapo." I asked for the year the truck was made and she whispered what sounded like "two" a couple of times and then said, "Maybe 1989."

43 Between the time I talked with Noreen Renier and the time I talked with the next psychic, the story of Carl Morris reached a conclusion in the local papers.

I don't know Carl Morris. I've never met him, never laid eyes on him, never had a conversation with him. All I know about him is what I've read in the newspapers, what a few attorneys and other people who worked in and around the county judicial system told me about him in private, and what Mama said. I haven't changed his name.

Carl Morris was a Baltimore police officer who lived in Columbia and commuted to work. I have no idea if he was a good police officer or a bad one. All I know about his career as a police officer is that he found his wife or his former wife, I don't know which it was, in bed with another man and he supposedly hit the man. I don't know if he hit the man a lot, or a little, or even if he hit the man at all. For however many times Morris supposedly hit the man, Morris was charged with using excessive force.

Morris had a brother who also lived in Columbia and who claimed to have been beaten by Officer Roland Meyers at one time or another. It was just one of many such claims that people had made about Meyers and that always ended with a determination by the police department that Meyers was just doing his job and that nobody but the police understood.

On the night Jon died, Morris, who still was a Baltimore police officer at the time, said he was following Meyers. Morris's brother was at a party that night and Morris said he was following Meyers because he didn't want Meyers to show up at the party where his brother was and do his job again. Morris said Meyers was in an unmarked police car and was wearing a police officer's uniform. Morris said that at eleven o'clock that night he had followed Meyers to a gasoline station that was in the same neighborhood as the backstop where Jon would be found the next morning. According to anything I'd learned, this excursion into Jon's neighborhood wasn't part of Meyers' alibi. In fairness, however, I must mention that the gas station was close enough to where Meyers lived at the time to have been a logical place for him to stop for gas.

In October, five months after Morris followed Meyers on the night Jon died, Morris was suspended from the Baltimore police department as the result of the excessive force charge. When I learned that Morris had been suspended from the police department for hitting his wife's boyfriend, and only after it became known that Morris was a witness in the Bowie case, I began to suspect there was more to the Carl Morris story than was getting in the papers. As everyone in America now knows, a whole crowd of police officers can hit a person on videotape and it might take two trials and some serious city-burning before anything gets done about it. A police officer being suspended for hitting his wife's boyfriend struck me as exponentially less likely than winning the lottery. Anyway, Morris was suspended at about the same time Sandra first learned that the FBI was investigating Jon's death.

Three months later, in January, Morris said he was in the bedroom of his home and he heard a crash and then heard his twenty-month-old son crying. He came out of the bedroom and found his son lying at the bottom of a six-step flight of carpeted stairs. A carpet cleaning machine that had been at the bottom of the stairs was lying on top of him. Morris called the rescue squad and administered CPR.

Morris's son died and Morris was charged with first-degree murder. In a newspaper article, a hospital spokesperson was reported to have said the injuries to Morris's son were not consistent with such a short fall.

While Morris was awaiting trial for the death of his son, the FBI interviewed him about Jon's death. Morris told the FBI he had followed Meyers on the night Jon died. Morris said Meyers was in uniform and in an unmarked car. Morris gave the FBI the license number of the car. The FBI contacted the Howard County police, who said Meyers wouldn't have been in uniform that night because he was off duty. They also said the license plate number Morris gave was not the license plate number for Meyers' police car. After more checking, the FBI determined that the police car normally assigned to Meyers was in the repair shop on the night Jon died. Meyers had temporarily been assigned an unmarked car. The license number of the car temporarily assigned to Meyers was the license number Morris had given the FBI.

The FBI gave Morris a lie detector test. I don't know anything about the results, but I know Tina Gutierrez asked the FBI to let Brisentine, the man who had tested Mickey, look at the results and maybe even test Morris himself. The FBI refused. I also know that when the FBI finished testing Morris, the FBI agent who had administered the test said to Morris, "Why would you want to *off* a fellow officer?" That's not very objective. I also know that.

Morris suggested to different attorneys that maybe his son hadn't fallen at all. Maybe, he said, it had something to do with the Bowie case. He might have been getting a little crazy if you take into account what his young daughter said.

The case against Morris finally came to trial in April of 1992. According to newspaper articles, doctors testified that Morris's son had an almost severed major artery deep within the abdomen. This injury was more likely to have come from a straight, direct blow than from a short fall. There also were bruises on the child's scalp, on his abdomen, his back, his buttocks, and his testicles. A worker for the county rescue squad said Morris hadn't been as openly concerned about his son as the rescue squad worker thought a father should have been.

In August of 1992, Morris was found guilty and sentenced to sixteen years for child abuse and ten years for involuntary manslaughter. The sentences were to be served concurrently. A newspaper article in the Flier reported that the judge said the crime was cruel and brutal and vicious, and that Morris, even though he was a police officer, had lied in front of a jury and hadn't shown any remorse. Morris said in the article he hadn't killed his son and, even though there had been a trial, he had been found guilty of two things he hadn't done.

Morris's young daughter was not called to testify, and she was not quoted in the article. Someone close to Morris's case in a professional capacity, someone who wouldn't want to be quoted, told me what Morris's daughter said.

"Daddy not push baby. Baby fall."

I called Mama.

"Tell me about a man named Carl Morris."

"Don't say too much," Mama said.

"I think he's black. He's thirty-four years old. He's a police officer. He's just been found guilty of killing his twenty-month-old son."

Mama called back a few nights later.

"I can't get a clear picture," she said. "When I try to get inside of him, all I get is a sense of great sadness, and injustice."

44 I talked on the phone with Nancy Myer in October. Ms. Myer liked to hold a photograph of the scene as she worked, so Sandra had sent her a police photo of Jon on the backstop. As with Ms. Renier, Ms. Myer didn't know any details of the case.

The feeling Ms. Myer got was that there were four people present in addition to Jon just before Jon died. Two young men knew there was going to be trouble and they had accompanied Jon in hopes of helping protect him. Two men who were present were engaged in a conversation about a sizable amount of money owed, perhaps as much as three or four thousand dollars. The two men were in their late thirties or early forties.

"They are putting a lot of pressure on him," Myer said, "to provide services that he is completely unwilling to provide involving the sale of drugs. And I believe there is also some pressure towards something to do with, ah... I think it would be called *fixing a game* or something like that. He is completely adamant. There is no way, you know, he's going to come up with the money. He talks about approaching a friend of his who has money. These men are not at all willing to delay their payment any longer. They start to get pretty hostile. Some physical threats are made. The boys try to leave. I feel very strongly that the bigger of the two men restrained the victim from leaving, and the two other boys did successfully leave. Unfortunately, they didn't call the cops."

Myer said it was nightfall when the altercations started, because there still was a sense of light in the sky. "But it was quite dark. So, either they were near a place that had those daylight lights and the lights went out, or the last of the daylight... of actual daylight... because it goes from being somewhat lit, not strongly lit, to being quite dark in the area where they are. And these younger men escape partly due to the darkness and partly due to the fact that they know the terrain a lot better than the men do. They are able to hide very rapidly, and they're not that far away. They can still hear what's going on. In fact, they don't want to leave him alone completely and, yet, they're not armed. They don't have any way to protect him. The two young men are discussing going for help, but they are afraid to leave. They're foolishly... they have the idea that, if they stay in the vicinity, somehow they'll be able to help him. There's a very nasty argument between the victim and the two men. He pleads with them that, you know, he will get the money. He'll get it to them by next week-end. And, apparently, they have been expecting payment from him for close to a month and a half, and the patience department is no longer there. They want an agreement from him having something to do with fixing a game, or sale of drugs. In other words, they're using his owed money to try and blackmail him into a position of illegal activity, and he will not agree to it."

The bigger of the two men was a white male with dark, thick, wavy hair that was medium length and came a little down over the ear. The hair came maybe as far as to the bottom of the ear, but not long down the back. He had rather large ears and the long hair might hide the fact that the ears protruded a little. The hair was slicked straight back and did not have a part. She suspected that the hair had a tendency to be unruly and would not be easy to part. He had a cowlick in the back, on the left-hand side. The man had noticeable scarring from acne all along the jaw line and down under the chin. The scarring was bad and a person would expect it also to be on the shoulders. His eyes seemed to be hazel or grayish; there was a little bit of blue, but the eyes were not clearly blue. He was very shifty-eyed. You couldn't get him to look you straight in the eyes. He had the appearance of a football player gone to seed. He was a big-boned man with broad shoulders and large hands and long fingers. A person who saw his hands would want to say *mitts* instead of hands. He had high, wide cheek bones.

"What does he do for a living?"

"I guess probably the easiest way to say it is he's an enforcer."

"An enforcer?"

"Uh-huh."

"Okay, what's the most distinguishing characteristic. The acne scars? Or is there anything else?"

"His size," she said. "I mean, this man is probably six-three or more. He may be as tall as six-foot-four. He's big."

"And roughly in his forties?"

I asked for this to be clarified because, if she was accurate, this would rule out Meyers. He was tall and big, but he was nowhere close to forty.

"I would say early forties, late thirties. Because of the way the acne's scarring, it's a little difficult to gauge his age. He probably looks actually a little older than he actually is. And he's, he's a heavy drinker, so there's a good bit of, you know, drying of the skin and everything from the alcohol."

"Where does he drink?"

She misunderstood the question and answered, "I would say mostly beer, and inexpensive whiskey."

"Does he have some place he goes normally?"

"Ah, yes. I would say that he hangs out in a bar that has a name having to do with cows."

"Cows."

"Uh-huh.

"Okay. Ah, how 'bout the other fellow?"

The other man was considerably smaller than the first. She thought he was around six feet tall, or just under six feet. He had more of a medium build and a constant nervous habit of messing with his teeth. He seemed always to have a toothpick or a pencil or something in his mouth and he chewed on it the way some people do when they've quit smoking. The hand that wasn't messing with his mouth would be in his pocket. He had medium brown hair and dark eyes. He looked Latin, not South American Latin so much as Italian Latin. He was fine featured with a long and a rather large nose. His eyebrows went almost straight across and, in fact, looked as if they partially met in the middle. He had deep-set eyes with the brow protruding a little bit. He wore corrective lenses and preferred the types of lenses that change color. In sunlight, the lenses would have a brownish tint. His glasses had light frames that weren't noticeable.

"Okay. Is there any place where this fellow hangs out?"

"He seems to be affiliated with, ah, I see a building that's like a three-story brick building, and it looks like an old-fashioned building. It's almost like an old school in the way it's built, but I know it's not a school. And it has something to do with city law enforcement, and he's around there a lot. But I don't think this is a police officer."

Myer said the two friends who had come in hopes of helping were devastated. "They just had no idea they were going to kill him. They expected a beating. That's what they were expecting. And they thought they would just go and get him and take him to a hospital."

There were others who also were aware he was in trouble. "There are probably nine or ten young men that knew he had a problem," she said.

She described the two young men. I don't care to go into the descriptions. She said there were serious safety issues involved.

"They came back," she said, "And when they realize he's dead, they panicked and ran. They were hysterical. Their car was parked about three-quarters of a block up from where this incident occurred."

The two young men, she said, ran back to their car and went to a nearby shopping center to use the phone. They called two friends of theirs to try to figure out what to do. She also had the feeling that they notified 911, but she wasn't sure there still would be a record of the call.

"Were these two young men at that party?"

"One of them was. They called the other one on the phone."

The two men were not particularly concerned about these two witnesses.

"They seem very secure that these kids are going to keep their mouths shut," she said.

She thought one witnesses wanted very much to help with the investigation, but he couldn't be open about it. "You will literally endanger his life," she said. "It's not a minor problem. That'll have to be taken into consideration. But he would work through an intermediary."

The name of another acquaintance of Jon's came up, and I asked if this young man was also at the backstop.

"[He] is not at the backstop," Nancy said, "but he led those men to this young man."

"So he might actually be a betrayer of some sort."

"Oh, yeah. But, again, in defense of [him], it never occurred to him, as it did not to these other two men, that he would be murdered."

"What is the likelihood," I asked, "that [he] would speak openly with some guarantee of safety?"

"Virtually... no. Because [he] does not believe there is any way with these particular men that his safety could be guaranteed. This is a problem. These men seem to be able to move about with tremendous impunity in that community, doing a lot of what they want with no one able to stop them. I've only encountered that kind of behavior when either the perpetrators are being condoned by law enforcement or are somehow connected to it. You just don't find that kind of brazenness very often. And there's this odd behavior on the part of these three youngsters of not expecting this. I mean, they expect the beating, but not murder. Now, why, when they're dealing with someone who enforces money owed, they would not have expected that problem... to me, you know, just looking now at all of the different murders I've investigated, that just strikes me as odd, unless they had some misguided reason for trusting the one man, the shorter of the two men."

Myer told me she had worked with the FBI before and, when the time was right, she would help me approach them. She said the case was complicated and she would have to get more involved.

"Don't worry about the money," she said. "You might have to come up for a visit eventually so we can sit down and go over this at length. Trust me, I'm not going to go away. We have to solve this young man's murder."

I thanked her.

I was unable to get in touch with Ms. Myer for some time after that. Eventually, the woman with her answering service said there had been a school bus accident and Ms. Myer's daughter had been seriously injured. I silently cursed myself for all the names I had called Ms. Myer in my heart when I had been unable to contact her.

I called Arthur Bellinger and he came to my office. I asked how we could protect a witness and he mentioned the witness protection program.

"No," I said. "I couldn't ask someone to do that."

It didn't occur to me at the time that a witness could simply provide background information in a quiet investigation, and I don't suppose it occurred to Bellinger, either. I gave Bellinger the name of an FBI agent Ms. Myer had said could recommend her to Bellinger.

I contacted a young man whom Myer thought would talk, but he said he wasn't the one. He said he wished to God it had been him, because he never would have remained silent so long.

I told Sandra about the conversation with the young man, although I didn't give her his name. She said, "Maybe he's just afraid."

"No," I said. "I think he was telling the truth. It was in his eyes."

———————————

Howard, the writer from New York, met with Iglesia several times, and Howard was getting more and more nervous. Iglesia's story kept getting more intricate. Iglesia was naming more local officers as well as officers in another county. He said these officers were involved in some sort of drug operation that Jon and he had gotten caught up in. Iglesia said that because he hadn't known Rogers originally, and had been suspicious, he had lied about not knowing anything about selling drugs. He said that, in truth, he knew quite a lot.

Howard did not want anyone to know when he was coming into town to interview Iglesia. He emphasized repeatedly that he couldn't promise an article in *Vanity Fair*, but he often expressed confidence that he could sell the story, either to that magazine or to some other with the help of editors from *Vanity Fair*. He said it was not at all unusual for a *Vanity Fair* article to be the precursor of a *60 Minutes* story. The people at *60 Minutes* were very cautious, he said, and usually did a story only in safe situations in which there was no chance the network could be embarrassed. He also said his editor was excited about the story, and was helping him with it. This, of course, gave Sandra considerable hope.

Sandra kept waiting for something to come out of the *Vanity Fair* thing, but there always seemed to be one more interview and one more thing to check out. Sometimes Howard's assurances were so positive I would drive to the nearest news stand to see if the upcoming issue was out and he simply had been too busy to let us know that there would be an article on the Bowie case that month.

Just before Thanksgiving of 1992, Howard scheduled a train trip from New York to Columbia to interview Iglesia one final time. Much ado was made about the need, for safety reasons, not to let anyone know Howard was visiting the prison.

On the day of the interview, Jane and I traveled to Ohio to visit Jane's family. Jane and I had just arrived at her sister's home in Ohio and I had started what I was hoping would be the first in a series of night caps at the kitchen table when Rogers called. Jane's brother-in-law handed me the phone and Rogers' voice was not just trembling. It was shaking.

"I think I've just had my life threatened," he said.

"Hold on," I said. Jane's brother-in-law was a successful salesman who made and took a lot of phone calls at home, and he had a long extension cord on the wall phone in his kitchen. I stretched the cord down the hall and around the corner and finished talking with Rogers in the living room.

"Tell me what happened."

"I just got a phone call," Rogers said. "The man didn't identify himself, but it sounded like Iglesia's brother, Carlos. All he said was, 'Tell him to back off,' and he hung up."

"It doesn't sound like an immediate threat," I said. "It sounds like Iglesia told somebody that Howard visited him, and that person doesn't like Iglesia being put in the spotlight."

We talked a while and Rogers calmed down. When he hung up I went back into the kitchen to finish my first night cap. Jane knew Rogers wouldn't casually have interrupted our visit to Ohio, and she asked what the call was about. She was beginning to have her fill of the constant interruptions in our lives that the Bowie case presented, and I kept the explanation as short as I could. She and the rest of the gathering, who had kept track of the story over various family visits, agreed that the threat did not seem immediate and seemed more directed at Howard, who was safe in New York, than at Rogers. Then Jane's sister pulled out photographs of fishing trips and weddings and I leaned back in my chair at the kitchen table and quietly drank to moderate excess.

Rogers made a point of visiting Iglesia again in prison. Rogers told Iglesia in rather clear language that he would no longer waste his time talking with Iglesia if Iglesia kept telling people every time Rogers or Howard came to see him.

Iglesia said, "What are you talking about? I haven't told anyone."

Rogers told Iglesia about the phone call and said something like that had better not happen again.

Iglesia said, "People know when someone visits me. I can't help that. I haven't told anyone. People just know."

I checked out bars and restaurants with names that seemed to have something to do with cows. There weren't that many, but they were spread across several counties. I pulled out maps and drew maps and drove around looking for these witnesses who might talk. The Sheriff's Department maintained an old stone building that looked a lot like a school and I photographed it. I photographed the local state police barracks, which was a three-story brick building that looked a lot like an old schoolhouse. I mailed the photos to Ms. Myer but, as I would eventually learn, her life had turned upside down and she was unable to deal with the investigation at the time.

I tried to piece together the things Ms. Myer had seen and began to piece together a scenario that involved some of Jon's friends. I was running this scenario by Sandra one evening at her kitchen table when she put her hands over her ears and sat up straight with a startled look on her face.

"I just heard Jon," she said. "He said, 'My friends wouldn't do this to me.'"

45 In December, I spoke with Sylvia Browne on the phone. I decided to take a different approach with Ms. Browne. It wasn't my goal to prove whether any particular psychic was good or accurate. I wasn't conducting a test. I wrote a very detailed background paper and mailed it to Ms. Browne. I told her, without drawing any conclusions, everything I could think of that might be related. I also told her what the previous psychics had said. I wanted to get beyond what I thought I knew, and I didn't want to beat around the bush. By the time I called Ms. Browne, she had read the material I sent her.

"First of all," she said, "let's get right down to the nitty gritty. He didn't commit suicide. Let's get that out of the way."

Two people did this to him, she said. One was a large, heavy-framed, dark-haired guy. The other was a large, light-haired, fat guy. In the background, there also was an oriental man. He was fairly short, maybe five-eight or five-nine, thin and wiry; he had a nervous habit of pushing his hair back off his face, and he worked in some kind of technical or auto-body place. She saw lots of mechanical or technical apparatus around him.

"Let's get this out of the way," she said. "Not because I work with police departments, because they can be just as crooked as anything, but I don't think this has anything to do with the police department. Even though there was abuse there, and a little bit of violence, this wasn't... See, I think he believed that the police were stalking him because I think he knew that he was being stalked, and the only place that he had to put it was he thought possibly it could have been the police. But it absolutely, beyond a shadow of a doubt before God, it wasn't the police department. Now, I'm not discrediting the fact... having a party and all that, and the officers and all that business... You know, you said Puffy claims to have witnessed Mickey being struck, and Chong Ko having a nightstick stuck in his mouth, and none of that do I appreciate. I think all of that is awful, but I don't think it went beyond that."

"So that was an isolated event."

"Exactly."

"How do we get to the bottom of it?"

"Well, I think you're going to see that everything starts coming to light in April." She said that there would be another crime committed against one of the people mentioned in the information I had provided. The explanation of Jon's death would come out of this other crime, she thought.

Ms. Browne thought there might be a brown truck with a sheared-off right fender involved with Jon's death. The license plate on the rear hung crooked.

I asked about the young man who, out of the blue, had offered to Sandra to have Meyers killed. Ms. Browne asked if his family owned a restaurant or deli in Columbia named Alfredo's. I didn't know. Ms. Browne said that a group of people who had information about Jon's death hung out at this Alfredo's. If I went there and hung around, I would find people who would be willing to provide details of Jon's death. This would be a starting point that could eventually lead to a solution. There were at least three or four people, she said, who knew things and were not saying anything because they were afraid. Knowing things didn't mean they were involved, but learning what these people knew could help me find out what had happened. Some people who knew things might not even realize what they knew.

Ms. Browne threw out a name that was completely new to me. She gave a first and last name and asked if I knew this person. She was very specific about the last name and even spelled it. She said this person was white and heavyset and lived north of Columbia, probably in Baltimore. I told her I didn't know the name, but, since it was an unusual name, we agreed that it shouldn't be too difficult to check out.

I asked, "Do you think one of these people will come forward and talk?"

"I know they will," she said, "and I know the reason why they will is because they are afraid for their life."

"Do you think they will talk to me?"

"Yeah, because they certainly are not talking to the police." She said that I didn't have to be overly concerned about my own welfare since I had kept a low profile.

Thinking that I would be looking for information at this place called Alfredo's raised in my mind the lingering question of what to do with any information that I learned. I asked, "Can I trust - now, I don't mean trust as a human being; I mean trust to actually do something effective about it - Police Chief Gus Ingersoll, if I come up with information?"

"Yes, you can," she said. "And, otherwise, I'd say back off, because we all know that there can be corruption anywhere in this world. Yeah, you can. I think he's just at odds with everything because he doesn't know..."

"He's caught in the middle."

"Yes, that's right. Exactly."

"But he would effectively work on legitimate information."

"Yes. Because I think that this crime is only the pop-up bead for what's going on as far as graft and payoffs. I don't mean necessarily the police department. I mean, you know, like years ago when they used to sell insurance for businesses and all that stuff. You know, in the time of Capone?

I think that we're talking about a real gang situation here, and I think that's why it goes so deep."

Jon's death seemed to her to have something to do with drugs. Jon wasn't involved in drugs, she said, but, wherever she looked around him, there were drugs. She said Jon was killed because he knew something about a gang. It was a gang sort of thing, she repeated. There also was a female involved in some way. Ms. Browne said, "I think the police are... I don't want to say scared, but I just think they've just backed off, because I think this thing is more... deeper than anybody realizes it is. He just happens to be the pop-up here. And I don't mean to seem that I'm not concerned about the way that he died. The thing that I'm glad about is that, thank God, the way he died was really fast."

I asked what steps she would suggest I take. She told me to concentrate on Alfredo's, and to look for the brown truck.

"Who do you think owns it?" I asked, referring to the truck.

I'll say the name she gave was Leonard, and she thought he owned the truck.

"White or black?"

"Black. And I think his name is... in fact I'm positive his name is..." and she gave a last name. It meant nothing to me."

"How old?"

"I'd say twenty-two, maybe twenty-one, twenty-two, twenty-three. No older than that."

"That's now. Not when Jon died."

"No, no. That's now."

Then she made an offer. "Let me work with you," she said. "You paid the first fee. That's okay. But let me work with you ongoing without charge. You find Alfredo's, then you find the truck, and then you find Leonard. Then you call me back and then we'll take the next step."

To be succinct, I didn't find Leonard, I didn't find Alfredo's, and I didn't find the brown truck.

There were no listings in the Baltimore, Columbia or Washington phone books for the men Ms. Browne had named. I drove by Meyers' home and his pickup didn't have a sheared off fender or loose license plate or any sign visible from the street of having been repaired.

There was no eating establishment named Alfredo's in the area. When the normal listings yielded nothing, I approached a cab driver in a shopping center parking lot. The cab driver called his dispatcher and the dispatcher had never heard of such a place.

There was an Alfredo's in Washington, and I drove down one week-end to have a look at it. It was one of a string of mezzanine walk-up food places inside a large office building. The only way for anyone to hang out there was to sit on the tray rail.

Ms. Browne had seemed so certain about some things, and, yet, they weren't checking out. I wanted to call her back, but I hadn't really come up with anything.

Sandra liked to buy presents for her friends. Outside of family, I wasn't so big on swapping presents myself, but it's embarrassing to get something from someone when you don't have anything to give in return. Just before Christmas that year, I bought Sandra a small angel made of dough and I took it by her house.

I said, "I think we're getting bad information."

Sandra was sitting across from me at her kitchen table and she got a concerned look. Her lips were pursed tightly and pushed off to one side of her face the way they got when she was open to listening but she hadn't really bought into an idea.

"What do you mean?"

"Think about it. We keep getting what seems like good information and it doesn't lead anywhere. There's no denying the reputations of the people who have provided it to us. They didn't suddenly lose the knack. There's something else going on here."

Sandra kept that pursed-lip look and I dropped the subject, which I didn't seem to be explaining too well, anyway. She thanked me for the angel and gave me a wrapped present which she said I wasn't to open until Christmas, and I left.

I was in a local convenience store getting milk and I asked the clerk, a man I'd put in his early sixties, if he'd ever heard of a restaurant called Alfredo's. He stepped back as if I had slapped him square across the forehead.

"You know Alfredo's?"

"No," I said. "I just wondered if you'd ever heard of such a place."

He pulled out his wallet and produced an ornate, tan business card, which he handed to me. The word *Alfredo's* was written broadly across the card in a thin, artistic script.

He said, "That's the restaurant where I will go into business with my brother. It's in South Carolina."

I made excuses and left. I called Sandra and said, "Alfredo's is not a place. It's a message."

"Are you sure?"

"What are the odds," I asked her, "that I'm running all over three counties looking for a place called Alfredo's, and this man pulls out a business card with *Alfredo's* written on it? It's a wild goose chase. That's the message."

"Just because you saw a business card?"

"No. Because I saw *that* business card in circumstances where it would hit me square in the face. There is no Alfredo's. We have to back up and remember who's in charge of this, and it's not us."

––––––––––

Sandra had been telling me for weeks that I would see an angel by January. I told her I wasn't too eager for that to happen, and I hoped she was wrong. I told her that if I did actually see one Jane probably would find me face up on the floor clutching at my chest.

That Christmas morning I opened the present Sandra had told me not to open early. It was a ceramic angel inside a glass dome fixed to a round, walnut base. I shook the dome to make it snow around the angel.

I smiled as I put the angel inside Jane's glass-front curio cabinet. It seemed to me that Sandra was hedging her bets. She was making sure I saw an angel by January.

46 Jane's Dad had reached an age when he needed care sometimes during the day. Jane's family bit the bullet and, after much searching, located a rest home where they had good reason to believe older people were treated with respect.

On the week-end of New Year's Eve, Jane was in Ohio helping her sister sort their dad's belongings and close out the apartment. It would be the first New Year's Eve Jane and I had spent apart since we were married. I was offered a couple of New Year's Eve party opportunities, but I wanted to finish some work I had committed to having done by the end of the year and that had taken longer than I anticipated. It felt odd going anywhere on New Year's Eve without Jane, so I worked late. I got home from work around nine in the evening and Jane called around ten. We told each other we would think of each other at midnight, if we could stay awake that long.

I drank a beer sitting at the kitchen table with my feet up on the counter, and I pondered. Despite what I had told Sandra about us not being in charge,

I was irritated that nothing the three psychics had said was checking out. I was tired of chasing wild geese, but I didn't know what to do next. I couldn't let it go and I didn't know how to hold on. I finished the beer and opened another, but my heart wasn't in getting tipsy by myself. I took a sip from the second beer and poured the rest in the kitchen sink and went upstairs.

I turned on the bedroom tv for background noise, set the tv timer for a little after midnight, and undressed. I read for a while but had difficulty concentrating. At midnight, celebrities hugged each other and wished each other Happy New Year. I wondered if Jane had been able to stay awake. I switched to a different channel in search of an only moderately interesting movie and, before I could figure out what the movie was about, I drifted off to sleep.

I was enjoying an interesting dream when, in the dream, I heard my younger son, Dan, say from the vicinity of the bedroom door, "Dad, can you help me?" Dan had told me he would be staying late at a friend's apartment and I was not concerned about him. In fact, as I awoke I began to realize he had spoken in a dream and was not at the bedroom door. In a rapid succession of reactions, I was at first irritated that he had awakened me from a most unusual dream, even though I was beginning to realize that he hadn't. I had already begun to rise up slightly and was turning toward the door to answer him. My next reaction was to redirect my irritation toward myself for being aggravated at my son for asking me for help. What kind of father was I, I scolded myself, if I couldn't respond openly when my son asked for help? I continued rolling over until I was on an elbow and looking toward the door. As I finished rolling, even though I had realized by then that it was a dream and that Dan would not be at the bedroom door, I was awake and no longer dreaming and I was saying out loud, "What do you need, Bud?".

The figure at the door was about six feet tall. It took a moment for my mind to clear to the point that I realized it wasn't Dan. It was a man, and he stood quietly studying me. He had a beardless face and thick, glistening, chestnut hair that fell in two rolling waves to the base of his neck. He wore a white robe and, although I couldn't see his feet, the location of his head near the top of the door frame suggested he was suspended about a foot off the floor.

I immediately did a reality check. I was awake. I felt suddenly frightened and then I was aggravated at myself for feeling it. To say that I was stunned is an understatement. It never occurred to me to speak and the man didn't speak, either. He looked straight at me for a long moment and then began moving, gliding across the room along the end of the bed. As he moved, his head turned so he kept looking at me. I was struck by his expression. It was neither smiling nor frowning, neither approving nor disapproving. It was both calm and firm. His eyes were a dark color and they seemed to know all about me there was to know. It occurred to me as he passed along the end of the bed that he was slightly translucent. When he reached a spot at the center of the foot of the bed, he vanished. There was no gradual dissolving; he simply was gone. The entire experience had lasted no more than a few seconds.

I did another reality check, and there was no denying that I was wide awake, half sitting up and leaning on an elbow. I waited, as if I half-thought something else might happen, but I didn't really expect anything. I didn't think I would be able to fall back to sleep and I decided to go downstairs and smoke a cigarette. The thought of walking across the same path that this image had just traversed brought back the fear. Irritated at myself again for having thought it, I shook it off and went downstairs. As I walked along the end of the bed, I had to fight off a chill.

I smoked two or three cigarettes as I sat at the kitchen table reliving the experience, running it again and again through my mind. I try not to lie to myself, and I try to be honest about what I see. He had been there, in my bedroom. I didn't know who he was. The word that kept coming to me was that he looked so *apostolic*. I tried to assess my feelings, but I found it easier to account for what I did not feel. I did not feel justified, or sanctified, or blessed or any of those kinds of things. I felt observed. I also felt a little scolded; not everyone, I thought, required an angel or whatever he was.

I couldn't stay up all night smoking cigarettes. If Jane had been home I would have dumped the ashtray into a paper towel and run water over the towel and discarded it in the trash. Since she wasn't home, I left the ash tray on the kitchen table. As I started upstairs the fear shot through me again, the fear that I would have to cross that path again. I shook my head and scolded myself. Figuratively speaking, I held my breath as I went through the door and along the end of the bed. Before getting back into bed I stood a moment looking across the room at the door. It looked like a door.

I looked at the clock and it was a little after one-thirty. There was no way I would get right back to sleep, so I found the remote control and flicked on the television. It was then I realized that the room had been dark when the image appeared. The television had turned itself off earlier and there had been no other lights. Still, I had seen the man clearly. I tried to recall if there had been any accompanying light or glow from within of the sort you read about, but I couldn't recall any.

I couldn't have predicted my reaction to this visit. It wasn't in my nature to put on a sheet and go up and down the sidewalk selling Bibles, but, if I had known what was coming, I would have predicted some sort of reaction that was at least humble, respectful. Instead, I went into a two-week pouting tantrum. Don't ask me why. I'm just reporting what happened. Then I heard another voice.

I had calmed down from my pouting tantrum and I came home from work one afternoon and laid down on the bed. I wasn't trying to concentrate or meditate or anything like that. I just wanted to close my eyes a few minutes and rest. The voice startled me.

"You have failed me."

I heard it only once, but there was no denying I had heard it. It didn't do a lot for my confidence.

For several days this voice saying I had failed always was in the back of my mind or farther forward than that. Failed how? Failed whom? It wasn't the kind of thing I felt inclined to discuss with friends, so I just thought about it and brooded over it. Should I have been more vocal on the Whitewash Committee? Should I have solved the mystery of Jon's death? Had I missed something obvious? Or, was I just wrong about the whole situation? Had I tried to do a good thing and had somehow misled myself and had done a bad thing instead? Sometimes it was an intellectual exercise. Sometimes I pouted. Sometimes I beat on the steering wheel and shouted such things as, "Well, you could at least tell me how I failed. What kind of chickenshit message is that?" I felt blind-sided, and I felt confused.

It took a while to calm down after that one, and, in all honesty, it still puzzles me some. Finally, I sat down and wrote Sylvia Browne a letter. I thanked her for her willingness to help and said I had reason to believe I should not continue working with her at that particular time. It wasn't that I thought there was anything wrong with Ms. Browne, or that I had any reason to doubt her abilities. I suspected that what it had to do with was that I was forgetting who was in charge, and it wasn't me.

I don't want to get into a religious discussion about having a visitor in my bedroom. I'm not qualified. For all the obvious reasons, I didn't tell a lot of people about it. Eventually, I told a few people.

I told Mama. She, of all people, should understand. I called her.

"I don't think I'd tell a lot of people about this," Mama said.

"Why not?" I asked her. "If something like this happened to me, it must happen to a lot of people."

"Well, I never told anyone," Mama said.

"You never told anyone what?"

"About visitors I had."

"What kinds of visitors?"

"Oh, you know. The usual. Saints, angels, things like that."

"Mama," I said, "when did someone first visit you?"

"I don't remember," she said. "I might have been about twelve. It's been going on for a long time."

Toward spring, I told Barbara Stewart. We sat in the swing on her back porch and she listened quietly as I told her.

"That's great," she said, when I had finished. "The only people who visit me are my grandparents."

"Excuse me?" I said.

"Oh, sure," she said. "They drop by once or twice a year to look in on me. They never say anything, but I'm always happy to see them."

I told Sandra, of course.

"That's wonderful," she said. "Now I don't feel so strange, like it only happens to me."

I told my sons. I was concerned that, because they were young, telling them would somehow do them emotional harm. They just sat and listened. I told them to remember it.

During a visit home to North Carolina, I told my youngest brother. We sat atop a picnic table in my parents' back yard. When I had told him, he looked at me and said, "You're not carrying a gun, are you?"

And I told Jane. We were sitting at our kitchen table.

"Good," she said. "It always bothered me that maybe you didn't believe as much as you should."

47 I spoke with Noreen Renier at length on the phone again in March of 1993. This time, Sandra sat in on the conversation at the extension I set up on my kitchen table.

The conversation with Noreen was again long and exhausting, and I'll summarize it and modify things or leave things out when I think that's necessary.

This time, Noreen described a different person to the police artist. She described a man with a long and somewhat oval face. He might have a long, drooping mustache and brown hair that possibly was dyed. The sideburns weren't particularly long. They couldn't grow long because he had a scar on one side of the face. He had a medium or "more thinnish" mouth. He had straight-across eyebrows, deep-set eyes that were fairly close together, a bony looking nose, perhaps broken at one time, and slightly flared nostrils. He wore hats a lot. He would be what would be called a country person. He had expensive tastes that might lead a person to wonder where he earned it all. He was about six feet tall and had a wiry build and strong-looking muscles. She could see the veins and muscles in his arms. The hair was unruly with some wave or curl in it and no obvious part. He had small ears that were close to his head. She would put him in his twenties. He was not full-blooded anything and his skin was light and looked more tanned than black. He reminded her of a tough Marlboro Man.

Noreen's assistant asked if this was the man most responsible for Jon's death and Noreen said, "I don't know he's *most* responsible, but he's clearly responsible."

Noreen described a pickup truck again. She thought it was American made, and wide. She said it was a Ford and then said she didn't know why she said that. "I don't know a Ford from a Chevy, but it would be one of those. A Dodge, or something like that." The truck wasn't new and she again felt a change in color. The back of the truck at the time had some sort of problem, maybe on the driver's side. The truck had a bench seat and a floor shift. It belonged to some sort of veterans' group. One window had a multi-colored sticker with a busy design. The sticker made Noreen feel very patriotic when she looked at it.

Noreen described the direction that one person responsible for Jon's death took as he left the backstop, and this person seemed to live within walking distance of the backstop.

I had never liked the Sam Long part of Jon's story. I couldn't get a stationary fix on it, but I didn't like it. It bothered me that the Internal Affairs Division of the police department had cornered Jon into saying Long might not have pressed a night stick against Jon's neck even though Jon had told Sandra he was convinced Long had done it. I asked Noreen about him.

Noreen paused a moment and said, "Sam doesn't have the guts."

"Okay," I said. "That's all I need to know about that."

Sandra asked if Noreen could stand in front of the killer's house, or even follow him to work.

The person Noreen saw lived with other people or it was someone else's house. It was an older house and not particularly fancy. The lawn was not well manicured. There seemed to be engines around. Maybe, Noreen said, this meant the person was mechanically inclined. She thought the house might be in the vicinity of where Sandra lived. She said there was a small, old-fashioned church on the street and the church might have been added onto or might be near a newer church that had been built to replace it. She described a stop sign, a traffic light, and a side road, and how these things were situated in relationship to the old church. She gave clock positions in a circle for each of these things, and for what looked to her like a water tower, an interstate highway, major old tracks, a large body of water, and a town.

Noreen's assistant asked if Jon knew the murderer and Noreen said, "I'm... I've known him. Everybody's known him and not known him... He's not a newcomer on the block. He's been here. Been almost, ah, convicted of another serious crime. Almost. Some technicality or in-..."

Noreen's assistant asked for something significant about this person.

"Music," Noreen said. "Maybe there was something with music to... bound us, or bring us closer together. I think because he was so different he attracted me. He seemed very free."

Jo instructed, "As Jon remembers a time when he was around this man responsible for his death, let Jon see and remember a place that they may have been together. Maybe a place they hung out. Jon remembering. He's comfortable. He's okay."

The atmosphere around the conversation seemed to change, to grow more intense, and Noreen said, "He hit me with a bat first. Hit me with something on my back first."

I asked, "Where are you when he hit you with the bat?"

"We weren't there. He had to drag or pull me there. It wasn't quite there. More toward the vehicles. That's where your witnesses were."

"Were you hit with the bat that night?"

"Yeah. Ah, early morning."

"You're wearing a watch, a gold watch," I said. "What time is it when you're hit with the bat?"

Noreen paused for several seconds and then whispered, "Gold watch. What time is it? I feel... five. It can't be five. Five... I... I... Three. Five. Wait, let me see. Let me see, Jon. We went over to someone's house. There was other elements involved. We went someplace else first and then all my - your suspects - say, 'Well, that's the last I saw of him. Last saw, last, last I saw of him.'"

Noreen asked if someone of a particular name was involved. It's the name I've been referring to as Leonard, so I'll say she asked if someone named Leonard was involved.

"We keep hearing the name," I said, "And we don't know one."

Noreen swore softly.

I asked, "How many people were there?"

"There's a bunch," Noreen said.

"How many of them were at the party and then went there?"

"I see at least three"

"All males?"

"No."

"How many females?"

"Lesser female numbers, and seems to be a lot of blondes."

"And this is the place where you were hit with the bat?"

"This is the place that first there were some drugs. Ah, I feel some injection in me, maybe after I was hit."

"Where? Where do you feel it?" I asked.

"I can feel it... they're holding... I'm on the ground, or I'm down, and I feel just, ah, in my vein. In the elbow. I feel something going in, in me."

"Before it goes in you, what time do you think it is?"

"Ah, the sun is either just coming up or going down. It's coming up, but it seems close to the earth. It's not high in the sky. It's either coming up or going down. I can't tell. Ah, twilight or daylight."

"Everyone says you left the party and 10:15. Did you?"

"Did I leave the party... I left the party at 10:15, but there were other people that left it with me. I didn't leave on my own, or voluntarily, but it was around that time. Maybe they backed it up a little bit. Maybe it was closer to eleven, or twelve-fifteen."

"When you left, did you know you were in trouble?"

"I... yeah. I, ah, yeah."

"When did you first know you were in trouble?"

"I knew I was in trouble at the party. I knew something was going on."

It wasn't clear to me that she meant that Jon knew that he was in trouble at the party where he had lost his keys, or if it had been afterward at some other gathering, so I asked if there had been another party.

"It, it was a party that was set up. A party that was set up. I go to one party, and, and leave it at 10:15, and we go someplace else, and that's where the trouble is. The trouble wasn't really all at the first party, but three of the people at the first party go on, and then there's more. Why? Why? I didn't do it. I didn't. I did. I really did. I, I, I, I... "

I would curse myself later for not asking what he did or didn't do, but I missed it at the time.

The second picture didn't look at all like the first. It really did resemble a rugged Marlboro Man sort. I took one of two Polaroid shots of the picture to Sandra's and she looked at it and set it on the table.

"No idea," she said.

There were two people who, to me, looked a lot like the picture. One was Kent, Meyers' attorney, and the other was Calvin Delight, the assistant state's attorney who had run the county grand jury that looked into Jon's death and the motel incident. Neither of those people was of mixed blood so far as I knew, and neither worked with his hands. I didn't seriously consider that either had anything to do with Jon's death. They just happened to be the only people I knew who looked like the picture.

I said, "I can't help thinking it's sort of a mixture of the first picture and something else, even though the two don't look alike. It seems somehow all mixed up."

I eventually thought to flip the picture over. A penciled note on the back said the second picture was a replacement for the first.

After a time I knew exactly how many traffic lights and county-maintained water towers there were in the county. I visited them all and checked out the areas for similarities with Noreen's descriptions. Then I discovered that private establishments had their own water towers and I started losing count. There was a military base in the next county over - I doubted that Noreen would have been aware of county demarcations - and it seemed there were water towers almost at every intersection. To this day I can't look straight at a water tower without flashing back. Sandra noticed one evening as we were walking through the ballfield behind the school that the press box over the football stadium looked a lot like a tower, and I had to throw in the towel for a couple of days.

Noreen had said in what sounded at the time like a moment of frustration that there couldn't be that many old churches or churches being added onto in the area. You'd be amazed. They were almost as plentiful as trucks with orange and black stickers, or water towers. It was as if every congregation of an old church had filed for a building permit.

Railroad tracks ran parallel to Interstate 95, and that seemed like the closest fit for the old tracks Noreen had said paralleled a major road, but there also was an old figure-eight race track, and the Laurel horse track, and numerous high school tracks.

I found a house across the street from a high school that stood next to a water tower and had lots of old cars and trucks in the yard. It wasn't within the radius I was supposed to stay in and the roads didn't run in the right directions to suit Noreen's points in a circle. I still kept driving by it every few days, as if I could look at it enough times and it would then be the right place. There was even an old white church nearby with the remains of a long-since-abandoned foundation for an addition beside it. I collected all the addresses off the mailboxes in the area and compared them to the street directory at the library. Nothing fit.

I drove two towns over to check the home of a the young man who had made himself conspicuous by offering to have Meyers killed and by showing up at Sandra's and snooping around when Amanda Garvey was there. I wanted to see if he drove the right color pickup. He did, but it was a foreign make and didn't have a sticker on the window.

I drew circles on paper and put the house we were looking for in the center and I triangulated all that we knew and searched all over town. Then I threw in the towel.

I did call Rogers and ask him to go in one more time and talk to Iglesia. I told him I wanted him to say we were tired of all the tap dancing, and Iglesia could either come clean or take care of himself. This had been going on long enough. If Iglesia seemed mildly receptive, I said Rogers should try to make a deal. I already had talked to an attorney without giving the attorney a lot of particulars, and the attorney had offered to serve as a go-between. I said Rogers should tell Iglesia that we would work for a deal in which Iglesia got something like a sentence reduction in exchange for full details that could be checked out.

"I can't do it," Rogers said.

"Why not?"

"I've already tried to get in to talk to him again. There's a new policy at the prison. Ministers aren't allowed to talk to prisoners without special clearance. There's no way I could get clearance to talk to him."

I said, "Well, ain't that a surprise."

I told Sandra I'd had it. We walked along the bike path that passed the backstop and I said I wasn't chasing after any more clues and I wasn't calling any more psychics and I wasn't getting involved in any more arguments with the local police.

"Do you mean you're giving up?" She asked me.

"Of course not," I said. "I'm going to write it all down, in a book. This is a story that needs to be told, and so much time has gone by there's a danger I'll forget things."

Carlen named her son Dakota. She said it so proudly that I didn't offer my opinion, which was that it was a bit on the unusual side. It did, however, have a certain ring to it. It's another name for a Sioux Indian, but I didn't know if Carlen knew that.

One evening in October when Dakota had reached the age of just talking, but not too clearly, Sandra had Dakota overnight. Sandra was in the bathroom with Dakota, giving him a bath. Dakota kept pointing over her shoulder and saying, "See? Mickey." Sandra looked and couldn't see anything, but there was a feeling of electricity in the air. Sandra got excited and she left the bathroom door open and went to her bedroom phone to call me and say she thought Jon was in the house. I wasn't home and Sandra went back in the bathroom. Dakota was standing outside the tub. He was dried off and he was holding his toothbrush in his mouth. Dakota could toddle around, but he wasn't old enough yet to get in or out of the bathtub alone or to reach his toothbrush over the lavatory.

"Who dried you off?" Sandra asked.

Dakota said, "Mickey. See?"

The next morning it was foggy and Sandra was afraid to walk the short distance from the house to the car. She and Dakota had to leave for the daycare center, but she didn't want to do it. She hurried to the car, and, as she helped Dakota get in, something like a white cloud came around the car from the rear. The cloud was about the size of a man standing. It hovered a moment and then went back around the car and started down the street, toward the backstop. Sandra cranked the car to warm the engine before getting Dakota into the seat belt. Dakota stood on the front seat and pointed out the window in the direction of the departing cloud.

"See? Mickey."

48 It was early morning and I was beginning to wake. The voice was very soft and yet perfectly clear. You could legitimately call it a *still, small voice*. It sounded to me like a woman's voice, but I wasn't certain. The message was quite long, and, as I listened, I became concerned that I would forget part of it. The voice repeated the message and some of the words were different but the message was the same. I found myself repeating the words inside my head almost simultaneously as the voice said them. I heard the voice a third time, again with some words slightly different, and yet with the same message.

I got out of bed and showered and prepared myself for work. I knew from the words that the message was for Sandra, but I was running late and I didn't see how I could possibly stop by the daycare center before work. I worried that I had made it up, or that it had been part of a dream.

I developed a toothache that morning, and I called my dentist and he worked me in-between his other patients. He couldn't find anything wrong.

The dentist's office was near the daycare center where Sandra worked, and, after the appointment, I decided to stop by. As I drove there I went over ways in my head that I could say what I had to say without it coming across as some absolute belief on my part that I was some sort of messenger for God. That was too awesome a responsibility, as I saw it, for me to run the risk of being mistaken.

Sandra was surprised to see me and had a puzzled look on her face when I asked her if she could step outside for a moment. She told her assistant she would be right back and we stepped outside and to the side of the building.

"Listen," I said. "I could be making this up, and it's possible that it's only me talking, but there's something I have to tell you." I told her about the voice and I could tell by her dead calm and intense silence that I had set her up for believing there was some source other than me, so I repeated my caution. "I'm serious," I said. "I mean, I heard the voice, but it could have been just a dream. The only reason I'm telling you is that I think it's something you need to hear, even if it's only me telling you."

"I understand," she said.

I told her I had heard it at least three different times, and the words changed a little each time, but I was pretty sure I could repeat it almost exactly as I had heard it. I told her it was long and she would have to be patient and hear me out. Then I told her what I had heard.

> *You know I love you like a sister, and I would never do anything to bring you harm or cause you pain, but you've been sad long enough.*

She gripped my lower arm and her eyes had a glazed and teary look, and she said, "Thank you."

"Wait," I said. "I told you it was long. There's more."

> *When you are sad, you deny God's truth. You deny His joy and His will for your happiness. If you do it because you want Jon to know that you love him, he already knows that. If you do it to show that you care, caring is its own proof. You've been sad long enough.*

"That's it," I said.

"Does your tooth still hurt?" she asked me.

"Not really," I said. "I'll take aspirin for a few days. I'm sure it'll be fine."

"Interesting timing," she said.

I was just beginning to struggle seriously with writing the book when Rogers called. Friends of his in the National Coalition on Police Accountability also belonged to the Presbyterian Church, USA. The Presbyterians, it seemed, were having a national convention and they wanted to make the Bowie case one of their national issues.

"Do you realize what that means?" Rogers asked me.

"Not really," I said.

"It means they'll contact the White House, and the U.S. Attorney General, and ask that the Bowie case be re-opened. There are over three million people in the Presbyterian Church. They have a reputation for taking on important social issues. Anything they send to the White House will get attention. They need you to send them some information."

I didn't have a lot of hope for the idea. The Justice Department already had investigated, and it goes against human nature to admit that you did something poorly and need to do it again. Still, there had been a Presidential election and there was a new administration in the White House. That could be used for leverage. The people at the National Coalition had been very supportive of Sandra. It was payback time. Somewhat begrudgingly, I put aside working on the book and pulled together a packet of information. There was considerable back and forth on the phone and through the mail and, all in all, it took up my spare time for the better part of a month.

After the Presbyterian Church passed a resolution asking that the Bowie case be re-opened, I prepared a press release for them and mailed it to the local papers. The Flier picked up on it and did a story, although the reporter who called me sounded a bit surprised and disappointed when she learned that I had written the press release. In the article that followed, a spokesperson for the local police was quoted as saying, essentially, that the case had already been investigated thoroughly, but the local police were willing to cooperate in the interest of justice.

Several weeks went by and Rogers called me at work.

"I think I just did a bad thing," he said.

As part of some national committee he was on, Rogers was supposed to meet with representatives of the Justice Department, and maybe even with the Attorney General. The head of the Criminal Section of the Civil Rights Division of the Justice Department, a woman named Linda Davis, had called him about the upcoming meeting.

"I know that name," I said. "That's the person who signed the letter from the Justice Department to Sandra saying that the case was closed."

"Are you sure?" Rogers asked.

276

"Yes."

"Now I know I've done a bad thing," Rogers said. Rogers explained that he had mentioned the Bowie case to this Linda Davis, and the letter from the Presbyterian Church asking that the Bowie case be re-opened. "She said the Bowie case had been thoroughly investigated, and the request from the Presbyterian Church would be denied. I went off," he said. "I mean, I really went off. I shouted at her for about five minutes. I shouted so long that, finally, when I calmed down, I felt that I had to apologize."

"So, the Attorney General let the same people who did the original investigation decide whether to re-open the case? Damn. That was stupid."

"You could look at it that way."

"How did she sound?"

"What?"

"This Linda Davis, how did she come across to you?"

"Professional, a bit of a bureaucrat, but very intelligent. She said she would be willing to look at any new information about the Bowie case, but that it had already been thoroughly investigated."

"Then I have to disagree with you. I think you did a good thing."

"I don't understand."

"She said, in essence, that legitimate information could persuade her to re-open the case. What else would you want her to say?"

"I don't know," Rogers said. "I'm afraid I got pretty abusive."

"So what? I still say that you probably did a good thing. She'll remember the Bowie case the next time it comes up."

"There's not much doubt about that," Rogers said.

On the Saturday after Thanksgiving it rained through the night in Columbia. There was a total reported rainfall of about eight inches. Unusual natural events draw families together, and Mickey drove up from the University of Maryland because so much rain had fallen and he wanted to look in on his mother. Sandra heard him walking up the stairs at around one in the morning and she got out of bed and went to the top of the stairs to meet him. She told him she was more worried about him driving in so much rain than she was about the rain itself. He brushed aside her scolding and said gruffly that he had been worried about her.

Mickey left the next morning to return to school and, at about one o'clock the following morning, Sandra again heard footsteps on the stairs. She got out of bed and stepped into the hall expecting to find Mickey coming up the stairs. At first she thought it was Mickey coming up the stairs toward her, but then she realized that it wasn't.

"You're not Mickey," she said.

He looked at her and smiled.

"You're right," he said. "I came to tell you something. You've been sad long enough."

He stood a moment smiling at her and then he turned to go back down the stairs. Sandra watched him go, thinking to herself how he looked exactly like himself and yet different. He looked calmer, older, more mature. Even taller.

"You're a very handsome man," Sandra said, and he turned and smiled again and then he was gone.

Sandra didn't think she could possibly sleep, but she got back into bed and immediately fell into a sound and peaceful sleep. The next morning she got up and had been getting ready for work for as much as fifteen minutes before it came into her mind that Jon had visited her. Then all she could think was that he looked good. He looked really good.

49 The set of portable bleachers near the backstop had been there for years. By portable, I mean that four or five grown men in reasonably good shape could drag and corner-walk it from one side of the field to the other and maybe only a couple of the men would get hemorrhoids from the effort. The bleachers usually were on the third base side but sometimes they were on the first base side. On this evening, the bleachers were on the third base side. The sun was going down, and Sandra rather concertedly didn't mention again how the press box over the nearby football field looked a lot like a tower.

"I'm not supposed to talk about this," she said, "but the county wants to settle the civil suit."

The amount of Mickey's civil suit against the county had increased from one to six million dollars. Jo Glasco had tried to explain to me how that had always been intended, but I didn't completely follow her explanation. At least twice before, the county had tried to settle the suit out of court; but, for one reason or another, it hadn't happened. The first time, as I recall, the offer was ridiculously low. If a person refused to settle a civil suit and then lost, Jo explained to Sandra and Sandra explained to me, the person could be liable for the cost to the county of defending the suit. There was the implication that the county's offer to settle could be a trick. Jo sent the offer back unsigned and without comment. A few months later the county came back with a substantially larger offer, but Sandra and the attorneys refused to consider that offer as well.

This time there was a different tone to Sandra's voice. She was distant, and yet still alert.

"What do you think?" she asked me.

"What do you think?" I asked back, hedging.

"I'm worried about Mickey," she said. "He said to me, 'Mom, I'll do whatever I have to, but these things take a lot out of me. It takes me weeks, months really, before I can sleep again after one of these things is over.'"

"You mean the court appearances and such."

"He has to sit there and have all those attorneys say that he's a liar and a delinquent, and that Jon was all those things, and just act like it's nothing. It's hard on him."

"Mickey's strong," I said. "I don't mean just strong. I mean that Mickey has a strength about him that even he doesn't realize. I noticed that about him when he was only eleven. If he has to, he can handle it."

"I know that," Sandra said, "but I'm his mother. If you had the choice of putting one of your sons through that, would you do it?"

"Maybe," I said. "I see what you mean."

"There's another thing, too," Sandra said. "We've done a lot. Maybe we've done enough. Maybe it wouldn't be good to do more."

"You mean give up?" I asked.

"No. I talked with the attorney who delivered the offer. I think she was a little surprised that I wasn't foaming at the mouth and crawling on the floor. I told her it wasn't about the money. It never was. I told her what happened to my sons shouldn't happen to anybody. That's what it was about, and if the county wanted to go to court then I'd have it all over the newspapers and television and there'd be the devil to pay. She said she knew that. I think that's part of the reason the county wants to settle."

"There's an election coming up soon."

"Exactly. The county's afraid of what we'll do."

"They should be," I said. "I talked with Rogers and he's ready to start faxing press releases all over the country."

"I think we could win," Sandra said. "The attorneys think we could win, too. I can't talk about the settlement, but it's significant. I mean really significant. Jim and I could get out from under, and the attorneys would be paid, and Mickey's education would be taken care of. Did you know that the attorney fees alone are over two hundred thousand dollars? I can't even imagine that much money. It's not the money, though. I hate to put Mickey through that again. And I really feel we have a responsibility to do the right thing." I sat for a while without speaking, and she finally added, "The attorneys should be paid. They've worked hard."

"So you think the right thing is to settle."

"I really do," she said. "I just don't know if I'm right."

"It sounds to me like you're worrying about what people will think even if you do what you believe is right."

"People will say I gave up," Sandra said.

"So. Somebody will eventually say anything that can be said."

"I think I should settle."

I didn't want to cave in just because she wanted me to. I knew she expected more of me than that.

"This offer the county made, have you seen it?"

"I've seen it. I didn't read it all that carefully, but I've seen it."

"Does it already have any signatures on it?"

"The County Executive has signed it, and the Office of Law."

"So they're not playing games. They really want it signed."

"I think it's the election," she said. "They're afraid of what we'll do."

The sun had gone down. We sat there on the bleachers a while, sometimes looking at where the sun had been.

"We should get back," Sandra said. "Jim's watching television and he'll think he has to come looking for us. He's put up with a lot. I hate to upset him."

Years ago, now, Alan Zindell said to me, "I'll tell you how this will come out so far as Meyers is concerned. After all the furor has died down, Meyers will be quietly eased out of the police department. I've seen it before. That's how police departments do things."

As it turned out, the county couldn't wait that long. On Christmas Eve, police were called to a trailer park just outside of Columbia to deal with a domestic disturbance. Somehow in arresting a man named Melendez, who had a .34 blood-alcohol level, Melendez died. The police said he died on the way to the hospital. In a newspaper article, the man's nephew was quoted as saying a police officer kicked the man in the back of the head as he lay face down and handcuffed on the living room floor. I'd done some research on blood alcohol levels and I knew a level of .34 was all but comatose. The man's family eventually sued the county for thirty-six million dollars. Meyers was one of the officers who responded to the call.

When Meyers did resign, it was mentioned in passing about two-thirds of the way through an article about the Melendez lawsuit against the county. A police source said in that article that Meyers' resignation had nothing to do with the Melendez case, or the Bowie case.

A few weeks went by before Sandra put two and two together and informed me that Meyers had resigned from the police department on the same day that Mickey graduated from the University of Maryland with a degree in criminal justice. Just before Christmas that year, I took a day off work and went to Mickey's graduation. About four months earlier, if memory serves me, the county had offered to set aside all the charges against Mickey. So that was finally off his mind as he walked up the aisle to accept his diploma, and Meyers walked out of the Howard County Police Department.

Sandra couldn't discuss the terms of the settlement of the lawsuit against the county. That was one of the conditions. She would be liable and the county could charge her with something or other. I didn't think the county was likely to charge Sandra with anything and risk putting her on a witness stand. Still, Sandra said it was a matter of honor. She had put her name on a piece of paper that said she wouldn't do it.

"You watch," she said. "They won't be able to keep it quiet. I just know it."

Sure enough, only a few days went by before newspaper articles said the county had settled the suit. An editorial in the Flier wondered why the county was so worried that it had to settle. The County Executive was quoted in a couple of articles as saying that the settlement had exonerated the police officers.

I told Sandra that since the county was talking about the settlement she should, too. Why stay quiet, I asked her, if the county already had cracked? At a minimum, I suggested, she could set the record straight by saying the agreement she signed didn't exonerate the police officers, but she wouldn't do it. She said if anybody asked her about it the only thing she would say was that maybe she would use part of the settlement to buy the County Executive a dictionary so he could look up *confidential*.

I made a point of never asking Sandra about the terms of her settlement, and she never told me what the terms were. Still, I have noticed a few things.

About a week after the settlement, Mickey started riding around in a new car. It was top of the line. If you asked him how he could afford such a car, he smiled that devil-in-the-eye smile and said his grandmother loaned him the money. Right.

A few weeks after the settlement, Jo Glasco moved into a new house. It was pretty big and had plenty of the newer doodads. She had a nice glow in her face when she gave me the tour. She talked about how she was thinking about semi-retirement.

Soon after the settlement, Jim and Sandra bought a house in another state. They left *New America*. There are lots of golf courses near where they moved. Sandra said before she left that she thought Jim had earned it. I couldn't say if buying this house had anything to do with the settlement. I know Sandra told me often enough that she and Jim had gone so far in debt they didn't know how they were going to get out from under, and then they bought the new house.

A reporter called me and asked if I knew the size of the settlement. I said I couldn't talk about that. I said it was bigger than a bread box.

The reporter asked, "How big a bread box?"

I said something ordinary, I don't remember what. What I should have said was, "Not big enough."

50 In July of 1994, before Jim and Sandra left *New America*, Sandra read an article about a psychic in New York who had helped police departments throughout the world solve cases. This time Sandra knew I wouldn't do it again, so she set up an appointment for herself. On the morning she was supposed to drive to New York, she had car trouble and couldn't do it. She called me at work and asked if I'd set up another appointment for the two of us.

"I'm not doing it," I said. "I told you."

"I know what you said, but this one is important. I'm sure of it."

"I'm not chasing anymore wild geese, and I'm sure as hell not going to follow up on something somebody else told you and you think you remember."

To make that long story short, I ended up calling the guy and making an appointment in August for the two of us. The day came, and Sandra and I left at around five in the morning. On the way up, we talked about what we expected to happen when we got there.

"This is not the last psychic for me," I said. "I told you I'd go see somebody after I'd finished the book. This one's a favor to you."

"You mean to get me off your back for a while."

"Exactly."

I'd read the article Sandra had read. The man was getting on in age. Although he had skills in channeling and other such things, he eventually had limited his work primarily to advising people on health matters. If a police department contacted him, he'd do what he could and, for that, he didn't charge.

"I just don't want him going into a lot a health things," I said. "If I'm going to have a heart attack or something like that, I'd rather find out at the time."

It rained and we missed a few turns and we got to the high-rise apartment building a few minutes before the appointment. I went first and Sandra waited in the man's living room. I sat in a high-backed leather chair in a small sitting room and he walked back and forth talking about my health and Jane's health and the health of various members of my family. Fortunately, all of us were healthy as horses, he said, and I was relieved. He told me a couple of vitamins to be sure I got plenty of. It soon became apparent that I would not be able to get him onto the subject of Jon's death. Whenever I tried, he either ignored me or simply refused.

"The book you're working on now is autobiographical," he said, which surprised me since I hadn't said anything about writing a book. I tried to explain that it was about the death of a young man I knew, but he interrupted me and insisted, "No. It's autobiographical."

"I suppose," I said, relenting. I asked if I could use his name in the book.

"No," he said. "What have I done?" Which is why I haven't described him specifically, or given his name.

He was pacing back and forth on the opposite side of the small sitting room and he turned away, looked back at me over his shoulder, and then turned to face me with a rather puzzled look on his face.

"You're a spiritual person," he said.

Such blatant, personal observations make me feel awkward, and I hedged.

"Well, in a way. I guess you could..."

He interrupted me again.

"It wasn't a question. I was just making an observation."

I supposed he had a sense of some of the things I would be discussing in the book, because he said, "I don't go around talking about angels, and look at what I do for a living." I took it as a caution, but I didn't follow up on the subject since, by that time, I was too far along with the book to change courses.

He went on about more health-related topics. He said that my father's heart problem was not congenital; it was a one-time shot that was over. It wasn't something I had thought to ask him about, and I hadn't mentioned it. My father's heart problem had to do with an aneurysm for which my father had major heart surgery a few years before.

He said it was ridiculous for Jane to worry about her weight the way she did since she was a healthy and tiny person.

"Women do that, though," he said with a sigh and a smile. "She's a very clever person. I like her. I like your mother, too," he said. He stopped and looked at the ceiling a moment. "I like her a lot."

The conversation went far over the allotted half hour and I never got him to talk about Jon's death. When I returned to the living room where Sandra was waiting she gave me a quizzical look, and I decided not to tell her anything. Maybe she would have more success than I had at getting him to talk about the case. Regardless, the man had impressed me as being very skilled, and I thought the session would be good for her.

The return trip from New York back to Columbia took several hours, and Sandra and I talked about nothing but the sessions. We talked about them at a gas station, in a hamburger joint, in a taco place, and throughout what normally would have been several hypnotically long hours of driving. Something about Sandra was different, and I kept looking at her, trying to figure out what had changed.

"I wouldn't let him off the hook," she said. "He kept saying, 'I should not be talking about this,' and then I'd ask him a question and he'd talk about it and then stop and say it again. 'I should not be talking about this.'" She mimicked him shaking his head left and right as she said it.

"And?"

"I asked him how Jon died. He said that, as I suspected, it was not a suicide. He said that the police know that he was murdered, but they are afraid."

"Did he say anything about how it happened?"

"I asked him. He raised his fingers to his throat." As she told me she raised the thumb and forefinger of her right hand to the base of her throat. "He said it was a martial arts thing. When he did that, he got tears in his eyes. He said he wished that he could help me, but that he was not supposed to do it. He got a distant look in his face and he kept saying, like he was saying it to himself, 'I can see the fingers on his throat.' Then he took his hand down and said, 'You realize, of course, that it didn't happen where he was found?' He was aggravated, and he said, 'How could any sane person even consider that he could have gotten himself into that position?'"

"Did you ask him where it happened?"

"Yes. He said, 'I'm sorry. That's all that I can say about that.' He said that maybe he had already said too much. He asked why I didn't simply have the body exhumed. 'You know that he was drugged,' he said. 'The medical examiners would not have known to look for that.' I said, 'Absolutely not. There would too much trauma for too many people.' I asked him why he wouldn't come to Columbia and talk to the police and he said there was no point. He said that as long as the same people are in power, they won't do anything. He said, 'What have they done about it so far?' They would simply try to hurt him, and me, say that we're crazy, and what would that accomplish? He said it eventually would be solved. He even told me some things about how, but he told me not to discuss it. You were right about one thing. He said that you and I won't solve it."

There were long silences during the trip home, and then Sandra would remember something else. During the silences, I would look at her when she was looking away. I still was trying to figure out what it was about her that had changed.

After one of the silences, she said, "He said that I should give up my fight with the police."

"He's right about that," I said. "It's gone on long enough."

It was late afternoon and we were just getting into Maryland when it dawned on me what it was about Sandra that was different. There was a calm and a peacefulness in her face I had never seen there.

"I was wrong," I said. "Going to see this man was a good thing. I don't understand it completely, but something about this trip helped you take a final step. You are healed."

"You're right," she said, and she laughed.

51 I finally figured out why Jon called me. He wanted me to help him save his mother. Sandra was desperate and beyond the edge, and someone had to help her survive. Someone had to save her.

Saved is a loaded word, and I'm not talking about the way the word is sometimes used. I'm talking about the way a person who's walking along a lake and sees another person drowning throws a line or jumps in and does what he can.

I got what Jon wanted me to do confused with a lot of other things, things like solving the case and being a hero. This was it, though. He wanted me to help him save his mother. There were other people who were to do the rest, whatever that meant. For reasons I don't fully understand those other things, and this, were things he couldn't do alone; and this was my thing to do. It was the reason he called *me*.

When I was younger I took a few courses in life-saving, and I know the smart thing almost always is to toss a line or extend a branch so the one doing the saving doesn't drown, too. I didn't do the smart thing. I jumped in. I grabbed Sandra and held on, sometimes with strength I never knew I had. Sometimes I almost had to let go, and it was her own increasing strength that saved her.

Then we both were ashore and she was all right. It was then I realized that, somewhere in the middle of all that, I had been saved myself.

I don't know any other way to say it.

I find, now that Sandra's healed and the book is nearly finished, that I've done my job. You can't put five years in a book.

I haven't heard any voices for a long time now, or had any visions or been visited by anyone. I was angry for a while that nothing the three psychics told us led to a resolution, but now I know it was a mistake to feel that way. All the long conversations and frenzied, clue-following episodes that were too numerous to include took time, time I thought I was losing but that I see now was time for Sandra to heal.

The psychic in New York said there is a person who will contribute significantly to finding out specifically how Jon came to be hanging at the backstop, which I now realize is not the same thing as finding out what happened to Jon. The psychic in New York gave Sandra the person's name, but he also told her not to tell the person. Things have to happen in their own natural way.

I know this person the psychic in New York named, and I have reason to believe the process has already begun. If this person comes to me for information, I'll share any information I have. In the meantime, I plan to spend a lot of time playing golf.

There were things I never checked out. Sometimes I felt blocked. For example, I called Sandra from work one day and said, "I think I know what happened."

"I just got a chill," Sandra said. "What do you think happened?"

"I don't want to tell you yet." I said. "I want you to ask if I have it right."

"I'll try," she said.

She called back an hour or so later.

"I don't understand any of this," she said. "I sat down during lunch and closed my eyes and I asked. Sometimes I use colors to help me, like green for yes and red for no. I asked if you had it right and all I could see was green. Then I saw the words *Green Feather* written across the green. I'm not usually very good at interpreting what I see, but I thought green must mean *Yes*. Then a red streak went like lightening down the center of the green, and I saw the words *Too dangerous*."

It was obvious to me what it meant. A year or so earlier, Sandra's father had been diagnosed as having terminal cancer and he was given only a few weeks to live. He quit chemotherapy and tossed his pills and checked himself out of the hospital and proceeded to live more than a year. Sometime during that year, I told Sandra I thought a green feather would make a good sign that someone who had died could use to let a loved one know he was all right. Sandra had mentioned this to her father, and he had said he liked the idea. He said he had always believed in such things himself but hadn't met a lot of people he felt comfortable discussing them with. A few weeks after Sandra's father died, a youngster at the daycare center found a green feather on the floor and gave it to Sandra. "Look what I found," the youngster said. "I wanted you to have this." So, the message was from Sandra's father, whom Sandra and I had started calling Green Feather. The green meant I was at least close in what I thought had happened to Jon. The red meant danger, and the words *Too dangerous* were to make sure I understood that.

It didn't matter if I was close to right, I told Sandra. We had to drop it. We could get ourselves or someone else hurt, and that wouldn't accomplish anything that should be accomplished.

A lot of people have helped Sandra and her family. I couldn't begin to name them all. As a tribute to all of them, I'll mention one.

To me she was a kid, although she has become a woman. We'll say for the sake of this telling that she was red-haired and bright and vivacious. The only reason I don't give her name is that it might cause her some embarrassment. She helped do a lot of things, some of which I know she wouldn't want mentioned or attributed to her. When she called Sandra and said she wanted to talk and Sandra called me, I said, "Sure."

We met in the mall and had pizza and sodas at a small table. We talked a while and then the conversation kept winding down but not stopping. When Sandra or I made gestures toward leaving, she always said, "What else?" "What else?"

Finally I said, "All right. Let's get down to it, then. Do you want to talk about any interesting dreams you've had?"

"Sure," she said. She sat back and let out a breath and it seemed we finally had come to the point of the meeting. "I had this really interesting dream," she said. I was asleep in my bedroom. At least, I think I was asleep, and I was dreaming that I was asleep in my bedroom. There was someone in the hall and I went to see who it was and it was Mickey. He looked at me and smiled and the dream was so real that I said, 'Mickey, what are you doing here?' He looked off to the side and I looked over and Mickey was standing there, too. Then I realized that the first Mickey wasn't Mickey. It was Jon. It was as if Mickey had to be there so I would know it was Jon, because I had never met Jon. When I realized who it was, he smiled and nodded his head and gave me a kiss on the cheek. Then he patted me on my back, tap-tap-tap, and I woke up. I felt good, as if I had been thanked for helping."

Sandra said, "I'm going to tell her."

Sandra told her about the visitor in my room and the kid sat listening and every now and then she looked at me. I started to feel uncomfortable and fought off the feeling. When Sandra had finished the kid said, "Is it true?"

"It's true," I said.

"Wow," she said. "Was it really an angel?"

I said, "Actually, I think it was a little higher up the organizational ladder. I was getting tired, discouraged, and what I think it was, was a good old fashioned butt-kicking, as if to say, 'Pay attention. This is an important thing that you asked to be a part of.'"

The young woman, who was Jewish, said, "I didn't want to tell anyone about my dream, but I feel better. And I'll tell you something else, too," and she looked away momentarily as if she wasn't sure she could say it. "I believe in God now. Maybe I should start going to church."

"It's two different things," I said. "If you feel you should do it, then do it. A lot of good people go to church. Just don't get the two things mixed up."

People still are waiting in the wings, waiting to help. When the time comes that they are needed, Sandra knows they are there. One is a man named Joe Allercia. Joe runs a company in Bethlehem, Pennsylvania called the American Detective Agency. Joe's made about all the money he needs and sometimes he takes on a case because it triggers something in him and he can't get it out of his mind. He took on the case of the young man who was found hanged in a county closer to Washington, the case that involved the son of the woman named Mary who sought out Sandra one morning. Mary introduced Joe to Sandra and the story of Jon's death triggered something in Joe. When Joe had read some of the documents related to Jon's death he found he couldn't let go of it, but it was too much for him to deal with all the way up in Pennsylvania. That's why Joe saw to it that I got a private investigator's license, so I could follow up on things for him. There hasn't been a lot for Joe to do lately since I've been working on the book instead of following up on things, but he's one of the people who's always there, waiting.

Carlen's husband was in the Navy, and Carlen and Dakota went with him when he was transferred to Italy. As Carlen was saying goodbye to Sandra, she told Sandra she just wanted to find some peace.

When Dakota was three, he came running into the kitchen from his bedroom. He said to Carlen, "Mama, do you know Uncle Jonathan?"

Dakota didn't know about Jon. The family protected him, because he was so young. Sometimes, when Dakota was shown a photo of Jon and Mickey together, Dakota would say, "Look. Two Mickeys," and no one corrected him or explained.

So, when Dakota came running into the kitchen talking about Uncle Jonathan, Carlen was surprised.

"How do you know about Uncle Jonathan?" Carlen asked.

"He's in my bedroom," Dakota said. "He said, 'I'm Uncle Jonathan.' Come see."

Carlen followed Dakota to his bedroom and she didn't see anyone. She said, "Where is Uncle Jonathan?"

"There," Dakota said, pointing toward his bookcase. "Can't you see him?"

Carlen stepped to the center of the room and looked in the direction of the bookcase.

"Hello, Uncle Jonathan," she said.

"Mama," Dakota said. "He says his real name is Carl Jonathan."

This was too much for Carlen. Dakota might have overheard Jon's nickname. He certainly was too young to know that it stood for Jonathan, and there was no way Dakota knew that his uncle's first name was Carl. Carlen slumped to the floor and sat there crying.

Dakota said, "Mama, why are you crying? Uncle Jonathan says he is glad to see you. He says he just wants you to be happy."